Mirror Mirror

Mirror Mirror

PATRICIA SCANLAN

POOLBEG

Published 1997
by Poolbeg Press Ltd
123 Baldoyle Industrial Estate
Dublin 13, Ireland

A catalogue record for this book is available from the British Library.

ISBN 1 85371 767 3

Cover photography by Michael Edwards
Mirror courtesy of JW Weldon Antiques, Dublin
Cover design by Poolbeg Group Services Ltd
Set by Poolbeg Group Services Ltd in Times 11/13.5
Printed by ColourBooks Ltd, Baldoyle Industrial Estate,
Baldoyle, Dublin 13, Ireland.

Acknowledgements

Once again I could not have written this book without the love and friendship of some very special people, and so it is with the deepest gratitude and love that I thank:

God is the Giver and the Gift. Thank you, God, for the gift of this book.

My mother and father, who helped me "rise above it".

My sister Mary and brother-in-law Henry, who got me through another one. Thanks especially for all the laughs in Wicklow (and for feeding me!).

My brothers Donald, Hugh, Paul and Dermot, who are the best.

My sister-in-law Yvonne, who has such a kind heart and whose "Three Stooges" joke couldn't have come at a better time.

Lucy, Rose and Catherine, sisters-in-law and dear friends.

And for all the wonderful hugs and kisses thanks to Fiona, Caitriona, Patrick, Laura, Rebecca and Tara.

And not forgetting Catherine, John and Jennifer. And Alison and Gillian.

To Maureen . . . keep working on the quilts!

For the first time in my writing career I didn't think I was going to be able to finish a book and then the cavalry came *galloping* to the rescue. Thanks:

To Breda Purdue, guardian of my career, and a true friend.

To Sarah Lutyens and Felicity Rubinstein, for your love, support, honesty and integrity. Good times are coming . . .

To Francesca Liversidge, only a phone call away, thanks for the editing and that lovely bedroom with the beautiful views.

To Annette Tallon, a great blessing in my life.

To Mary Fanning, Teresa Hanaway, Maura Lundberg and Suzy Kate, who help me along my path.

To Anne Schulman, who knows *exactly* what it's like.

To Deirdre Purcell, who makes it look easy!!!!

To Margaret Daly, who's always there.

To Anne Morahan-Wiley for the brunches.

To Angela Rohan, thanks for editing and proofing no 7 so conscientiously. And thanks for all the others.

To Gareth O'Callaghan, Marian Keyes, Lia Mills and Cathy Kelly, for all the care and support.

To Joe Lang for sound advice, hearty laughs, not to mention bachelor's buttons, "heavenly blue" and *white tulips*! And especially for the pink roses.

To Alil O'Shaughnessy, who listens.

To Tony Kavanagh for the hugs.

To John Condon, sound as a bell!

To Kieran Connolly . . . what can I say? Still waiting . . .

And to the divine Dave Wickham, the nicest pilot I know. (The only pilot I know!) I still don't trust computers!

To Michael McLoughlin, who told me I was at no 1 and who owes me lunch!

To Ivan Kerr for keeping in touch, and ditto lunch!

To John Carthy, who worked wonders on my back.

To Dr Frankie Fine, the best in the world.

To all in Transworld, who make me feel so cherished, and to Kevin Redmond for being concerned.

To Treasa Coady, Deirdre Moore, Peter Orford, Jimmy in Desktop Systems (Baldoyle). To the gang in Mac's Gym and congratulations to our new gladiator! To Susan O'Brien, Nikki and Jean at Nikki's Hair Studio. To Pat and all the make-up girls in RTÉ (thanks for the cheekbones!). Thank you all for helping me out.

My thanks to Sara Farrelly for a beautiful cover and for being so nice always, and thanks to Paula, Elaine, Conor, Emer, Karen, Simon, Nicole, Lucy, Peggy and Derek.

And finally a big thanks to all the lovely people who came to my signing sessions across the country (especially the gang of three in Belfast) and to all those who wrote to me. I really hope you enjoy *Mirror Mirror*.

I dedicate this book to Marty, Ciana, John, Dave, Bridie,
and all the wonderful gang on *Twelve to One*, not forgetting Noel
(who shared his cigarettes) and Eddie, Michael, Dennis,
Walter and all the floor gang who looked after me. I had a ball.
They were happy days. Thanks for letting me share them.
I loved being part of "the family".

Yet each man kills the thing he loves,
By each let this be heard,
Some do it with a bitter look,
Some with a flattering word.
The coward does it with a kiss,
The brave man with a sword!

(*The Ballad of Reading Gaol,* Oscar Wilde)

Mirror Mirror

Chapter One

Today will be a day of letting go. Ellen's eyes widened as she read her horoscope in the evening paper. Sometimes the forecasts were uncannily accurate.

Today she'd let go of Chris Wallace. After seven years of emotional turmoil, of loving and never really knowing if she was loved in return, she'd finally closed the chapter on the turbulent, passionate, savagely painful love that had left her life in tatters and her spirit crushed.

Seven years ago, she'd never have had the strength to turn her back on Chris. She'd always forgiven him, made excuses for him, let him control and manipulate her. The *I love you's, I'm sorry's, You're the only woman who understands me's,* the words that had promised a love which had never been delivered, had always got to her as he knew they would. They'd always stopped the pain for a little while at least, because she had so badly wanted to hear them.

Chris knew how vulnerable she was. He'd always counted on that and on her compassion. He'd played with her emotions. She'd danced to his tune. But not any more. Now she was free of him. She'd put the past behind her and taken a step towards a new life.

Doug Roche would give her all she wanted. Kind, decent, caring Doug, who was as strong and dependable as Chris was weak

I

and shallow. Chris with his insincere lies would promise you the moon . . . Doug would get it for you.

Ellen had always believed Chris because she wanted to believe him. Willing that there was some decency and goodness and truth in him. Time and time again he'd let her down. Chris would never change. Not for her, not for anyone. He hadn't it in him to put another person's feelings before his own. In a way, Ellen felt sorry for him. He had never really known the joy of loving someone. He had never known what it was like to be happy for someone when something good happened to them. He'd never known what it was like to truly share.

In all the years she'd known him and loved him, he hadn't changed at all. He hadn't grown or learned anything. He was still the centre of his universe and as long as she let him treat her the way he did, as long as she gave him permission to behave so badly towards her and with such lack of respect he would continue to do so. She had to accept responsibility for herself. Hard as it was, she had to finally draw the line and say *enough*. She had to value herself. It had finally dawned on her that she couldn't put all the blame on Chris.

It was a painful realisation. Ellen wanted to shy away from the thought, but that was cowardly and she'd never been a coward. She'd allowed him to treat her like dirt. She'd never said, "I don't accept the way you treat me. It's not decent. It's not nice." She'd let him think that his emotionally abusive behaviour was perfectly acceptable to her. And that was very wrong. Very demeaning. She was worthy of much more. And it was wrong of her to let Chris think that the way he treated her was all right. He'd never had to face the consequences of his actions. Ellen doubted he ever would. Accepting personal responsibility for his actions had never been Chris's way.

For some reason Ellen suddenly remembered a very kind nun called Sister Michael who used to teach her religion at secondary school. Sister Michael had been different to any other teacher they'd ever had. She'd believed women should go to university and get degrees and have careers. "You can be anything you want, girls. Don't limit your vision," she used to say. She'd been talking one day about *Loving your neighbour as yourself.*

"And girls," she'd said. "How hard it is to love yourself. But if you don't love yourself how can you love your neighbour? Don't ever *allow* anyone to treat you badly. Stand up for yourself and know what you are . . . a soul of infinite value to God. If you *allow* someone to abuse your mind, body or spirit, *you* are guilty of the sin of not loving yourself. And girls, that is like slapping God in the face, because he has made you perfect."

Ellen hadn't really understood what Sister Michael was trying to tell a class of thirty giddy sixth years who only had one thing on their minds . . . boys. She'd always thought that loving yourself was a very selfish thing to do. But now all these years later, as she sat thinking and thinking about her relationship with Chris, she suddenly saw what that wise nun had been talking about.

She had *allowed* Chris to treat her badly because of her desperate need for his love. And when he'd left her, she'd considered herself worthless. And then, after all the pain and suffering, after all the torment of rejection, she'd taken him back and *allowed* it all to happen again. If she had respected and *loved* herself she'd never have let that happen.

Tears pricked her eyelids. She felt ashamed of herself and her weakness. She'd been pretty pathetic really. No wonder Miriam, her sister-in-law, used to get mad at her. But it was very hard not to keep making excuses for someone when you loved them. She had let him do it to her . . . twice. How little self-worth she had. She'd let Chris manipulate and control her and done *nothing* to protect herself. Never *ever* again would she allow anyone to do that to her. Even if she were never to be involved with anyone again. Even if it didn't work out between her and Doug. At least she'd have peace of mind. And she did want peace of mind and a good life for herself and Stephanie, her beautiful little daughter – the one good thing that had come out of her relationship with Chris.

Ellen felt tiredness seep from every pore. It had been a long day. She was drained and exhausted. She folded up the paper and switched off the lamp. Five minutes later she was curled up in bed.

Stephanie was staying over at Miriam's. She loved going on "holidays" to be with her cousins. And it was kind of Miriam to take her so that Ellen could have a night out.

She and Doug had planned to go down to the Glenree Arms for a drink and then, because the night was so mild, Doug had suggested they drive to Howth and go for a walk along the pier. Then Chris had come knocking on her door and she'd nearly died.

Tonight certainly hadn't turned out the way she'd expected, she thought ruefully, as she stared at the patch of star-studded black velvet sky through the square skylight that sloped down her pine ceiling.

To think, though, that Chris had called to her door, yet again expecting her to take him back after all his shitty behaviour. This time he'd found the well of love *had* run dry. Did he think she would put up with his selfishness and his lies for the rest of her life? Did he think he could go on taking, while he gave nothing back? Did he think he could walk all over her for as long as he wanted?

Lying alone in her bed, Ellen felt a fierce anger. How could he not have loved her the way she loved him? Would that have been so difficult? He'd always taken her love for granted. He'd always known it was there for him. And she *had* loved him. Passionately. From the first time she'd met him, seven long years ago at her brother Vincent's wedding.

Now that she had finally closed the door in his face, wasn't it just typical of her to start wondering if she'd done the right thing? She *knew* deep in her heart that she had. She'd better cut this nonsense out now, Ellen told herself crossly, ashamed of herself for being so stupid.

In the last few months she'd had time to think and sort herself out. Hadn't she? She knew Chris would have stayed in her life for ever if she'd wanted. Flitting in and out as it suited him. But she *didn't* want it any more. She was weary of all the emotional trauma. He was a shit. He always had been and always would be. A sexy, charming, selfish, fun-loving child-man who had always run to her for comfort when times got tough. Nothing and no one could change him. She'd never change him. Suzy, his attractive blonde dolly-bird wife wouldn't change him either. He would never give emotional stability to any woman because he was so deeply engrossed in himself.

With Doug it was very different. Doug always made her feel that she was special. He was always interested in what she was doing. In little ways that meant a lot to her, Doug showed her that he cared about her. He always held the car door open for her. He walked on the outside when they were walking together. He mowed her lawn. He never let her carry anything heavy. He made her cups of tea when she was watching *The Late Late*. Doug couldn't have been more different to Chris.

Chris had never made her a cup of tea once. It wouldn't even dawn on him. She had always danced attendance on him and he'd expected it of her. Ellen lay in bed trying to think of one time that Chris had ever done anything nice that had made her feel cherished. He'd given her a cheap birthstone ring when he'd been trying to persuade her to resume their relationship. So that didn't count. There'd been an ulterior motive behind that.

He'd never done one nice thing for her, Ellen thought sadly. She'd loved a mean, self-centred, weak man. Tears slid down her cheeks. If Doug hadn't been there she wasn't sure if she would have had the strength to send Chris away. She did miss him. She couldn't deny that. True, she'd kept herself hectically busy so she wouldn't have time to think about him. Opening her new deli with Miriam and her old schoolfriend Denise was all that occupied her thoughts but at night in the dark, by herself, it was hard to shut out thoughts of Chris. Maybe tonight she'd crossed that final barrier. There was no going back. It was time for a fresh start. Chris was out of her life for good. She just had to be strong. And Doug would be there to help her.

Doug Roche took a faded photo from his wallet. He stared hard at Geena Kingston's image. He'd been crazy about her once. He'd wanted to marry her until he found out that she'd been seeing someone else behind his back. He'd suffered his heartache, just as Ellen had. But tonight had been a turning-point, he mused, as he struck a match and watched the flame curl around Geena's photo. Why he'd kept that photo so long he didn't know, but now as the ashes fell into the fireplace, he knew that Geena was a chapter in his past that was well and truly closed.

He wanted to make a future with Ellen and Stephanie and tonight, for the first time, he'd felt there was a chance. He wasn't a fool, though. Ellen loved Chris, Doug knew that. He'd seen her glowing and radiant those first weeks after they'd started seeing each other again. And then gradually he'd seen the unhappiness, the stress, the preoccupied look in her eyes, as the months had gone by.

When he'd seen Chris Wallace standing at Ellen's front door, so arrogant and cocky, so sure that Ellen would fall back into his arms, Doug had wanted to land him one right in the jaw. Had that bastard no conception of what he was doing to Ellen? Of the suffering he'd caused her? Why had he come back into her life again? He was a married man with young children. He was obviously a thoroughly selfish man. And he was a bloody idiot too, Doug thought contemptuously. He should have realised what he had in Ellen and married her years ago. When she'd closed the door on Chris tonight, he knew it was the hardest thing she had ever done in her life. If she could put Chris behind her, once and for all, Doug knew there was a good chance that he and Ellen could be happy together. There was a very close bond between them, a mutual respect and friendship. Maybe in time it would turn to love. There were different kinds of loving. What he'd felt for Geena was totally different to what he felt for Ellen. If only Ellen could come to the same sort of realisation, that would be half the battle. All he could do was hope and wait.

❧

Chris Wallace had never felt so angry in his life. The further he'd driven from Ellen's the angrier he'd become. How dare she turf him out as if he was just some piece of flotsam! How dare that creep she was with more or less threaten him! Just where did he get off, this Doug guy? How *could* Ellen want to be with him?

Chris shook his head in disbelief as he drove at speed along the back roads. He didn't care if he crashed. That would give Ellen something to think about. If he was killed in a smash-up *then* she'd be sorry, Chris thought self-pityingly as he scorched around a narrow bend forcing another car to pull in sharply. The driver blared his horn and shook his fist.

"Up yours," Chris snarled, unimpressed.

How could Ellen reject him the way she just had? Never in a million years had he expected that Ellen Munroe would shut him out of her life. Even a few months ago when she'd told him that it was over, he'd thought it was a phase she was going through. Women could get funny ideas into their heads. He'd called her bluff. Stayed away. He'd even started a little fling with Alexandra Johnston, his wife Suzy's best friend.

Well, it hadn't actually happened like that. He hadn't initiated the affair. Alexandra had. She'd *thrown* herself at him. It wasn't a huge surprise to him. He had a way with women. He liked them. They found him attractive. What was a man supposed to do? He'd always been of the opinion that you should take your chances as you found them. Fidelity was overrated. Men were different to women. Their biological drives were much stronger and, if women were going to flaunt themselves at him, he was no saint and he never had been. They all knew that. Ellen, Suzy, Alexandra.

Ellen knew him better than anyone. And he'd thought he knew

her. He'd thought she was happy being with him again. Their times together had been loving and immensely satisfying. It had been a huge shock to him when she'd said she wanted to end it. She'd gone all moral, saying she didn't like the lies and deceit. She'd even thrown his marriage in his face, saying he had responsibilities to Suzy and his kids. She'd known all that when she took him back. Her scruples hadn't mattered then, Chris thought angrily as he pulled into a lay-by at the back of the airport and watched a Viscount take off. He wished he was on the bloody plane.

A couple in the next car were snogging passionately. He and Ellen had often come here to court years ago. He felt horny thinking about it. He'd been so sure that he and Ellen would end up in bed tonight. He'd been longing for it. The sex with Alexandra was good enough but he knew it wouldn't last. Alexandra was a cold fish. She'd none of Ellen's warmth. He'd loved making love to Ellen. She was so giving and passionate. Had she slept with that bearded bastard of a builder? Jealousy seared his heart. How could she let another man touch her? How could she kiss anyone else? Would she whisper the kind of endearments that she'd whispered to him to that other fucker? A builder! Was that the best she could do? Chris was so angry he wanted to drive back to Glenree and smash his fist into that smug bastard's jaw. How dare he stand there issuing threats! Who the hell did he think he was? Showing off for Ellen. No doubt she'd been listening upstairs, lapping it up.

Well, it wasn't over. It wasn't over by any manner of means. Ellen loved *him*. *He* was the father of her child. Stephanie was *theirs*. And nothing would change that. He had every right to get to know his own daughter, Chris thought self-righteously. He'd be able to find out from Emma, his first cousin, what was going on. Emma was married to Ellen's brother Vincent. Emma would be his spy in the camp. Oh no, Ellen had not seen the back of him. Not by a long shot, Chris vowed as he started the engine and headed for Alexandra's pad.

Alexandra Johnston raised an eyebrow as her doorbell shrilled impatiently. She glanced out the window. Chris's red Peugeot was parked down in the car park.

How flattering, she thought smugly. He couldn't keep away. They hadn't made an arrangement to meet tonight. He and Suzy usually went out on Friday night. He must have told fibs and said he was working late and decided to surprise her, Alexandra decided. But that wasn't playing the game. What did he think? That she was sitting in *waiting* for him to call? That she had no life of her own? *Big* mistake! *She* was calling the shots. Not Chris.

Chris Wallace was finally going to find out that there was *one* woman who wouldn't dance to his tune. Alexandra would use him as long as it suited her. And then . . . when Mister Right came along . . . bye bye, lover-boy. Casanova Wallace had broken enough hearts. Now it was time for him to get a taste of his own medicine. And she was the one to give it to him.

Alexandra smirked. She liked being in control and tonight she felt extremely in control as she watched her lover stalk morosely to his car, glowering up at her window as he did so.

"Tough, baby," she drawled as she lit a Carroll's and took a slug of her G & T. By the time she was finished with Chris, he wouldn't know which end of him was up.

He was having an affair! She knew it. Suzy Wallace paced the bedroom floor. He'd told her he was working late. He hadn't used the hoary old auditor's excuse this time. He'd said that he and his dippy little secretary, Ethel, were putting in a new system to increase efficiency in office procedure. He was only an insurance broker, for God's sake! Suzy thought viciously. Not a business magnate like Aristotle Onassis or the like. Increased efficiency and new systems, her ass!

She'd phoned the office. She kept getting an engaged tone. He couldn't be on the phone that long. It got to her so much that she dumped the twins into the back of the car and drove all the way into town from Sandymount, to find her husband's office in darkness and not a sign of his car anywhere.

Maybe he'd just left. Maybe he'd be home when she got back. She tried to reassure herself. She'd had a knot the size of a melon in her stomach as she turned her car into the drive, hoping against hope to see Chris's flashy red car. The kids were bawling in the back. They were tired. It was long past their bedtime. They weren't even three yet, and it was a bit late to be dragging them around.

Suzy felt like bawling herself. For the past six months her life had been a misery. She was in turmoil. Tormented. Chris stayed out late, saying he was working. It was lies . . . all lies. But then Chris was an accomplished liar. She saw it all the time. If he didn't want to do something that didn't suit him, he lied. He lied to clients to get them to take out bigger insurance policies. He made his secretary tell lies if he didn't want to take calls. If he didn't want to have dinner with his mother, he lied. Charming plausible lies that were always believable, especially when he looked directly at you with those seductive blue eyes. Lying was second nature to Chris. And Suzy knew in her heart and soul that he was lying through his teeth to her.

It must be that bitch in Glenree, she thought frantically as she carried her two whingeing toddlers into the house. That Munroe woman and her illegitimate kid. Suzy peeled a banana each for her little son and daughter. That soothed them. While they were eating, she dialled the office number again and got the engaged tone.

"The conniving shit," she cursed as she slammed down the phone. He was so devious. She was going to have it out with him yet again. Definitely. She'd had enough. When the kids were in bed, she'd ring Alexandra, her best friend, and get her advice.

How had she never seen his deviousness when she'd started dating him? She'd known he had a past. Known that he loved women. But she'd convinced herself all that had ended when he'd married her. How dumb she had been, to be so blinded by his suave, charming, seductive ways.

She was just about to bring the twins upstairs when she heard the sound of the car engine. That threw her. Had he just left the office? Had she just missed him? Maybe he *had* been working late? If he was seeing someone, would he come home quite this early? It was just gone twenty to eleven. Maybe the mistress had to put up with a quick fuck. That was Chris all over. *Mister-Fuck-and-Run.*

He was like a demon as he barged in through the front door.

"Why aren't the kids in bed?" he snarled.

"Where were you? I rang the office and I couldn't get an answer," she snapped back furiously.

"The bloody phone is out of order. For crying out loud, I'm working my butt off to give you a decent standard of living, the least you could do is have the kids in bed at a reasonable hour and the house a bit tidy," Chris fumed as he kicked a toy duck out of his way. "What the hell is wrong with you these days, Suzy? Don't you think I have enough on my plate with the chaos at work without coming home to this mess?" He marched into the lounge, poured a whiskey and switched on the TV.

Suzy stood, wracked with confusion and anger. Was the phone out of order? Had he really been working late? He looked dreadful. Strained and tired. Not like someone who'd been having a good shag. Chris was always in a good humour after sex.

She didn't know what to believe any more. She wanted to believe him . . . badly. Maybe she was just paranoid. Alexandra was always telling her that she was. Maybe Chris wasn't telling her lies. Was it was all a figment of her imagination?

The twins started fighting.

She'd better put them to bed before he really lost his cool. Suzy sighed tiredly. She had a thumping headache and she couldn't think straight. Maybe Chris was telling the truth about this goddamn system of his. Perhaps there wasn't another woman. She had to be more trusting. If you didn't have trust you had nothing, Suzy thought unhappily as she undressed the twins for bed.

She heard Chris pound upstairs into their bedroom. He closed the door none too gently. He was going to bed without even saying goodnight. Tears welled in her eyes. No one could make her feel miserable the way Chris could. He was a master at it. How much longer could she take it?

Chapter Two

Sheila Munroe was not in a good humour as she prepared a chicken casserole for her husband Mick's dinner. She always cooked a chicken casserole on Monday if they had chicken on Sunday. She'd asked her daughter-in-law Miriam to make a dozen pots of blackberry jam for the annual sale-of-work for the Upkeep of the Parish Fund. Miriam had told her bluntly that she didn't have time. She was too busy making curtains for this new coffee shop or deli thing she and Ellen were opening in Glenree.

Sheila's nose flared in disdain. Deli indeed! Why couldn't they call it a plain ordinary coffee shop? It wasn't New York they were living in. It would match Madam Miriam better if she'd stay at home and look after her family instead of all this nonsense about setting up a business. She was getting ideas beyond her station. There was a time when Sheila could depend on her. Sheila chopped an onion with venom. She wasn't used to having her requests refused. Especially by Miriam, who'd always been a little in awe of her.

It was all this talk about women's lib. That's what it was. Putting ideas into girls' heads. She was going to have a word with Ben about it. Her youngest son was far too soft and easygoing. She didn't want to see him or the children neglected because her daughter-in-law was "doing her own thing", as Ellen had put it when Sheila had tried to express her grave concerns about the venture. Ellen had more or less told Sheila to mind her own

13

business. But that was typical of her daughter. Ellen had always been wayward. She'd given Sheila and Mick more trouble than Ben and Vincent put together.

Not that Mick saw it that way. He was far too soft with Ellen. There she was, living in the lap of luxury with Stephanie in the flat over Mick's butcher's shop, and now he'd given her a lease on the coffee shop next door, to set up her deli.

Considering Ellen's circumstances as a mother with an illegitimate child, she should have stayed at home, living on the farm with her and Mick. She had a good job as a cashier in his butcher's shop. Wasn't that enough for her? Sheila shook her head as she sliced a carrot. Ellen shouldn't be drawing attention to herself. She had this bee in her bonnet about setting up this deli business. Why couldn't she just be content to live a quiet life and stay in the background? Even though Stephanie would be seven on her next birthday, the circumstances of her birth were still a trial to Sheila. She held her head high in public all right, but the superior looks of her ex-best friend Bonnie Daly and her cohorts still had the power to wound her pride.

Sheila sprinkled some chopped fresh herbs into the casserole and slid it into the oven. She decided to ring Vincent, her elder son. His wife Emma was coming home from hospital today. The baby, unfortunately, was premature and had to stay in an incubator for another week or two.

Emma was not the world's greatest housewife. In fact, in Sheila's opinion, her snooty daughter-in-law was a lazy little madam who lived a far too frivolous life. It would match her better if she'd learn to cook and bake properly and feed her husband proper food. Her daughter, Julie Ann, would turn into a baked bean if Emma wasn't careful. The child hardly knew what a real vegetable was. If Sheila didn't send over a bit of home baking now and again, all Vincent would get were shop cakes! Sheila didn't approve of shop cakes. Only the lazy housewife bought them.

She'd baked scones and Julie Ann's favourite, chocolate sponge, to celebrate Emma's homecoming. Julie Ann's nose would surely be out of joint with this new arrival, Sheila mused. She'd been the centre of attention for nearly seven years and now she had to share the limelight with a new baby brother. Well, it would do her no harm, Sheila thought firmly. Julie Ann was a precocious little miss. It would do her all the good in the world to have to share.

She went out to the hall and dialled Vincent's number. "It's his mother," she told his secretary in her posh voice. She was very proud that Vincent had a secretary. He was a partner in an Estate Agent and Valuer's and his firm was doing extremely well. There was even talk of expanding and opening another office.

"Hello, Mam," Vincent's deep voice came down the line.

"Vincent, dear, I've baked some scones and a chocolate sponge for Emma and Julie Ann. What time are you bringing her home? I'd like to be there to greet her."

There was a pause at the other end. Sheila got the distinct impression that Vincent was not too enamoured of the idea of her being there.

"Well actually, Mam, Emma's a little bit weepy. You know how it is? Maybe if you left it for a day or two, until she's settled in again. I don't think she's quite up to visitors," Vincent said diplomatically. His diplomacy was wasted on Sheila.

"I'm not a visitor. I'm your *mother*. But far be it from me to intrude where I'm not wanted. Perhaps you'll kindly let me know when I *can* call. Goodbye, Vincent." Sheila clattered the receiver down none too gently. She felt highly indignant.

That Emma one was so dramatic, making a fuss out of everything. Of course women got weepy when they had babies. But you just got on with it. What made her so different from everyone else? She was spoilt rotten, that's what was wrong with her. She had her own car. Her own horse. She could spend whatever she wanted on clothes and the like. She'd nothing to do in that magnificent house. She had a lady to "do" for her, just like the gentry. She had a nanny for the new baby. A *nanny*!! Whoever heard of such a thing? It was a poor sign of the times when a mother couldn't look after her own child. Didn't Emma know how lucky she was? What business had she being weepy? Vincent was far too soft with her.

Well, if they didn't want her to visit, she wouldn't visit. An interfering mother she was not! Sheila was so vexed she abandoned her plans to make Mick an apple crumble. He'd have to make do with the chocolate sponge instead.

Vincent heard the abrupt click and stared ruefully at the receiver. His mother and her huffs were the last thing he needed. He knew Emma wouldn't want Sheila fussing about. She'd more or less told him that she didn't want anyone calling for a few days at least. It would be worse though when the new baby came home. Vincent's heart sank at the thought of it. His mother would have a comment on everything.

The baby has too much clothes on!
You shouldn't hold him like this. You should hold him like that.
Don't pick him up when he cries. He'll get spoilt.

She'd nearly driven Emma mad when Julie Ann was a baby. No doubt she'd be making snippy remarks about the new nanny. Sheila just had to stick her nose in. Her way was always right. She did it all the time with Miriam as well. And got away with it, Vincent thought grimly. He loved his mother, but there were times when he dearly wished that she'd mind her own business.

He glanced at his watch. He should go and collect Julie Ann. She was spending the day with Emma's mother. They were making it a special day for her. New dress, day off school. Vincent knew Julie Ann was already having difficulties in accepting that there was a new little Munroe on the scene. It was hard on her, she was looking for a lot of reassurance. Today was her day alone with her parents. Vincent knew his daughter well enough to know that once little Andrew came home for good, there'd be more than a few fireworks.

Julie Ann skipped along happily holding her daddy's hand. They were going to collect Mummy. Daddy had let her have a day off school. That baby was staying in the hospital. She was very glad of that. She'd decided that she'd prefer not to have a new baby. Everyone was making far too much fuss about him. Her cousins Stephanie and Rebecca kept saying that they were *dying* to see her new brother. They kept asking about him. They wanted to wheel him in his pram and bath him. They kept asking her silly questions about him all the time.

Julie Ann just wanted things to be the way they were when there was only herself and Mummy and Daddy. She'd had a great idea last night. Her cousin Stephanie used to live with Nannie and Grandad Munroe. Now she lived in her own house and she'd a really brilliant bedroom like the nursery in *Mary Poppins*. But Nannie missed Stephanie. Julie Ann had heard her mummy and daddy talking about it. She knew just what to do. *They* could have the new baby. Then they wouldn't be lonely at all. And they'd think that she was very very kind for giving him to them. They might even think she was a saint. She'd been learning about saints at school. Julie Ann rather liked the idea of being a saint. She wanted to grow a halo. Maybe it was already growing, she thought excitedly. She must have a look in the mirror in her mummy's bedroom to see if the light had started to shine around her head.

It was a great relief to have worked it all out. Julie Ann ran up the steps of the hospital eagerly, dying to tell her mummy about her plan and anxious to see if the longed-for halo had started to shine.

Emma Munroe applied a light touch of *Wild Rose* lipstick and sprayed some *Chanel No 5* on her neck and wrists. She was a little sorry to be leaving the hospital. It had been nice being fussed over and pampered. She'd come down off her double high of having the baby and presenting Vincent with a son. Even though Vincent had got a nanny for Andrew, it was only from nine to five and after that she'd have to get used to feeds and nappies and disturbed nights all over again. She dreaded the idea.

Still, at least Andrew was the last child she'd ever have, Emma comforted herself. She'd never have to get pregnant again. Vincent was going to London to have a vasectomy. She sighed. It was a big step to take. Sheila would be horrified if she ever found out. She'd say it was tampering with nature and God's plan. Emma would have had six kids if her mother-in-law had her way. What a thought! It was all right for Sheila, she'd never had toxaemia and nearly died. She didn't suffer from high blood pressure like Emma.

Emma scowled. Her two pregnancies had been dreadful! No woman should have to endure what she'd endured. It was nearly enough to put you off sex and Emma liked very much making love with her husband. Not that she'd be making love for a while. She was still very sore down there. She'd been having salt baths twice a day. Her boobs were like two big balloons. She was bigger than Jayne Mansfield had ever been. She, who'd been a perfect size ten, was now a big fat lump of blubber. It was disgusting. Maybe Vincent wouldn't even want to make love to her. Emma burst into tears.

What was wrong with her? She kept crying at the slightest thing. Not that a waist as wide as Nelson's Pillar was a slight thing. A horrible thought struck her and made her cry even harder. Maybe she had that postnatal depression thing. Maybe she was going to be depressed for months.

A nurse came in and saw her weeping. She put her arms around Emma. "Don't cry, Mrs Munroe, you'll be able to bring Andrew home as soon as he puts on a bit more weight," she said soothingly.

Emma felt a stab of guilt. She hadn't even been thinking about poor little Andrew. As well as being fat and frumpy she was a thoroughly selfish mother. The thought made her cry even harder. She cried herself into such a state that the house doctor decided she needed a mild sedative and told her he was keeping her in hospital for another day or so.

Vincent and Julie Ann arrived just then. When her daughter heard that she wasn't coming home she threw such a tantrum Vincent had to carry her yelling out of the hospital. It was all extremely stressful. The sedative they'd given her made her feel nice and woozy and spaced out. Another day's reprieve from real life, Emma thought drowsily as she snuggled down under the crisp starched sheets. Maybe she might try and persuade Vincent to take her away for a week while Andrew was still in hospital. The South of France would be nice. Miriam would mind Julie Ann. She was always very obliging. Julie Ann would enjoy staying with her cousin.

That's what she'd do, Emma decided. A week away was just what she needed before she faced into the trauma of taking care of a new baby.

Miriam Munroe sat at her sewing machine sewing like a fury on the curtains for the new deli. They'd be opening as soon as Doug had completed the renovations.

She was sizzling with suppressed rage. Her husband Ben had told her that Mrs Munroe had the nerve to say she was concerned that he and the children were going to be neglected when she started working in The Deli. The nerve of her. The absolute *nerve*!

Miriam had been married to Ben for thirteen years and she'd put up with a hell of a lot from that woman. She'd been a doormat for far too long. Well, not any more. She was thirty-eight years old. She'd had enough of Sheila Munroe's bullying. It was time her mother-in-law realised that they were living in the twentieth century, not the eighteen-nineties. The Seventies were almost upon them. Miriam was going to start the next decade a new woman.

This time she really was going to let Ma Munroe have it. Miriam had never neglected Ben and the children. They were the most important part of her life. To be accused of neglect made her so mad. Ben had told her as a bit of a joke. But it was no joking matter. She wouldn't dare say something like that about Emma, Miriam thought resentfully as she straightened a seam. She wouldn't get away with it. Vincent would hit the roof if she suggested such a thing. Ben should have put his mother in her place. He was too easygoing sometimes.

If there was neglect, then poor Julie Ann was the neglected one, in Miriam's opinion. She might have the best clothes and her own pony and the like, but that child was always being dumped on anyone who'd take her so that Emma could get on with her hectic social life. And did Ma Munroe have anything to say about that? She did not. Well, Miriam was going to send her off with a flea in her ear this time. Enough was enough. She had her own life to lead and people could start getting used to it. And Emma needn't think for one minute that she was going to land Andrew on her the way she did Julie Ann. Those days were over, Miriam vowed as she stabbed a pin into her pincushion with a savagery that was most unlike her.

Chapter Three

"I think you're mad, Miriam! You've enough on your plate without minding Julie Ann for a week," Ellen chastised her sister-in-law as they sat in Woolworth's cafe sipping hot sweet tea and eating cream cakes. They were having a rare morning in Dublin together.

"What could I do?" Miriam asked irritably. "Emma was almost in tears when she was asking me to mind her. She's very down, you know. She's depressed."

Ellen snorted. She had very little time for Emma and the feeling was mutual. Their relationship was very much of the Walking-on-Eggshells variety. It annoyed her the way Emma took advantage of Miriam. "For crying out loud, Miriam. Depression, my hat! You know Emma, the way she exaggerates. If she gets a headache she's got a brain tumour! She's just playing on your good nature. And you'd want to put a stop to it. Once we get The Deli open you'll hardly have time to look after your own three."

"I know. I know. I wish people would stop telling me what to do," Miriam scowled.

Ellen raised an eyebrow at her companion's tetchy tone. It wasn't like Miriam to snap. She was usually very placid.

"I wanted to say no to Emma. But I just couldn't bring myself to when I saw the tears in her eyes. She's very pale and wan-looking. She did have a rough pregnancy," Miriam murmured defensively.

Ellen forbore to say anything. Miriam was a softie. That would never change.

"Your mother thinks I'm going to be a neglectful wife and mother," Miriam confided glumly as she took a doughnut from the plate.

"*What!*"

"She gave Ben a real earful. I was so mad I nearly went and had it out with her."

"Why didn't you?" Ellen demanded.

Miriam shrugged. "I got as far as Blackbird's Field and then I lost my nerve. Your mother's a very intimidating woman."

"Who are you telling. The cheek of her to say that about you. The trouble with Mam is she's got no one to boss around at home now. Well, she needn't think she's going to start interfering in our business, Miriam. I'm telling you now. Don't take any nonsense. Put your foot down once and for all."

"Yes, Ellen," Miriam said meekly. Grinning.

Ellen laughed. "Sorry."

"Have you heard anything from Casanova?"

"Nope."

"He'd know better than to tangle with Doug, I'd say," Miriam said scornfully. "He was always good at running away when the going got tough."

"Ah Miriam, stop," Ellen said unhappily. Just because she'd refused to let Chris back into her life didn't mean that she didn't still love him. Even though Miriam spoke the truth, it hurt to hear it. Ellen was trying not to think about Chris at all. It was much easier to blank him out of her mind than to torment herself with *If only's* and *Why's.*

"Did you hear what Jimmy said to Denise?" Miriam changed the subject. A year ago their friend had found out that her husband, Jimmy, was having an affair with Esther Dowling, the bank manager's secretary.

"Whatever Jimmy says wouldn't surprise me. He's an ignorant two-faced shit," Ellen declared.

"Yeah, well wait until you hear this. He told Denise that once she starts working with us, he's reducing her housekeeping money. Esther's buying a house in Swords and Mister Generosity's going to help furnish it, even though he's still living at home with Denise most of the time."

"I don't believe it."

"Isn't he a peach? He doesn't give two hoots about his kids. Esther says jump. He says how high? And Denise still does his washing for him." Miriam shook her head at her friend's folly.

"She's crazy. I hope we make a fortune. I hope we make so much money that she can tell him to go and take one big running jump for himself. You don't know how often I say thank God I'm not dependent on anyone for money. If I was married to someone like Jimmy McMahon, I'd shoot myself."

Miriam, with admirable restraint, refrained from saying that in her view, Chris Wallace was just as big a rat as Jimmy McMahon.

"What on earth does Esther Dowling see in that long lanky streak of misery?" Ellen wondered.

"What does *he* see in Esther Dowling? Did you ever hear anything like her? Yakkity, yak, yak, yak!" Miriam retorted.

"I know. And she's such a man-chaser. Remember years ago we all went to Cora Nugent's wedding and Esther got the hots for Dermot Dunne and made him give her a lift home?" Ellen grinned.

"Yeah, and she left her jacket in the back of his car on purpose so he'd have to see her again. Then she rang him to say she had tickets to go to the Abbey. And he was too nice to say no thanks, so he went drinking for the afternoon and then fell asleep and snored the whole way through the performance. I'll never forget him telling us about it afterwards."

They guffawed at the memory.

"Dermot Dunne's a gas man. He's a great sense of humour," Miriam said fondly.

"He'd want a sense of humour to go on a date with Wishy-Washy Dowling," Ellen drawled.

"It's lovely having a few hours to ourselves, isn't it?" Miriam was enjoying her morning immensely. It was now the first week in September and the children were all back at school. Miriam was making the most of her few hours freedom every day. She and Ellen had driven into town to buy tiles for the kitchen area of The Deli.

"We'd better get a move on, I suppose. The kids will be off school in another hour." Ellen finished her tea regretfully. It was nice being a lady of leisure for a while.

"I need to get some golden syrup. Julie Ann loves it on her rice pudding. She never gets rice pudding or semolina or apple crumble at home. Ice cream and jelly seems to be Emma's only dessert recipe." Miriam neatly arranged her plate and cup for the waitress to clear away.

"I know. Emma can't cook for nuts. Julie Ann *stuffs* herself when she comes to stay with me," Ellen remarked as they walked down the narrow stairs that led on to Henry Street.

"I couldn't go away knowing my baby was in an incubator in hospital. Could you?" Miriam asked. She'd been shocked when Emma had asked her to mind Julie Ann so that she could go on holidays to the South of France for a week.

"I couldn't either. I'd be worried sick but that's Emma for you. Maternal she ain't," Ellen said dryly as she pulled up the hood of her anorak to protect her from the drizzling rain that an autumnal wind whipped into their faces.

Emma stretched catlike on her lounger and yawned. She'd been having a wonderful snooze. The sun was warm on her limbs. The fragrance of *Ambre Solaire* mingled with the scents of rose, jasmine and magnolia on the breeze. Vincent had gone for a game of golf and she was content to laze beside the pool in the lush grounds of the hotel.

The afternoon sun sparkled on the turquoise water of the enormous kidney-shaped pool. Big urns of scarlet and pink geraniums were a riot of colour against the whitewashed balustraded steps that led up to the hotel. The emerald cushions on the loungers were soft and luxurious. Huge umbrellas offered shade from the harshest rays. Palm trees dotted the verdant lawns. Emma was in her element. She'd give anything to spend another week here with Vincent. It was wonderful to be away from all her worries. As though she'd jumped into a time warp, the way they did in *The Twilight Zone.* If only she could stay here. She didn't want to go home.

Andrew was going to be in hospital for another ten days at least. Julie Ann was at Miriam's. Emma wasn't the slightest bit concerned about her. Miriam was a born mother. There was no reason, really, why they couldn't stay longer. Unfortunately, Emma knew Vincent wouldn't be keen about the idea. He wasn't happy about leaving the baby, even though he'd had to admit Andrew was in the safest place possible. One week without his parents wasn't going to make any difference to his progress.

They phoned the hospital twice a day, morning and evening, and the reports were satisfactory. Vincent had phoned his mother today. Emma hadn't bothered to talk to Mrs Munroe. She didn't want to hear disapproving sniffs down the line. Emma knew Ma Munroe was scandalised because she'd gone abroad for a week. Tough! It wasn't any of the old bat's business. Emma dismissed thoughts of her mother-in-law without a qualm. Life was too short to worry about the likes of her.

Tomorrow she'd go shopping for a nice present for Miriam and she'd seen a beautiful red taffeta dress that would look gorgeous on Julie Ann. Even though it cost a fortune she'd buy it. Julie Ann would love showing off in it, Emma thought with satisfaction as she smoothed more oil onto her golden arms, regretting bitterly that she couldn't get into her bikini. It was such a waste having to lie covered up in a beach wrap. By Christmas she was determined she'd be back to her svelte self.

Emma picked up her Mills & Boon romance, took a sip of her Pimm's and settled back to enjoy her read.

Julie Ann sat with her cousins Rebecca and Stephanie as they ate their lunch and drank hot dark Bovril in the little white cups from Rebecca's flask. They couldn't go out to play because it was raining.

Her mummy and daddy were on holidays in a very sunny place. They said that her new brother was in the hospital but Julie Ann wasn't convinced about that. She had a deep suspicion that they'd brought him on holiday and left her at home.

Julie Ann was most worried about this. Her plan to give him away to poor lonely Nannie Sheila hadn't worked. Daddy had said Nannie was too old to take care of a baby. This was a big shock. How could she become a saint if she couldn't give her baby brother away? Her halo hadn't started to grow even a tiny bit, she thought despondently as she brushed her hand over her hair to see if there was any sign of it.

What a pity Nannie Sheila was too old to take the baby. Nannie Pamela would be too old as well, although she didn't look as old as Nannie Sheila. Nannie Pamela always smelt of lovely perfume and she wore lipstick and eyeshadow. But she was always going away on holidays, just like Mummy and Daddy, so she wouldn't have time to mind a baby.

The baby would have to be given to someone who wasn't too old. Someone who never went away on holidays. Someone who needed a baby. Julie Ann had been racking her brains for days to find such a person.

Stephanie hiccuped. "'Scuse me," she said politely.

"When I get the hiccups, my daddy gives me a fright and then it stops," Rebecca said helpfully.

"My daddy puts a cold sixpence on my back and then he lets me spend it," Julie Ann boasted. She stared at Stephanie. Stephanie had no daddy. She lived with Auntie Ellen over the butcher's shop. Julie Ann had an idea. A great idea.

"Sure you've got no daddy, Stephanie?"

"I do have a daddy. He just lives far away an' I've never seen him," Stephanie retorted. She hated when Julie Ann said things like that.

"I know that," Julie Ann said impatiently. "But if he doesn't live with you, he can't put a seed in your mummy's belly button with his willie, sure he can't?"

"No," agreed Stephanie doubtfully, not sure where this was leading.

"So that means your mummy can't get a baby, doesn't it?" Julie Ann declared triumphantly.

"You leave my mammy alone," Stephanie scowled.

"But maybe she'd like a baby," Julie Ann persisted. "Wouldn't *you* like a baby?"

"Well, I might get one, one day." Stephanie sighed. It was her greatest wish to have a baby.

"But you *can* have one," Julie Ann announced magnanimously. She felt like Cinderella's fairy godmother. "You can have my baby brother. I'll give him to you."

"Auntie Emma won't give me her new baby," scoffed Stephanie unimpressed.

"Yes, she will," Julie Ann declared airily. "She won't mind at all, 'cos she knows you're poor and have no daddy. Besides my daddy has lots of seeds I'm sure. He can always make another baby if he wants to."

"Really?" Stephanie began to get excited. She hadn't realised it was as easy as that.

"You lucky sucker, Stephanie," Rebecca said enviously. "I'm going to ask my daddy to make a new baby."

"So do you want him?" Julie Ann demanded.

"Yes, please." Stephanie was thrilled. Wait until her mam heard the news that they were getting a new baby.

Julie Ann felt a huge wave of relief. No one could say Auntie Ellen was too old. This was even kinder than giving the baby to Nannie Sheila.

"I'm giving him away, because it's a very kind thing to do. Saints do very kind things and I've decided I'm going to be a saint. I think my halo is starting to grow. It probably will grow when I give you the baby. When we stay in your house, Stephanie, I'll dress up as a saint an' you an' Rebecca can pray to me. I might even make a miracle," Julie Ann decreed.

"Ooohh yeesss!" the other pair agreed eagerly. Julie Ann was great for thinking up new games.

"An' we can see if my cloak will grow an' cover the land just like Saint Bridget's did."

"Yeah!"

"Brill!"

The cousins couldn't contain themselves. To be sitting beside a saint who made miracles and gave babies away was the most exciting thing yet.

"Mammy, Mammy, guess what? We're getting a new baby."

Stephanie raced into the kitchen where Ellen was making scrambled eggs for tea.

"What?" Ellen's jaw dropped.

"Don't say what, say pardon, Mammy," Stephanie rebuked, much to her mother's amusement.

"Sorry. *Pardon?*"

"Julie Ann is going to give us her new baby 'cos we've no daddy to put a seed in your belly button. An' if she gives us a baby, she'll be a saint, an' grow a halo and make miracles. Isn't it *reeelly* exciting?" Stephanie was hopping from one leg to the other, her pigtails swinging, her eyes bright with excitement.

Holy Mother! Ellen thought in dismay. What was all this about seeds and babies? "Julie Ann can't give away her baby brother, pet. Auntie Emma wouldn't like that," Ellen explained patiently, ignoring the reference to seeds and hoping that Stephanie would forget about it. She didn't want to get into explanations about the facts of life. Trust Julie Ann to have a convoluted idea about the gory details. Belly buttons indeed!

"But Mammy, Julie Ann *said* I could have her new baby! She said Auntie Emma wouldn't mind. Uncle Vincent has lots of seeds to make new babies with," Stephanie explained earnestly.

Oh Lord! There were times she could strangle Julie Ann. What a little madam she was. Ellen looked down at her daughter and felt enormous love for her.

"Would you like if I'd given you away when you were a baby?"

Stephanie's face fell. "No."

"How do you think poor Andrew would feel if he knew he was given away?"

"He'd probably feel a bit sad." Stephanie was crestfallen.

Ellen put her arms around her daughter. "It's very kind of Julie Ann to want to give us her brother. It's nice to know she wants to be a saint. But you can see why we can't take him, can't you?"

"Yeah, Mammy. I'd really have liked a new baby though," Stephanie sighed.

Ellen prudently changed the subject. "I've got nice scrambled eggs for tea and as a special treat I bought us a cream slice when I was in town."

"Oh yummy!" Stephanie forgot about new babies. Cream slices were her absolute favourites.

"Wash your hands and hurry up, tea's nearly ready," Ellen smiled, mightily relieved that the discussion was at an end. She knew the time was coming when she'd have to explain the circumstances of Stephanie's birth in more depth than she had. She didn't relish it.

They ate their eggs and toast and Ellen had just taken a mouthful of delightfully gooey cream slice when her daughter fixed her with a piercing stare.

"Mammy, you know my daddy who lives far away?"

Ellen's heart sank. "Hmmm," she murmured non-committally.

"Could you not ring him and ask him to put a seed in your belly button so you could get a new baby."

"No, love, I couldn't," she said gently.

"Why not?" Stephanie asked innocently. Ellen knew she could pass it off and say that Chris lived in another country, or make some such excuse, but she'd always sworn to herself that she'd never lie to Stephanie. She took a deep breath.

"Your daddy lives with another lady now, love. So I couldn't ask him to do that."

"Is he married to her?"

Ellen nodded. Stephanie looked at her with big trusting blue eyes. Those beautiful blue eyes, just like her father's.

"Did my daddy not love you enough to marry you?" The honesty and innocence of the question nearly made Ellen cry out as a stab of intense pain imploded in her chest. The cake in her mouth tasted like sawdust. She took a sip of tea to help her swallow it.

"No, he didn't, Stephanie." Her calm voice belied the turmoil she was feeling.

"Did he not love me enough to stay and be my daddy? Did he not love me when I was a baby?" Stephanie's eyes were two pools of bewilderment.

"He never saw you when you were a baby. If he'd seen you I'm sure he would have loved you very much." Ellen struggled to remain composed.

"Will we ever get a daddy of our own?"

Ellen smiled. "We might. We could ask Holy God if he would send us one. We could pray for a Special Intention."

"It would be nice if he sent us one with lots of money. I'd love a pony like Julie Ann's," Stephanie confided.

"Well, maybe while we're waiting for our prayers to be answered, we might get a little kitten. Wouldn't that be nice?"

"Oh, Mammy! That'd be brillo!" Stephanie beamed. "We'll ask Doug to make a little house for it. We'll get a special saucer for the milk. Oh thanks, Mammy."

"You'll have to take care of it, now," Ellen warned.

"I will . . . I will. Wait until Julie Ann hears about this. 'Cos she's not allowed have a cat, you know. Auntie Emma doesn't like cats. But I'll share mine with her. I might grow a halo myself."

"My goodness! Two saints in the family. I'll have to remind you you're a saint when you get cranky when I call you to come in at night," Ellen teased.

"Stop it, Mammy. I do come in."

"I know. You're a great girl for me and I love you very much."

"I love you too, Mammy. An' I'll really love my dear little cat." Stephanie finished off her cream slice with relish.

Children were amazing, Ellen thought as she lay in bed that night. They were so resilient. Stephanie had accepted that her father hadn't loved her enough to be a father to her. There were no more questions after that. It was all the kitten this and the kitten that.

Chris was a bastard, Ellen thought bitterly. All those years when he hadn't come near her. All the years she'd raised Stephanie alone and he'd never even lifted the phone. How could someone be so callous about their own flesh and blood?

When Stephanie had asked did Chris not love Ellen enough to stay with her, it had cut her to the quick. She'd never actually admitted it. She'd made excuses about him being immature and not ready for commitment. She'd never permitted herself to think it was because of a lack of love. And Stephanie with all the honesty and simplicity of a six-year-old had seen straight away what Ellen had always denied to herself. Chris hadn't loved her enough!

As she lay there in the dark, the pain came back. Waves of grief and anger and hurt and rejection. She started to sob. Great heaving racking sobs that shook her body. "He didn't love you enough. He didn't love you enough." She made herself say it out loud over and over again to try and finally get herself to face it.

Why? Why? Why are you doing this to me, God? I've gone through all this before. I've endured it. Why can't I just get on with it and forget him? she screamed silently. She knew she was being utterly illogical, but deep down, even though she'd told him she wanted to end it, even though Doug had warned him off, it hurt that he hadn't phoned in the weeks that had followed. He'd just run away . . . the way he always did when things got too tough for him.

What kind of bloody idiot was she that she could even think that way still, she thought in disgust, as she wiped the tears from her cheeks with the back of her hand. Why couldn't she give Doug a chance and forget someone who clearly had no real interest in her?

This was the last time that she was ever going to cry over him, Ellen vowed. She was going to get him out of her system once and for all.

⁂

"You look a bit shattered," Doug commented the next morning when he arrived to take some measurements for the renovations of the coffee shop. "What's up?"

"Ah, nuttin'," Ellen said offhandedly.

"Stick the kettle on and spill the beans before I start work," Doug ordered.

Ellen stared up at him. Doug had the kindest eyes she had ever seen and when he smiled at her she had to smile back.

"Did Chris phone?"

"No, no," she said hastily.

"Good." His crisp reply had all the directness she expected of him.

"Stephanie asked about him last night."

"Oh!" Doug's eyes met hers. "That sounds tough."

"She asked me did he not love me enough to marry me." Ellen's lip trembled. "My six-year-old asked me the question I didn't have the courage or the honesty to ask myself. Especially when I knew the answer so well." Tears welled up. Doug put his arm around her and held her close.

"It still hurts, Doug. Isn't that crazy? I want to forget him, I want to be happy. Why?"

"I dunno, Ellen. I'm no expert. I wish you could get him out of your system. I wish you could try and be happy with me."

"I want to try and be happy with you. But I have to be honest with you, Doug. I'll never tell you a lie. I'll always be dead straight with you."

"I know you will, love. I don't want you ever to pretend to have feelings for me that you don't have. If it's going to happen, it will happen."

"Yeah, well I'm sick of going around like a weeping willow. I've had enough of this nonsense," Ellen sniffed. "I don't know how you put up with me."

"I'll put up with a lot for one of your steak and kidney pies," Doug teased.

"You've to make a house for a cat, too." Ellen hugged him tight.

"Have I? How come?"

Ellen told him the story of Julie Ann's impending sainthood and the cat saga.

"Seeds in the belly button." He wrinkled his nose. "Not as much fun as the proper way."

"Behave yourself you." Ellen gave him a dig in the ribs.

"There's nothing wrong with good honest sex," Doug said primly. "We were all found under cabbages in my family."

Ellen guffawed. She felt much better. Doug never made her feel under pressure about her feelings for Chris. He was so easy to talk to. She knew she was very lucky to have him as a friend.

They drank their tea and had a chat before Ellen went downstairs to the butcher's to do the accounts for her father.

Doug washed their tea mugs and emptied the teapot. He'd known the minute he'd seen Ellen that morning that something was troubling her. Instinctively, he'd known it was about Chris. Doug sighed. It was natural that Stephanie was going to start asking about her father. As well as deserting Ellen, Chris had deserted Stephanie. Ellen understandably felt anger and bitterness about that.

At least she'd been able to talk about it to him. That was very encouraging, Doug thought optimistically. Time would heal. He just had to give her time. The phone rang. He picked it up. "Hello?" he said. The line went dead.

He knew it was Chris. He was glad he'd been there to answer the phone. It might give that bastard food for thought, he scowled as he replaced the receiver. Much as he hated the idea, Doug knew that Chris Wallace would be a part of Ellen's life until she finally and irrevocably cut her ties with him. Could she do it if Chris kept pestering her? Doug didn't know. But he knew the relationship that he wanted with her would never happen as long as Chris was in her heart. And he had to face the fact that Ellen was still entangled in Chris Wallace's net.

What the bloody hell was that Neanderthal doing in Ellen's flat at this hour of the morning? Chris thought viciously. He'd phoned Ellen's work number earlier and a strange woman had answered and said Ellen wouldn't be in until later. He'd tried to concentrate on his work but it got too much for him and he'd tried the flat. And that redneck culchie had answered.

What kind of a game was Ellen playing with him? How could she prefer that builder to him? They must be lovers if he was in her flat at this hour of the morning. What about her scruples about Stephanie seeing her with someone now? Chris fumed. She'd thrown that in *his* face as one of her excuses for ending it with him, a few months back. His daughter was seeing Ellen in bed with a man she wasn't married to. It was outrageous – she should be protected from that sort of thing. And some day he was going to let Ellen know his feelings on the matter. Chris frowned self-righteously as he lifted the receiver again to phone Alexandra.

Alexandra swanned into the foyer of Stuart and Stuart's, eyes aglow and a smile on her lips despite the fact that she'd only had a few hours sleep. She felt on top of the world. Chris was pretty good in the sack. She had to give him that. They couldn't keep their hands off each other. They'd done it three times last night and each time had been better than before.

He looked much more relaxed. *She* knew how to look after him. *She* understood him. Suzy had driven him away because she'd pushed him into the background once the twins had arrived. She'd neglected him. Alexandra had no problems justifying her affair with her best friend's husband.

Chris needed a lot of attention and he just hadn't been getting it. He was the type of man who had to be the centre of attention. Not in the Hail-Fellow-Well-Met tradition. He was much more subtle than that. Chris needed to know that he and his problems were of more concern to a woman than any other matter on the planet. He loved the idea of being deep, complex and unfathomable. When really, Alexandra thought with an amused little smile, he was selfish, shallow and very, very devious.

She had to admit though, she hadn't enjoyed herself so much in ages. It gave her immense satisfaction to toy with him. She'd watched Chris manipulating women all the years she'd known him. And now the master manipulator was being manipulated himself. And he didn't even know it. Alexandra had never felt so powerful in her life.

She took the lift to her second-floor office, and buzzed for one of the clerk typists to take dictation. She had several letters that she wanted to get out of the way. She was taking a client to lunch in the Shelbourne at midday. She intended being on top of her paperwork by then. Alexandra dictated rapidly, watching the young girl's pen fly over her pad as she took it down in shorthand. At least this one had good speeds and was competent, Alexandra mused. Some of the girls she'd had were so inept. She wasn't a popular boss, she knew that. She demanded the best from her minions. It didn't bother her that the girls preferred to work for the bosses in the Advertising Agency. Alexandra managed more clients in the PR division than anyone, because she was the best. She intended keeping it like that. When Malachy MacDonald, the smoothie chairman and MD of Stuart and Stuart's Advertising Agency, one of the oldest established firms in the city, had decided to branch out into PR he'd gone looking for the best. She *was* the best, Alexandra reflected smugly. Weldon's had been sorry to lose her.

Right now she was in the middle of working out a publicity campaign for the launch of a new upmarket women's magazine. It was immensely challenging. Alexandra thrived on it.

"Get those letters typed up as soon as possible," she instructed her subordinate crisply and nodded in dismissal.

"Yes, Miss Johnston," the clerk typist said sullenly as she closed her notepad and left the office. Alexandra's direct line bleeped. It must be Chris! Well, he'd have to sod off. She hadn't time to talk to him now.

"Yes?" she said coolly, in her best *Don't-Disturb-Me* tone.

"Alexandra, do you know what time Chris got in last night? Well, it wasn't even last night – it was 5 a.m. this morning. I know he's having an affair. He's a bastard! I hate him." Suzy Wallace burst into tears at the other end of the phone.

Oh no! Alexandra groaned inwardly. Suzy's moaning was the last thing she needed.

"Suzy, you knew what Chris was like when you married him. You knew he wouldn't be faithful. So what if he's having an affair? You just go out and have one yourself and enjoy it. And show him that you can do it too. He'll come running back then. I can guarantee it," she advised briskly.

"I don't want to have an affair, Alexandra. I love Chris. He's my husband. I bet he's out with that bitch in Glenree. What can she give him that I can't?"

"Look, Suzy, listen to what you've turned into. You're smothering him. You know Chris, he can't stand being stifled. The more you go on at him, the more he'll withdraw. Go and get your hair done, buy some new clothes and some new make-up and start going out yourself. Make yourself interesting and mysterious to him again. Remember how he was when he was trying to get you back, years ago? Remember how you kept him dangling and he was going crazy? Do it again. It's easy with Chris. All he needs is the challenge. The unobtainable. Now I have to go. I'm up to my eyes. Talk to you soon." Alexandra hung up decisively.

Suzy had turned into such a moan. No wonder Chris had started playing the field. Hadn't the girl an ounce of sense? Once a glamorous, with-it, cool sophisticate who knew how to play the game, she'd turned into a clingy, dependent, whingeing wife. The worst possible thing she could do with a man like Chris. Suzy really had a bee in her bonnet about that woman in Glenree. Alexandra knew all about the love child. Suzy had confided that piece of news to her as soon as she'd discovered it herself.

It didn't surprise Alexandra that Chris had a love child . . . she was surprised that there weren't a few more. Chris had always been a womaniser. It was surprising that he'd lasted so long in his marriage without cheating. If Suzy had copped on to herself and handled him the way he should be handled, he might even still be faithful. In a way, though, it was good that Suzy thought Chris was having an affair with that woman out in the sticks. She'd never ever think of suspecting Alexandra.

Alexandra didn't feel the slightest bit guilty about her affair with Chris. If it wasn't her, it would be someone else. That was life. Suzy needed to grow up. She'd always been far too inclined to feel sorry for herself. She had so much. A lovely house, two children, an idyllic lifestyle, kept by and provided for by Chris. She didn't have to pay her own mortgage or support herself and work like a Trojan day in day out like Alexandra did. Suzy needed a good kick in the butt, Alexandra thought irritably.

She'd boot Chris out when she was good and ready. Their affair meant nothing. She'd never love someone as weak as him. But for the time being he had his uses. It was a diversion she was enjoying and the sex was super.

Suzy walked slowly upstairs into her bedroom. It wasn't her fault that Chris was having an affair. It was very mean of Alexandra to imply that it was. Alexandra just didn't understand what it was like being married and having children. She couldn't be a dolly-bird the way she used to be before she had the twins. She shouldn't *have* to be a dolly-bird. She was Chris's wife. He'd made a commitment to her on their wedding day and she'd made a commitment to him. She'd been a good wife, she didn't have to defend her behaviour to anyone.

Suzy stood in front of her dressing-table mirror and studied her reflection. Blonde hair down to her shoulders. Her fringe, too long, brushed tired green eyes. A fine web of lines, lightly grooved, curving around her eyes and mouth caused her heart to sink. She was starting to age. No longer a fresh young woman. She looked pale. Well, of course she did, Suzy thought angrily. She was so full of anger, resentment and suspicion, she couldn't sleep properly. Her trauma was showing in her face and she cursed Chris for it.

Chris had told her when he got home in the early hours that he'd taken a client to a night club. How many nights had he used that tired old excuse or the one about working late in the office? Did he think she was a fool? She'd had enough of this crap, Suzy decided as she listened to the happy yells of the twins playing Tarzan downstairs in the dining-room. It was time to do something about this torment and misery that her life had become. She had to know one way or another if Chris was having an affair. There was no point in asking him any more. He just kept denying it. She'd have to deal with it some other way. She'd just have to catch him in the act with that woman in Glenree.

Chapter Four

Ellen, Miriam and Denise McMahon stood in a semicircle around Ellen's kitchen table studying the architect's plans for The Deli. The excitement was mighty. To see their hopes and dreams down on paper in a most attractive plan made it all very real.

"Doug says he can have it ready in a couple of months. We're going to be open for Christmas," Ellen beamed.

"I can't believe it." Miriam stared at the drawing on the table. "Do you really think we can make a go of it?"

"Of course we can," Denise said firmly. "If the two old dears who ran the coffee shop made a living out of it, I don't see how we can fail. Glenree needs something a bit more upmarket than the coffee shop and a bit less pricey than the Glenree Arms. Most people don't want to have lunch in a hotel. They want to drop in somewhere and have something tasty and inexpensive to eat. Don't say you're going to chicken out before we even get going?"

"No . . . no . . . " Miriam said hastily. "I just have visions of us being left with loads of food or else running out of things."

"We'll have to play it by ear and see how it goes. We'll keep the menus fairly simple at first. If the business is there we can always expand. I think we should try and buy as much fresh produce as possible from the local farmers. It will save us having to go into Dublin at the crack of dawn to get to the market," Ellen interjected.

"None of us would really be able to go to the market," Denise frowned. "You wouldn't be able to leave Stephanie. I couldn't leave the girls. You'd be stuck too, wouldn't you, Miriam?"

"Well, I suppose it would depend on Ben's shift. As long as I was at home in time to let him go to work."

"No," Ellen said. "We can't make life complicated for ourselves. We need to suit ourselves as much as we can. Tell you what?" She grinned. "Let's nip over to that new place in Swords and see how they're getting on. We'll have a cup of tea while we're at it and work out a strategy. It's only half ten. We've loads of time before the girls get out of school."

"You're on." Denise was game.

"Why not?" Miriam agreed. "It's research."

"You housewives have a great life," Ellen teased. Until very recently she had been the cashier in her father's butcher's shop. Now, having trained in someone new, she only did the books for him. The freedom to come and go as she pleased during the day was a rare treat.

"We better make the most of it – we're going to be career girls from now on," Denise retorted. "We won't be able to go gadding over to Swords for coffee."

"No, we'll probably end up being our own best customers," Ellen laughed as she locked the door after them.

Twenty minutes later they were seated in a small tea room in Swords. There were a few other customers at various tables. Mostly elderly women.

"The tables are very small," Miriam murmured.

"And they're too near each other. Too cramped." Ellen kept her voice down.

"I like the china plates decorating the top of the window pelmets," Denise whispered.

"Mmmm. The curtains are a bit psychedelic though." Miriam studied the menu. "They do a good selection of sandwiches."

"Sandwiches are boring," Ellen argued.

"The service is very slow," Denise noted.

They grinned. They were enjoying their little bitching session.

By the time they left, they'd decided on table mats rather than tablecloths, to cut down on washing. They were adamant that they would never add packet soup to their home-made soups, after tasting the vegetable soup. Their tables were going to be spaced well apart to avoid a sense of claustrophobia. They were going to nick the pelmet idea. Miriam had suggested displaying old china teapots and brass kettles. The other two thought this was a great idea. They were well pleased with their foray. The more they prepared now the fewer mistakes they'd make when they were finally up and running, they assured each other confidently as they drove home to Glenree to get down to the mundane tasks of preparing dinner for their respective families.

It was hard to settle down. Even her tan was fading. Emma felt depression settle on her like a cloud. A great, grey gloomy cloud just like the sullen skies that hung over Glenree.

She was on her way home from seeing Andrew. He was getting bigger and stronger. That was a relief. When she'd seen him that first visit after getting back from France, it had been nice to cuddle and hold him. That had surprised Emma. She'd never had maternal feelings like that for Julie Ann. Looking back at the weeks and months that had followed her daughter's birth, all Emma could remember were feelings of panic and fear in case anything should go wrong.

The idea of having a nanny this time was most reassuring. Maybe that was why she was more relaxed with Andrew. To think she was a mother of two children! It made her feel so *old*. How nice it would have been to stay with Vincent in the South of France for a month. When would she ever get a proper holiday with him again? Years from now. She simply couldn't ask Miriam to mind two children. And anyway Miriam was going to be working with Ellen in their cafe. Just as well she was getting a nanny – she wouldn't be able to rely on her sister-in-law any more to mind Julie Ann.

Emma thought Ellen and Miriam were mad to be taking on all the work that running a cafe involved. Especially Miriam. Hadn't she enough on her hands with a husband and three children? It must be awful not to have enough money to enjoy a good lifestyle. Thank God Vincent was rich, Emma thought fervently as she drove along Main Street. She saw Ellen, Miriam and Denise McMahon getting out of Ellen's car. They were all laughing uproariously looking not the slightest bit oppressed by their deprived lifestyles and lack of cash.

The sight of the laughing trio depressed Emma even more. They all seemed to be having such fun. Her time for fun was over. The baby would be home from hospital soon. Lord knows how Julie Ann was going to react. All she could think about was giving poor little Andrew away. She'd thrown a sensational tantrum the day they came back from France when she'd informed them that she was giving Andrew to Stephanie.

When Vincent had very gently told her that Andrew was not being given away to anyone she'd screeched, "But I want to be a saint. How's anyone ever going to be a saint in this house when they're not allowed give things away?"

She had this thing about being a saint and growing a halo. Whatever were they teaching her at school? Her daughter's religious fervour certainly wasn't inherited from her, Emma thought wryly. She found it hard enough to go to Mass on Sundays. If it wasn't to show good example to Julie Ann, Emma wouldn't bother.

She wondered what Ellen's reaction had been when she'd heard that she was getting a present of Andrew. Emma glanced in her rear-view mirror and saw Ellen opening the door to her flat. Chris wouldn't be a bit pleased to know that she was enjoying life. When he'd come to visit her in the hospital and poured his heart out to her, saying that he really loved Ellen, Emma had been truly stunned. To think after all these years he had come to the conclusion that it was Ellen he loved and not Suzy. It was such a mess. Poor Suzy. How awful to be married to a man who didn't love her. Emma would *die* if she ever found out that Vincent didn't love her. She adored him. He was the most wonderful husband.

Emma knew how lucky she was. None of her friends had a husband as good as Vincent. In fact Diana Mackenzie's husband was hardly ever home he worked so hard and Declan Mitchell had left Lorna for that little cat, Nina Monahan. And as for Frank, who was married to her best friend Gillian, he'd never in a million years change a baby's nappy or cook a dinner the way Vincent often did. For Vincent's sake she had to get out of her postnatal depression, Emma told herself firmly. Maybe they might get away for a weekend after Christmas. The nanny might agree to mind the two children for them. The thought cheered her up no end. Maybe she'd phone Chris and get him to meet her for lunch tomorrow. Her cousin always made her laugh. He was such good company, even if he was a stinker where women were concerned. Imagine him having a fling with Alexandra Johnston! He'd confessed that to her as well, when he'd brought champagne into the hospital that night.

He really was something else, Emma thought, half-revolted, half-amused. Married to Suzy, in love with Ellen and having a fling with Glamour Girl Johnston. Emma wouldn't be able to tell Vincent that she was having lunch with her cousin. Vincent hated his guts for what he'd done to Ellen. It was very awkward so the best way to deal with it was to say nothing. Emma had always stayed friends with Chris. They were mates and always had been. If there was one person guaranteed to cheer her up it was Chris. He was the perfect antidote to postnatal depression, Emma assured herself as she drove up the shrub-lined drive of her beautiful big house, the likes of which had never been seen in Glenree.

"She was laughing and joking!" Chris was aghast. Emma had just informed him that she'd seen Ellen yesterday, looking like a million dollars, laughing and joking with her friends in Main Street.

"Chris, you'd want to put Ellen out of your head. I bet she never even thinks of you now. She's doing a steady line with that guy I was telling you about. He's renovating her cafe," Emma said earnestly, her big brown eyes wide with concern.

If only she knew the half of it, Chris thought wryly. He hadn't told his cousin about his last visit to Ellen in Glenree. Emma had no idea how *destroyed* he really was.

"Look, why don't you end this thing with Alexandra and make a fresh start with Suzy?" Emma advised. Chris knew she was enjoying her role as marriage counsellor and confidante.

"Yeah, maybe," he said wearily.

"I've some brilliant gossip for you." Emma's eyes twinkled.

"What?" Chris grinned. Emma was great fun.

"Guess who Vincent and I saw canoodling in Nice?"

"Who?"

"John Carey and Elaine Pender. Can you believe it? They nearly *died* when they saw us."

"Well, well, well! *Mister-Family-Values* himself. What a bloody hypocrite. At least I don't go around preaching about being the great family man the way he does. I thought Elaine Pender was going out with his best friend for a while?"

"She was. It's all a bit sick. All that swapping around. How could she sleep with John after sleeping with Maurice?" Emma's gorgeous retroussé nose wrinkled in disdain. Then suddenly realising what she'd said and remembering Chris's own entanglement with his wife's best friend, she blushed.

"Oh, for heaven's sake, Chris . . . well, it's – it's . . . I don't know."

"Easier than you think," Chris said dryly.

"Guess who was caught with his hand in the till by his boss?" He changed the subject.

"Who?" Emma's jaw dropped satisfyingly.

"Desmond McMurrogh."

"Wow!" Emma was gobsmacked by this magnificently juicy titbit. "Gayle won't be swanning around in her Chanel suits any more. How did it happen? Tell me *all.*"

They spent two hours having a wonderful catch-up and Chris really enjoyed himself for the first time in ages. As they finished coffee, he said quietly, "Do you really think Ellen is serious about this bloke?"

"Yes, I do," Emma answered honestly.

"Don't you think I should try and get to know Stephanie? Do you not think it's important for her?" he asked, hoping against hope she'd agree.

"Look, Chris, Stephanie has got by without you up until now. As far as I know she gets on very well with Doug. Leave them be. If Ellen marries him, Stephanie will have a father and there'll be no complications."

"That's not very fair on me," Chris said sulkily.

"Try not to be more of a selfish bastard than you are, darling," Emma advised coolly. "I just don't understand you. Years went by and you never asked about them even once. Why now?"

"I'm getting soft in my old age." Chris tried to keep his tone light.

"You soft. Ha! Go home to Suzy and the kids. Cop on to yourself, Chris. If she ever finds out about you and Alexandra, that'll be the end of it. Suzy's not the forgiving type."

"Well, she won't find out unless you tell her," Chris frowned. "I keep my tracks well covered."

"Don't be ridiculous. Of course I'm not going to tell her. I'm just warning you about what'll happen if she ever does find out. You'll be out on your charming ear," Emma retorted.

"That'll be the day." Chris snorted. Suzy might be unforgiving but she'd never kick him out. He was her meal ticket and anyway when all was said and done, poor old Suzy was crazy about him. That thought didn't make him feel much better, he thought crossly as he paid for lunch. Suzy was crazy about him, Alexandra was crazy about him and the one he was crazy about was off having a ball. Laughing and joking as if he'd never existed. Right this minute he hated Ellen almost as much as he loved her. He'd had enough of this carry-on.

He walked Emma to her car, got into his own and drove back

to the office. He dictated some letters, made some calls and then told his secretary he was leaving work early. "If anyone's looking for me, tell them I'm with a client," he instructed briskly.

He hoped Suzy wouldn't phone. She was really paranoid these days. The tension at home was unbearable. One good thing about Alexandra, she wasn't a hysterical female type. She didn't go off the rails or make demands the way Suzy and Ellen did. She was far too controlled for that, he reflected as he got into his car. He had the perfect mistress. Life was full of irony, Chris thought wryly as he drove out of the car park and eased his way into the flow of traffic.

"Mammy, there's a man at the door that wants to talk to you," Stephanie called upstairs.

"Hell," muttered Ellen as she stirred the big pot of chutney she was making. She, Miriam and Denise were all up to their eyes in their respective kitchens, making home-made jams, pickles and chutneys from the harvest fruits, to stock up their deli larder. She took the pot off the heat, wiped her hands in her apron and hurried downstairs. It was hardly the pools or insurance man – it wasn't their day. It must be a door-to-door salesman. Maybe someone selling encyclopaedias. She was in no humour for the hard sell from anyone, she thought irritably. She was a busy woman. She got to the top of the stairs, polite refusals at the tip of her tongue when she caught sight of the man at the door and nearly fainted.

Chris stood nonchalantly, smiling down at Stephanie, making light small talk with her.

Ellen's throat constricted. She opened her mouth to speak but nothing came out.

"Mammy, please please can I go out on the green? Gwen and Niamh out of my class are there," Stephanie begged. She'd lost another front tooth and she looked so endearing as she gazed up at Ellen entreatingly.

"All right. Put your anorak on, it's cold," Ellen heard herself say calmly. She didn't know where her voice was coming from or how she sounded so composed. Stephanie was gone in a flash. Not in the slightest bit curious about the stranger at the door.

"How could you, Chris? For God's sake, come in. I don't want people seeing you on my doorstep. It's broad daylight. How could you?" she hissed. She closed the door behind him and glared up at him.

"You'd have only hung up on me if I'd phoned. Wouldn't you?" he said accusingly.

"I told you I don't want you in my life. I told you I didn't want to see you again," Ellen said heatedly.

"No . . . you let lover-boy do your dirty work for you. You didn't tell me yourself to my face. I wanted to hear you say the words yourself," Chris said harshly.

"I did tell you. I told you that last night we were together. I told you I wanted peace of mind. But you just can't leave me be. Why, Chris? Why won't you leave me alone?"

"Because I love you, you stupid woman. I *love* you. And she's my daughter and I want to get to know her. I have that right."

"You have no rights. You're seven years too late, Chris." Ellen's voice rose an octave.

"Tell me you don't love me," he said. "Look me in the eye and tell me you don't love me."

Ellen looked into his blue eyes ringed with thick dark lashes. He stared back at her intently. "Say it," he challenged. "Say you love him more than you love me."

"Oh Chris, you're a cruel bastard," Ellen said quietly. She did love him. She couldn't lie to herself. It was a love that went so deep, nothing would ever quench it. But loving him led to misery. His love, which had given her the greatest joy and happiness in her life, had also given her the deepest hurt and sorrow.

"You *do* love me." Chris went to take her in his arms.

Anger flared in her. "Don't!" she snapped. "Whether I love you or not, I don't want you here. I can't believe that you'd let

Stephanie see you. I can't believe that you are so completely and thoroughly selfish, Chris. Go away. Please, please go away and never come back."

"You don't mean that, Ellen." He gripped her by the arms.

"I do. I do." She was sobbing now. Distraught.

"Ellen. *Listen* to me. I love you."

"Well, you don't love me enough. You never did and you never will. If you really loved me, you'd have married me. If you really loved me, you wouldn't have left me all those years without a word. Actions speak louder than words, Chris. You're very good at words. But that's all they are to you. You don't really love me. If you did, you'd never have come to the door in broad daylight for Mam, Dad, Miriam or Emma to see. If you loved me you wouldn't be putting me through this torment."

"I never thought you'd be such a hard, cold bitch, Ellen. You talk about *me* being selfish. Do you not think it's selfish of *you* to stop Stephanie from getting to know her father? All I hear is me, me, me. People in glass houses shouldn't throw stones," Chris raged.

"Get out of my house, Chris." Ellen was as pale as a ghost. She felt sick.

He looked at her, frustration and anger written all over his face.

"I'm going. But you have a good hard think about what I've just said. And whatever you think . . . I do love you." He let go of her arms and turned and walked out the door.

Ellen sat on the bottom of the stairs with her head in her hands. Why was it that every time she'd managed to regain some emotional equilibrium in her life Chris waltzed back in and left her utterly confused and in turmoil?

When he'd told her to tell him that she didn't love him, she couldn't do it. What did that say about her feelings for Doug? She did care for Doug very much but if she still loved Chris how could she ever hope to love him? Was she being unfair to him? Was she being unfair to Stephanie in not allowing her to get to know Chris? What was the best for her? Ellen sat, numb, breathing slowly and deeply, trying to slow the frantic beating of her heart.

Her thoughts raced around her head in mad confusion as she sat attempting to come to terms with this latest episode in her roller-coaster relationship with Chris.

She felt very much alone. It wouldn't really be fair on Doug to tell him about the visit. She didn't feel she could talk to Miriam about it. Miriam had such antipathy to Chris. She'd go crazy if she thought Ellen was even considering letting him get to know Stephanie. They'd fallen out over Chris once. Ellen didn't want to risk that again. Denise would be very antagonistic towards him because of what she was going through in her own marriage. She wouldn't be able to view it objectively. This was a decision Ellen was going to have to make on her own.

Five . . . ten minutes later – she wasn't sure how long had passed – the doorbell rang. Her heart somersaulted. Maybe it was Chris again. Ellen was terrified any of the family would see him. If Sheila got wind that he'd called to see her there'd be the mother and father of a row. She saw a blue colour reflected in the glass and knew it wasn't him. He'd been wearing a dark suit. Wearily she opened the door.

Her mother stood there with a purposeful expression on her face. Ellen's heart sank. Sheila was the last person she could cope with right now. Fear chilled the pit of her stomach. Maybe she'd seen Chris. There couldn't have been much time between his departure and her arrival.

"Hello, Ellen, I was in with your father and he told me you'd be here. I want to know how many books of tickets you're going to take for the church fund raffle? Or will you have time, now that you've become an *entrepreneur*?" She gave a disdainful sniff.

No one could sniff quite as eloquently as Sheila or flare their nostrils so expressively, Ellen thought wildly.

"Come in, Mam." She tried to make her voice sound as normal as possible.

"I don't want to take you away from any pressing business. Yourself and Miriam don't seem to have a minute these days." Sheila's tone was brittle.

Mother, not now, Ellen groaned silently. "Of course I'll sell some tickets, Mam. Give me three books." Ellen made a supreme effort to keep patient.

"Thank you." Sheila was somewhat mollified. "Where's Stephanie?"

"She's over playing on the green. Would you like a cup of tea, Mam?"

"If it's not putting you out I wouldn't say no." Sheila wheeled her bike into the hall. "You look pale, Ellen. I hope you're not biting off more than you can chew. I certainly think Miriam is. She does have three children and a husband to look after as well. I worry that they'll be neglected."

Don't get into it, Ellen silently warned herself, biting down the irritable retort that she was tempted to make. She ignored her mother's comment. It was a typical Sheila ploy. *Be Made to Feel Guilty.* Obviously Sheila considered Ellen to be the main culprit, having come up with the idea in the first place. It was Ellen who was leading Miriam astray therefore Ellen too should be made to feel guilty for being the cause of familial neglect.

"Excuse the mess, I was making chutney." Ellen cleared away a space on the table.

"What on earth are *you* making chutney for?" Sheila was astonished.

In spite of herself, Ellen was amused. When she'd lived at home, she'd shown very little interest in domestic matters. She could understand her mother's surprise.

"We'll be using as much home-made produce as we can in The Deli so we're all making jams and chutneys and marmalades and crab-apple jellies and stuff," Ellen explained as she filled the kettle and cut and buttered a couple of slices of tea brack.

"Make sure you don't make it too watery." Sheila cast an experienced eye over the pot of sweet-smelling chutney. "I'd blend in a little cornflour with that if I were you."

"OK. You know if you wanted to make sponges or bracks or cakes or tarts we could always buy them from you," Ellen offered.

"Well, I don't know if I'd have the time, Ellen. I *am* president of the guild this year you know. It's a very responsible position. I have a lot of organising to do." Sheila gave a martyred sigh.

God! You can't win with her. Ellen bit her lip. She'd thought to make her mother part of the adventure so that she wouldn't feel left out.

The doorbell rang. Ellen jumped. She couldn't help it. What if it was Chris again?

"You'd better answer that," Sheila remarked.

Ellen hurried downstairs. The afternoon was turning into a nightmare.

"Hiya, Ellen." Doug stood smiling cheerfully at her.

Guilt enveloped her. If Doug knew what had just transpired between her and Chris he wouldn't be at all happy.

"Doug, come in," she said with forced heartiness.

"You OK?" he eyed her concernedly.

"Mam's upstairs." She threw her eyes up to heaven, hoping he'd leave it at that.

"Oh! I see. There, there, there," he teased, patting her shoulder. "I won't stay then. I've to go over to Swords and I'm expecting the electrician in half an hour. Will you be here to let him in?"

"Yeah, no problem, Doug. I'll see you later then."

"Well, you won't, Ellen. Remember I told you. I've to bring my sister in to the Mater to visit an aunt of ours."

"Oh, I forgot. How is she?"

"Ah, the poor old soul. She's on the way out. We're the only relations she's got left. We'll stay as long as they let us."

Ellen reached up and touched his cheek. "You're very kind, Doug."

"And you look tired. Go and have an early night for yourself. I'll see you tomorrow." Doug leaned down and kissed her on the cheek.

"Bye, Doug." Ellen felt like crying. Why couldn't she love him the way she loved Chris? Doug was such a decent man. He deserved much more than what she could give him.

"Who was it?" Sheila wanted to know when she went back upstairs.

"It was Doug."

"He's a very nice fellow, I must say," Sheila commented. "I'm surprised he's not married. He'd make some woman a good husband."

"I think a girl let him down once," Ellen murmured. There was nothing subtle about her mother, that was for sure. Ellen knew it was Sheila's greatest wish to see her walk down the aisle wearing some man's wedding-band on her finger. Then, and only then, would her mother consider Ellen to have redeemed herself. She'd finally be respectable.

"I'd better go, Ellen. I've a committee meeting tonight. Bonnie Daly is trying to get us to change our committee meetings from Monday night to Thursday because it suits her better. She's started playing *bridge*. So *we* all have to change our night to suit Queen Bee! Well, as president, I informed Madam Daly we would have to have a vote on the matter. I have to be seen to be impartial. And would you believe it, Ellen? She's taken me up on it!" Sheila declared indignantly. "So we have to vote on it tonight. She doesn't mind a bit who she's putting out with all this nonsense of two-no-trump and suchlike. Just so she can hobnob with Father Larkin and the O'Deas. Did you ever hear such rubbish?"

"That's a nuisance all right, Mam," Ellen agreed. That was all her mother had to worry about. Her intense rivalry with Bonnie Daly would last as long as they lived. Sheila thrived on it. She had no conception of the worries and torments Ellen endured. Sheila didn't know how lucky she was. Ellen sighed as she followed her mother downstairs.

"I'll need the tickets sold by the weekend," Sheila said briskly as she pulled on her gloves. "And maybe Stephanie would like to come and stay on Friday night. She hasn't stayed for a while now. She can help me make a fruit cake for the whist drive we're holding."

"She'll enjoy that, Mam."

"She's a good little girl. I miss having her around." Sheila looked sad.

"Mam . . . you know she asked me about her father recently.

Do you think she has a right to know him?" It burst out of her. Ellen had to hear what someone else had to say. She was scared that whatever decision she made would be subconsciously affected by her own desires.

Sheila looked startled. She paused from buttoning her anorak and said slowly, "You know how I feel about that man, Ellen. He's a no-good fly-by-night and I would hope and pray that Stephanie has as little to do with him as possible. But he is her father and you have to ask yourself, dear, whether it would do more harm than good to prevent her from meeting him if it ever comes to that. I'll do a novena to Saint Jude about it."

"Don't say anything to Stephanie about it on Friday night, Mam."

"Oh no, no. Not a word," Sheila agreed. "Try not to worry about it, Ellen."

Ellen could see that Sheila felt awkward. They weren't close. Her pregnancy had been the greatest blow to Sheila. It had put an immense strain on a relationship that had always been stormy.

"I won't. And thanks, Mam."

"It's starting to drizzle. Tell Stephanie to come in," Sheila instructed as she cycled off home.

Ellen was touched by her mother's advice. She'd fully expected her mother to disapprove of any contact with Chris. She certainly hadn't got the answer she'd wanted to hear, Ellen thought unhappily as she waved Sheila off and called her daughter in from play.

The days that followed were difficult for Ellen. She half-expected Chris to phone or land on her doorstep again. She felt guilty for keeping his visit from Doug. She was trying to keep up the facade of normality when all the time she was racked by confusion and unhappiness. At night in bed she tossed and turned wondering how in God's name she could be so stupid as to still love a man who caused her nothing but sadness. Over and over she told herself that there was no future for her and Chris. Only a sordid half-life existence of furtive visits and snatched moments of togetherness.

How did you get someone out of your head? What did you have to do? She was weary of it. And she was heartily sick of herself for being such a pain in the ass. But then, every time she did make the effort and got on with things, he was back annoying her, tormenting her, reminding her of her love. It wasn't all her fault. She was only human, she'd try and comfort herself. She'd look at Denise and see what grief she was going through because of the break-up of her marriage and take a small comfort knowing that she certainly wasn't the only woman in the world to suffer heartache.

One day, about three weeks later, Doug was mending a puncture on Stephanie's little bike. It was late, Stephanie was in bed and Ellen was working on her father's accounts. Out of the blue Doug looked up at her and said quietly, "Chris has been in touch with you, hasn't he?"

"How did you know?"

"Aw come on, Ellen. You're not on the planet these days. You're miles away. You're not sleeping. You've shadows around your eyes. You're trying to be bright and breezy and it's a huge effort. And you're keeping me at arm's length. I don't have to be Sherlock Holmes to work it out." There was a trace of anger in his voice.

"If you get mad at me, Doug, I just won't be able to handle it. So don't start," Ellen said shakily.

"I'm sorry," he apologised. "I just hoped that you'd finally made a decision about him and us that night he called to the door when I was there."

"Oh Doug, I swear I want him out of my life. I really really do. But as much as I want to I just can't block him out and shut down all the feelings I had for him. If I could I would, Doug, you have to believe that. There's no comparison between you and him. You're a thousand times the man he'll ever be. I know that. But I'm not going to lie to you and say I don't still have feelings for him." Ellen came over and knelt beside Doug and put her arms around him.

"What did he want?"

"To get back with me. He says he wants to get to know Stephanie. He says it's his right."

"What did you say?"

"I told him to get out and leave me alone. I don't know what's the right thing to do. Maybe I should let him get to know Stephanie. But I'm afraid she'll get hurt. Chris's top priority in life is himself. His children are way down the list. I think he's using Stephanie to get at me. I don't believe after all this time that he's genuine about wanting to get to know her. How could he be?"

"Why didn't you tell me about all this?" Doug stared hard at her. "I thought we were friends. Why couldn't you share it with me?" He was still angry.

"Ah Doug." Ellen shook her head. "I didn't want to hurt you. It's my problem. I have to work it out myself. If you want to go and try and find happiness with someone else, I'll understand. I do love you in a very different way to him. I just don't love you the way you want me to, yet." Ellen's gaze never wavered. It was the only honest thing she could say.

"I'm not going anywhere," Doug sighed. "I'm in this for the long haul, Ellen." They held each other tight for a long time, finding a sort of comfort and unspoken reassurance in their embrace.

It was coming home tomorrow, Julie Ann thought dispiritedly as she sat in bed colouring Cinderella's beautiful ball gown a deep shade of pink.

She'd tried and tried and tried her best to give him away so that she could become a saint but her mummy and daddy just wouldn't allow it. She couldn't even make a miracle because her halo hadn't grown one tiny little bit. Julie Ann had studied her reflection intently from all angles, but no sign.

You'd think that her parents would be delighted to have a saint in the family, Julie Ann thought indignantly as she coloured Cinderella's hair reddy brown, just like her mummy's. All the *fuss* about a baby. Her old nursery had been decorated in blue for Andrew. He was getting a new cot and loads of new clothes and toys. Everybody kept bringing presents for him. If it was Baby Jesus, she'd understand all the fussing. After all, the three Wise Men had come to visit him, and the Angel of the Lord had told the shepherds about him, but Andrew was just an ordinary old baby. No angels had heralded his arrival. No star had shone brightly in the East.

Julie Ann sighed deeply. Her mummy and daddy had gone out for a meal because they wouldn't be able to go out so much when the new baby was home. They wouldn't be leaving him on his own with Mrs Kelly, the babysitter, the way they left her, she thought resentfully. It just wasn't fair. A very odd feeling made her face hot. There was a funny sort of a lump in her chest. Julie Ann stared at her beautiful picture and then holding her crayon tightly she scribbled as hard as she could all over the face of Cinderella.

This time Suzy was going to be prepared for him. Tonight was the night that she was going to catch Chris red-handed with his slut. He'd told her he was going to an insurance brokers' meeting. He was a bare-faced liar. He looked at her, straight, with those innocent blue eyes and told her he wouldn't be home from work that evening so she needn't cook dinner for him. And then he'd the nerve, the *nerve* to kiss her on the cheek before he grabbed his briefcase and hurried from the house.

How her palm had itched to slap that smooth jaw. Well, tonight she *would* slap his face, hard, when she caught him with his floozy of a mistress out in Glenree. She had to get petrol, Suzy reminded herself as she poured hot milk over the twins' cornflakes. It wouldn't do to run out of petrol on the back roads to that godforsaken hole.

Suzy fed the twins their breakfast and then wiped their hands and faces before wrapping them up warmly in hats, coats and scarves so they could go out and play on the swing in the back garden. It was good for them to get fresh air, but today in particular she was glad that the sun was shining and that depressing grey drizzly sky they'd had over the past few days had cleared. She had a reason for wanting the children to be outside this morning. She had a task that needed all her attention and she didn't want Adam and Christina asking awkward questions.

Suzy washed up quickly and hurried upstairs. She pulled two large suitcases from deep in the recesses of her floor-to-ceiling fitted wardrobes and flung them on the bed. In one she packed Chris's underwear, socks, shirts and pullovers, in the other she crammed his suits.

A cold rage fuelled her actions. He could have his slut but he was going to lose everything else. A forgiving wife she was not going to be. She wasn't going to close her eyes to his infidelity for one minute longer. Chris had betrayed her and their children and ruined their marriage. He'd treated her like dirt. He was so smug, he thought he could keep rubbing her nose in it and get away with it. Well, he'd picked the wrong woman to put up with his crap, Suzy fumed as she shoved his expensive leather shoes into a holdall. And tonight he was going to learn that to his cost. She was exhausted by the time she carried the lot out to the car.

By the time her babysitter came at four, Suzy was a coiled knot of nerves. She hadn't been able to eat all day. She could barely manage to take a few sips of tea. She gave the girl a few brisk instructions and hurried out to the car, palms sweaty.

She parked discreetly down the road from Chris's office twenty minutes later. She got out of the car and hurried to the car park at the side of his office. She had to make sure Chris was still there or her whole plan would collapse. Heart pounding, she saw his red Peugeot. So far, so good. Now all she had to do was wait.

Suzy had to wait for almost an hour before she saw her husband's car nosing out into the traffic. Sick with anticipation, petrified that he'd see her in his rear-view mirror, she allowed a few cars to come between them before she edged out into the lane and started the chase.

She was indicating to turn right at Pembroke Street Lower, sure that her husband would do the same to head north along Leeson Street, when she realised that he was continuing south along

Baggot Street. How odd, Suzy thought, as she cut in in front of a Mini and earned herself an irritated blast of a horn. She had fully expected Chris to drive towards the city centre and the northside of town, instead he was driving southside. What was he up to? Maybe he *had* a brokers' meeting. If he had, she'd have to race home and unpack all his damned clothes.

"Hell! Hell! Hell!" she swore. Where was he going? They crossed the canal into Upper Baggot Street. Maybe he was going to Jury's. Maybe that's where the meeting was. No, not Jury's, she thought as he carried on towards the American Embassy. He was heading towards Ballsbridge. Why would he be going to Ballsbridge? She was thoroughly confused.

She followed him towards the Merrion Road and then saw him indicate right for Anglesea Road. Why was he going down there? The meeting was hardly in the RDS. He passed the side entrance and continued on. In a minute he'd be passing the apartments where Alexandra lived, Suzy thought irritably. What kind of a wild-goose chase was he leading her on? Maybe he'd seen her in his mirror. Maybe he was trying to throw her off the scent. But she'd been very careful to leave cars between them and he certainly wouldn't expect her to follow him from work. She'd just have to keep after him and see what he was up to. They were almost at the entrance to Alexandra's apartments. She should call in to her friend and forget this nonsense, Suzy thought wearily when her eyes widened with shock as she saw Chris's car glide up the discreet tree-lined drive.

What on earth was Chris driving into Alexandra's pad for? He couldn't stand Alexandra. They never had a good word to say about each other. Suzy drove on, flummoxed. As soon as she had a chance she did a U-turn and headed smartly back. From across the street, half-hidden by shrubs and trees, she could see her husband standing on the steps of Alexandra's apartment block with a bouquet of roses in his arms.

"Oh my God!" *It's Alexandra! He's having an affair with Alexandra!* The realisation was like a hammer-blow to her skull as she watched Chris disappear behind her best friend's front door.

Chapter Five

Suzy sat in the car, her heart thudding. She was so utterly shocked she had a sensation of complete unreality. This wasn't happening. This was a nightmare. Chris couldn't be having an affair with Alexandra. They couldn't stand each other. They never lost an opportunity to insult each other with snide barbs.

But he was here on her doorstep with a bunch of flowers. He'd told Suzy he was going to a brokers' meeting. Instead he was at her best friend's place with flowers. She'd seen it with her own eyes.

All her instincts about him having an affair were true. But she'd got it terribly wrong about the other woman. She'd been convinced it was Ellen Munroe. She'd kind of got used to the idea, strange as it seemed. Never in her wildest moments had she suspected Alexandra of being her husband's mistress. *Alexandra!* Her best friend. The pain of it. The pain of it. It was as though she'd swallowed a burning rod right down to her solar plexus. It was a physical ache that overwhelmed her and made it difficult to breathe. Did they both think so little of her? Did they both consider her feelings of such little consequence? Chris knew Alexandra was her best friend. Alexandra knew how much she loved Chris . . . she'd even advised her on how to get him to pop the question all those years ago and still she'd betrayed their friendship in the worst possible way a friend could betray another.

Grief, anger, hurt, fear, ripped through Suzy.

She'd have got over Chris having an affair with Ellen Munroe, eventually. They had a past history and a child together. Suzy'd always intended teaching Chris a lesson until he came to his senses and ended the affair. That had been her thinking about the Munroe woman. Now she knew their marriage was well and truly over. *This* she could never forgive or forget or put aside, even for the twins' sake. She could have forgiven an affair but she'd never be able to get past the sheer callousness of Chris and Alexandra's betrayal. Her feelings meant nothing to either of them. There hadn't been the most infinitesimal drop of loyalty towards her. In their eyes, she was a nothing.

The emptiness that she felt at that moment was the worst emotion she'd ever experienced. Feelings of loss so strong she felt as though she'd never ever climb out of the void of despair she'd just been flung into. She'd never really trusted Chris, deep down. But she *had* trusted Alexandra. And trusted her with all her fears about Chris's infidelity. How that bitch must have been laughing up her sleeve at her. The hypocritical, sly, lying husband-stealer.

Suzy burned as she remembered how she'd confided the most intimate details of their marriage to Alexandra. Alexandra knew all about their sex life. She'd even given Suzy a book about sex with tricks to spice up their love-making. Some of them had made Suzy blush even to read about. No doubt Alexandra had used all her erotic techniques on Chris.

How could she sit and listen to Suzy giving out about Chris and look her in the eye. All the nights they'd gone out, even as recently as last week when they'd gone to a make-up party together and they'd laughed and gossiped as usual. And, all the time, Chris was screwing her. How long had it been going on? Maybe months. Maybe they'd been deceiving her for years. It was obvious Chris's marriage vows meant nothing. Why had he bothered to marry her? Suzy wondered desolately. And why had Alexandra encouraged it if she'd been interested in Chris herself? What kind of sick game had they been playing all along? What warped, twisted, dirty, seedy charade? A cold fury replaced her devastation. She'd make them pay. By the time she was finished with them, they'd suffer as much as she was suffering. They weren't going to treat her with such contempt and get away with it.

Suzy sat rigidly in her car for a good thirty minutes waiting until she saw a BMW drive into the complex. She got out of her car and hurried across the street. She didn't want to drive in herself for fear Alexandra or Chris would spot her car. She couldn't get into the building unless someone was going in or out. If she rang Alexandra's bell herself, they'd know she was on the warpath.

"Hi, I'm just going in myself," she said breathlessly as the man who'd been driving the BMW inserted his key in the lock. "I'm a friend of Alexandra Johnston's."

"Ah, Alexandra." The man smiled.

You've probably fucked her too, Suzy thought bitterly as she stepped past him and hastened up the carpeted staircase to the first-floor landing where Alexandra's apartment was located. She heard the man go into his own apartment downstairs.

Suzy swallowed hard. Right this minute, Chris and her best friend were probably going at it hammer and tongs, grunting and groaning their passion. Chris liked his women to groan and moan – it made him feel good. Made him feel like he was the world's greatest lover, Suzy fumed. Well, he wasn't. For the last few years he'd been a selfish shit in bed. Once he was satisfied, that was it. Forget it. She was going to give them something to groan and moan about, she vowed as she rapped on the door. Hard. She kept rapping until eventually Alexandra opened the door, dressed in a silk gown, her hair dishevelled.

"Yes, what is it?"

She saw Suzy and her face drained of colour. "Suzy! What are you doing here? How did you get in?" The famous Johnston self-assurance was lost momentarily.

Suzy shoved past her and raced into the bedroom. Chris, stark naked, lay spread-eagled on the bed, his hands bound to the brass bedstead with the cord of Alexandra's dressing-gown. His eyes bulged in panic when he saw her.

"Fuck you, you fucking bastard!" Suzy screamed as she clawed at his face with her nails. "You lying toad! You worm! You're the lowest of the low."

He twisted and turned, kicking out as he tried to avoid her and struggle free, but he was bound too tightly.

"Suzy! Suzy, cut it out! Get off! Alexandra, get these knots open!" he yelled.

Alexandra hovered by the door, shaken by the wild woman clawing and screaming and shouting obscenities.

"Calm down, Suzy, he's not worth it. It means nothing," she announced in her husky voice. Suzy stopped her attack on Chris and advanced, face contorted in fury, on Alexandra, who ran into the lounge.

Suzy followed and grabbed the bunch of flowers that lay on the coffee table.

"You lying, two-faced, cheap slut whore!" she yelled, battering the other woman with the red roses. "I'll make you pay for this, Alexandra. You'll be sorry, you sly, conniving, evil bitch." She punched her former best friend in the nose as hard as she could and felt a fierce satisfaction when two crimson streaks gushed out. Alexandra collapsed in a heap, howling in pain.

Chris was yelling from the bedroom, "Suzy, get the fuck out of here! Alexandra, cut me free. If I get my hands on that mad bitch I'll kill her."

Suzy ran back to the bedroom and picked up one of Alexandra's white stilettos. With all the savagery she could muster she whacked Chris across the face and then, even more satisfyingly, she jumped up on the bed and kicked him hard in the balls.

Chris went green, groaned, and doubled up.

"Yeah, groan, baby, I'm not finished with you by a long shot," Suzy panted as she landed one on his pasty ass for good measure. "I have your clothes packed in suitcases. I'll leave them outside. I want a cheque from you every week with the housekeeping. And you make sure you keep paying the mortgage on that damn house or by God I'll create such a stink, you fucking shit."

She marched out of the room to where Alexandra was cowering in the corner. "You're going to regret this, Alexandra, believe me," she said emphatically. "And I hope your nose is broken," she added furiously. "You and Chris are welcome to each other. You're two of a kind. And don't forget you took my kids' father away from them. I hope you can live with that, you underhand bitch."

"*You* drove him away, you stupid cow! With your complaining!

What man wants to come home to a pigsty and a wet rag of a wife who never shuts up about him having an affair, even when he's not having one? You pushed him into my arms, Suzy. You better take some of the blame. You had it all. A sexy husband, loads of dosh, a fab house and two kids. What more did you want? You were never satisfied. You knew what he was like when you married him. Don't blame me because he came to me when he couldn't put up with your carry-on for another minute. You're a stupid, frivolous, silly little airhead! He needed a real woman and that's what he got. I'm sick of you whingeing and moaning. At least I won't have to put up with that any more," Alexandra ranted as she tried to staunch the flow of blood from her nose.

"Yeah, well at least I don't go around stealing other women's husbands!" Suzy shrieked at the top of her voice.

"Shut up, you blithering idiot! I don't want everyone to hear this racket," Alexandra exploded.

"Don't you call me a blithering idiot!" Suzy launched herself on the other woman and they tussled and struggled on the floor, pulling hair and hitting and kicking. Moments later Suzy felt herself being pulled away.

"Get out of here, Suzy, before I break your goddamn neck!" Chris yelled as he manhandled her to the door. He gave her a violent shove that sent her sprawling along the landing and slammed the door shut behind her.

Panting, breathless, Suzy lay, shaken to the core. She heard the click of a door and looked up to see an elderly dowager type peering through a slit in a door opposite.

"Disgraceful! Disgraceful!" she rebuked, scandalised.

"Piss off," muttered Suzy as she dragged herself to her feet and staggered downstairs on very unsteady legs. She made it to the car and collapsed in a heap behind the wheel, sobbing her heart out. She felt sick, only an immense effort of will stopped her from vomiting. After a little while she regained some composure. She drove the car into the grounds, unloaded his belongings from the boot and left them at the bottom of the steps. She looked up at the window of the apartment and saw Chris looking down at her.

Suzy stared back with a hatred so strong she could almost taste it.

She gave him a vicious two fingers, got back into the car and drove straight out on to Anglesea Road without looking left or right. If she got killed, she got killed. That would serve them right. They'd have to live with the guilt of that for the rest of their miserable lives. And she'd haunt them. They'd never have a minute's peace.

Suzy started to cry again. All she wanted to do was to get home to her own house and drink herself into a stupor, to forget for an hour or two the nightmare that was now her life.

"Look at my face! Jesus, I'll be scarred for life," Alexandra wept as she stared at her pumping nose and her marked cheeks.

"Look at mine, for chrissake. She could have blinded me. I can't go into work looking like this." Chris was horrified at the sight that was reflected in the mirror. Deep gouge marks that had drawn blood ran the length of his face from temple to jaw. A purple weal over his right eye, where Suzy had hit him with the stiletto, was swollen and red-raw. He still felt nauseous from the hard kick she'd given him. The pain a sickening reminder that she might have damaged him for life, for all he knew.

He wiped his poor battered face, gingerly. He couldn't believe how savage Suzy'd been. It had been unbelievable. He'd never have thought his wife was capable of such passion.

Chris felt extremely apprehensive. He didn't like what he'd heard about housekeeping cheques and mortgage payments. He wasn't getting out of his house. He'd give Suzy a day or two to calm down and then he'd have to persuade her that it was all over between him and Alexandra.

What a bloody nuisance. He didn't want all this hassle. He turned to look at Alexandra. She was sitting on the side of the bath with her head back holding a towel to her nose. He'd better be nice to her. He'd have to stay with her for a day or two.

"Are you OK?"

"You *are* a fucking shit. All you care about is your own face!" Alexandra snapped.

"Hey, hey. Stop this. I *am* concerned about you. And anyway what was all that about me not being worth it? You told Suzy it meant nothing," Chris retorted angrily.

"Well, I had to say something to calm her down. And besides it's not as if we're madly in love with each other."

"Why are you having an affair with me, Alexandra?" Chris demanded.

Alexandra looked at him through swelling eyes. "It seemed like a good idea at the time. Right now I don't know."

"Don't you feel anything for me?" he asked, shocked by her dispassionate response.

"I like you OK, sometimes. Like I said, we're not madly in love with each other."

"What about when we're having sex?" Chris was most taken aback by her attitude.

"Sex is sex," Alexandra drawled. "You satisfy my itch for now and I satisfy yours."

"You *are* cold." Chris couldn't believe his ears. He felt . . . he searched for a word to describe his feelings. *Used* . . . he felt used by her. All he was was someone to satisfy her sexual needs.

"I'm merely doing what you do, Chris. I'm just doing what all bastards do. They use women as playthings, to entertain and satisfy them, and then they discard them and move on to some other poor unfortunate. It's called sauce for the gander."

"You're a real ball-breaker, Johnston, you know that," he said disgustedly.

"I am what I am. You are what you are. We know each other, we don't have to pretend a niceness that isn't there. That's one good thing about you and me."

"Do you want to end this?" Chris barked.

Alexandra shrugged. "I'm easy either way."

"You don't do much for a man's ego, that's for sure."

"Listen, darling, I've enough to do looking after my own ego without looking after yours. I'm not into a real heavy scene with you. That stuff about me taking you away from your kids is crap. I'm not taking the blame for that."

"Suzy didn't mean that. She'll cool down." Chris sat on the side of the bath beside his mistress and put his head in his hands. He'd a thumping headache.

"Don't be so stupid, Chris. Suzy'll never take you back. If you think she will, you're a fool. It's finished. She'll never forgive you and she'll certainly never forgive me. For someone who's had so many women, you know fuck all about them."

"Look, Alexandra, I pay the bills. That's my house she's living in. They're my kids and if she doesn't like that, she can walk. I'll get someone in to mind them. In fact I think that's the best idea all round. I'm fed up of women grinding me into the ground. Let Suzy stand on her own two feet if she wants to."

"Well, just keep me out of it. It's nothing to do with me," Alexandra scowled.

"I can't go home tonight. I'll have to stay here. She's left my cases outside. And I can't go in to work tomorrow either. Look at the state of my face!"

"Your face! Look at *mine*. The vicious bitch. I won't be able to go to work for a week." Alexandra glowered at him. Her nose started bleeding again. "I think you better bring me to hospital. That cow's broken my nose. If I have a lump on it, I swear I'll have her arrested for assault."

"You can't do that! You can't do that," Chris said hastily. Visions of a court case and all the juicy details splashed over the papers were enough to give him palpitations. That's all he needed. A society scandal. He'd be ruined. He'd be a laughing stock. And his mother would disinherit him. Chris felt his blood run cold. This thing was taking on a life of its own. Suddenly he felt hugely oppressed. He looked at Alexandra, pale and bloodied. He'd better handle her with kid gloves or there could be trouble. "OK, love. I'll bring you to hospital. We'll say we were in a car crash or something. We don't have to tell them all the gory details. You get dressed. Don't worry about a thing. You'll be fine," he said reassuringly. A casualty unit was the last place he wanted to go but if it would shut Alexandra up he'd put up with it. Besides, he might need stitches over his eye. It was a deep gash. He could murder Suzy for the havoc she'd caused. She'd better cop herself on, he thought furiously. Or else she'd be very much the loser.

Chapter Six

Suzy opened one eye, tentatively, and groaned. Little hammers beat a tattoo behind her eyeballs. Her mouth was dry. A wave of nausea overwhelmed her. She closed her eye again, hastily.

"Mummy, my bottom keeps pirping. I need to do a pooh." Adam poked her impatiently.

"Mummy, I'm hungry. Can I have my cornflakes? Mummy, where's Daddy?" Christina climbed up onto the bed.

Where was Chris? Suzy thought groggily. Realisation struck. Dread engulfed her. Chris was with Alexandra. He'd betrayed her with her best friend. Her marriage was over. She was on her own with two children. Her insides turned to liquid. Her heart began to race. Last night she'd drunk a half-bottle of gin.

Fuck them! she thought grimly. She wasn't going to let them turn her into a lush. She was going to get on with her life and she was going to make their lives a misery. That thought and that thought alone got Suzy through the day. She dragged herself out of bed, took care of her children's needs and arranged for a locksmith to change the locks on the doors immediately.

Chris would never set foot in his house again. He'd made his choice. He could go and live with that two-faced tart who'd called herself a friend. Alexandra could wash his smelly socks and cacky underpants. That would soon take the romance out of their seedy little affair. He'd come crawling back sometime. He'd never last being stuck with Alexandra day after day, week after week. Oh no! Suzy lit yet another cigarette and inhaled deeply. The chase and the challenge and the intrigue and uncertainty were fuel to Chris's fire. When it all turned mundane and normal and unexciting, he'd get bored. Any hint that Alexandra expected a commitment and Chris would be gone like a shot. Suzy knew that much about her husband.

That afternoon, while she was lying on the sofa, drained and hungover, watching the twins playing in front of the fire, the phone rang. She tensed, expecting it to be Chris. It was his mother.

"Suzy," Katherine Wallace said in that clipped snooty accent that always grated on Suzy's nerves. "I phoned Christopher at his office and his secretary told me he was out sick. What's the matter?"

Suzy took a deep breath. This was where revenge started.

"You want to know what's the matter, Mrs Wallace? I suggest you call Chris at his mistress's flat and ask him. It's Alexandra Johnston. She was my best friend once. Her number's in the book and that's where you'll find him from now on. Our marriage is over. I never want to see him again."

"I beg your pardon!" Katherine was aghast. "What do you mean your marriage is over? What about the children?"

"Oh, Chris doesn't give a hoot about the twins, Mrs Wallace. But then that's not surprising, given his track record."

"What on earth do you mean by that, Suzy? I don't understand any of this," Katherine retorted sharply.

"Well actually," Suzy said coldly and with great satisfaction, "I'm talking about your other grandchild out in Glenree. Stephanie Munroe. She's nearly seven now and, as far as I know, Chris has never contributed a penny to her upkeep. That's the only one I know about. God knows how many other grandchildren you have, Mrs Wallace. Chris was playing the field long before I knew him. He still is. Fidelity is not his strong point," she added, really putting the boot in. "Good afternoon, Mrs Wallace."

Suzy hung up briskly. Her mother-in-law's horrified gasp at that piece of information was music to her ears. Katherine Wallace had no idea until now that she had another grandchild and an illegitimate one at that. Now the cat was really among the pigeons. Her mother-in-law disapproved of such behaviour. She was rather strait-laced – a result no doubt of her own husband's philandering. Although she'd never admitted that Jeffrey Wallace was a womaniser. Like father like son, Suzy thought in disgust. Chris was very much in awe of Katherine. It fascinated Suzy to see how her husband still craved his mother's good opinion.

Soignée. Classy. Rich. Katherine Wallace lived life to the full among the crème de la crème of high society. A scandal would be anathema to her. Petite, reed-thin, she looked as if a puff of wind would blow her away, but she was one of the most controlling women Suzy had ever known.

Maybe Chris treated women badly because he resented his mother's authority. Or maybe he was just a complete louse. Suzy didn't care which. She could analyse him until she was blue in the face but it didn't change the fact that behind the dependable, solid, successful, family-man facade that he projected so convincingly, he was an out-and-out self-centred liar!

How he could have sunk so low as to have had an affair with Alexandra was beyond her comprehension. Suzy's brow furrowed. Over and over the unanswered questions danced around her brain. Had he no sense of decency at all? Didn't he have any feelings for her? Why had he married her? Why? Why? Why? Pigs would fly before she'd get an honest answer from him. Her husband had treated her as though she were his worst enemy. Now he was going to find out that he'd picked the wrong woman to mess with. Mrs Wallace would certainly give Chris a very hard time. *Good!* It was only the beginning of the misery Suzy was going to inflict on her betrayers. She had a lot more planned for them.

Katherine Wallace lit a Rothman's with trembling fingers. She had another grandchild, almost seven at that. And Christopher had walked out on his family to have an affair with that dreadful brash young woman, Alexandra Johnston. It was outrageous. It was . . . it was *common*. The Wallaces did not behave like that. Even Jeffrey, when he'd been misbehaving, had been discreet, Katherine acknowledged grimly. Her husband's infidelities were something she rarely permitted herself to think about. It was easier to pretend they didn't exist. Now, like history repeating itself, Christopher was emulating his weak, dishonest cad of a father. It had always been her greatest fear that her sons would inherit their father's genes and grow up with bad character defects. Lacking in moral fibre and backbone. Flawed pedigree.

She'd always denied it to herself when Christopher, her favourite child, showed weaknesses that mirrored his father's shortcomings. Even as a child, Christopher had never been able to tell the truth, or accept responsibility for any of his misdeeds. He'd always used his charm and ability to amuse to wriggle out of trouble, just like his father.

That poor young woman in Glenree, what must she have endured giving birth to a child out of wedlock? Katherine shook her head in disbelief as she walked into the lounge. To think that Christopher had turned his back on her and the child. And now he was turning his back on his wife and children for that Johnston hussy. It was unforgivable. Christopher had better realise he had responsibilities. And he couldn't walk away from them no matter how much he wanted to. He'd always had life too easy. It was time he began to face a few harsh realities, Katherine thought coldly. He was going to end this sordid little fling and go back to his wife and children and he most certainly wasn't going to disgrace the Wallace name.

Munroe. The name sounded familiar. Emma, her niece, was married to Vincent Munroe. What was the connection? Did Emma's mother know anything about this?

With shaking fingers, Katherine dialled her sister's number.

"Pamela, did you know that Christopher got a girl into trouble and she had a baby nearly seven years ago?" she demanded.

"Actually, as a matter of fact I did," Pamela Connolly answered calmly.

"Well, why didn't you tell me, Pamela?" Katherine was furious.

"Because it wasn't my place to tell you, Katherine. That was up to Chris."

"Good God, Pamela! I should have known about this before now."

"I thoroughly agree," Pamela said dryly. "How did you find out?"

Katherine paused. She was reluctant to tell her sister the shocking news she'd just heard from her daughter-in-law. Maybe the marriage could be salvaged. She didn't want to admit to Pamela that her son's marriage was on the rocks.

"I just heard," she said evasively. "Was it a relation of Vincent's?"

"His sister. Ellen," Pamela answered.

"Oh! That must have been awkward for you and Emma . . . I'm sorry." Katherine felt most uncomfortable. She was furious with her son for putting her in such an embarrassing position.

"Yes, it was awkward. Very awkward. They're a nice family and it was a great shock to them. But you don't have to apologise to me, Katherine. It had nothing to do with you. Christopher got the girl into trouble and ran out on her and that's the sorry truth that neither you nor I can change."

"Did that girl ever get married?"

"No."

"I see. And Christopher didn't look after them?"

"No, Katherine. I'm sorry to say he behaved very badly towards them. They were left to their own devices. Ellen had to rely on the goodness of her parents."

"It wasn't the way he was raised, Pamela," Katherine snapped. "And if I'd known about it at the time, I'd have seen to it that Christopher attended to his responsibilities."

"Well, they've managed without him all these years and she's a lovely little child, Emma says, so don't distress yourself."

"Just imagine how you'd feel if you found out you'd a grandchild that you didn't know about. And how you'd feel if you found out that one of your children has behaved despicably." Katherine was pale with fury.

"Katherine, he's a grown man. You did your best for him. It's not your responsibility."

"I suppose you're right. I'll talk to you soon. Bye bye."

Katherine hung up and inhaled deeply on her cigarette. She was disgusted with Christopher. Disgusted! To get a girl into trouble and walk out on her and leave her to accept all the burden, and then to have an affair with his wife's best friend and walk out on his marriage as if he had no responsibilities whatsoever – it could not be countenanced. His grandmother had often said Christopher was spineless but she had always vigorously denied the charge and defended her son. It looked now as though his grandmother had been right. It wasn't acceptable behaviour. If he didn't grow up and start acting like a man, he was out of the will. And she was going to tell him so, just as soon as she could get her hands on him.

"I think I might try going home and see what sort of reception I get." Chris stared moodily out the window of Alexandra's flat. He was like a cat on a hot tin roof. He just couldn't settle. He hated being out of work but his face was black and blue, his eye swollen to twice its size. He couldn't let any of his clients see him in that state.

He was furious with Suzy. How dare she pack all his clothes in suitcases and throw him out of his own house! He'd no intention of moving out to live with Alexandra. She wasn't exactly falling all over him, begging him to stay either, he thought, miffed.

The phone rang in the hall. He wondered if it was Suzy. Alexandra got up to answer it. A moment later she stood in the doorway looking somewhat startled. "It's your mother."

"*What!*" Chris was horrified. "How does she know I'm here? I'll break Suzy's goddamn neck. The bloody-minded little bitch," he raged. "What does she want?"

"She wants to speak to you. She doesn't sound too happy," Alexandra drawled.

"What did you tell her I was here for?" Chris growled.

"Don't be ridiculous, Chris. The woman obviously knows you're here. She's only going to keep calling you until she gets to speak to you. We're not fourteen-year-olds. We're adults. Tell her to mind her own business. And tell her not to phone here again," Alexandra said coldly.

"Sorry about that," Chris muttered. He walked out to the hall and picked up the phone. "Yes, Mother," he said in his best *Don't-Trifle-with-Me* tone.

It cut no ice with Katherine. "I want to talk to you, Christopher. I'll be at home for the rest of the evening."

"It's not really convenient, Mother. I'll phone you later this week. And Alexandra has asked me to ask you not to phone here again," Chris said firmly.

There was a long pause. Chris felt he'd been admirably resolute.

His mother's frosty tone arrowed down the line. "You may tell *Miss-Fur-Coat-and-No-Knickers* that phoning her is the last thing I want to do. It was distasteful enough to do so once. As for you, Christopher, I want to see you this afternoon. *Make* it convenient."

There was a decisive click as Katherine hung up. Chris's mouth was agape in shock. *Miss-Fur-Coat-and-No-Knickers!* Where had his mother got such an expression? It was totally uncharacteristic language for Katherine.

Chris gazed at the phone in impotent fury. Just who the hell did she think she was talking to? A five-year-old? He was a grown man with a successful business, a big house, a big car. A wife, a mistress and two – no – he thought of Stephanie – three children and still his mother could make him feel like a powerless, naughty little boy awaiting her chastisement.

Today he was going to tell her where to get off. Today he was going to tell her to butt out of his life. And she needn't threaten him with "The Will". She could take her will and stuff it up her aristocratic ass. Chris was angrier than he'd ever been in his life. He was sick of all of them. He was sick of hassle. If they didn't all get off his back he'd . . . he'd *emigrate!*

"You better do some shopping. I can't go out like this."
Alexandra grimaced. She had a black eye, scratches and there was
still some puffiness around her nose and cheek. She didn't look as
bad as Chris, but she was determined not to set foot out of the flat
until her bruises had faded.

"Look at the state of me!" Chris exploded.

"Well, if you don't go shopping, you can starve. For heaven's
sake, Chris, go somewhere you're not known and stop making
such a drama out of it."

"Shut your bloody mouth, Alexandra! I'm not in the humour
for it, OK!"

They scowled at each other. After almost twenty-four hours of
close proximity their tolerance levels were starting to wear thin.

"Make out a list then, I'll do the shopping after I've seen
Mother," Chris ordered as he marched into the bedroom to get his
tie.

Twenty minutes later, after another row about the list, he sat in
his car trying to decide whether to drive home to Suzy or to go see
his mother.

Maybe he'd go and see Katherine while he was still as mad as
hell. He'd need his anger if she started laying down the law. This
time, for once in his life, he was going to tell her to bugger off. She
could stuff her inheritance. It was an awful pity he wasn't more
financially secure, he thought ruefully as he drove towards
Foxrock. His inheritance had always been a safety net for him. He
didn't like to think of the possibility that it could be withdrawn.
What in the hell had Suzy been thinking about to go blabbing
their personal business to his mother? Katherine was so
conservative about such matters. Probably because his father had
had a few flings that meant nothing. That was the way with men,
Chris thought irritably as he drove past RTÉ.

His father had told him once that Katherine was a cold fish in
bed. He'd been pissed and maudlin. "Find yourself a warm-hearted
woman, they're the best," Jeffrey advised drunkenly. Chris thought
of Ellen. She'd turned her back on him too, he thought self-
pityingly. If it wasn't for her, if she hadn't kicked him out of her

life, he'd never have had the fling with Alexandra. Suzy would never have found out and he wouldn't be in the mess he was in now. It was all Ellen's fault.

He arrived at his mother's fifteen minutes later. His heart raced as he let himself in to the house. He dreaded the meeting with his mother. She was in the lounge, sitting at her writing desk. Her thin, fine-boned face flawlessly made up. Her outfit, an elegant cream and navy shirt-waister dress, with matching cream shoes, simple yet utterly chic.

"Good heavens, Christopher! What happened to your face?" His mother's face wrinkled in distaste as she saw his black and blue bruises.

"Nothing. It was a slight accident in the car," he muttered.

Clearly she didn't believe him.

"Sit down, Christopher." Her eyes were cold, contemptuous.

He felt flustered. Now that he was here, his mother had reduced him to his usual feeling of inadequacy.

"Now just wait a minute, Mother," he retorted defensively. "I don't know what Suzy's been saying, but whatever difficulties we have, it's our business and you stay out of it."

"Why didn't you tell me about that girl in Glenree who had your baby?" Her sharp glacial rejoinder halted him in his tracks.

"It was a long time ago," he blustered, stunned.

"That's no excuse." Her voice was like a whiplash.

Chris was rigid. He'd expected a lecture about Alexandra but Suzy had really played dirty telling Katherine about Stephanie. It shocked him that she would go to such depths. And it had given his mother a hell of an unfair advantage.

"How could you do that to a woman? How could you turn your back on your own child? What kind of a son did I raise? And, if that's not bad enough, now you're sleeping with your wife's best friend. I'm ashamed of my life of you, Christopher. I didn't think even you could sink so low." His mother's eyes flashed disdain. "You end this tacky little fling with that dreadful woman and sort yourself out with Suzy, and if I ever hear of you carrying on again, I won't leave you a penny."

Tell her to stick it, Chris raged silently. He struggled with himself, torn between the enormous desire to tell her exactly what he thought of her and her money but knowing that if he did, he'd be on his own if anything ever went wrong in the business.

Speechless, he turned and walked out of the room, still his mother's prisoner. A hostage of his own cowardice. How dare she treat him like that? How dare she look at him with such scorn? How dare she *talk* to him like that? Suzy would pay for opening her big mouth. She'd pay dearly. He'd break her bloody neck.

Suzy heard the crunch of gravel under tyres and her stomach gave a lurch. She'd been expecting her husband's arrival ever since she'd hung up the phone on her mother-in-law.

She'd asked a friend to take the twins for the night. She wasn't quite sure what Chris was capable of. He might try and break in when he found the locks had been changed. She didn't want the children to hear any rows. She didn't want them to realise that she'd locked him out of their lives. He was their daddy and they loved him. Even though he'd been spending less and less time with them over the past year, they always wanted to be with him.

She hurried upstairs. She felt safer there. She hid behind the curtains in Christina's bedroom and watched as Chris, purple with temper, strode over to the front door and inserted his key. She couldn't see his face, just the top of his head beneath her, but she could hear the furious juggling as he tried to get his key to open the lock. She saw him step back a pace and look up at their bedroom. He was livid.

"Open that fucking door, Suzy, or I'll smash it down. I swear I will. This is *my* house, and you malicious bitch, when I'm finished with you, you'll be sorry."

The silence enraged him. He hammered on the door with his fists. Suzy's heart hammered in unison with each blow. She was thankful for the solid oak strength of the door. She'd often nagged him to get it changed for a glass door, to allow more light into the hall, and he'd kept putting it off. She was heartily glad of that now. She was glad, too, that the ground-floor windows were quite high off the ground – even if he did smash the glass he'd need a chair to climb in. He wasn't at all athletic.

"Let me in, Suzy!" he roared through the letterbox.

She came and stood at the top of the stairs. "Go back to your whore," she said coldly. She wasn't going to show that she was afraid.

"You let me in, you bitch. I'll break your neck for telling my mother to ring Alexandra's place. How dare you tell her our business? How *dare* you tell her about Stephanie?"

"And that's not all I'll tell her. If you touch me or do any damage trying to get in here, I'll call her right now. If you want to talk to me we'll meet somewhere public for lunch to make arrangements about when you can see the kids and about our finances. I'll call you at work next week to fix a time and place." Suzy came halfway down the stairs. She wasn't afraid any more. She felt very much in control of the situation. Chris could rant and rave as much as he liked but, as long as she didn't back down, he'd have to give way.

"Open that door!"

"Get lost, Chris. You made the decision. You made the choice. Now live with it. Our marriage is finished. I *might* have got over a fling with a stranger. But you decided to rub my nose in it by having a seedy little affair with my best friend. So there's no going back. She's welcome to you. She can tie you to her bedstead for the rest of your crummy little lives, as far as I'm concerned. I hope I have as little to do with you as possible. You revolt me."

"I'm just telling you, Suzy. This is *my* house. And I'll come and go in it when and where I please. I've no intention of living with Alexandra for the rest of my life. So you have a key cut for me the next time I see you or I'll cut you off without a penny."

"Don't threaten me, Chris. There's a lot more I'll do to you. Just wait and see."

"You're a crazy bitch. I'll have you committed. I'll sign you in somewhere and say you've lost your marbles. I'm warning you. I've got friends in the medical profession."

"It's not me that's lost my marbles. How could even *you* lower yourself to having an affair with the Ballsbridge Bike? She's put more men through her hands than you've had hot dinners. I thought you had some taste, Chris. I was obviously very wrong. You're pathetic and I'm not standing here arguing any more. I'm busy."

Suzy turned and walked back upstairs. The truth was, she wanted to open the door and attack Chris with anything she could find to hand. Coolness and calmness had given way to jealousy and hatred. Tears smarted her eyes. "Bastard, bastard, bastard," she muttered as the huge knot of pain, hurt and deep deep anger flared up and engulfed her in a cloud of dark, oppressive anguish that frightened her with its intensity.

Would she always feel like this? Torn apart? Had that poor woman in Glenree felt like this when Chris had left her, pregnant and alone? Would Alexandra eventually feel like this when he left her, as he surely would? They'd never last together. Or would they? Was Alexandra the one who could give him what he wanted and needed? Would she succeed where all the others, herself included, had failed?

This thought caused Suzy such grief she thought she was going to die. Chris had called Alexandra a ball-breaker once. He'd always despised her. How could he want to be with her? Was their sex wild and passionate? Perhaps if she'd been a bit more adventurous Chris might still be with her. She'd never thought of tying him to the bedstead. Trust Alexandra! She'd probably done every position in the Kama Sutra with him. It tormented Suzy to know that Chris preferred making love to Alexandra than to her. It was such a rejection of her as a woman. Why, why, why couldn't it have been a stranger? To lose your husband to your best friend was the most grievous betrayal imaginable.

Suzy sank her head in her hands and bawled her eyes out as the silence downstairs told her that Chris had retired, defeated.

She wasn't getting away with it. If she thought for one minute that she was going to kick him out of his own house, she was sadly mistaken.

The nerve of her. By God, Suzy Wallace was going to come to earth with a bang. And to think that he was going to have to pay for the locks that were keeping him out of his own house. It was outrageous.

Chris drove towards town with no clear idea where he was going. He didn't feel like going back to Alexandra's. He didn't want her to think he was depending on her for a bed.

He was heartily sick of women. All they meant was trouble. All they'd ever done was to give him grief. He was damned if he was going back to Alexandra's. She was the worst of the whole lot of them. She was so damned cold. Good in bed but very brittle afterwards. She wasn't fun. She couldn't care less about his work. The only woman who'd really been interested in him was Ellen.

Chris felt a deep pang of heartache as he thought of Ellen. She'd make him happy, she really would. He had to get her back, he thought miserably. He had to. Otherwise what would he do? Where would he go?

He was alone, he thought sadly, feeling immense pity for himself. A man alone.

He drove into the Burlington car park. To hell with the whole lot of them, he'd book in here. Tonight he was going to order a good steak and an expensive bottle of fine wine and after that he was going to spend the night getting rat-arsed drunk with a bottle of brandy in his bedroom. He might as well spend his money on himself and enjoy it. It would mean less for Suzy. He might even treat himself to the weekend in the hotel doing just as he pleased. If he didn't look after himself nobody else would, that was for damn sure.

Where the hell was Chris? He'd been gone for hours. She was hungry. Alexandra paced the floor impatiently. She was dying to know what had happened between him and his mother. *And* to know had he called to see Suzy.

What a wildcat she'd turned out to be. Alexandra traced a finger along the puffiness of her cheek and eye. It still hurt like hell. She'd never thought that Suzy was capable of such passion. And over Chris. It was amazing. She really did love him.

Well, she could have him back. As far as Alexandra was concerned it was over. She'd tell him tonight when he got back with the groceries.

It had been an interesting little fling. She'd enjoyed it. But it was all getting too heavy now. The balance had changed. She hadn't bargained on him *living* with her. A couple of nights of good sex, dinner and champagne had suited her fine. She hadn't wanted anything more. Now it looked as if it was being forced on her. So tonight she'd dump him, Alexandra decided firmly.

The phone shrilled out in the hall. She hurried to pick it up. It was Chris. She listened astounded as he informed her calmly that he was spending the weekend in a hotel to "think".

"And what about me?" she demanded.

"I'll talk to you Monday," Chris said impatiently.

"But all your clothes are here. You'll need a change of clothes." Alexandra couldn't believe her ears.

"I'm going to treat myself to some new clothes tomorrow. I'm going to go shopping," Chris declared.

"And what about the groceries you were supposed to get? I've nothing in the fridge. I can't go out like this!"

"Go to a small corner shop where they don't know you. Put your dark glasses on and you'll be fine. Look, I need time to be alone to think. I'll call you." The abrupt click as he hung up left Alexandra with her mouth open.

Was he dumping her? That wasn't the way it was supposed to work. *She* was going to dump *him*. Just what kind of a shit was he? How dare he leave her . . . foodless . . . and with a face like the back of a bus while he lounged in a hotel room . . . *thinking*? He needn't think it was over. It would be over when *she* decided and not before.

Chapter Seven

The noise *it* was making. Julie Ann tutted as she raised her head from her sums. The baby was yelling and the new nanny, Mrs Murdock, couldn't get it to be quiet. He'd been here for two days now and such a fuss that was being made of him. *Everyone* wanted to see him. He was getting loads of presents. Her daddy kept looking at him in his pram and smiling.

Yesterday she'd been singing *The Hills are Alive with the Sound of Music* and doing her ballet twirls just like Julie Andrews and her mummy had told her crossly to "sshhh" because she'd wake the baby up. She'd got really mad and said she wasn't sshhhing because she was practising to be a film star, and how was anyone supposed to practise being a film star in this house if they couldn't sing? And her mummy had got very cross and told her not to be cheeky or she'd send her to boarding school. *That* was scary. She didn't want to go to boarding school. It was all that new baby's fault. Julie Ann scowled as he kept bawling.

She'd had enough. She flounced out of the sitting-room and went upstairs to her bedroom. If she didn't get her sums done, she'd be a dunce at school tomorrow. Rebecca and Stephanie always knew their tables and their spellings because their mummies helped them with their homework. Her mummy was never at home. It wasn't one bit fair at all.

Julie Ann stared at her reflection in the mirror. It really was time she started wearing lipstick and eyeshadow, she decided. Then maybe she could leave school and not have to do sums and spellings. Everyone would think that she was grown up and she could go shopping and have lunch with her friends just like her mummy did.

She could hear Mrs Murdock singing to the baby downstairs. She sounded like a crow, Julie Ann thought scornfully.

"The hills are alive with the sound of music," Julie Ann trilled at the top of her voice as she pirouetted into her parents' bedroom, coming to a breathless halt in front of her mother's dressing-table. She opened the middle drawer. Lipsticks, powders, eyeshadows, eyebrow pencils and mascara all lay neatly in front of her. *"I am sixteen going on seventeen,"* Julie Ann warbled as she sat on Emma's dainty little seat and began the serious task of putting on her make-up.

"Aunt Katherine's found out about Stephanie – wow! Did she go bananas?" Emma sipped a cup of coffee but refused the chocolate biscuit her mother offered her.

"She was extremely distressed. She wanted to know why I hadn't told her about it. But it wasn't my place to tell her." Pamela tapped her fingers agitatedly against the table.

"Of course it wasn't," Emma soothed. "Chris should have done that."

"Tsk," Pamela snorted. "That pup wouldn't know what it was to do something honest and decent. Mother was right about him. She always said he was spineless. I pity Katherine. Between him and Jeffrey she's never had a minute's peace. He gets more like his father every day."

Oh dear, Emma thought. *Chris certainly isn't in the good books today.*

"Is Aunt Katherine going to get in touch with Ellen and Stephanie?" Emma asked delicately. Vincent mightn't like the idea. He had no time for Chris because of the way he'd deserted Ellen when she got pregnant with Stephanie, but as far as he was concerned the past was over and done with. He wouldn't want Aunt Katherine interfering, raking over old coals.

"I didn't like to pry. You know Katherine – she can be prickly. I think she should just let things be," Pamela sighed.

"I think so too. It's a bit late now anyway."

"Knowing Katherine, though, I should imagine she feels bad that Chris never supported them, Emma. Katherine has moral fibre, Chris has none. I'd imagine she has some sense of obligation and duty towards her grandchild. I know I would in her position," Pamela mused.

"It's a mess," Emma murmured. Chris must be going ape now that his mother had found out his dark secret. How on earth had she found out? He hardly told her off his own bat. Or maybe he had. Maybe he *was* serious about wanting to get to know Stephanie. How odd that this was all happening after all these years.

A thought struck her. She'd be having a christening party for Andrew. Now that Ellen and Vincent were on speaking terms again, she'd have to be invited. Hopefully they wouldn't have a row at *this* party like the one that had caused the falling out a few years back. That had been nasty. It would be much easier not to invite her but it would be a very obvious snub if she wasn't. Emma couldn't do that to her sister-in-law. They might not be bosom buddies, but Ellen had been very good about letting Stephanie play with Julie Ann. She hadn't carried her bad feeling over into their children's relationship. And for that, Emma had to admire her.

Aunt Katherine, too, would be invited to the christening. She'd see Stephanie for the first time. Well, not the first time exactly. Ellen and Stephanie had been at a service for Emma's late grandmother but Katherine wouldn't have known anything about Stephanie then.

She sighed. Maybe she should reconsider and just have a small family gathering. Grandparents only. But how boring that would be, she thought crossly. She was looking forward to having a big bash. Gillian and Frank had thrown a big do for their wedding anniversary last month and they'd really gone overboard. They'd put up a marquee in the back garden, even though their garden was only the size of a postage stamp, and invited about two hundred guests. It was ridiculous. All the gang had thought so. But it was the first time any of their set had done it. Gillian and Frank were like the cats that got the cream. For once, Emma had felt outdone.

She'd been racking her brains to see how she could outdo the marquee. She didn't want anything vulgar and ostentatious. Style was what it was all about. Style and elegance. Gillian and Frank wouldn't know style if it came up and smacked them on the nose, Emma thought scornfully. She'd been thinking of having a pianist or – even better – a harpist. That would be so different to her friend's excesses. Much more sophisticated.

Damn Chris and Ellen and Aunt Katherine. They weren't going to stop Emma throwing a party that would be the talk of the town for its style and elegance, she decided there and then. Anyway it would be good for Aunt K to be taken down a peg or two. She was always so superior about everything. She'd actually told Pamela years ago that she'd been worried about Vincent and Emma getting married.

"He's not quite of our class," she'd declared. Emma had never forgiven her aunt for that. It wasn't out of any egalitarian belief on Emma's part. Katherine Wallace could have made such an observation about any other couple and Emma could very possibly have agreed with her. But she'd cast aspersions on Vincent. And no one was allowed to do that. Aunt Katherine would see just how of their class Vincent was. She'd never attend such an elegant soirée as she would for the Andrew Michael Edmund Munroe christening, Emma vowed.

"Don't you think you've been away from Andrew long enough?" Pamela interrupted her thoughts, her tone faintly censorious. "He's only home from hospital after all."

"Mother, I do have a nanny." Emma was defensive. "And she's extremely capable. I've only been out a couple of hours and I told her I'd be calling to see you after lunch. She has your number if she needs to call me."

"Nevertheless, Emma, you should be there when he's so young."

"Oh, don't fuss, Mother, I'm going," she snapped irritably. She hated feeling tied down and she was annoyed with her mother for making her feel guilty. What was the point in having a nanny if you didn't make the most of her?

"Tell Julie Ann I send my love," Pamela instructed calmly, ignoring her daughter's exasperation.

"She's getting to be so naughty." Emma wrapped her fur coat snugly around her. It had been a surprise present from Vincent after she'd given birth to Andrew. Gillian had been pea-green with envy when she'd seen it and Diana Mackenzie couldn't even bring herself to compliment Emma on it, she was so jealous.

"Of course Julie Ann's being naughty. She's looking for notice. Don't forget, her poor little nose is out of joint. She's been queen of the castle for so long and now she's got this little intruder on her patch. Pay attention to Julie Ann, Emma," Pamela warned.

"I do, Mother, I do. Believe me, it's impossible not to," Emma retorted dryly.

She thought about her mother's words as she drove home. Julie Ann had always been hard to handle. Wilful, stubborn and a handful at the best of times, she'd become unbelievably naughty since Andrew's birth. Emma marvelled at Vincent's patience with her. She had none. It was just that Julie Ann always seemed unerringly to know exactly when to play up. Usually in front of Miriam and Ellen. It always made Emma feel woefully inadequate. Her two sisters-in-law had no trouble at all controlling their respective offspring. But when she told Julie Ann what to do, her daughter argued or refused to do what she was told or, worst of all, ignored her. It was mortifying. Emma often let Julie Ann get away with things for the sake of a quiet life. She knew she should be stricter with her. It wasn't fair to leave all the chastising to Vincent.

Emma sighed. Tonight she'd make a fuss of her. She'd read her one of her favourite Brer Rabbit stories. Emma hated reading stories and saying nursery rhymes. Miriam and Ellen were much better at that kind of thing, she thought ruefully as she overtook a Morris Minor driven by an ancient crone. She really wasn't cut out to be a mother. If she'd never had any children it wouldn't have troubled her in the slightest. Vincent was her life. He was enough for her. But she had two children now and she had to make the best of it. She really should be more motherly, Emma resolved. More like Ellen and Miriam, otherwise poor little Andrew might end up like . . . Emma cast around for someone suitably deprived of a mother's nurturing care. Her eyes widened as she thought of Chris. Aunt Katherine was a distant sort of mother and look at the way *he'd* turned out. A charming, lying, cheating rotter. *No!* That would never happen, Emma comforted herself as she left the suburbs and drove along the winding road past St Pappin's church. Andrew had Vincent's genes in him. Not weak, shifty, feckless traits like Jeffrey Wallace. Traits that had very unfortunately been passed on to Chris.

Andrew would be like his father. Strong, moral, dependable and very kind. The thought gave Emma enormous comfort.

She had to accept her responsibilities as a mother, though. Pamela was right. And she would. Emma felt a surge of optimism. She'd start tonight. She'd play with Julie Ann at bath time, and read her a story and let her feed her brother. It was most important that Julie Ann should start caring for her baby brother. Emma was almost looking forward to it, she decided as she drove past the airport.

The evenings were certainly getting short. Soon it would be time to start thinking about Christmas. But first she'd have to have the christening party. She'd sit Vincent down tonight and they could discuss it. She'd get a formal photograph taken too. She'd seen one recently of the Queen, Prince Philip and their children. It looked most impressive. Emma had a vision of herself, sitting regal and straight-backed, holding Andrew in his christening robe, with Julie Ann at her knee and Vincent standing protectively behind them.

Full of good intentions she turned into her driveway and took pleasure in the still blooming roses and the rich-berried pyracantha that grew green and orange against the boundary walls. The lamps were lighting and the house was cosy and inviting in the deepening dusk.

Humming, she let herself in. The house was very quiet. Emma peeped into the sitting-room and saw Mrs Murdock dozing on the sofa with Andrew fast asleep in her arms. They looked very contented. Emma smiled. What a nice scene to come home to.

She could hear Julie Ann's falsetto rendition of *Edelweiss*, à la Julie Andrews. Since they'd got her the LP of *The Sound of Music* they'd had to listen to it morning, noon and night. Actually Julie Ann had a good little voice and she was quite theatrical. Maybe she'd send her to classes to learn to sing and dance properly, Emma thought as she hurried upstairs to ask Julie Ann to keep her voice down. She didn't want Andrew woken until she'd given her daughter her tea.

"Darling, darling," she called quietly as she poked her head into Julie Ann's bedroom. She wasn't there. Emma saw the lamplight spilling out from her own bedroom. She tiptoed in and gave a shriek at the apparition that greeted her. Lipsticked, rouged, mascaraed, Bette Davis and Joan Crawford couldn't have done better.

"You naughty, naughty girl! Just wait until your daddy gets home!" she exploded, all good intentions gone with the wind.

Miriam yawned as she ironed Ben's shirt. She hated ironing and the pile in the linen basket was heart-sinkingly high. It was after midnight. Sometimes, when she was tired, she wondered if she had bitten off more than she could chew. She'd spent the day sewing aprons. The three of them had decided that overalls were a bit clinical. Aprons lent a more homely air. And they wanted their deli to be homely.

Because she'd spent all day sewing, she'd been late getting the dinner, much to her son Daniel's annoyance. He was playing a football match and he informed Miriam that he probably wouldn't be able to run fast enough to score a goal because he'd be too stuffed after his late dinner.

When she'd suggested he leave his dinner until later he'd exclaimed indignantly, "What do you want me to do? *Faint* from lack of food?" Sometimes her son could be as dramatic as Julie Ann, Miriam thought in amusement.

It was going to be difficult to keep to routines and have a full-time job. She'd just have to become more organised. Get up earlier to get her washing and cleaning done. And she'd have to start putting her foot down about making the kids help more in the house. They were all old enough now to make their own beds and wash up the dishes after their breakfast. She was too soft with them really, Miriam mused. When she'd been their age she'd been well able to polish and tidy and do washing-up. It had been expected of her.

The extra money she'd be making would be spent on little luxuries like a holiday in Butlin's. A new spin-rinse that would halve washing time. A new Electrolux that would halve cleaning time. Miriam had seen one in Clery's. It was as light as a feather and had great suction. She'd promised herself she was going to get one with her first week's wages.

They'd be opening shortly. Doug and his workmen were doing a marvellous job. The place was transformed from the shabby coffee room that had been there for years.

Miriam felt a surge of energy. She lifted up her linen basket. She was mad, ironing underwear and tea towels and sheets. Pillowcases yes, but from now on sheets were only going to be ironed on the folded side.

Sheila'd have a fit if she ever found out, Miriam couldn't help the niggle of guilt that nagged as she skimmed lightly over the folded edge of the sheet with her iron. Sheila even ironed dusters! Well, it was none of her mother-in-law's business, she thought defensively. Let her run her house the way she wanted to. Miriam was a modern woman. She was going to have a career. The Seventies were going to be the best of times for her. It was a great omen for their deli. A new business for a new decade. "*The times they are a changin!"* She hummed the Bob Dylan song and felt very with-it. If she really kept at it, she'd be finished in half an hour and then she was going to tumble into bed.

"I was just thinking, Doug – " Ellen stepped back a pace to look at the facade of The Deli. "Do you think I'd be a good candidate for hanging geraniums?"

"Where? One in each ear?" Doug grinned.

Ellen guffawed and gave him a thump. "Behave yourself, you." She studied the doorway. "I think two hanging baskets would be gorgeous. Would you put up two holders for me? One on each side of the door?"

"You could stick a couple of window boxes along the window sills as well if you like. I could put up a little edging to keep them secure and you could paint it the same colour as the door. Have you decided what colour you want the door and windows painted?"

"We think we'd like to whitewash the walls and we'll use either coral pink or pale blue on the door and windows," Ellen declared.

"I see." Doug kept his face straight.

"What's the matter with that?" she demanded.

"Pink!"

"Coral pink," Ellen corrected.

"I should have known pink would get in some way. You're a pink freak, Munroe."

"I know. It's my weakness."

"Well, my good woman, if pink is what your little heart desires, pink is what you will have," Doug smiled affectionately at her. Ellen felt very close to him. She put her arms around him and gave him a warm hug.

"You're a real pal," she murmured against his chest.

"Bonnie Daly's coming down the street." He smiled down at her, his hazel eyes twinkling.

"Who gives a hoot about Bonnie Daly, she thinks I'm a Jezebel anyway," Ellen scoffed.

"You're the nicest Jezebel I know. Is there steak and kidney pie for lunch?" he asked hopefully.

"Typical." Ellen gave him a dig in the ribs. "Here I am trying to say something nice to you and all you're interested in is your stomach."

"It's a most interesting stomach, especially if it's full of steak and kidney pie," Doug teased.

"Well, my good man, if steak and kidney pie is what your little heart desires, steak and kidney pie you will have," Ellen retorted.

"See what saying yes to pink does?" Doug kissed the tip of Ellen's nose.

She felt cherished. He was good to her. She knew that he'd been upset about Chris's visit but he hadn't gone all huffy or withdrawn. It was time really that she put the past behind her. She and Doug could make a go of things if she'd let it happen. She really enjoyed his company. They could talk for hours about everything. She was very comfortable with him. And just as importantly, so was Stephanie.

The past was the past. It had held her a prisoner for far too long. It was up to *her* to close the chapter and move on.

"Doug," she said quietly.

"What?"

"You're the nicest man I know."

He stared down at her. "Ellen, don't feel you have to say things like that to me. Promise me that you'll never say anything to me unless it's what you really feel."

"I promise, Doug. I'll never tell you a lie about how I feel. I wouldn't do that to you. And I really mean it. I've never known anyone, apart from my dad, who's as nice as you. No one has ever been as kind to me as you have."

"You're easy to be kind to, Ellen."

Doug held her tight and Ellen felt a rare moment of happiness. A feeling that she wanted more of. A feeling that she knew could be hers for ever if she could just put Chris Wallace behind her, once and for all. The choice was hers. Emma and Vincent were going to have a party for Andrew's christening. She'd ask them if she could bring Doug. It would be a nice way of announcing to the family that they were a couple.

Chapter Eight

All that weekend she'd thought about them. Suzy just couldn't get the images of Alexandra and Chris having fun, eating, sleeping and, most of all, making love out of her head. Thoughts of their intimacy consumed her every waking moment. Her anger was so fierce it made her feel ill. Schemes for revenge addled her brain. Though she hated Chris and despised him, she truly hated Alexandra more.

She'd make Alexandra pay, Suzy vowed. She'd rub her nose in it, just as Alexandra had done to her. She'd make sure her erstwhile friend would sink to the depths of the abyss. She'd hurt her where it hurt most. Alexandra was a highly respected PR woman. She'd climbed the ladder of success the hard way. She'd elbowed and shoved her way to the top in a man's world. Slept her way to the top, too, Suzy ranted as she hung out the washing. She didn't care if the neighbours heard her talking to herself. She didn't care about anything except getting even. By the time she was finished with Margarine Legs Johnston she'd be a very sorry woman that she'd tangled with Suzy Wallace.

Suzy jammed a peg savagely onto her sexy lacy bra. It had cost a fortune and a fat lot of good it had done her wearing it. Her husband had cheated on her with a better-endowed woman.

What would be the best way to smite her now sworn enemy? What would inflict lasting pain and damage? Her mind was a bubbling cauldron of malevolence as she sought ways to wound her betrayers.

It was such a pity Alexandra was manless, except for Chris. It would have given Suzy immense pleasure to tell her friend's partner about her infidelity. It was a shame the tart still wasn't with that Will bloke – she could have caused a huge row.

What could she do? Suzy's brow furrowed in concentration. She could slash her car tyres, she supposed. But that would only be a temporary setback. Besides she might be arrested for criminal damage or something. No! It had to be something permanent and lasting. Something that would make Alexandra really hate her. Something that would come between her and her sleep.

A germ of an idea glimmered in her brain. Suzy focused her thoughts. A grim smile played around her mouth.

Yes! she thought exultantly. Yes! Yes! Yes!

Alexandra glanced at the typed envelope that she'd found among several letters in her mailbox. It was Monday morning and she still felt she couldn't face work. She'd phoned in sick earlier. It was unusual for her to be out sick so at least she didn't feel bad about taking a few days off. She deserved them. Stuart and Stuart's got far more of her time and attention than they merited, although it would be just like that miserly streak of misery Ron Evans to dock her wages. Alexandra loathed the company accountant. Her battles with him were not for the faint-hearted. He could never look her straight in the eye and she didn't trust him an inch. With good reason. Ron had a very devious way of doing business. He'd tried to underpay her the first week she'd worked there, figuring that being new she wouldn't question it. Big mistake. She'd soon sorted him out. And kept a sharp eye on him since. Alexandra sighed deeply. She had enough to contend with without worrying that Mister Sharp Practice Evans would do her out of her salary.

She'd probably have to stay out for the rest of the week. Her bruises were a hideous yellowy purple. She couldn't face the questions she'd undoubtedly be asked. Alexandra hurried back upstairs to the sanctuary of her flat although, to be honest, it was beginning to feel more like a prison. She was definitely suffering from cabin fever. Maybe later she'd wrap herself up in her coat and scarves and put on dark glasses and drive to Dún Laoghaire and go for a walk on the pier.

She sat down at the kitchen counter, poured herself a cup of coffee and flipped idly through her mail. Two bills. A card from a friend on holiday in India. Junk mail from *Reader's Digest*, and a letter in a cream envelope. Alexandra slit the envelope with a knife and perused the typewritten page. Her eyes widened at the contents and she sat up straight.

"Bloody hell!"

It was a letter from her landlord giving her a month's notice to quit, due to complaints from other tenants about unruly and disturbing behaviour. There was also a complaint about her entertaining men overnight.

Alexandra was horrified. That stupid cow, Suzy. Now look what she'd done! Surely the landlord couldn't *evict* her? How mortifying. The letter made it seem as though she was some sort of cheap woman. It was intolerable. Could she sue for defamation of character or something?

Who could she ask? She couldn't very well ring her solicitor and tell him that she was being kicked out of her flat because her best friend had caught her seducing her husband and caused a fracas. She had an image to maintain. Image was all-important.

Which of the tattle-telling brown-noses had gone scuttling off to the landlord with their breathless little tales? Alexandra seethed as she tore the letter up in bits and dropped it into her wastepaper basket.

Miss Kirwan across the hall for sure. And probably prim little Mr Deasy upstairs. It was hardly Jonathan Butler on the ground floor. He was a real ladies' man. He and Alexandra had had a mad passionate fling once, but it had fizzled out when she'd met Will, and he'd taken up with a tarty actress who was a real luvvie-darling who couldn't act for nuts apart from faking an orgasm, as Alexandra had told him waspishly, much to his amusement. No, it certainly wasn't Jonathan. He would have been most entertained by the contretemps.

She toyed with the idea of phoning the landlord. But that would be so undignified. If she phoned him, it would seem as if she were defending herself from the accusations. Pride wouldn't let her do that.

She was on the horns of a dilemma, then. "Damn you, Suzy! Damn you, Chris!" she swore angrily. She liked this flat. It was posh and plush and not wildly expensive. It suited her image to have a Ballsbridge address. Dublin 4 was *the* place to be. Any move from there would be a retrograde step. She'd just have to look around and see what was on the market. But first of all she was going to phone Chris and give him a piece of her mind.

She dialled his number. "Chris Wallace, please."

"Who may I say is calling?" his secretary asked in a bored sing-song voice.

"It's personal," snapped Alexandra.

"Yes?" Chris came on the line seconds later. He sounded wary.

"I got a letter this morning giving me a month to get out of my flat, all because of that stupid feather-brained wife of yours, Chris. And I'm not one bit happy about it," she complained.

"Well, do you know what she did on me? She changed the locks on the bloody door. So I might as well be homeless. You're not the only one out on their ear," Chris growled.

"Yah! Well, *I* can't afford to stay in hotels *thinking* like some people can!" Alexandra retorted sarcastically. What did he want? For her to offer him a shoulder to cry on? She was the one who was being harassed.

"Don't be like that, Alexandra. I was thinking of you too. I felt you were getting fed up with me," Chris wheedled.

"*You* were getting fed up with *me*."

"No I wasn't. I've a lot on my plate. Suzy won't let me into the house. My mother's on my back. I'm not very good company right now."

"That makes two of us, I suppose," Alexandra had to agree. Now that she was in the pickle she was in, she felt the need of some support. If she was going to have to move she'd need a man to help. She might as well hang on to Chris until she was sorted out. Better him than no one.

"How about if I come over tonight? I'll buy the evening papers. We can go through the accommodation-for-rent pages together," Chris said dryly. "I may have to get a place until Suzy comes to her senses."

"I'm telling you here and now, Chris. Suzy won't forgive and forget. Underneath it all she's a tough little cookie. Don't forget I know her longer than you do."

"I don't bloody care whether she forgives or forgets. I just want to get back home. I'm paying through the nose for it as it is." Chris sounded extremely tetchy.

"Well, the best of luck getting back, darling. See you tonight," Alexandra retorted. It didn't matter a whit to her whether Chris and Suzy got back together or not. She had much more important worries. Such as where she was going to live. The sooner she found a new pad the better. She didn't want to stay here a minute longer than necessary now that she'd received that dreadfully insulting letter. She'd better start trawling through the papers, she thought morosely as she finished her coffee and filled a basin for the wash-up.

Chris doodled on his notepad. He'd picked up the phone to ring Suzy at least three times and each time he'd lost his nerve. It was ridiculous. A man shouldn't be locked out of his own home. It was *his* house. His name was on the deeds. His money was paying the mortgage. Legally, Suzy didn't have a leg to stand on. But was that what he was going to have to do? Take legal action to get back into his own property. Suzy'd have to see reason. And besides, he wanted to see his kids. Now that he was deprived of their company he wanted to see them.

She couldn't separate him from his children. They were *his*. He had as much right to them as she did. She was as bad as Ellen Munroe, he thought savagely. Stephanie was his, too. What right had Ellen to stop him from seeing his own daughter if he wanted?

Women! They were witches. They had the upper hand in everything. Suzy, Ellen, Alexandra, his mother! They were all taking their pound of flesh and it damn well wasn't fair. Chris was so agitated he actually felt like crying. He wanted to put his face in his hands and bawl his eyes out. But he was a man. He couldn't do that. That was unmanly behaviour. Woman had it so easy. They could cry and rant and rave and whinge to their friends, but men had to bottle it all up inside. Wetness stung his eyes.

He was losing it, he really was. Imagine if his secretary walked into his office and saw him like this. He'd never be able to look her in the eye again. She'd never respect him. She'd given him a very strange look when he'd walked into the office this morning still fairly battered and bruised. He'd told her he'd been in a car crash. He hoped she'd believed him. Chris brushed the tears from his eyes and blew his nose.

He wanted to phone Suzy and arrange to meet her for lunch as she'd demanded. But he was scared. Just say she hung up on him. What would he do? Should he go around to the house and physically break his way in? Was that what it took? Chris mulled over his options. They were few and far between. He didn't want to frighten the twins. His heart started pounding. His palms were sweaty and his tie felt very tight around his neck. This was crazy, he thought frantically. He was the one in control. He held the purse-strings. He'd better start acting like it.

Chris picked up the phone and dialled his home number.

Suzy answered after a dozen or so rings.

"Hello?"

"It's me," Chris said brusquely.

"What do you want?" She sounded very hostile.

"I want to know how my kids are. I want to know when you're going to stop this madness. You said you wanted to meet for lunch. Meet me today in the Burlington." He kept his tone cold and curt.

"Don't dictate to me, Chris. Don't forget I'm not the one whoring around the country. You weren't thinking about the kids when you were seducing *Miss-Big-Boobs*. How long was it going on for? All through our marriage? Or before?"

"It's only been going on for a couple of months," Chris said through gritted teeth.

"*Liar!* Liar, liar, liar! Don't take me for a fool, Chris."

"I'm telling you the truth," Chris said desperately. The venom in her tone shook him.

"And I don't believe you, Chris. I'll never believe a word out of your mouth again."

"Look, this is pointless. I'm coming home and you better let me in. I want to see the kids. I need to get some paperwork. You can't keep me out of the house for ever. It's *my* house. Don't forget that."

"You can come home and get your papers and you can spend some time with the kids but as regards coming to live here again, you can forget that. Our marriage is finished."

"That's fine," snapped Chris, at the end of his tether. "If that's the way you feel, *you* leave. I'll get someone to take care of the kids."

"Oh no, Chris. I'm not going anywhere. I'm not the one who's having an affair. Go and live with your little tart. You're welcome to each other."

"I don't want to live with Alexandra! I'm not walking out on my kids!" Chris exploded.

"Oh, I see. You just want to screw her and have some peace and quiet when things get too noisy and stressful here. That's called having your cake and eating it, Chris. You won't make a commitment to me and you won't make a commitment to her and you'll use the kids as an excuse. Well, it won't work. I don't want you. You revolt me. I despise you. I don't want to be near you. And not even for the kids am I going to swallow all this and let you back to live here as if nothing had happened. If Alexandra doesn't want you, go and get a place of your own."

"I can't bloody well afford a place of my own. You know that, Suzy!" he shouted.

"Well, you'll just have to work harder then, won't you?" Suzy shot back. "Or else go and see if that other woman you did the dirty on years ago will take you back. You could live with her over the butcher's shop rent free and be a good daddy to your other poor unfortunate kid!"

Chris winced as the phone was slammed down noisily at the other end.

Suzy really was vicious when she got going. Maybe Alexandra was right. Maybe she meant it when she said their marriage was over. He felt impotent. Helpless. She couldn't dictate like that. He wasn't going to be walked on by his own wife. He was going to go home and demand a key and he was going to live in his own house if he damn well wanted to.

Half an hour later he drove into his driveway. The twins were playing on the front lawn. They screamed with excitement when they saw his car.

"Daddy, Daddy! Where were you?" Adam raced over followed by Christina.

Chris was touched by their pleasure at seeing him. At least they cared about him, he thought forlornly. He got out of the car.

"Daddy, what happened your face?"

"I was in a small crash. I had to go to hospital," he fibbed.

"Daddy, we missed you. Can you play with us now?" Christina flung her arms around him and he scooped her up.

"Sure I can play. I just have to see Mummy first. I'll be out in a minute." He walked around to the back of the house.

The back door was open. Suzy was drinking coffee and smoking a cigarette. She looked ghastly. Very pale and tense and strained. Her eyes were shadowed and dark, sunken into her face. Obviously she wasn't sleeping well. It was her own fault. Chris felt no sympathy for her. She was making the mountain out of the molehill, not him. It was only a fling. These things happened and she was a fool to think otherwise.

Her eyes flashed hatred when she saw him. It hardened his resolve. He faced her. "It's like this, Suzy. If you want to leave, you leave. This is my house. My home. And they are my kids. Don't cause a scene in front of them. I'll move into the spare bedroom. If you don't like it . . . walk!"

"No, Chris, let me tell you the way it's going to be," Suzy retorted tightly. "You can come and see the kids whenever you like. But that's it. You get your own place."

"And you're going to make me? Do you realise you haven't a leg to stand on, legally? Forget it."

"If you don't," Suzy continued, ignoring him, "I will make an appointment to see a tax inspector and I'll present him with copies of a certain set of account books. I had copies made of them this morning. You remember, the black leather-bound ones in the safe?" she said sweetly.

Chris felt the blood drain from his face.

"You wouldn't dare!"

"Wouldn't I? Try me, you bastard. You might get away with lying to me but you won't get away with not paying your taxes. It's called fraud! You're a thief as well as a liar!"

"Are you crazy? God Almighty, Suzy! That would ruin me . . . and you."

"Well then, we'll both be ruined together, won't we!" Suzy's tone was brittle. "I begged you for years to stop messing about with the accounts and get your tax in order, after that crooked accountant of yours let it slip one night when he was pissed that you had two sets of account books. I was always petrified you'd be caught and that the taxman would come knocking on the door. Whoever would have thought that one day I'd be glad of those account books?"

"Declan Carney would be jailed for false accounting. You wouldn't do that to him. He's got four kids." Chris felt as though he'd been hit by a ten-ton truck.

"Declan's a toadying worm and I couldn't care less about what happens to him. And anyway it's up to you. If you don't want any trouble, just get out and leave me alone."

"You are *low*, Suzy." He was so angry he wanted to thump her.

"I had a good master. Didn't I? I was taught by the best." Her face was contorted with detestation.

"I hate you, you fucking bitch," he hissed.

"And I hate you, you two-faced bastard." She turned and walked from the room, leaving him standing with his hands clenched at his sides.

He'd been completely outmanoeuvred. She had him by the short and curlies and she knew it. She was capable of turning him in to the tax people. He'd seen the hatred in her eyes. He'd shot his bolt with Suzy. She was out for revenge. He'd misjudged her, badly.

How could all this be happening to him? Was he in some sort of nightmare? Things were rapidly going from bad to worse.

Well, it looked as if he'd no option but to get a place of his own. At least for the time being. Maybe in a month or two, Suzy would start being rational about things.

Chris went into the lounge and poured himself a stiff whiskey. He needed it. And damn it, it was still his whiskey. He had to review his options. He was going to have to stick with Alexandra for a while longer. At least until he got sorted out with a place. She'd been given a month's notice. He had a month to sort out his living arrangements. And he was going to have to find more clients to fund this added expense.

He felt utterly oppressed. He had no one to turn to in his hour of need. Alexandra wasn't interested in his problems. Ellen had shut the door on him. He had no control over anything. Chris felt very much alone. It was an immensely disturbing feeling. More than disturbing, strangely frightening. He felt as though he was standing on shifting sands. Everything had changed. He'd no idea where he was going or what was going to happen to him. He was going to have to think of some strategy to get back on top of things. But where to start, he did not know.

Suzy had promised herself that they would pay. The expression on Chris's face when she'd told him that she'd shop him to the taxman had been immensely gratifying. That had been an absolute brainwave. It had come to her in the middle of the night as she'd tossed and turned, tormenting herself with visions of Alexandra and Chris together. Asking herself questions she had no answers to.

She'd puzzled over how she could stop Chris from coming back home. And then it had hit her. His little secret. The second set of accounts, the real set, that he kept in the small safe he'd had installed under the stairs. For the first time in their relationship, she had the power and control. It was a bitter triumph. He was under her thumb now. And that was where he'd stay. He owed thousands to the taxman. One word from her and he'd be in it up to his neck. She'd seen fear in his eyes. He didn't know whether she'd do the dirty on him. He'd been afraid to call her bluff.

He'd want to be afraid, Suzy thought grimly. If he started messing her about, she would tell. She'd show him the same loyalty he'd shown to her. None! Chris Wallace would rue for the rest of his miserable life the day he betrayed her with Alexandra Johnston.

But whatever animosity she bore towards Chris, it was nothing to the hatred that she felt for Alexandra.

Alexandra would suffer. That grudge would be borne for ever.

Suzy sat down at her dressing-table and began to write. This would hit that bitch where it really hurt, she thought spitefully. By the time she was finished, Alexandra Johnston wouldn't be able to face anyone in Stuart and Stuart's.

Chapter Nine

Emma surveyed her dining-room with enormous pleasure. She'd had it redecorated especially for the occasion. The cream and gold was *gorgeous*. Rich gold damask curtains hung on the floor-to-ceiling French doors. The walls were painted a warm magnolia and her new parquet floor, burnished bronze, gleamed in the watery winter sun that streamed through the windows. When her guests arrived after the service, the fire would be lighting and the lavish hot and cold buffet would be laid out on a long trestle table covered with pure Irish linen cream tablecloths. Champagne flutes and Waterford crystal wineglasses sparkled with rainbow prisms of light, from the rays of the midday sun.

Emma was glad the sun was shining. The weather had been miserable for the past few days. The gardens had looked so gloomy and dreary. Now, with the sun shining on the crisp pile of russet-gold leaves and the berry-laden shrubs and hedges, vibrant against the blue sky, the grounds looked most impressive.

Eat your heart out, Gillian, she thought happily as she walked between the sliding doors into the lounge. Andrew was cooing in his cot.

"My darling's getting christened today. Oh, my little pet! There's my good little boy." She picked him up and gave him a cuddle. He was such a dotey little baby with his big trusting brown eyes. Emma felt a rush of love for him. He was a very placid baby. He slept well at night. And because she had Mrs Murdock to take care of him during the day, Emma wasn't half as nervous as she'd been with Julie Ann.

"Mummy, will you put him down and do my hair, please?" Julie Ann stood at the door holding a black velvet ribbon and a hairbrush. Emma gave Andrew a little kiss and laid him back gently in his carry-cot, careful not to crease his silk and lace christening robes. He beamed up at her.

"Doesn't he look pretty?" She smiled at her daughter.

"Don't be silly, Mummy. Boys aren't pretty. Only girls are. *I'm* pretty."

"Of course you are! You're the prettiest little girl in the world."

"I'm prettier than Stephanie and Rebecca, aren't I?"

"It's not really nice to say things like that," Emma demurred as she began to brush Julie Ann's hair. "Everybody is different. Stephanie has dark hair and blue eyes and you have blonde hair and brown eyes."

"And Rebecca has freckles. I'd hate to have freckles."

"Yes, but don't say that to her," Emma said hastily.

"They're not as rich as us either. They don't have parties like us and they don't have a pony and a horse. Stephanie doesn't even have a daddy living with her."

Oh Lord! Emma gave an inward sigh. Julie Ann was constantly comparing and contrasting. It was as though she needed to know that she was superior to her cousins.

"Do you want a ponytail or a plait?" Emma changed the subject hurriedly.

"A plait. Mummy, when we're having our dinner in the playroom today, aren't I in charge, 'cos it's my house?"

"Yes, yes, just don't fight!" Emma quelled her impatience as she laced Julie Ann's fine blonde hair into a plait. "Now, go and get your fur muff and bonnet."

"I think Daddy should buy me a fur coat too," Julie Ann fixed her mother with a determined stare.

"When you're a little bit older."

"Well, I want one now."

"Julie Ann, don't start!" Emma warned. "You're to be on your best behaviour today. Nannie Pamela and Nannie Sheila and

Grandad Edmund and Grandad Mick won't want to see a naughty little girl."

"I'm not a naughty little girl," Julie Ann pouted.

"Just be good today for your brother's christening."

"Huh!" snorted Julie Ann, totally unimpressed. "Actually I think I'd prefer a ponytail," she announced calmly, untying her hair ribbon and shaking free her plait.

Emma felt her blood pressure rise. There were times when she could strangle her daughter . . . and this was one of them. Breathing heavily, she brushed out Julie Ann's hair and tied it up in the required ponytail. She had a sinking feeling that her daughter was just beginning her shenanigans for the day.

Ellen felt a sense of trepidation as she walked into the church holding Stephanie by the hand. Doug walked beside her and she was glad of his reassuring presence. She wondered if Chris would be at the service. He and Emma were close. She might have wanted him there and, even though Ellen was sure Vincent would object, Emma had a way of twisting him around her little finger when she wanted something.

She hoped against hope that he hadn't been invited. Seeing him in the flesh always brought back memories she preferred left buried. Memories of good times always softened her towards him. He only had to look at her with those intense blue eyes and say something to make her laugh and she'd find herself thinking, *Maybe he's not that bad.*

Besides, if he was invited, it would be awkward for her parents. Surely Emma would have more tact than that. She glanced around at the gathered guests as she took her seat beside Miriam and Ben and their children.

She could see Pamela and the Judge, and a very elegant, slim woman seated beside them. The woman's eyes were the colour of cornflowers and Ellen instantly recognised her as Chris's mother. She was looking intently in her direction. There was no sign of Chris.

Infuriatingly she felt a stab of disappointment. Sometimes she drove herself mad! She didn't want to see him, she wanted him out of her life, and yet she had just felt disappointment because he wasn't here. Who was she kidding? She wasn't over him. There were times she feared she never would be. It seemed such an impossible obstacle and yet, intuitively, Ellen knew if she could make that final leap and leave him behind, she'd find a lifetime of happiness with Doug.

Chris's mother kept up her scrutiny. It was unsettling. Why did she keep staring? As far as she knew, Chris had never told her about their relationship. He certainly hadn't told her about Stephanie.

Ellen looked down at Stephanie, who was whispering to her cousin Rebecca. She looked so pretty in her new red coat. The colour brought out the vivid blue of her eyes and highlighted the rich bronze glints in her wavy chestnut hair. She was a beautiful little girl. The greatest blessing in Ellen's life. How ironic that the rich, refined socialite just across the aisle should be deprived of the joy that was Stephanie – her grandchild.

Julie Ann pranced over to them and edged past Doug.

"Hello, Auntie Ellen, can Stephanie come up and sit with me? Mummy said I could ask."

"Well, there's to be no giggling! And what about Rebecca? You can't leave *her* out."

"She's with Daniel and Connie an' anyway Auntie Miriam wouldn't let her move 'cos she has to stay with her family."

"Well, maybe Stephanie should stay here with *her* family," Ellen said firmly.

Julie Ann fixed her with a *Don't-be-Silly* look. "But she doesn't have a proper family, Auntie Ellen. She hasn't got a daddy. She's only got you."

Ellen was momentarily speechless at this dismissive put-down. But Julie Ann wasn't being cheeky, she was just presenting the facts as she saw them. It pierced her heart.

She hasn't got a daddy. She's only got you.

Children could be so cruelly honest.

Doug frowned. "Go back to your own seat, Julie Ann. You shouldn't be talking in church." He was livid. His eyes were like

flints. Julie Ann ignored him. Ellen had to admire her niece's
nerve. Doug wasn't easily ignored, especially when he looked the
way he looked right now.

"Please, please, Auntie Ellen. She'll be in the most important seat,
'cos it's *my* brother that's being christened," Julie Ann wheedled.

"Do you want to go up and sit in the front with Julie Ann or
do you want to stay here with Doug and me and Rebecca?" Ellen
murmured to Stephanie.

"Oh, can I go up to the front, Mammy? Can I see the water
being poured all over Andrew?" Stephanie asked eagerly.

"But you won't be able to hold him. Only *I* can hold him. I
might give you a go later," Julie Ann interjected, laying down the
ground rules.

"OK," Stephanie agreed.

Ellen felt like telling Julie Ann to get lost. She was such a little
consequence. Dishing out orders and making conditions.

"Well, if there's any messing that'll be the end of it. Stephanie'll
have to come back here," Ellen decreed.

"There won't be." Julie Ann gave a toss of her ponytail as she
shoved her way past Doug, followed by her excited cousin.

"I want to go too, Mammy," Rebecca demanded.

"No, Rebecca. Stay where you are like a good girl." Miriam
threw her eyes up to heaven.

Rebecca's lower lip trembled. "It's not fair. I always get left out."

"Don't be silly, Rebecca. If you go, Daniel will want to go. Stay
here with us now."

Two big tears plopped down Rebecca's cheeks. Ellen put her
arm around her. She understood her niece's misery perfectly.
Typical Julie Ann, causing consternation as usual.

"You can come and stay the night with Stephanie tonight if you
want to," she whispered.

"Can I?" Rebecca brightened. "Can we have cocoa for supper?"

"Of course. And maybe beans on toast."

"Oh yum! Thanks, Auntie Ellen." Ellen gave her a squeeze.
Poor Rebecca was a real little softie, just like her mother. Julie Ann
made mincemeat of her.

"That young one should be seen and not heard," Doug hissed.

"She's only a child, Doug, she knows no better," Ellen murmured.

"She'd know better if she was mine, the little brat."

Ellen giggled. She couldn't help it. Doug was really put out. And Julie Ann had ignored him so magnificently.

Doug caught her eye, scowled and then, in spite of himself, had to smile. "This is going to be an interesting day all round, I'd say. We still have the meal to get through. Maybe the priest might do us all a favour and drown the little she-devil in the font."

"Stop it, Doug!"

"Well, I'm just telling you one thing. If Stephanie ever wants a daddy, tell her I'm applying for the job."

"Oh Doug, that's not fair," Ellen said miserably.

Doug sighed. "I'm sorry, Ellen. I didn't mean to say that. I just felt for Stephanie. She's a great kid. Forget it."

Ellen slipped her hand into his. He gave it a squeeze. She felt like crying. His loyalty to Stephanie really touched her. He'd make a hell of a better father than Chris ever would, she thought dolefully.

This was supposed to be a happy event. She'd better cop on to herself and stop behaving as though she were at a funeral. She really was a pain in the ass. How Doug put up with her, she didn't know. She wasn't going to give Chris Wallace one more thought today. She was going to enjoy the christening and the party afterwards. And that was all there was to it.

The priest came out on the altar and silence descended on the congregation as they stood to begin the service.

Katherine Wallace felt a pang as she watched the two little girls in the front seat of the church. One dark and one blonde head, close together giggling and whispering. Stephanie had such a look of Chris around the eyes. She was a little beauty. How could her son have turned his back on his own child?

She wasn't maternal herself. She admitted that. She'd always considered the rearing of her children as an obligation. A duty and responsibility to be endured rather than enjoyed. When she saw Stephanie she felt somehow that she had failed as a mother. Perhaps Chris had turned his back on his child precisely because she had communicated too strongly this sense of encumbrance. Accepting responsibility had never been her youngest son's strong point.

If theirs had been a warm, compassionate, affectionate type of relationship would things have turned out differently? Was it her fault because she'd been too austere and reserved? Was it a case of the sins of the mothers . . . ? Katherine sighed deeply. She was what she was. She'd always found it difficult to show affection and let her barriers down. Maybe that was why Jeffrey had turned to other women. She'd never refused him but sex had always been a duty, not this great pleasurable event that young people of today seemed to think it was. Was it because she was frigid? If Jeffrey had been kinder to her, more understanding of her fears, her inhibitions, would their sex life have improved? He hadn't given it a chance.

His rejection of her had been the most devastating trauma of her life. When she'd found out that he'd been having an affair during her first pregnancy, she'd gone into a depression that had lasted for years. He'd ended the affair but things had never been the same between them. She hated it when he touched her. They'd struggled along for a year. She got pregnant again with Chris. After that she never had sex with her husband again. In fact, she'd never had sex again.

Katherine frowned. What on earth was the matter with her? She'd repressed that side of herself so thoroughly, why was she thinking about it now at sixty-five years of age? In a church, at a christening, she was thinking about her sex life. It was absurd.

Why couldn't it have been good for her? she thought, wrathfully. Why couldn't she have been normal? She wondered why Jeffrey couldn't have given her pleasure, as he'd undoubtedly given to the women whose lives he'd drifted in and out of until he'd died suddenly at the age of sixty-three, leaving her a very angry, troubled but rich widow.

Outwardly she'd always presented a serene, controlled facade. What was happening to her now? Where was this sudden turbulent emotion coming from? Why did she feel that she'd failed dreadfully as a woman and as a mother? She was the one who'd suffered. She was the one betrayed. She was the one who'd borne the burden of responsibility while Jeffrey was off enjoying his flings. She didn't like this one bit. Katherine bit her lip. She would *not* take the blame. She had nothing to reproach herself for. Her behaviour had been honourable and dignified.

Katherine Wallace took a deep breath and stood ramrod straight as the priest began to pray.

Sheila cast a sideways glance at Pamela Connolly. The woman was amazing. Today she was wearing a royal blue cape and matching blue beret. Black gloves, black patent shoes and a black patent handbag. She looked the height of elegance. And half her age.

Sheila had been quite confident in her heather tweed suit and smart little purple hat and shoes. She just didn't have Pamela's élan. She hadn't realised Pamela would be accompanied by her sister Katherine. Katherine was Chris Wallace's mother. Stephanie's other grandmother. How would she feel if she knew that Stephanie was her grandchild?

Sheila felt a flush mottle her face. Even after all these years it was still mortifying. Her daughter had been defiled before marriage and Stephanie would always be a reminder of that. If Ellen had married, people might have, in time, forgotten her shame. Well, not everyone, she conceded tightly. Bonnie Daly would never forget. She never lost an opportunity at their guild meetings to make sly digs about young people's loose behaviour.

Bonnie was a thorn in her side that would have to be borne until one or the other of them passed away. If only Ellen had behaved herself, she'd be able to enjoy a gathering such as this with pride. The Judge and Pamela might be well off, but they didn't own land like the Munroes. It was the Munroes who had provided the site for their daughter's magnificent home. A magnificent home built for her by Vincent.

Yes, thought Sheila sourly, this would have been an exceptionally proud moment if it hadn't been for Ellen. It was difficult to endure sometimes. She didn't have her husband Mick's forbearance. Stephanie's illegitimacy was a cross and she had to bear it. But Ellen could at least *try* and get a husband for herself. This chap that she was friends with seemed like a nice steady sort. Maybe with the grace of God something might work out there. Sheila dropped her head into her hands and began to pray to Saint Jude, the patron saint of hopeless cases, that he might intercede to the Almighty and get a husband for Ellen to make a respectable woman of her.

"A harpist, Frank! Who does she think she is? The queen of Bunratty Castle, for God's sake!" Gillian hissed through clenched teeth as she and her husband sat sipping champagne and forking morsels of delicious poached salmon into their mouths. The christening had passed without a hitch and the assembled guests were tucking into a feast fit for a king.

"There's not half as many people here as there was at ours, though," Frank said smugly. "We had *everyone*."

"Precisely," Gillian said dryly. "Don't you see the point Emma is making? Quality not quantity. It makes our party seem so tacky."

"Oh, stop taking it so seriously! It's not a competition. Just enjoy yourself. The grub is scrumptious."

"Do you hear who's talking? You nearly had a fit when Vincent bought that new BMW. *And* you promised you'd get me a fur coat when Emma got one. I'm still waiting," Gillian retorted sulkily.

"You will get one." Frank scowled. "Hell, Gillian, Vincent's making a bomb. If I had his dosh I'd be grinning from ear to ear. Give me a break."

"It's just, looking at Emma swanning around thinking that she's absolutely *it* would drive anyone nuts. She always lands on her feet."

"Thanks," Frank snapped huffily. "That makes me feel really good. Maybe *you* should have married Vincent Munroe!"

"Oh, be quiet, Frank! Here's Diana. Put a smile on your face, for God's sake." Gillian composed her features and beamed at her friend. "Darling, you look stunning. I love the trouser suit. Lilac is your colour."

"I bought it in this fabulous boutique off Carnaby Street, when I was in London last month. I'll give you the name if you're thinking of popping over," Diana boasted.

"Thanks," Gillian said tightly. She was furious with herself. She'd really walked into that. Diana never lost an opportunity to go on about her shopping trips to London. She knew Gillian had as much chance of *popping over* to London on a shopping trip as the man in the moon.

"What do you think of the harpist?" Diana murmured.

"A bit *de trop*, if you ask me," Gillian bitched. She liked to throw in a bit of French here and there. It sounded ever so sophisticated. "*Entre nous*, of course."

"Of course," agreed Diana, who hadn't the foggiest notion what *de trop* meant. But Gillian's tart tone made it clear it was something rather OTT.

"I like the colours in her new dining-room."

"A wooden floor's very noisy with kids." Gillian was dismissive.

"True, but then her kids would never be allowed in here. Where's the little Princess?"

"Having her lunch with her cousins, thank heavens. Such a show-off! Did you hear her singing *Edelweiss*? Talk about confidence. Shirley Temple's got nothing on her."

"Emma's sending her to speech and drama classes, I believe," Diana remarked.

"She would." Gillian sighed. If her kids heard about Julie Ann going to speech and drama – as they would, because Julie Ann would certainly rub their noses in it – they'd want to go. And Frank would have a fit. Another expense he wouldn't want.

"I was thinking of sending mine, actually. It would be good for them. Give them confidence," Diana said.

That was it, Gillian decided firmly. Her two were definitely going to speech and drama no matter what Frank said.

"Do let me know when and where, I'll send mine along to keep them company. Who knows, we might have a budding Olivier in our midst." Gillian gave a little trill of laughter.

"Well, Julie Andrews would want to look to her laurels, for sure," Diana drawled as Emma made her way over to them.

Gillian laughed.

"Girls, good to see you enjoying yourselves. Do help yourselves to more food. There's oodles. Frank, have some of the lobster. I know you love it and it's fresh. The chef collected all the seafood from Howth this morning, straight off the trawlers. The scallops are out of this world and so are the prawns."

"Right, Emma, I will," Frank agreed with alacrity.

I'll kill him. I'll kill him. You'd think he never had lobster and scallops before. You'd think he was never fed at home, Gillian fumed as she watched her husband stride up to the buffet.

"Could Chris and Suzy not make it?" Diana asked.

"No, unfortunately," Emma said lightly. "And neither could Tom and Margaret. They've gone to Paris."

"Have they?" Gillian was astonished. "I thought his business was in trouble."

"It was. Did you not hear? They sold most of their back garden to a developer who's building two mews and six luxury apartments on it. They got a fortune for it because it's in Ballsbridge."

"I don't believe it."

"I'm telling you. Vincent looked after the deal. It's all signed, sealed and delivered. So they're in the money again."

"But for how long?" Gillian said dryly. "You know Tom's fondness for the horses."

"I know," Emma agreed. "I don't know how Margaret puts up with it. I'd hate to live with a gambler."

"Darling, you'd have it spent before Vincent got time to gamble it," Gillian retorted.

"Just as well he's got plenty to spend," Emma said airily. "Have more Moët or do you prefer Bollinger? There's plenty of both, so drink up. Talk to you later." She glided over to her mother and aunt, who were chatting to Sheila.

"Sometimes she's insufferable," Gillian said through gritted teeth.

"Oh come on, let's get another bottle," Diana urged. "There's no point in leaving it there. And I'm going to have more salmon. If you can't beat them, join them."

That's because you're easily impressed, Diana Mackenzie. You've no class! Gillian wouldn't lower herself. If Diana and Frank wanted to make gluttons of themselves, that was up to them.

"I'm fine, thanks," she said coolly. "But do go ahead by all means. I know you adore champagne."

Diana got up and headed for the buffet. Gillian could be such a moody madam. They were at a party. There was loads of booze and food. What was the point in sitting there like a prune, just because she was mad with Emma for outdoing her bash. Diana spooned some scallops onto her plate. They looked delicious. She helped herself to some more. Gillian didn't know what she was missing, she thought crossly, annoyed because her friend had made her feel like a greedy lush.

Sheila watched Mick and the Judge laughing heartily and envied them. Her husband was at ease in any company, she thought fondly. It was all the same to Mick if you were a prince or a pauper, he'd find something to talk to you about. He took people as they were and wasn't at all impressed by the trappings of high society.

She felt uncomfortable with Pamela and Katherine. Katherine in particular had none of her sister's charm. She was much more aloof and stand-offish than Pamela. Her brittleness was extremely off-putting and she'd such a clipped way of speaking. To think that she was Stephanie's grandmother. She might not be so snooty if she knew her son had an illegitimate child that he'd never accepted any responsibility for.

Sheila glanced at her watch, it was after two. How long would she have to stay before she could leave without seeming rude? Most of the people here were posh friends of Emma and Vincent. They might be posh, she comforted herself, but they didn't have land and property like her and Mick. If she and her husband wanted to, they could go and dine in the Russell and the Shelbourne any time they liked. They could hobnob in *dozens* of fancy restaurants if they cared to.

Half of them probably couldn't cook anyway. No wonder Pamela and Katherine were as thin as knitting needles. They never had home-cooked food. Look at Emma, feeding her family out of tins and packets. The thought of her superiority over the South Dublin brigade was comforting to Sheila's spirit. She had to admit that the chef who'd cooked the buffet had done a good job. She might as well make the most of her day off, she decided. The lemon cheesecake looked luscious. Sheila edged her way over to the buffet and helped herself to an extra-large slice. She deserved it.

"You know, Ellen, your sister-in-law can really cook. Do you think she's got any building jobs that need doing?" Doug inquired as he helped himself to seconds.

"She didn't cook this, you idiot." Ellen laughed at the idea. "Emma can't cook an egg. She got someone in to do it."

"Oh! And here I was thinking that Vincent was a lucky man. She can't cook! I couldn't marry a woman who couldn't cook."

"You're managing fine without one," Ellen snorted.

"Ah but it's a sad and lonely life and my poor tum longs for home-cooked grub."

"I'll be crying in a minute," Ellen jeered.

"Your sister is a hard-hearted woman, Ben," Doug winked.

"Doug, stick to your guns. I married a woman who can cook and I've had a very good life, and so has my stomach – as you can see," Ben guffawed.

"You'll be doing a lot more cooking when I'm working," Miriam interjected.

"Not at all. Won't you be bringing home lovely nosh from The Deli?"

"You're not going to eat our profits, Ben Munroe," Ellen warned.

"Don't mind him, Ellen." Miriam smiled serenely. "Our profits are going where they belong. Into our saving accounts."

"I'd say we're eating a hell of a lot of Vincent's profits today." Ben grinned.

"It's a tasty feast whoever cooked it." Doug ate a stuffed mushroom with relish. "That one in the purple get-up is really enjoying it too. You should have seen the plateful of scallops she took."

"*Doug!* Don't be so pass-remarkable," Ellen chided.

"Well, it's the truth. She might have a dead posh accent but her manners leave a lot to be desired. She snaffled the last piece of buttered brown bread right from under my nose," Doug said indignantly. The others laughed.

Ellen was glad she'd invited Doug. He got on well with Ben and Miriam and they were having a great laugh. Her discomfort over Katherine Wallace's presence had eased. There were plenty of guests mingling around. Ellen had no trouble avoiding Stephanie's grandmother. Besides, the woman didn't know about her. She sipped her champagne and felt herself relax. She'd had mixed feelings about coming to Andrew's christening. But now that she was here, with Doug, it wasn't too bad at all. In fact she was rather enjoying it. She was daft to have worried about it at all.

Katherine Wallace toyed with a mussel on her plate. She wasn't really hungry. It was a very nice meal. Emma and Vincent had gone to a lot of trouble and hadn't stinted on anything, Katherine thought approvingly, but she wasn't in the mood for a party.

She was uncomfortable knowing that she had an unacknowledged grandchild in the same house. Poor Sheila Munroe didn't know where to look and what to say to her or Pamela. The conversation had been stilted and awkward. The girl, or rather woman as she was now, that Christopher had got into trouble seemed happy enough with that nice bearded man she was with. She was certainly better off with him than she would have been if she'd ended up with Christopher. Maybe the Almighty had broken a bigger cross for her, Katherine reflected as she studied the dark-haired woman laughing with her friends.

Emma had certainly struck gold with Vincent Munroe. She'd had her doubts about that wedding, admittedly. She'd never heard of the Munroes. Socially the families weren't on a par, but Vincent knew how to conduct himself and he'd become extremely successful. And they seemed very much in love with each other after years of marriage, Katherine thought enviously as she watched them slip out of the room hand in hand.

She'd never really known what it was to be loved. She'd loved Jeffrey, very much. But he had never really loved her . . . or desired her. It was a bitter cup to drink from. No matter how much she tried to bury it, it kept edging into her consciousness as if to say *I'm here, deal with me*. She didn't want to deal with it. She didn't want to look back and see how much she'd failed. She didn't want to admit that she was a sour elderly woman whose life, behind the superficial facade of social success, was empty and unfulfilled. She was too old now to have a great love affair. To have the passion she'd missed. Why had she been so afraid of it? Why couldn't Jeffrey have loved her? Why even after all these years did it still cause her pain?

She'd want to stop all this nonsense and put the past behind her, Katherine thought wearily. But it was difficult, especially when her youngest son was behaving so like Jeffrey. It brought back all the misery and made her feel a complete and utter failure.

"It seems to be going OK, doesn't it, Vincent?" Emma gave her husband a quick hug. They were opening more wine in the kitchen. The lunch was over and the guests were nicely relaxed. Diana Mackenzie had drunk one glass of champagne too many and was giggling like a schoolgirl.

"It's going fine, petal. Stop worrying. Look at our two dads – they're going over every fish they've ever caught and the battle they had to catch them gets more fierce with every telling." Vincent laughed as he uncorked a bottle of red wine.

"It's a pity that I had to ask Aunt K, but Mother said she would have felt very snubbed if I hadn't. If she didn't know about Stephanie it wouldn't be so bad. What dreadful timing for her to find out."

"Emma, stop fretting. It's not your fault that Chris is a rat, and your Aunt Katherine is Stephanie's grandmother. It's her problem and she'll have to deal with it. It's awkward for all of them, Mam included. There's nothing we can do about it except hope that they're having as nice a time here as they can," Vincent pointed out firmly. "Ellen's not letting it bother her."

She wouldn't, Emma thought crossly.

"Come on. It's a great party. The food was out of this world. Relax and enjoy it." Vincent enfolded his wife in a hug and kissed her tenderly.

"Gillian's so miffed," Emma grinned. "When I told her the seafood was fresh off the trawlers in Howth, she was fit to be tied. You wouldn't catch me serving chicken supreme and salads. She hasn't a clue really."

"She's her own worst enemy. She's always trying to keep up with the Joneses – or rather in this case the Munroes. Life's too short."

"Well, I'm just glad we've plenty of money to throw decent parties. I'd hate it if we hadn't," Emma admitted. "I'll have to put my thinking cap on for our New Year one."

"Get over this one first," Vincent advised.

"You're right. And hasn't Andrew been such a treasure? Everyone thinks he's gorgeous."

"He's not gorgeous, Mummy! He keeps *farting*." Julie Ann marched into the kitchen.

"Julie Ann!" Emma was horrified. "What a dreadful word. If you have to say that, say windy-popping. And don't say things like that in company."

"Well, he does keep farting." Julie Ann ignored her mother's dictate. "We're trying to play *The Sound of Music*. I'm Maria, and he keeps exploding in his pram and the others all laugh and it's very annoying," she declared indignantly.

Vincent turned his back. He was afraid he was going to burst out laughing.

"What do you want?" Emma changed tack.

"I wanted some more Toy Town biscuits."

"Please," Vincent reminded.

"Please," Julie Ann said irritably.

"Don't make yourselves sick," Emma warned as she filled another plateful.

"Of course we won't, Mummy." Julie Ann grabbed the plate and hurried back to entertain her guests in the playroom.

"Poor little Andrew. He certainly won't get a swelled head with his adoring sister around."

"She'll adjust," Vincent soothed. "Come on. Let's get back to our guests. They'll all think we're smooching in the kitchen."

"Hmmmm," murmured Emma as she entwined her arms around his neck. "I love to smooch."

"Me too," grinned her husband as his arms tightened around her in preparation for a serious smooch.

"I can have two and even four if I want. This is my house and my party and he's my baby brother." Julie Ann scowled at her cousins. She'd been handing around the Toy Town biscuits and had taken two for herself, much to their annoyance.

"You're just a greedy guts, Julie Ann Munroe," Rebecca declared.

"I am not!" Julie Ann was outraged at the slur. "I told you, it's my party."

"It's not your party, it's Andrew's," Stephanie corrected her. "And your Guardian Angel can see you being greedy. She saw you putting a biscuit in your pocket and so did I."

"You just shut up, Stephanie Munroe. And mind your own business. You're only jealous 'cos you don't have a baby."

"No I'm not."

"Yes you are. And I know something you don't know."

"No you don't."

"Yes I do."

"OK. What is it then?"

"I'm not telling."

"See. See. You don't know," Stephanie declared triumphantly.

"Yes I do. I know who your other nannie is!" Julie Ann stood with her hands on her hips, glaring at her cousin.

"I don't have another nannie. I've only got Nannie Sheila."

"You do have another nannie! I heard my mummy and daddy talking about her."

"Have I?" Stephanie was unsure. "I think you're telling fibs, Julie Ann Munroe. *Liar! Liar! Pants on fire!*"

"I am *not* telling lies!" Julie Ann was stung at the unfairness of the accusation. "You come with me, Stephanie Munroe, and I'll show you your other nannie. She's in our house, you know."

"Well, I don't believe you," Stephanie retorted, hating the idea of her cousin knowing something about her that she didn't.

"Come on, let's go to the dining-room and I'll show you. You can see with your own two eyes if you don't believe me," Julie Ann challenged.

"Can I come?" Rebecca asked.

"You can *all* come," Julie Ann said importantly. "Except Andrew. He can stay in his pram." She didn't want Andrew taking away from her spotlight.

Like the Pied Piper, she led her curious cousins across the hall towards the dining-room. She took Stephanie by the hand and led her in, scanned the room, found who she was looking for and marched over to stand in front of Katherine Wallace.

"That's your other nannie, Stephanie! See, I told you!" she declared triumphantly at the top of her voice, conscious of her audience. Julie Ann smiled happily, delighted to be the centre of attention.

Heads turned in their direction and a horrified hush descended on the assembled guests as Julie Ann's loudly spoken words penetrated their chatter.

"*Julie Ann!*" Emma nearly fainted. "Vincent, do something!" she hissed.

"Are you my nannie?" Stephanie fixed Katherine Wallace with a curious stare.

"Jesus, Mary and Joseph," Ellen whispered, rooted to the spot. Sheila went pale.

Katherine wanted to sink through the floor. Thanks to that

obnoxious child of Emma's the gossip about Christopher's love child would spread through their set like wildfire. He had put her in an impossible position.

She looked at the little girl standing in front of her. It wasn't the child's fault. And not, by the flicker of an eyelash, was she going to let these people see how upset she was. Poise was everything. She was noted for her poise. She'd been in worse situations than this. Jeffrey's mistresses had often been invited to the same parties that she'd been at and she'd always handled that with aplomb. Taking a deep breath she said clearly, for all to hear, "Yes, Stephanie. I'm your grandmother. It's about time we met."

She took Stephanie by the hand and walked over to Ellen. "How do you do, Ellen?"

Ellen, dry-mouthed, took the outstretched hand. It felt thin and bony in her own. Katherine's blue eyes stared into hers. She didn't know what to say to the woman.

"How do you do?" she murmured awkwardly. "I'm sorry about this."

"Well, maybe about the circumstances of our meeting, but may I congratulate you on your beautiful little girl. Perhaps you might bring her to visit some day?"

Oh no! Ellen groaned inwardly. "Certainly," she agreed.

"If you're my nannie, what's my daddy's name?" Stephanie inquired interestedly.

You could have heard a pin drop as Katherine, two red spots of mortification staining her cheeks, stared down at her grandchild.

"His name is Christopher, dear."

"Like Christopher Robin? Me an' Nannie Sheila always sing that song."

There was a sympathetic titter from the guests.

"I'm sure you do," Katherine said calmly.

"Right," Vincent interposed. "All children back to the playroom. We're going to play Musical Chairs."

"Goody!"

"Brillo!"

"Yippee!"

Assorted cries of delight and a stampede back to the playroom ensued.

"We'll talk again, Ellen, this isn't the time or the place," Katherine said quietly.

"I am sorry about this, Mrs Wallace," Ellen said miserably.

"Please, don't distress yourself. Now go and enjoy the rest of the party. Emma, I think I'd like to go home. Perhaps you'd be good enough to call a taxi for me."

"We'll bring you home, Katherine," Pamela said firmly. "We brought you."

"No . . . no, really, Pamela, I'd prefer to be alone." Katherine shook her head.

"I'll call a taxi now," Emma murmured. She was in a state. She could murder Julie Ann. In fact she probably would, she decided as she phoned for a taxi. She'd been watching Diana and Gillian. Their faces were a study. Gillian had practically got lockjaw. Now it would be all over town about Chris and Ellen. She'd better warn him, she thought angrily, although he certainly didn't deserve that courtesy.

Sheila walked into the hall. She was pale with fury and dismay. "It's really time you did something about Julie Ann, Emma. She has no manners whatsoever. I've never seen such a display," she said sharply.

"Mind your own business!" Emma exploded.

"Well, I can see where she gets her bad manners from. I'll never set foot in this house again," Sheila raged. "I'll get Mick and we'll go."

Emma burst into tears.

Gillian and Diana, who'd overheard the row, looked at each other in delight. This was the best ever! Who'd have thought that Chris Wallace had a love child with Emma's sister-in-law? This was the juiciest of gossip. They couldn't wait to spread the news.

The party was in disarray. Emma was weeping. Guests were starting to leave. Andrew Munroe's christening do was the best bash they'd been at in ages, the two girls assured each other gleefully, as they drank another glass of champagne and observed the dramas unfolding around them.

Chapter Ten

Ellen walked along the hall to the playroom to collect Stephanie. She didn't know whether she was on her head or her heels. If she could get her hands on Julie Ann, she'd wring her precocious little neck for her. Imagine marching up to Katherine Wallace like that. Why Vincent and Emma had to discuss adult issues in front of her, Ellen could not fathom. The child knew far more than was good for her and this was the result.

What a mess, she thought distractedly. The first time she'd been at a party in Emma and Vincent's in years and all this drama had to happen. She'd never be invited again. Trust Julie Ann!

It was a disaster for Emma. Katherine Wallace knew about her grandchild and all Emma's hoity-toity friends knew about Chris having an illegitimate child. Ellen had heard the gasps and seen the whispered asides of the astounded guests. It would be the talk of the town. It didn't particularly bother Ellen that they knew. She'd never see them again. She didn't move in their circles. She deeply regretted her mother's embarrassment though. Poor Sheila had been absolutely mortified in front of Pamela and Judge Connolly. She'd gone pale and then got very flushed. She'd feel the burning humiliation of that episode for years to come. And now, unfortunately, she'd stormed out of Emma's in a huff, so that was going to have major family repercussions. Life would never be dull in the Munroe family, Ellen thought dryly as she made her way through a chain of excited children, waiting for Vincent to stop the music in Musical Chairs.

"That was unfortunate," Vincent said gruffly when he saw her.

Ellen shrugged. "Kids will be kids." *And Julie Ann would want to be told how to behave,* she added privately. "Look at them, they've forgotten it already."

"I thought it was best to get them playing." Vincent stopped the music and there was a mad scramble for chairs. "Is Emma OK, the poor love? This'll be very upsetting for her."

Ellen felt a surge of irritation. To hell with Emma. What about how upsetting it was for *her?* The least he could do was to apologise for his daughter's dreadful behaviour. Typical of Vincent. Ellen's feelings were of no consequence. They never had been. Was she a non-person? Were her feelings any less important than Emma's? Obviously yes. Right then, Ellen decided she was sick and tired of being treated as a lesser being. Vincent did it to her, her mother did it to her, Chris had always done it to her.

"It's been distressing for *me,* and for Stephanie. If you don't mind I'm going to take her home."

"There's no need for that," Vincent said hastily. "Julie Ann will get upset if Stephanie goes."

Tough. She could do with being upset now and again, Ellen thought unsympathetically.

"Look, Vincent, I'm not making a big deal out of it. I simply want to go home. I feel like someone in a zoo in there. I have feelings too." Ellen knew it was pointed but she didn't care. She was making a stand and that was it!

"For God's sake, poor Emma's gone to a lot of trouble for this party. Katherine's leaving. You're leaving. It's a bit ungracious, Ellen."

Ellen drew a deep breath. She and Vincent had always sparked off each other. She could let fly and tell him what she thought of his selfish attitude and cause another family row or she could save her energy. The old Ellen would have launched a counter-attack. The new Ellen, with great difficulty, let his comment pass.

"Stephanie, pet. Come outside for a minute," she said quietly.

"But Mammy, I'm playing Musical Chairs."

"Now, Stephanie." Her tone was firm.

"OK, Mammy." Stephanie obediently followed her from the room. "Good girl," Ellen approved, thankful beyond belief that she could rely on her daughter's good behaviour. She might have had a child out of wedlock and have very little money for ponies and parties and the like, but she'd brought Stephanie up well and no one could take that away from her. Julie Ann might have everything money could buy, but she was a disobedient little brat who hated sharing and who rarely did what she was told. Vincent and Emma had little to be proud of in the rearing of their daughter.

She knew it was childish to make comparisons but it made her feel better. She knelt down beside Stephanie.

"Listen, love, I know you won't make a fuss, but you and I and Doug are leaving a little bit early."

"But Mam, I want to play Musical Chairs an' Rebecca's staying an' it's not fair," Stephanie protested. "Please let me stay."

Ellen's heart sank. Stephanie was right. It wasn't really fair to drag her away, just because Ellen was uncomfortable with what had happened. Stephanie was the innocent party in all of it. If she made a stand and left because her feelings were hurt, Stephanie was going to suffer. When was it right to make a stand and when was it not? She looked into her daughter's blue eyes and saw the resentment and anxiety there. Ellen made her decision. Today wasn't the day to make her stand. "OK, pet, you go back in and play. And have fun."

"Thanks, Mam. Thanks." Stephanie was gone like a flash, back to her cousins – a new grandmother, social dramas and family friction taking second place to the important priority of the day . . . play.

Ellen walked back up the hall. She really didn't want to go back into the lounge. She could hear Emma sobbing upstairs and Pamela murmuring words of comfort. Katherine stood at the front door awaiting her taxi.

The two women stared at each other.

"I think this is a party that won't be forgotten in a hurry," Katherine said dryly. "I hope your mother and Emma don't have a serious falling out."

"It'll blow over. My mother's a bit sensitive about it all. And Emma's excitable."

"Don't I know it," Katherine said wryly. "And Julie Ann is certainly her mother's daughter." They shared a smile. Ellen felt a strange affinity with Chris's mother.

"Stephanie is a beautiful child," Katherine remarked a little awkwardly.

"Yes, she is."

"For what it's worth, I think my son behaved very badly. I didn't raise him to turn his back on his responsibilities. He takes after his father, unfortunately."

"Oh!" Ellen replied, unsure of how she should respond.

"My husband turned his back on me too." Katherine's tone was brittle.

"I'm sorry," Ellen reached out and touched the older woman on the arm. "It's a hard thing to endure, being rejected by someone you love."

Katherine grimaced. "I've never admitted that to anyone before. I can't believe I'm saying it to you, someone I've never met before. I can see why Chris was drawn to you, Ellen. But I'm telling you something now, maybe it's as well things happened as they did. You might have the chance of a happy marriage some day. You might meet a man who will value you. Don't ever put up with being second best. Not like me. My marriage was a sham. I should have walked away from it and made a new life for myself. Now all I have is bitter memories and a feeling of emptiness that can never be filled. Do you understand that?" Katherine asked. Her eyes were bright with emotion, her cheeks were flushed.

"Yes, I do," Ellen said quietly. It was clearly out of character for this reserved woman to speak of such private matters.

Katherine took a deep breath and some of the tension went out of her ramrod-straight body. "Isn't it ironic? I never had a daughter to share my feelings with. Thank you. You're the last person I should burden with my problems. I really don't know what came over me." She gave an embarrassed little laugh.

"Maybe only a person who's experienced a betrayal can understand the pain of it. We might be poles apart socially, Mrs Wallace, but we've each been rejected and have had to deal with it. Our feelings aren't so different."

"No . . . no, I suppose not," Katherine agreed tiredly. "It's a little difficult when you've suppressed them for a long time and they come back with a vengeance."

"Someone once told me that when your past holds you prisoner you should let it go. I, of all people, know that's easier said than done, but maybe you should think about it," Ellen offered.

"I think I'm too old to change now." Katherine shook her head. "Sometimes anger and bitterness are more comfortable to live with than making the effort to move on. I don't have youth on my side as you do . . . better the devil you know and all that. Goodbye, Ellen. Here's my taxi."

"Goodbye, Mrs Wallace."

Ellen watched Chris's mother walk briskly to the taxi. She was a strange mixture. Clipped and reserved for the most part but with a core of vulnerability and sadness that, Ellen suspected, was rarely revealed. Ellen was glad she'd seen it. It made Katherine seem very human. If she'd shown that side of her to Chris, maybe he might have understood how women could be hurt. Ellen sighed. Maybe's. If's. But's. She was a fine one to be telling Mrs Wallace not to live in the past. She'd want to start practising what she preached.

"Are you OK?" Miriam came to stand beside her.

"If I went home, now, would you drop Stephanie back when you're going? She doesn't want to leave the party but I want to get away from here," Ellen asked.

"Of course I will. We won't stay that much longer ourselves. I think Emma would be just as happy if we all left."

"I know. It's just that I don't want to drag Stephanie off and make her feel she's missing something. It won't be so bad if your gang are going as well. And I promised Rebecca she could stay the night."

"Are you sure, about Rebecca, Ellen? She can stay another night if you don't feel up to having her."

"Rebecca's no trouble, Miriam. Stephanie's looking forward to it. I just want to get away from here. Because if Vincent says one more word about how upset Emma is I'll split him. And if Julie Ann says one more time that Stephanie has no daddy, I won't be responsible for what I do to her."

"Maybe you should go, quick," Miriam grinned. "I don't think poor Emma could cope with murder just now. Your mother storming out saying she'd never set foot in this house again was the straw that broke the camel's back, I think."

"There's no need to be insulting to camels. If you were a camel, would you like to be compared to Emma?" Ellen retorted nastily. She'd had enough of "poor" Emma.

"Go home!" Miriam ordered.

"Just ask Doug to come out, will you?"

"Right!"

Ellen got their coats. She hoped they'd be gone before Emma came back downstairs. She didn't particularly want to speak to her sister-in-law. She was sure Emma bitterly regretted inviting her and Stephanie to the christening. Well, it was her own fault. If she had more control over her daughter, none of this would have happened.

"Miriam said you wanted to go." Doug walked over to her.

"You can say that again," Ellen said dryly.

"Do you want to say goodbye to Vincent and Emma?"

"Nope."

Doug raised an eyebrow at her surly tone but he made no comment and followed her from the house.

They walked to the car in silence. Doug held the door open for her.

"Thanks." Ellen sat into the car.

"How's Stephanie?" Doug got in beside her and started the ignition.

"Playing. Musical Chairs."

"Water off a duck's back?"

"Yeah!" Ellen sighed.

"But . . ."

"Well, what a way to find out about your father and your grandmother. In front of all those people. Gossip fodder. I could wallop Julie Ann!" she exploded. "I mean, Doug, what are they up to, talking about things like that in front of Julie Ann? She's only a child, for heaven's sake. It was embarrassing in there, not only for me but for my parents. I'm sure it was embarrassing for you. You had your first taste of a typical Munroe family get-together."

"The food was good though," Doug murmured.

"Oh Doug! Be serious." Ellen gave him a dig in the ribs.

"Look, get it off your chest. Get it out of your system and forget about it. Stephanie already has and surely she's the one that counts."

"I know you're right. But Ma's not going to forget it, or Emma or Vincent."

"Well, you can't take on their feelings. You've enough to do looking after your own. You can moan for another ten minutes and then that's it. OK? I'm not having the rest of the evening spoiled."

"That's magnanimous of you," Ellen snapped.

"I'm a magnanimous sort of guy," Doug said calmly.

"You don't have to spend the evening with me."

"I know that. Do you want me to go home?"

"Suit yourself, Doug," Ellen said huffily.

"I might go back to the party and see how I get on with the apparition in the lilac trouser suit. I think she fancied me." Doug was unperturbed by her moodiness.

In spite of herself, she had to laugh. It was impossible to row with Doug. He was too good-humoured.

"Smarty-pants!"

"I know you're mad and pissed off, love, but what happened happened. Maybe it's time to talk to Stephanie and tell her the facts as simply as you can so that Julie Ann can't come out with any more little shocks," Doug advised.

"I know. I've been putting it off for as long as I could. She's only a little girl, Doug. I don't want her to be troubled or upset."

"I know that, Ellen. But kids can accept things. Look how quickly she got back to playing after discovering she had a new grandmother."

"Do you think I should let her get to know Chris?" Ellen asked quietly.

"If *you* do, Ellen. I'd do it because it's what Stephanie wants. Not what Chris wants."

"Or what I want."

"I didn't say that."

"Did you think it?"

"Ellen, I can't exorcise Chris out of your head. Much as I'd like to. You're the only one that can do that. I just wish you'd get on with it."

"Well, episodes like today don't help," she said irritably.

"There's going to be more of them, Ellen, one way or another. You might as well get used to that idea," Doug retorted as he pulled up outside the flat.

He was right, Ellen admitted to herself. This was only the start of it.

❦

"Mammy, you know my new nannie that we met today?" Stephanie looked up at her mother, who was making the cocoa for the supper. Rebecca was in the sitting-room playing with Lego.

"Yes."

"Do you think she'll give me a Christmas present?"

"I don't know, pet."

"Oh!" Stephanie was disappointed. Now that she had two nannies she was hoping for an extra present. Julie Ann always got two presents from her nannies and grandads and she only got one.

"You know my daddy Christopher, that that lady told me about, maybe he doesn't know where we live. Maybe if he did, he'd come and see me. He might even bring me a present."

Her mammy looked sad. Stephanie knew she shouldn't have said that. She knew her mammy didn't like talking about that daddy because he didn't love them enough. He was a mean daddy, she thought angrily.

"I don't want his smelly old present anyway." She put her arms around her mammy and hugged her tightly. She didn't like it when Ellen was sad. It made her feel worried and frightened. She'd heard her crying in bed at night sometimes. That was very very scary. Big people weren't supposed to cry, especially mammies.

"Would you like to meet that daddy?" Her mammy bent down and looked at Stephanie. She smelt nice. Stephanie nuzzled her neck. Ellen's curls tickled her cheeks.

"What does he look like?"

"He's got blue eyes like yours."

"Where does he live?"

"He lives with the lady he got married to, in a house in Dublin. He's got a little boy and a girl."

Stephanie was intrigued. "What are their names? Are they my cousins like Julie Ann and Rebecca?"

Her mammy gave a funny little smile. "No, love. They're not your cousins. Because Chris . . . *Christopher* is your daddy as well as theirs. So you've got a half brother and sister."

"I've got a brother and sister?" Stephanie was amazed at this news. A brother and sister. Just like Rebecca had Connie and Daniel and Julie Ann had Andrew. This was brill! "Can I go and see them?"

"Maybe sometime, Stephanie. It's a bit awkward at the moment, because I'll be opening the new cafe and you and me will be very, very busy."

"Well, they could come and see us. They could have tea in our new cafe. And the daddy Christopher could bring the new nannie too." Stephanie beamed at Ellen. This was going to be great. Even

Julie Ann couldn't do better than this. She wouldn't be able to treat people in a cafe 'cos she didn't own one.

"We'll see," her mammy said and Stephanie had the feeling it was one of these things that was going to be put off for a while. Mammies always said "We'll see," when they were putting things off. Her little bubble of excitement got smaller. She'd better not say anything to her cousins until it was arranged, in case anything went wrong. She didn't want Julie Ann to make her feel silly.

That night, lying in bed, listening to Rebecca grinding her teeth, Stephanie lay looking out at the stars in the window above. She loved looking at the stars. Venus was her favourite. She always pretended that Venus came out to play and that the moon was her mammy. Sometimes Venus was bold and the mammy moon had to give out. Stephanie usually played this game until she fell asleep. But tonight she had another game to play. She patted her Guardian Angel on her shoulder, said goodnight to Holy God and then closed her eyes. She liked lying in bed with her eyes closed because then she went into her imagination-box and had great dreams. It was brill having an imagination-box right in the middle of her forehead. Tonight she was going to think of the new brother and sister and the daddy having tea in the cafe with her mammy and Doug. Julie Ann would be looking in the window, wishing she could come in. Stephanie'd let her in after a while. But she'd have to sit and do what she was told, because it was Stephanie's cafe. This was going to be a great new dream, she thought happily as she hugged her teddy close and snuggled in under the bedclothes.

"I've never been so humiliated, Mick. That child has no raising and it pains me to say that about my own grandchild." Sheila was so livid her hand shook and she slopped milky tea into her husband's saucer.

"Tsk! Now look what I've done."

"Sheila, would you calm down like a good woman." Mick took

the cup and saucer from his wife. He'd listened to Sheila's tirade since she'd marched out of Emma and Vincent's house vowing never to set foot in it again. He knew his life wasn't going to be worth living for the next week at least. She'd raged all the way home in the car and now she was really getting into her stride.

"That child has far too much to say for herself. It's going to get her into trouble some day. And I'm going to give Vincent a piece of my mind about it."

"Don't interfere, Sheila."

"Don't interfere! That's all right for you to say. She's my grandchild and, if I'm affected by her impudence, I certainly will interfere. What, for example, if Bonnie Daly ever gets wind of this, Mick? She'll make my life a misery," Sheila fretted.

"How is Bonnie going to hear about it?" Mick strove to keep his patience. Sheila was indulging herself now. Looking for sympathy. "Emma isn't friendly with her now, is she? She's hardly going to go up to her and say, 'Bonnie, we had a bit of an upset at Andrew's christening, wait until I tell you what happened.' Sheila, be sensible."

"Well, you just never know. And how am I going to face Pamela Connolly again?"

You'll hardly be facing Pamela if you're never setting foot in the house again, Mick was sorely tempted to retort but he restrained himself admirably. "Sheila, it will all blow over."

"But Emma was so rude," Sheila complained indignantly. "She told me to mind my own business."

"She was upset. You know her. She's highly strung. She didn't mean it," Mick soothed for the umpteenth time.

"Mick, I try not to interfere. You know that," Sheila declared. "But they can't let Julie Ann behave the way she does. Look at the trouble she caused today."

"I know, love. I know." Mick's eyes glazed over. He longed to have a little nap in front of the fire. He'd eaten too much fancy food in Emma's and he was having many happy returns. He didn't know which was worse. His indigestion, or his wife's moaning.

"What did the Judge say?"

"About what?" Mick had lost her train of thought.

"About the . . . the carry-on, of course." Sheila glared at her husband.

"He didn't say anything. We were making an arrangement to go fishing."

"Well, heavens above, Mick Munroe, there was our family being shamed in public and all you care about is your fishing. You're the limit, Mick. The absolute limit! I'm so vexed, I've a thumping headache. I'm going to lie down!" Sheila marched out of the room in high dudgeon.

Thank God for small mercies, thought her husband gratefully as he threw another log on the fire, settled himself more comfortably in his armchair and closed his eyes, ready for a nice nap.

"It was a disaster, Vincent. An absolute disaster. I should never have invited Ellen and Stephanie and Aunt Katherine all to the same party."

"What could you do? We'd have caused great offence if we'd left any of them out."

"But it's nothing to do with us. That's between Chris and Ellen and Aunt Katherine. Why did it have to ruin our party?" Emma demanded.

"Well, it *was* Julie Ann that brought it up," Vincent pointed out.

"If they weren't there, she couldn't have." Emma was in no humour to be rational. "Gillian and Diana enjoyed every minute of it. I could see them whispering and sniggering. It's going to be all over town."

"I think most people know Chris is a shit by now, Emma," Vincent said tightly.

"Well, it takes two to tango, Vincent. It wasn't *all* his fault." Emma jumped to her cousin's defence.

"I didn't say it was. But he didn't act like a man when he got Ellen pregnant. I heard the other day that there's rumours that he's having an affair with Alexandra Johnston. That's how much of a shit Chris Wallace is. He's having an affair with his wife's best friend. So you needn't be so quick to take his side."

"I don't want to talk about it. I just don't want to talk about it. And another thing, Vincent, since you feel so free to criticise *my* family. Your mother was very rude to me. And I won't put up with that in my own home. I certainly won't be visiting *her* house again."

"Go to sleep, Emma, and forget it. That's the last party we're having," Vincent snapped.

"That suits me just fine." Emma turned on her side and pulled the blankets up over her ears. She was so mad she felt like sleeping in the spare room. How dare Vincent be so unsympathetic. She'd just gone through a terrible trauma and he obviously couldn't care less. Who did he think he was, lecturing her about Chris? His precious sister was just as much to blame for her predicament. Chris was always painted to be the black sheep. Ellen could have said no and used her wiles on him to get him to propose to her. If she hadn't been so free with her favours Chris might have married her. Every woman knew that one way to keep a man dangling was to tease him, lead him on and then say no. It was a technique that had worked since time immemorial.

It infuriated Emma that Vincent always put all the blame on Chris. How had he found out about Alexandra Johnston? The gossip must be doing the rounds. She'd better phone Chris and warn him that his little secret was out. It wouldn't do if Suzy got wind of it, Emma thought tiredly. Then the fat really would be in the fire. Alexandra was supposed to be Suzy's best friend. She'd be shattered if she ever found out Chris was sleeping with her.

She'd phone Chris first thing in the morning and make an appointment to have lunch with him. Anyway she needed a comforting shoulder to moan on after her disastrous party. Chris always provided a good shoulder to cry on, which was more than could be said of her husband right this minute.

"Bloody hell, Emma! You should put a sock in that child's mouth. What did Mother say?" Chris stared at his cousin in horror. They were having lunch in the Gresham and he'd just been regaled with the details of the previous day's christening party.

"She was very gracious about it, actually," Emma admitted. "She handled it extremely well. And she was very nice to Stephanie. I think she liked her. I just thought you should know what happened in case she says anything to you about it. Gillian and Diana enjoyed it immensely," she added dryly. "It's going to be around town like wildfire, so be prepared."

"Sod them!" Chris scowled.

"I think you should know, as well, that rumours are going around about you and Alexandra. Vincent said it to me last night. I didn't let on that I knew anything." Emma looked him straight in the eye.

Chris shrugged. It was all beyond his control now. Nothing in his life was going right. If the whole world knew about it, there was nothing he could do.

"You might as well know, then, that Suzy's found out about it and she's kicked me out. She won't let me live at home, so I'm going to have to get a place of my own."

"How did she find out? Did someone tell her? How beastly!" Emma was horrified.

"I don't know how she found out. All I know is she showed up at Alexandra's flat like a mad woman and caught me there and she went crazy. She was really vicious."

"I suppose I can understand that," Emma murmured.

"Yeah, but for crying out loud, Emma, it's a bit much kicking me out of the bloody house! I can't afford to live somewhere else. She'll have to come to her senses."

"Why did it have to be Alexandra Johnston? She was Suzy's best friend, Chris. You can't expect a woman to get over knowing her husband's slept with her best friend. A stranger wouldn't be so bad. If I thought Gillian or Diana had slept with Vincent, I'd die. I really would. I'd never ever want to see them again. It was an awful thing to do, Chris. You should never have got involved with her. You should have nipped it in the bud when she gave you the come-on. Suzy was entitled to that much loyalty from you. It's clear Alexandra was no friend to Suzy. She obviously couldn't care less about her feelings."

"Look, Emma, I don't want a lecture from you. Right?" Chris snarled.

Why did women take these things so seriously? So, he'd had a couple of shags with Alexandra. You'd think he'd committed murder the way the women were reacting. His father had had affairs left, right and centre and he hadn't left home. Emma needn't be so smug about Vincent. If Boy Scout Munroe ever got the chance, he'd be no different, Chris reckoned. Practically all the married guys he knew had had a fling at some stage. It was no big deal! They'd just been luckier than him at getting away with it. Anyway Emma had no business interfering.

"I'm only trying to make you see it from Suzy's point of view. I can't believe even you are that insensitive," Emma ignored his sulks.

"Oh quit nagging, Emma. I'm sick of being nagged."

"Where are you living now?" She changed the subject.

"With Alexandra. She's been given notice to quit by the landlord. I might bunk in with her for a while in her new pad until I get sorted."

"Couldn't you move in with Aunt K for a while?"

"Are you joking, Emma? Why the hell would I want to move home? Imagine the lectures I'd have to put up with there!" Chris was taken aback that Emma would even suggest such a thing.

"I was just thinking it wouldn't be so expensive. But you're right, of course. It wouldn't work."

"You can say that again. I've been threatened with "The Will" already," Chris confessed glumly.

"Oh dear!" Emma made a face.

"I wish I could tell her to stuff it but I need to know that money is there. You don't know the pressures I'm under, Emma.

You were dead lucky getting that site for nothing. And getting your house built at cost price. My place is costing me a fortune. And Suzy doesn't have any damn money to look forward to. That's what I get for marrying a pauper."

"Chris! Stop it."

"Well, she has no money behind her, the way you'll have eventually. Vincent knows he's cushioned."

"He doesn't look at it like that at all, Chris."

"Yeah, well, we're not all making money hand over fist like he is. Suzy'd want to remember that if she doesn't want to end up in a two-up two-down," Chris growled.

"You'll have me in tears in a minute," Emma drawled.

Chris chuckled. His cousin was the only one he couldn't bullshit and get away with it.

"What did Ellen say yesterday, when it happened?" he asked diffidently.

"Nothing much, really." Emma daintily wiped the side of her mouth with her napkin and sat back. "She was with Doug Roche."

"Bully for her!" Chris felt his throat constrict. The piece of steak in his mouth tasted like sawdust. Jealousy seared him. How could Ellen prefer that bearded bogman to him? Did they talk, the way he and she had? Holding nothing back. Revealing deepest secrets. Did they hold each other tight after they'd made love and feel that they were the only two people in the universe? Did they laugh and tease and cuddle? How could she do all that with another man and not think of him and all they'd shared together? Was he really just a memory? It was inconceivable.

"Did she talk to my mother?" he asked curiously.

"They said a few words to each other. Aunt K asked me to phone for a taxi for her because she was upset. And then Old Bat Munroe came out and ate the face off me about Julie Ann and I told her to mind her own business and she stormed off in one of her huffs. Gillian and Diana overheard it too. It was so upsetting, Chris, I just burst into tears and went upstairs. By the time I came down, your mother had gone and so had Ellen. I don't know whether she's annoyed or not. And I don't want to know either. I'm sick of the lot of you, frankly. My party was ruined over something that has nothing to do with me, not that I'm getting any sympathy from anyone. And Vincent and I aren't speaking," Emma complained plaintively.

"We all have our problems, don't we?" Chris pushed his plate away. He'd lost his appetite. "At least you and Vincent will make it up. I'm up shit creek."

"Well, you've got one friend, even if you are an idiot." Emma softened and reached across the table and squeezed his hand.

"Thanks. I need one."

"I won't be able to offer you a bed for the night, unfortunately, if ever you need one. Vincent wouldn't be too impressed. But I'll buy lunch today."

"I'm not in the poorhouse yet, Emma."

"I insist. After all, I will be a woman of means. And besides, I'd hate to see Suzy in a two-up two-down."

Chris laughed at her sarcasm. He always knew where he stood with Emma. Right now she was his only ally. It made life a little more bearable.

Having lunch with her had been a normal kind of event in his suddenly abnormal life. He felt uprooted, at sixes and sevens. It was most unsettling. Like a nightmare that was dragging on and on. He was going to have to come to some sort of solution soon.

Later that afternoon, he sat doodling in his office. Thinking of how to resolve his problems. Imagine Emma suggesting he go home to his mother. Was she barking mad? It might make economic sense but he'd never stick Katherine day in day out. He'd feel utterly smothered. Besides, his mother wouldn't exactly welcome him with open arms. She'd told him to end the affair. But whether he did or not, Suzy wasn't going to let him darken the door for the foreseeable future.

He didn't want to live with Alexandra. If he moved into a new apartment with her he'd have to pay half the rent. That would cost an arm and a leg. If he got a place of his own, that would be even more expensive, unless he got some kippy little flat in Rathmines or Ranelagh. But he couldn't be expected to live in those sort of conditions. Chris hastily dismissed *that* option from his list. If he could only live somewhere rent free for a while, until Suzy came to her senses. And what if Suzy didn't come to her senses? What would happen to him then?

Chapter Eleven

Would she do it? Could she do it? Suzy sat at her breakfast counter and stared at what she had just written. She'd spent days writing and rewriting words that she knew would do the greatest damage to Alexandra's reputation. Chris would kill her for it. Because if she did what she wanted to do, their private business would be in the public arena. Everyone would know about his seedy little affair.

Fuck him! She wanted everyone to know. She wanted everyone to see what a horrible sneaky pair they were. She wanted family, friends and acquaintances to see what a lying, cheating, selfish irresponsible shit Chris was. The charm, the wit, the sophisticated hail-fellow-well-met, trust-me-I'm-a-great-guy front that he presented was just a facade. He'd shown himself in his true colours. Now he could live with it. She was damned if she was going to be the loyal little wife, pretending that all was rosy in the garden. She'd been cruelly wronged. To hide that from the world would be almost a denial that it had happened. It *had* happened and she was suffering grievously and she wanted people to know what Chris and that bitch had done to her. He'd forfeited any claims to her loyalty the instant he'd betrayed her with Alexandra. Why should he get away with it? Why should she? Why should they be happy together when she was in hell because of them?

It wasn't getting any easier, Suzy thought despairingly. She was tormented with thoughts of them. Anger and bitterness, plots of vengeance, were her daily companions. From the moment she got up in the morning to the moment her eyes closed at night. She couldn't eat. She was smoking like a trooper. She felt ghastly. Most of the time she was living in a weird imaginary world. Picturing scenarios involving Chris, where he'd come crawling back to her saying he'd made a huge mistake, begging her to take him back. He'd tell her he was crazy about her and that Alexandra was a cold-hearted, bossy manipulator who was consumed with jealousy for all that Suzy had. Sometimes, in her fantasy, Suzy took him back and she would imagine them making love. But the memory of her husband tied to Alexandra's bedstead always came back to haunt her and she'd end up eaten up with bitterness, rage and jealousy and the harsh realities of her life would still be there to taunt her.

Tears brimmed. What was to become of her? Would she always feel like this? There they were, Chris and Alexandra, having a wonderful time, and she was husbandless, best-friendless, with two small children depending on her. Would she ever have fun in her life again? Would she ever have love and sex? Knowing Chris and Alexandra, they were probably at it like rabbits. Would she ever get turned on by a man again? Suzy just couldn't imagine kissing or being intimate with another man. It would be so awful having to go through all that dating business again. She'd never ever let herself put her hopes and faith in a man. That was certain. It was far too risky. Even though she'd known what Chris was like when she married him, she'd hoped against hope that he'd change for her. She'd kidded herself that he'd realise she was the only woman for him and value what he had in her as a wife. She'd pitted herself against the temptations other women held for him. His fidelity was the way she measured her worth. And now events had proved that when the crunch came she was truly worthless in her husband's eyes. Her deepest fears had been realised.

How ironic, she thought, suddenly terrified. She was going to turn into a replica of her mother-in-law. Was that the fate in store for her? Misery and more misery? Well, if she was miserable she'd make sure they were too. Katherine might have been a lady, turning a blind eye to her husband's infidelities. But she wouldn't act the lady, Suzy vowed. She'd play as dirty as they had . . . and worse.

Slowly, carefully, in her best handwriting, she signed her name and invested every letter with pure venom.

***

"I just need another week and then I'll be back, right as rain," Alexandra informed her colleague calmly.

"Fine, Alexandra, everything's covered," Thomas Scully said smoothly. Too smoothly for Alexandra's liking. Thomas Scully was a smarmy git who was constantly trying to get one over on Alexandra. He licked up to the senior partners, making himself out to be the best thing since fried bread. If Superman Scully could cope so efficiently they might decide to give him some of *her* work. Maybe another week was pushing it.

"Talk to you soon, Thomas," Alexandra said briskly and hung up. She certainly wouldn't let that baldy little toady know that she was in any way perturbed. He'd love that. Thomas Scully was a shit-stirrer. Some day he was going to fall into it face down and she wouldn't be there proffering a helping hand. It would give her immense pleasure to watch Master Scully getting his come-uppance, some day. Alexandra stubbed out her cigarette and began to apply heavy make-up to hide the discoloured bruises, which, thankfully, were beginning to fade.

She was going to view an apartment today. A new two-bedroom one off Herbert Park. How absolutely classy. The tree-lined roads around there reminded her of London. It was a very affluent area and it would be a feather in her cap to rent there. They'd be pea-green with envy at work.

Chris was meeting her for lunch to discuss it. He was going to be her lodger! Alexandra smiled to herself. Things weren't working out too badly after all. She was going to rent a bigger apartment. He, hopefully, would pay half the rent but her name would be on the lease. So when she met someone she wanted to get serious with, she'd just boot him out. Chris needed her more than she needed him, which suited her just fine. Suzy was adamant that he couldn't go back home and he couldn't afford to spend a fortune on rent. Chris was at her mercy. Alexandra liked that. It made her feel in control. She'd enjoy her fling with him and then when it was over he could fend for himself. That day might be coming sooner than he thought, Alexandra mused.

She had a client, Marcus Lynn, whom she'd fancied for ages. He was tall, at least six two, and he carried himself very straight. Some tall men had a way of hunching over, but Marcus had great bearing. He had jet-black hair that was just beginning to go grey at the temples. His brown eyes were ringed by the longest darkest lashes. He was sallow-skinned. Always tanned, he had a cleft in his chin that was incredibly sexy. Sean Connery had nothing on him.

He was thirty-five, a very wealthy successful hotelier and he wasn't married. He was dating a country girl. Some hick who'd been widowed young and left with a child. Marcus had met her when she spent a weekend in one of his hotels. He'd been very taken with her. It was the talk of the dinner-party circuit. Marcus Lynn could have his pick of women and he was involved with a little mouse from the back of beyonds, it was ridiculous. Alexandra dismissed the other woman from her thoughts. It was clear Marcus only felt sorry for her. It wouldn't last.

But Marcus Lynn and Alexandra could be a pretty powerful couple. Since she'd taken over his advertising campaign his hotel's image had been thoroughly revamped and he was more than pleased with her. They had an extremely good business relationship. Alexandra admired his decisiveness, his directness, his commanding presence. Marcus was no pushover. Alexandra felt that in Marcus she'd found the man she'd always been looking for. The man who would not be controlled. The man who was stronger than her in every way. A little shiver ran down her spine. Imagine being married to someone like Marcus. Imagine being a wealthy wife, never having to worry about money. Imagine travelling the world and staying in the best hotels. Imagine seducing and being seduced by him . . . it gave her goose-bumps to think of it.

The snaring of Marcus Lynn was going to be given top priority.

As soon as she was settled in her new pad Alexandra would go all out. It was time. Another year or two and she'd have crossed that very frightening line between *Independent-Career-Woman-who-Loves-her-Fascinating-Job* to *Pathetic-Spinster-who-has-to-Work-to-Keep-Herself*. The idea of not finding a man to keep her in the comfort in which she wanted to be kept was too awful to contemplate. Even if it didn't work out, the security of the ring on the finger could not be denied.

Look at Suzy. Alexandra had to admire her tenacity and determination in not letting Chris walk all over her. Suzy was living in the comfort of her elegant home, while Chris had been evicted.

Not that if . . . no . . . *when* she married Marcus, she would ever give him grounds for an affair. She would be the perfect wife, Alexandra decided. She, who knew so much about men, couldn't possibly fail.

Ellen, Miriam and Denise grinned from ear to ear as Doug hammered in the final nail of the striking white-and-pink sign with its gorgeous lettering *The Deli* emblazoned for the citizenry of Glenree to see.

"We'll put up a Christmas tree in the window," Miriam exclaimed.

"Oh yes! And boughs of holly and ivy," Denise added.

"Girls! I've just had a brilliant brainwave!" Ellen's cheeks were red with excitement.

"What?" the other two chorused.

"Let's have Santa do the official opening."

"Munroe, you're a genius!" Denise clapped her on the back. "Who'll we get to do Santa?"

With one accord the three turned to look up at Doug, whose expression changed from one of amusement to consternation.

"Oh no! No! No! And definitely no!"

"Ah Doug, go on," Ellen pleaded.

"You'd be perfect," Miriam cajoled.

"The kids love you," Denise flattered.

"No way," Doug declared from atop the ladder.

"I'll make you steak and kidney pie any time you ask me," Ellen bribed.

"Sorry, the answer's still no. I'm not doing Santa to the mad hordes of Glenree. Can you imagine me trying to be nice to the likes of Julie Ann Munroe?"

The girls guffawed.

"Ah Doug, please," Ellen begged. "You've been part of it all since the beginning. It would be perfect."

"Aw, Ellen. Have mercy," Doug groaned.

"It would only be one hour of your life and I'd be grateful for the rest of mine," Ellen twinkled.

"Why did I ever get involved with you lot and your mad hare-brained ideas?" Doug grumbled as he came down the ladder. "I used to have a quiet life. Early to bed and early to rise. My eyes were clear, and so was my head. And now look at me. A wreck of a man. Go in and make me a cup of tea, woman, and while you're at it, feed me a few goodies to build up my strength."

"You can act like this for a week, Doug, and then forget it," Ellen grinned.

"You better be nice to me, Ellen. I could lose my nerve and get stage fright. Us actor types are very fragile." Doug minced into The Deli followed by the three grinning proprietoresses. Later, having served Doug tea and coffee slices, they sat making plans for the opening.

"I'll make the Santa suit." Miriam wrote it down on her list.

"I'll go in to Hector Grey's and get some colouring books and crayons and bits and pieces for Santa's sack," Denise offered.

"I'll get the posters organised. Debbie White is brilliant at art work. I'll get her to do a flyer and get them printed and we can drop them in the houses in the village and out in the new estates. The kids can help, they'll enjoy that. We better get cracking," Ellen declared.

A hectic week followed. The children, infected with the adults' excitement, were more of a hindrance than a help. The idea of Christmas cheer coming earlier than normal was most exciting.

As well as preparing for the grand opening of The Deli, Miriam was preparing for Christmas. Baking cakes and puddings, making

Doug's Santa suit, as well as doing her normal household chores left her more than frazzled.

It was with a sinking heart that she saw her mother-in-law cycle past the front door several days later.

"Good morning, Mrs Munroe," she said politely when Sheila marched into the kitchen.

"You're at home then," Sheila remarked tartly. "I've called twice this week and there hasn't been a sinner around."

"Well, Ben's at work. The children are at school and I've been down at The Deli," Miriam explained.

"Hrump. It will all end in tears, believe me. You've too much to be doing, Miriam, with a husband and three children. You shouldn't be putting all this work on yourself. It's not fair of Ellen to impose on your good nature."

Mrs Munroe's false sympathy made Miriam want to scream.

"Don't let it bother you one whit," she said firmly. "Everything's under control and Ellen isn't imposing in the slightest. I'd offer you a cup of tea but I'm just off to Swords with Ellen. We've a few bits and pieces to get yet."

"Oh! Tsk! Soon I'll have to make an appointment to see the pair of you," Sheila said huffily. She was most put out. She'd never come to Miriam's house without getting tea and cake. "Well, the reason I came over was to ask you if you'll bake the usual three dozen mince pies for the Christmas fair. I'll need them for Sunday fortnight. And I'll need a bit of sewing done. We're making new curtains for the parish hall. I told the guild you'd do two windows for them."

"Oh! Oh!" Miriam got into a fluster. Where was she going to get time to make thirty-six mince pies and sew curtains for the parish hall? How typical of Mrs Munroe to volunteer her services without even asking. She knew she was up to her eyes. Miriam knew she had to make her stand. It was now or never. Inwardly she quaked. Sheila Munroe was a formidable woman. For years, Miriam had let her browbeat her into doing work for the parish. Church works, as Mrs Munroe called them, were most important. It was a duty and an obligation. As well as turning her back on Mrs Munroe, it would seem as though she were slighting the parish. Guilt assailed her. She always cooked mince pies for the Christmas fair.

Stop it! Stop it! she ordered herself silently. Miriam took a deep breath. "Mrs Munroe, I just don't have the time this year. And I won't be able to sew the curtains either. I'm sure you'll understand. I'll buy a couple of cherry logs for the fair. And, while you're here, now that I'll be working full-time I won't have time to bake for the monthly bring-and-buy sales and I won't be coming to the quilting classes any more. I'm sorry, but I just won't have the time."

Sheila stared at her in horror. "Well, Miriam, this is very upsetting. I always thought I could rely on you. This is what the world is coming to. You young women have no time for the church or the parish. It's all me, me, me. It's a sorry day when the young married women of Glenree haven't time to do some charitable work. No wonder the world is the way it is. What kind of example is that to be giving to Connie and Stephanie?"

"Mrs Munroe, I'll bring up my daughters as I see fit. And they won't be lacking in good example. Now excuse me, I'm going out. Good day." Her voice shook with the effort of defying Sheila.

Miriam was raging. How dare her mother-in-law imply that she was an unfit mother giving bad example? How she longed to emulate Emma and tell her to mind her own business.

Sheila's nostrils flared and she and her cheeks flamed.

"Well, Miriam Munroe, you're a sad disappointment to me. I've treated you with kindness from the day you first set foot over my threshold, when Ben brought you into this family. And this is the thanks I get. I'll not be asking you for a favour again." Sheila was livid. She stalked out the door, got up on her bike and cycled down the path like a fury.

Miriam stared after her and burst into tears. Her mother-in-law had just succeeded in making her feel like a naughty, ungrateful little girl. She was disgusted with herself. It was infuriating. She was a grown woman with a family of her own. Why did she feel like this, at her age? It was ridiculous. Or was it the same with all mothers-in-law? None of them could be quite as bad as Sheila. Miriam was sure of that.

The ungrateful little snipe, Sheila raged as she cycled at speed out of Miriam's drive. It was hardly credible. Miriam had behaved in a most disgraceful manner. Sheila felt snubbed and humiliated. Miriam had not acted out her part. She'd responded as an equal, which was something she most emphatically was not, Sheila fumed as she swerved to avoid a large puddle. It was most disconcerting. After all she had done for that girl. Taken her into the bosom of the family and been a mother to her since her own was dead. How dare Miriam rebuff her! What was she, only the daughter of a penny-farthing farmer from the back of beyonds? Sheila's face was as dark as a thundercloud as she cycled along the wind-chilled wintry-hedged back road. She came to the turn that led to Glenree. She could see the church spire and the rooftops framed by winter foliage in the distance. She'd planned to cycle into the village to call on the priest's housekeeper to discuss whether Father Kevin would prefer a roast of beef, a pair of chickens or a side of pork as his Christmas box from Mick. There'd be a bottle of port as well, of course.

She'd been looking forward to it. Taking tea with the priest's housekeeper, Fanny Burke, was something she always enjoyed. Being the priest's housekeeper conferred a status of sorts on Fanny, who kept her distance from the majority of the parishioners. Only the privileged few were invited into the presbytery to partake of tea and ginger cake. By dint of making sure that Mick provided Fanny with the choicest cuts for the Reverend's dinner, and because of her position as president of the guild, Sheila was one of the few to enjoy Fanny's favour. A position she guarded zealously. It was an alliance that caused great grief to Bonnie Daly, who, years ago, made a supreme error of judgement and criticised Fanny's cross-stitch in a craft competition that she and Fanny had entered. Fanny had never forgiven the slight to her sewing skills and the privilege of tea in the presbytery had instantly been withdrawn, never to be restored. It was something that came between Bonnie and her sleep and she rued the day she'd opened her big mouth.

Sheila never failed to mention at the guild meetings that she had taken tea in the priest's house just so she could watch the pinched look of envy on her enemy's sly, sharp face. She'd been looking forward to tea with Fanny today in particular, because she'd wanted to find out whether it was true that Dentist Donovan's wife had gone up to John of God's in Dublin, to dry out. Fanny knew everything that happened in Glenree and was the source of jewels of gossip that were sparingly dispensed, depending on her humour. If she was in good form and you got her going, the rewards were well worth enduring an hour's complaints about her hiatus hernia, and her "delicate tummy". Sometimes when Fanny was in one of her moods, she'd be sharp-tongued and snippy and the visit would be a complete waste of time, apart from the social kudos of being seen entering the presbytery.

Sheila ignored the turn and cycled straight on towards home. She wasn't in the mood to listen to Fanny Burke's complaints today, not even to ferret out news of Dentist Donovan's nervy wife. Miriam had upset her. She was probably on the road behind her, on her way to Ellen's. Sheila was glad she hadn't been overtaken by her ungrateful ibex of a daughter-in-law.

Oh, the quiet ones were sly. Give them an inch and they'd take a mile. She was far more offended by Miss Miriam's cheek than by Emma's outburst at the christening. Emma was a spoilt high-strung little madam. She'd expect no better from her, but she *did* expect that Miriam would know her place and show some gratitude and consideration. After all, Ben had given her a very nice house and a far better standard of living than she could expect on a poky little farm in the middle of nowhere. She'd married into a respected and well-off family. Her position in society had risen a hundredfold and this was her attitude.

"I haven't time!"

The impertinence of it. Sheila was so vexed and indignant, her concentration so addled, that she failed to notice the crater of a pothole beside the iron gates to Blackbird's Field. The bike juddered. Sheila lost control and went flying over the handlebars at speed. A brief instant of surprise, shock, then fright engulfed her before she hit the ground with force, a jagged rock jamming sharply into her ribcage. Inky darkness closed in on her and she lay spread-eagled, bleeding and unconscious on the gravelly winding country road.

Chapter Twelve

"I feel a bit mean, Ellen. You know how guilty your mother can make you feel?" Miriam confided as she and Ellen washed their new crockery and cutlery in preparation for the gala opening.

"Look, Miriam, Mam's got to get used to the idea that you're going to be working and that you won't be available to bake and sew for the guild. She doesn't ask me. She's never asked Emma. She only asks you because she knows you won't say no. You're too soft with her, Miriam. Mam can be an awful bully if you let her. And I know that's a terrible thing to say about your own mother, but I've seen her imposing her own will on people. That's why we've never really got on. I won't let her do it to me."

"Yeah, but she does great charity work for the parish. She made me feel I was letting the church down." Miriam polished soup spoons with a vengeance.

"Charity begins at home, Miriam. If she wants to bake and sew for the parish, fine. That's her choice. And anyway she's got loads of free time now. She doesn't have a young family to take care of. You have your own path to follow and it's not up to her to dictate it or tell you whether it's wrong or right," Ellen argued firmly. She'd had enough of Sheila whingeing and moaning and making disparaging remarks about neglected children. Nothing would give her mother greater satisfaction than for the business to be a disaster, so that she could be proved right. It wasn't meant maliciously, Ellen knew. It was because it was something Sheila had nothing to do with and therefore she had no control over. It suited her to be able to drop into Miriam whenever she wanted with requests for sewing and baking. Why would Miriam want to be anywhere but at home taking care of her husband and family? Ellen knew exactly what her mother's thoughts were about Miriam's part in the deli venture.

In Sheila's view a woman's place was in the home and all this talk about working women and feminism and women's lib was hugely threatening. Many times, watching *The Late Late*, she was scandalised listening to young women arguing the cause of women's rights in a very forthright and frank way. The old ways were changing but Sheila was hanging on grimly, afraid of what was on the other side of change. Apart from which, she had always been a pessimist, seeing the negative side of everything and everyone. It was very wearing and Ellen had learned, with great difficulty at times, to ignore it. It was easier now that she was living away from home but there were still times when her mother could leave her fit to be tied. She could understand how Miriam, who was such a softie, would find it hard to say no to Sheila.

"I wonder if I'll be like that with my girls when I'm your mother's age?" Miriam remarked. "Will they be doing things that I object to and rearing their families differently to the way you and I are rearing ours? Will we be saying, what are young women coming to?"

"I don't know." Ellen wiped her sudsy hand against her apron. "You and I wouldn't leave our kids on their own in the house but look at Angie Nolan. She leaves her three on their own when she's working in the bookie's and she doesn't see anything wrong with it. I'd be afraid of my life something would go wrong if I left Stephanie on her own for even twenty minutes."

"Yeah, well I saw young Kenny Nolan kissing the face off that young McGrath one and he's only twelve. It's kissing now. What will it be in a few years time when he has the run of the house and he's inviting those young ones in? You have to draw a line somewhere and take responsibility when you're a parent." Miriam frowned.

"It's hard, really, knowing what's the right thing to do for your child. I mean, should I let Stephanie get to know Chris if she wants to? Have I the right to stop her just because I want to keep my distance from him? She's asked me about him after the palaver at the christening," said Ellen, broaching the subject she'd been reluctant to bring up with Miriam.

"Oh dear." Miriam shook her head. "That's tough. But it was bound to happen sooner or later. What are you going to do? What do you feel for him now, Ellen? After all that's happened?" she asked curiously.

Ellen smiled at her and put the kettle on. She was dying for a cup of tea. In the distance an ambulance siren wailed. It was an uncommon sound in Glenree. She hoped it was for no one that they knew.

What did she feel for Chris? He'd been the great passion of her life. There was no denying that. Once, she would have done anything for him. Once, to hear him say *I love you* would have made her the happiest woman in the universe.

"I suppose when trust and respect go, there isn't much left. Part of me will always love him. There's a bond there that's survived all the lies and pain and hurt and rejection. If he'd given it a chance, we could have been happy maybe. But then, knowing Chris and knowing me, I would have been the one doing all the giving and he would have been the one doing all the taking. It would have been a very unbalanced relationship. Perhaps I was protected from that in some strange way. It's funny the way things work out. Five years ago I wouldn't have said that in a blue moon. Up to a year ago he was still all I wanted in life. Maybe I've got sense."

"He was the big loser there, Ellen, not you."

"Maybe, maybe not. I don't think he'd ever see it that way."

"Well, he was always an idiot," Miriam declared tartly. Time had not improved her opinion of Philanderer Wallace. Privately she thought Ellen was well rid of him and she couldn't understand her sister-in-law's hesitancy about nabbing a gorgeous, kind, decent man like Doug.

"Chris is what he is and he's not going to change and if Stephanie gets to know him she's going to find out that he's not a very dependable person. I want to protect her from that. I want her to think well of her father. I really respected my father. He's been the rock of support in my life. Knowing I had that kept me going through the really tough times. Stephanie would never have that with Chris."

"Maybe not. But she'll certainly have it with you, Ellen. In that respect she's a lucky little girl. If I were you I'd take it one step at a time and see how it goes."

"What will be will be, I suppose, Miriam. I can't protect her from life's hard knocks, much as I'd love to. I suppose poor Mam thinks she's doing her best too. I know in my heart and soul I was a grave disappointment to her as a daughter and it hasn't been easy knowing that. Sometimes I feel she let me down by judging me so harshly. I just hope Stephanie won't feel I've let her down as a mother."

"She won't, Ellen. Don't be daft." Miriam turned to the biscuit tin, the source of all consolation in times of stress. "Here, stick this in your gob and stop your nonsense. Tomorrow we're going on a diet. Right?"

"Right." Ellen laughed. The famous diet was always starting tomorrow. It was good to have Miriam to confide in. Her friendship gave Ellen great comfort.

They were cleaning the inside of the windows a little while later when they caught sight of Emma as she got into her car after doing some shopping.

"Would you look at Barbarella Munroe? Who does she think she is in that get-up? Jane Fonda?" Ellen snorted. "Bonnie Daly can't believe her eyes." Emma was wearing a black catsuit that emphasised her slender figure quite daringly. A short fox fur jacket hung casually over her shoulders. It was obvious from Bonnie's expression that she was utterly scandalised as she walked past the totally oblivious Emma.

Miriam giggled. "Look at Bonnie. Her face would stop a clock! I heard her once describing Emma's mini-and-white-leather-boots outfit as an 'occasion of sin'. She told Nora Bennet that Emma was responsible for leading the young men of Glenree into bad thoughts and whoever designed the mini is destined for the fires of hell! Poor Bonnie, it's just as well she's never seen Emma in her Ursula Andress bikini. You have to admire our Ems, though, she doesn't give a hoot about what people say. I'd love to be like that. I'd love to have Emma's confidence."

"How does she keep her figure, that's what I want to know?" Ellen demanded enviously. Her voluptuous curves would be too much for a clingy catsuit. She'd never have the nerve to wear something like that anyway. Nor would she have the money to buy such treats. Emma spent a fortune on clothes and was always dressed in the height of fashion. Her geometric sharp-cut bob of recent years had grown into a longer softer style of flicked-out curls which was ultra-glamorous. She looked like a film star. Her make-up was flawless and immaculate . . . as usual.

Ellen looked at her spattered jeans and bobbly red woollen jumper and felt a real dowdy frump compared to her sister-in-law. She should make more of an effort, she thought glumly. Still, she might be curvy but she'd kept her weight down. That was a real triumph. She'd get her hair done and dress up smartly in her black trouser suit and wear the rose chiffon blouse and treat Doug to a meal at the weekend. She'd done Harry Dowling's accounts as a favour and he'd given her two pounds to spend on herself.

A sudden flurry of rain against the windows turned what had been a light drizzle into a full-scale downpour. Emma took off in her car and Bonnie hastened towards the shelter of the post office.

"I suppose wintertime isn't really the ideal time to open a cafe," Miriam remarked.

"On a day like today it might give us a few more customers anxious to escape the rain," Ellen said sanguinely. "It's going to be a real adventure, isn't it?"

"Yeah, it's great." Miriam's eyes sparkled.

"Oh look, here's the sergeant. I wonder what he wants?" Ellen said curiously as Sergeant Doyle knocked on the door.

"Come in," she invited, opening the door to him.

"Ellen, I've some bad news for you and I want to tell you first before we go in to tell Mick," Sergeant Doyle said gruffly, his weather-beaten face troubled.

Ellen felt sick. Fear gripped her. Stephanie! That's who the ambulance had been for.

"What? What? Tell me. Is it Stephanie?"

"It isn't Stephanie. It's your mother. She came off her bike over by Blackbird's Field. She's been taken in to the Mater. Fintan Collins found her and phoned for the ambulance. He doesn't know how long she was lying there."

"Oh Jesus!" exclaimed Miriam, pale as a ghost. "That's all my fault. She was so mad when she left. Maybe she had a heart attack or something. I should have baked the bloody mince pies for her." She burst into tears.

"It's not your fault, Miriam. Look, will you take care of Stephanie for me? I better get Dad and go in to the hospital. Will you ring Vincent and Ben?"

"Yes, yes. I'm sorry, Ellen, I'm really sorry."

"I better go. I'll phone from the hospital," Ellen said distractedly. She was dreading telling Mick. To think she'd been saying those awful critical things about her mother and all the time Sheila was lying unconscious in a heap on the road. Guilt and anger swamped her. If her mother died, she'd have to live with that guilt for the rest of her life. Trust her mother to add yet another burden to those she already carried.

Mick was carving up chicken portions when she went into the butcher's, his cleaver making firm sharp cuts. He smiled when he saw her.

"Here's the business tycoon." He saw the expression on her face and saw Sergeant Doyle following behind. "What's up?"

Ellen recognised the fear in his eyes and wanted to shelter and protect him from the pain of what was to come.

"Dad, Mam's had an accident. She fell off her bike and she's unconscious. The ambulance has taken her to the Mater. I'll bring you in now."

Mick sagged. He loved Sheila in a way no one else did. He loved something that only he saw in her, Ellen thought with a pang. Just as she loved Chris, and loved something in him that touched no one else but her.

"As far as we know, she fell off the bike, Mick. There were no other vehicles involved," Sergeant Doyle said ponderously, hiding his distress for his old friend behind his policeman's formality.

"We'd better go quick." Mick hastily removed his apron and hat and went to get his coat.

"Should I go home and get some nightdresses and things?" Ellen suggested.

"We can get them later. I don't want Sheila to be alone among strangers. I want to be there in case she needs us. In case anything happens . . . " Mick said urgently.

"Oh Dad." The tears that came to her eyes were for him. If anything happened to Sheila, Mick would have to go through a bereavement and the thought of her father's pain and loneliness was hard to bear. He didn't deserve it. He was the kindest, most compassionate soul. He shouldn't have to suffer, Ellen thought angrily as she followed him to the car and they began their journey to the hospital.

"I was always telling her to watch out for the potholes. You don't think she's had a heart attack or anything, do you, Ellen? Your mother's a very healthy woman for her age." Mick twisted his cap in his hands, his normally ruddy face ashen.

"Yes, she is, she's very healthy. And very fit too," Ellen agreed reassuringly.

"I can always get someone in to run the shop if I have to." Mick was talking to himself almost. Ellen's heart sank. Everything had been such a shock she hadn't given a thought to the implications of her mother's accident.

If Sheila had had a heart attack or a stroke or some such disabling illness she would need caring for. Ellen was the only daughter. She didn't have a house like Ben and Vincent. She didn't have a husband. It would be expected of her to leave her little haven over the shop and move back home. And how would that affect The Deli? How could she run a business if she had to take care of her mother? Ellen felt a fear deep in the pit of her stomach. She didn't want to go back to living at home. She'd never be able to cope with the smothering restrictions that had nearly driven her over the edge, before she'd made that life-enhancing leap and moved out to her own place. It would be a disaster for her and Stephanie.

Dread seeped into every pore. *Please God! Please, please, please don't do this to me. Please give me a break. I've paid my dues,* Ellen prayed silently, fervently. She saw her father's lips moving in soundless prayer and felt a sense of disgust and shame that she should be so concerned for herself when, right this moment, her mother might be fighting for her life, or even dead. What sort of a human being was she at all? she thought in dismay. Was her real nature selfish and callous? Miriam had far more compassion for Sheila than she had. Imagine if one day she was in Sheila's shoes and Stephanie thought the way Ellen was thinking.

Sick at heart, petrified of what the future held, Ellen drove towards Dublin in a daze trying to shut out the horrible thoughts which crowded her mind.

"Please, God, let her be all right. I'll bake her mince pies for her. Just don't let her die because of me," Miriam prayed aloud as she washed out the tea towels. She'd phoned Ben and Vincent and told them the terrible news. All she could do now was get the children's dinner and wait.

To think that Mrs Munroe had fallen off her bike and had been lying for God knows how long in that damp drizzle. And it was probably all her fault. Mrs Munroe had been furious when she left. Maybe her anger had brought on a heart attack or a stroke. If

Miriam had agreed to bake the mince pies this might never have happened.

She started to cry. This was a horrible thing to happen. If Mrs Munroe died, it would be her fault. How would she live with that? And would Ben ever forgive her?

What a nuisance, Emma thought irritably. She and Vincent had planned to have a meal in the Savoy Grill before going to the pictures. She'd really looked forward to it. She needed a night out. The last film she'd seen was *Butch Cassidy and the Sundance Kid*. Paul Newman had been so sexy in it. He was *almost* as sexy as Vincent. She hadn't been to the cinema for ages! Once upon a time she'd gone to the pictures every week.

She was *exhausted* looking after Andrew at night. All the feeding and nappy changes and broken sleep were getting to her. She just wanted to be normal again for one measly night and have fun and forget her cares. And Ma Munroe had to go and throw a wobblie and fall off her bone-shaker of a bike. Poor Vincent was terribly upset. He was going straight to the hospital. He felt bad that Sheila had left the house in a huff the day of the christening. He'd asked Emma several times to apologise for her outburst, for the sake of peace. She'd refused. Why should she apologise? It was Sheila who should apologise for her rudeness.

Emma sighed. She couldn't very well carry on the tiff if Sheila was in hospital. She'd have to go and visit her mother-in-law. Vincent would be most put out if she didn't. It was *such* a pain in the ass. With any luck Sheila only had a few bumps and bruises. Emma sincerely hoped so. She hated visiting people in hospital. That horrible antiseptic smell and the sound of old people coughing and wheezing. It gave her the goose-bumps even to think about it.

"Your wife is still unconscious, Mr Munroe. There's swelling on the brain which is a cause for concern. We may have to operate. She has several broken ribs, severe contusions, a fractured wrist and lacerations. We need to perform tests as soon as she's conscious."

"But will she be all right?" Mick asked desperately. "How long will she be unconscious for?"

"I'm afraid we don't know the answer to that. We must wait and see," the doctor said kindly. "Why don't you go and have a cup of tea with your daughter?"

Mick nodded, unable to speak. His eyes filled with tears. His Sheila, always so strong and full of life, with a thousand and one things on the go, was lying motionless and white in the bed looking as if the life was draining out of her second by second. And there was nothing he could do to help her.

Chapter Thirteen

Her mother's bed was beside one of the long windows that faced out onto Eccles Street. Ellen was glad Sheila had a window bed. It gave her a little more privacy in the rectangular bed-lined ward. The curtains around the bed were semi-drawn, for which Ellen was grateful. Mick sat holding Sheila's hand.

It was visiting time. People trooped in bearing brown-bagged grapes and bottles of crinkly orange cellophane-covered Lucozade. Chairs were pulled up beside beds. Trays were pushed back. Bunches of limp carnations were stuck into great thick glass vases which reminded her of her schooldays. Mass cards hung over the iron bars of the bedsteads.

The hum of chatter rose as more people arrived. Ellen wanted to tell them all to shut up. Didn't they realise that her mother was very ill? How could there be any rest or peace in this noisy, foot-clattering, trolley-banging, chair clanging bedlam?

An elderly woman, yellowed from cancer, face drawn in pain, cried quietly in the bed opposite Sheila. She was dying and alone. But there was no peace to her dying, just noise and strangers casting quick glances of curious, detached pity. What a way to end your life, Ellen thought angrily. It was distressing.

Sheila lay pale and still under the starched white sheets, a purple-red bruise on her temple, vivid against the pallor of her waxy skin. Her dentures had been removed and her cheeks were sunken. For the first time, Ellen realised that her mother was on the threshold of old age. It came as a shock. Somehow she'd always thought of Sheila as invincible. Other people got sick. Other people grew old. Not Sheila. Sheila went on for ever.

A nurse padded quietly to the end of the bed and cast an experienced eye over her. "I'm going to take her blood pressure. Just step outside for a moment," she instructed calmly.

"She hasn't got any worse, has she?" Mick asked anxiously.

"No, no, Mr Munroe. This is just routine," the nurse soothed.

"Come on, Dad," Ellen said gently. Her heart went out to him, standing there, lost, bewildered, unable to conceal his fears for Sheila.

They stepped outside the cubicle as the nurse whisked the curtains around the bed. People looked at them inquisitively.

"Any improvement?" asked the middle-aged woman in the bed beside Sheila. Ellen shook her head. She didn't really want to get into conversation with the woman. She was loud and irritating as well as being an absolute know-all. She was thoroughly enjoying her stay in hospital where she was the centre of attention. She'd had her gall bladder removed. She'd suffered complications, she'd proudly told Ellen. *And* had to be opened up again. This was declared as though it was an added bonus. It was her badge of honour and each visitor was regaled with details of every incision, every stitch, every ounce of drama that could be squeezed out of it.

"Who's she under?"

"Professor Dean," Ellen said through gritted teeth.

"A good man," *Centre-of-Attention* said knowingly. "He looked after my sister-in-law when she had angina. Mind you she's poorly at the moment. Has to have the womb removed," she mouthed, lowering her voice momentarily. "She'll be coming in here under Dev. He did me when I had my fibroids and the repair job done."

"Goodbye," Ellen murmured and moved away, not in the least interested in this utter stranger's medical history. It was obvious she knew every specialist in the hospital.

"She's upset. You can see it." *Centre-of-Attention* took the snub graciously, speaking *sotto voce* to her two visitors.

Ellen felt like crowning her. The dry cloying heat from the huge brown radiators and central-heating pipes and the smell of antiseptic that could not quite disguise the odours of sickness made her feel queasy. It was a long time since breakfast.

"Let's go and get a cup of tea, Dad."

"Maybe we should stay." Mick was reluctant to leave.

"No. Come on. A bit of fresh air will do you good. We can have a cup of tea in the Roma cafe over there on Berkeley Road," Ellen said firmly. "Maybe you should eat something too."

"I couldn't eat a bit," Mick sighed.

"You should try. It's going to be a long day." She took his arm and they walked out of the ward, down the crowded corridor, towards the stairs.

On their way back to the hospital, after a cup of hot sweet tea and a cheese sandwich, they slipped into Berkeley Road church. In the gloominess of late afternoon, the flickering flames of small white candles lent an air of serenity that was vaguely comforting. An elderly woman threaded Rosary beads through her fingers, praying silently. Apart from her, the church was empty. Ellen followed Mick into a pew, glad to postpone the moment of return to the hospital. Lost in their own thoughts, they knelt and prayed, fearful of what they would find when they returned to Sheila's bedside.

Miriam's stomach was tied up in knots. Her heart was racing. She had a throbbing headache. It was the longest day of her life. The last she'd heard from Ellen was that Sheila was still unconscious and the doctors thought they might have to operate. She felt desperately guilty. If Mrs Munroe died, she might as well have murdered her.

This was her punishment for being selfish and not helping her mother-in-law out. Baking a few mince pies for the Christmas fair wouldn't have killed her. But she had wanted Mrs Munroe to realise that she, too, was very busy and that she would have very little spare time once she started working. *And* that she was fed up being treated like a dogsbody.

Mrs Munroe never treated Emma the way she treated *her*, Miriam thought resentfully as she cleared the kitchen table of dirty dishes. It was as though she had much more respect for Emma. Well, she was worthy of respect too, wasn't she? Was it so wrong to stand up for herself? How come other people seemed to do it with ease and yet when Miriam made a stand, she was made to feel as though she was stepping out of line and being selfish.

Maybe she *was* only thinking of herself by going into this business with Ellen and Denise. What if Sheila was right and her children did suffer because she wasn't able to give them her full attention? They were all in the sitting-room in front of the fire, making a get-well card for their nannie. Miriam could hear them arguing about what colour to use for the rainbow over her hospital bed.

Nagging doubts began to gnaw. Maybe she should give up the whole idea. But then Ellen would be dreadfully disappointed and she'd be letting her down. And besides she'd already invested money in the venture. She couldn't very well go looking for it back.

All the good had been taken out of it now, Miriam thought miserably. Just this once in her life she'd badly wanted to do something. It had looked as if it was all going to be perfect and now this had to happen. It wasn't fair. She'd always tried her best to be a decent person. Couldn't something nice happen to her once in a while? Miriam burst into tears as she washed the dishes after the children's dinner.

Peggy Kinsella slipped her long orange sleeveless cardigan on. It had got cooler and the foyer of Stuart and Stuart's Advertising Agency was always draughty. The black skinny-rib jumper she was wearing wasn't very warm but it showed off her figure admirably. And Peggy wanted to be noticed. That was why she only put her cardigan on when it got really chilly. She liked when the partners looked at her admiringly. She didn't plan to be a receptionist for ever. She wanted to be like Alexandra Johnston. A fully-fledged PR woman, planning promotions and advertising campaigns. Wining and dining clients in the best hotels.

All her friends said she was very lucky to have a receptionist's job in an advertising agency. It was much more interesting than their boring old jobs. She *was* lucky. But deep in Peggy's heart burned a flame of ambition that had been ignited the day she'd first laid eyes on Alexandra in her smart Prince of Wales check suit with her expensive black gloves and patent leather shoes and handbag. She exuded confidence and sophistication as she swanned into the lift to her second-floor office. There and then Peggy had vowed she was going to be like Alexandra some day. The fact that Alexandra was a sarcastic wagon only added to her glamour. Some day she, Peggy, would issue orders and take typists and secretaries to task for "sloppy incompetence" – Alexandra's favourite term of reprimand.

The afternoon post had just arrived. She liked sorting the post. One day letters would be addressed to her. And a receptionist would bring them to her very own office.

A large garish card in psychedelic reds and purples caught her eye. It was way-out, Peggy thought admiringly as she studied it. She had a Beatles poster something like it hanging up in her bedsit. She flipped the card over and saw that it was addressed to her heroine.

Peggy's blue eyes grew round as she read the opening sentence.

"Oh my Gawd. Oh! *Oh!*" she exclaimed aloud as she read further.

June Whelan from the typing pool happened to be passing.

"Hey, June! June, quick, look at this!" Peggy called urgently, knowing that never again would a nugget of gossip of this magnitude be hers to enjoy.

June tottered over on her newly acquired platform shoes and

took the card eagerly. This was obviously something out of the ordinary. Peggy didn't usually associate with a mere typist.

"Holy Moly," June stuttered as she read it. "Is this some sort of a joke?"

"I wouldn't think so. Can you believe it? No wonder *Miss-High-and-Mighty's* out sick."

"She'll be even sicker when she reads this," Peggy declared as she took back the card and reread it just to make sure she wasn't seeing things.

***

"Well, what do you think?" Alexandra drew deeply on her cigarette and exhaled a long thin stream of smoke.

"My bedroom's a bit small," Chris said sulkily.

"Darling, don't be silly. We can do the woo in my bed. We'd better make up our minds today, though. These pads are going to be snapped up."

"Twelve pounds ten is a bit steep."

"Well, it's not as if you're paying the full whack! It's six pounds five shillings each, Chris. Don't be a cheapskate," Alexandra drawled.

"Look, Alexandra, I have a business to run and a mortgage to pay. It's nothing to do with being a cheapskate."

"Fine," she snapped. "Go and get a kip of a bedsit in Rathmines."

"All right, all right, but as long as it's understood it's not a permanent arrangement. I'm only staying until I can persuade Suzy to let me home again. I can't afford this carry-on," Chris said irritably.

"Darling, you've no idea how good you are for my ego," Alexandra said dryly.

"Well, it was always only going to be a fling, wasn't it? It's not as if we're madly in love with each other." Chris jammed his hands in his pockets.

"You could lie to me a little," she pouted, stubbing out her cigarette in the fireplace. "You're so good at it normally."

166

"It takes one to know one."

"Bastard!"

They glared at each other.

"Let's do it now. On the floor!" Alexandra urged, excited.

"You're a crazy bird! You're wild," Chris muttered as he drew her to him.

"Yeah, that's me. Wild and crazy, baby. It takes one to know one," Alexandra murmured huskily as she unbuckled his belt and drew him down beside her on the bare wooden floor.

Her head hurt. Everywhere hurt. She felt very, very strange. Sheila tried to open her eyes. Her eyelids felt like lead. It was too much of an effort. Someone was calling her name. Go away, she wanted to say, but the words wouldn't come out.

"Mrs Munroe, Mrs Munroe." The voice was very insistent.

Sheila made a supreme effort. The light hurt but after a moment or two she realised that a nurse was bending over her, smiling at her.

"That's very good, Mrs Munroe. Everything's all right. Look, someone's just come to see you."

The face she loved most in the world became more focused.

"Mick, Mick," she croaked.

"You're all right, Sheila. Don't worry about a thing." Her husband's dear familiar voice was very reassuring. He gave her hand a comforting squeeze. Sheila closed her eyes. Mick was here, that was all that mattered.

"I'd better postpone the opening. I'll probably have to go home to look after Mam when she comes out of hospital." Ellen couldn't keep the despondency out of her voice. It was late and she was at home with Doug. Miriam had kept Stephanie. But Ellen had insisted that Mick spend the night with her. She didn't want him to be on his own. He was fast asleep in her bed, worn out after the shocks of the day.

"Don't make a decision now, Ellen. You're too tired. You've had a rough day. Things will look different in the morning," Doug advised. "This is a good time to open. There's going to be lots of people doing extra shopping for Christmas. You know the way it's always busy. There's queues in your dad's shop for the turkeys. Some of those people would enjoy a cup of coffee or a bite of lunch. And you have Miriam and Denise."

"I know. But it's going to be really awkward. I can't let Dad handle all this on his own. And I wouldn't see Mam stuck."

"I know you wouldn't, Ellen. I'm just saying this is a good time to open The Deli and, if you can get around it at all, try and keep to your original plan. I'll do anything I can to help."

Ellen reached up and stroked his beard. "Did anyone ever tell you you're a big softie?"

"I beg your pardon, woman, no one's ever cast aspersions on my credentials before," Doug said in mock indignation.

Ellen giggled. Doug's humour was always such a tonic.

"Idiot!" She smiled up at him and cuddled in close beside him on the sofa. It was so good to have someone to share her woes with. She'd carried her burdens alone for such a long time she'd got used to aloneness. This sharing with Doug was very comforting. Was this what a good marriage was like? she wondered as she gazed at the flickering flames. Was this really what it was all about? Not the wild passion and trauma and roller-coaster emotions that characterised her relationship with Chris?

She couldn't imagine Chris offering to muck in to help her out of a fix, she thought wryly. Other people's crises were of no interest to him. His own were far too absorbing.

At least her mother hadn't had a stroke or a heart attack. There was light at the end of the tunnel. She'd really done a job on herself, though. She'd broken three ribs, fractured her wrist and given herself an awful concussion. She was going to be in hospital for at least a week. After that, she'd need time to recuperate. Ellen had more or less resigned herself to spending Christmas at her mother's. Her eyes drooped tiredly. She was jaded. She sagged comfortably against Doug.

"I think it's time you went to bed." He gave her a gentle shake.

"I don't want to move. You've got very comfortable shoulders," Ellen protested, too lazy to get up.

"They're one of my best attributes, true. Women go mad about these shoulders, you know? But flattery will get you nowhere. It's time for bed," Doug teased as he hauled her up off the sofa.

"Aw, Doug."

"Aw, Ellen."

He leaned down and kissed her lightly. "I don't want to go either. But you've had a long day. And there's a lot to be done tomorrow, so lock up after me and hop it." He put the guard in front of the fire, carried the cups out into the kitchen and rinsed them before shrugging into his leather jacket.

"Night, love."

"Goodnight, Doug. Thanks for everything."

"Go to bed." He smiled his lopsided crinkly smile, took her hand and led her downstairs. "I'll see you tomorrow."

Yawning, Ellen closed the door behind him. She had the strangest feeling that if her dad hadn't been staying with her, she would have asked Doug to stay the night. They had become so close, she wanted to be with him. It was the first time she'd really felt that way and it gave her a little shock. Did it mean she was finally over Chris?

She was too tired to think about it. Or maybe she didn't want to think about it. Committing to Doug would mean giving up on Chris and there'd be no going back. She wanted to be absolutely fair to Doug. Chris would have no part in her life if she turned to Doug. It would be a very final step to take. Could she take it? Why was she so hesitant about it? She wouldn't think about it tonight. It was much easier not to and she'd had a very long day.

Weary to her bones, Ellen barely washed her teeth before getting into Stephanie's snug, hot-water-bottle-warmed bed. She was asleep in seconds.

"Miriam, Mam's accident isn't your fault. These things happen," Ben explained patiently.

"Yeah, but she was mad when she left. I should have just agreed to bake the damn mince pies. It wouldn't have killed me," Miriam said heavily.

"Miriam, you were right to say no. Mam's just got to accept that you're going to be busy with The Deli. You can't spread yourself everywhere, love. And you've always helped out until now. You've done more than your share."

"I was half-thinking maybe I've made a mistake about The Deli. Maybe I shouldn't take it on. I'm going to be up to my eyes with it and maybe it's not fair on the kids and you."

"Are you nuts?" Ben sat bolt upright. "I don't want to hear that kind of talk again, Miriam. You've been looking forward to this for months. The kids are looking forward to all being together after school and I'm looking forward to having a rich wife. Right?"

"Oh, Ben, I'm serious," Miriam said in exasperation.

"And so am I, Miriam. I don't want to hear this bull. Mam's going to be OK. She'll be out and about again, I guarantee you that. And you're *not* going to sit here and bake mince pies for the parish and let a chance like The Deli pass you by. Over my dead body." It was rare for Ben to get worked up about something. He was very placid usually.

"Are you sure you don't mind me doing it? Are you absolutely certain you won't feel I'm neglecting the children?" she asked doubtfully.

"I'll be really disappointed in you if you don't do this, Miriam," her husband said quietly.

"Thanks, Ben." Miriam was so touched by his support and belief in her that tears came to her eyes. Ben always made her feel good about herself. She was very lucky to have him.

"What am I going to do with you?" Ben drew her close and they sat in the firelight, arms entwined, and suddenly things weren't so gloomy. Miriam felt a flicker of excitement again at the thought of the adventure to come.

❦

Emma lay next to Vincent, listening to his even breathing. She was in a state. He'd gone in to the Mater to see his mother and had come home distressed at her injuries. He'd made her promise that she'd go and visit Sheila and make up their tiff.

Then later, he'd come out with his bombshell. He wanted to take Sheila home to their house when she came out of hospital so she could recuperate. After all, they had Mrs Murdock – she could help out, he'd suggested. Emma had been so stunned at this proposition she was practically speechless.

"But your mother might prefer to go to Ellen's or Miriam's," she'd managed weakly.

"It's out of the question, Emma. They wouldn't have time to look after her with this cafe business," Vincent pointed out reasonably. "She should come to us. It's the best option. It will only be for a week or so."

Emma was horrified. A *week*! What a nightmare. Two hours of Mrs Munroe's company was more than enough to endure.

She couldn't really argue, unfortunately. After all, Vincent was her husband and he was very good to her. He rarely asked her to do anything that put her out. Emma had to be honest about this, much as it pained her. She couldn't very well cause a fuss. Vincent would be hurt if she dug her heels in and said an emphatic no. She was his wife, she had to be helpful in difficult times. But the thought of having Mrs Munroe in their house for more than a couple of hours was a heart-sinking, dread-inducing prospect. This would be a major test of how good a wife she was.

Blast Ellen and Miriam and their silly little cafe, Emma thought irately. All the fuss about it, you'd think it was the blooming Ritz. Who in their right minds would want to spend hours cooking food, serving it to people and then washing up after them. They were mad! If it wasn't for that, Ellen could look after Mrs Munroe.

After all, she was her daughter. It was her place to look after her mother, not Emma's. And besides Emma had only had a baby a few months ago. It was exhausting looking after him and trying to cope with Julie Ann as well. Mrs Murdock was extremely efficient, to be sure, but it was still very tiring and everyone knew she'd had a most difficult pregnancy, Emma thought indignantly as she lay in the dark feeling very sorry for herself.

But she couldn't get out of this, she admitted glumly. If Vincent wanted his mother to come and stay with them and Sheila agreed, that was that. She'd have to pretend to accept with good grace. It was a major pain in the ass. She tossed and turned and fretted and fumed while Vincent slept, oblivious, beside her.

The next few days were exhausting for Ellen. Between the hospital visits twice a day, cooking a meal for her father and trying to keep his spirits up, and preparing the finishing touches for the grand opening, Ellen didn't know if she was on her head or her heels.

Sheila was crotchety and in pain and kept asking for things like blancmange and chicken broth, that had to be specially prepared and brought in at each visit. Now that the shock had worn off and she'd got over the worst part she was feeling contrary and sorry for herself. She resented the fact that Ellen and Miriam weren't dancing attendance on her, as she thought. She was playing the old soldier. But Mick had told Ellen that she was to open her deli as planned. Now that Sheila was more herself, he was taking charge in his own quiet way.

"Once I hear your mother complaining, I know she's on the mend. So you keep going and don't worry, we'll work things out," he assured Ellen.

Much to her relief. If she'd thought for one instant that Mick would have preferred her to postpone things, she would have. Her father had supported her when she'd needed it. There was no question of her support for him.

Denise and Miriam worked like Trojans to get The Deli shipshape. The night before the opening, after she'd been to visit her mother, Ellen joined them to take a look at their immaculate and very impressive deli cafe. Mick was minding Stephanie.

Shining pine tables and chairs lined the walls and windows. The counter and delicatessen bar faced the door. Two pine dressers resplendent with sparkling delph stood one on each side of the counter. Crisp lemon and blue curtains adorned the windows. Old teapots and gleaming brass kettles graced the pelmets. Starched lemon and blue napkins that matched the curtains stood folded artistically in their pine rings, in front of each place setting.

The fire, piled with logs and turf, was waiting to be lit. The mantel over it held a huge vase of orange- and red-berried foliage. Boughs of holly decorated the walls above it. Beside the fire stood the magnificent Christmas tree that the children had decorated with much care and excitement. Santa would be switching on the lights. Small wooden stairs at the gable end of the room led to the upper dining area where banquettes lined the wall. Tables for two nestled beside the windows. The pine-covered ceiling and walls glowed in the soft lamplight lending a cosy intimate air.

The girls were thrilled with it. All the hard work was worth the effort and they stared around at the result of their endeavours with enormous pride.

Ellen went to her big carrier bag and pulled out a bottle of champagne. "I bought this when I was visiting Ma today. We deserve it, girls. I want to thank the two of you for being such pals."

"Thank you, Ellen, for having the brainwave in the first place and for letting us be part of it." Denise gave her a grateful hug. "I'm really glad you decided to open. Once we get going and get into our routines, we'll be flying."

"I hope so. I told Ma I wouldn't be in to see her tomorrow. She's a bit huffed."

"God, Ellen, you've been in to see her twice every day. That's a bit unreasonable." Miriam made a face.

"You know Mam. Anyway," she continued briskly, "tomorrow's our day, so get the glasses, Miriam, and let's drink up."

"I better not go home pissed, or Jimmy'll have something to say," Denise demurred when Ellen filled her glass with the bubbling gold liquid.

"Sod Jimmy. The time is coming, Denise, when you can tell him to get lost. You'll be an independent woman. And you can tell Specky Spinster Dowling she's welcome to him," Ellen retorted firmly.

"I suppose so," Denise said doubtfully. But Ellen suspected that her friend would never have the nerve to cut her ties with her philandering husband.

"I must say, I've never seen a more Santa-looking Santa than Doug when I put the suit and beard on him," Miriam tactfully changed the subject.

"He's dreading it," Ellen laughed.

"He'll be grand." Miriam held out her glass. "Fill me up again. Between yourself and Emma I'm developing a taste for the bubbly."

They drank the champagne and relaxed for a while until Denise said she really had to go. They washed up the glasses and went into Ellen's hall through the door that Doug had put in to connect the two buildings.

"This is so handy," Ellen remarked as she locked it after her. "The kids are all excited at the idea of being here together."

"It'll be mad." Miriam grimaced.

"One thing, no matter what rows or arguments *they* get into between themselves, let's promise that we'll never fall out over the children," Denise said firmly.

"Absolutely," Ellen agreed.

"Girls, by the time we've got through the day we won't have the energy to fall out with anyone. Now I'm off," Miriam declared. "I want to cook a stew tonight so that Ben can give it to the kids for their dinner tomorrow."

They said their goodnights and Ellen closed the door on her friends with tiny little butterflies of apprehension. Just say they had no customers and the whole thing turned out to be a flop? All that money they'd spent renovating the place would be lost.

"Don't think like that," she told herself sternly as she switched out the lights downstairs and hurried up to let Mick go home. They had a quick cup of tea and when he was gone she slipped into a scented bath to ease away her tension. It was her last night of freedom. From tomorrow she'd be a businesswoman, with all the hard work and worries that it entailed.

Sheila lay in bed twisting and turning. She was sore. The painkillers she'd been given earlier had worn off. The woman beside her, Mrs Redden, snored resoundingly, her ear-splitting snorts and gurgles rising to a climax every couple of seconds. Sheila gritted her teeth in irritation. She hadn't had a decent night's sleep since she'd landed herself in hospital. She missed her own comfortable bed and Mick's comforting arm around her. The sooner she got out of here the better. Mrs Redden started to cuck.

"Jesus, Mary and Joseph, will you be quiet!" Sheila hissed. Mrs Redden cucked serenely on. She was a loud-mouth during the day and a loud-mouth at night. She truly was an irritating woman and trust her luck to be beside her, Sheila thought resentfully. The old wooden windows seemed to rattle in harmony with her neighbour's snores as gusts of wind caught them every so often. They were the creakiest windows she'd ever heard. Sheila yawned tiredly.

The new woman in the bed opposite coughed, a dry harsh racking sound. She'd only been admitted today. The poor creature who'd been in the bed before her had died yesterday.

She should give thanks for small mercies, Sheila sighed. At least she was alive, on the road to recovery, and not on the road to the cemetery. But it was all such a nuisance what with Christmas coming and all that she should have been doing for the guild. No doubt Bonnie was taking advantage of her illness. Making herself indispensable.

And there was poor Mick at home with no one to look after him. Ellen was feeding him, and though she and Miriam had asked him to stay with them, he'd gone back home. Mick liked his own place best. She didn't like to think of him on his own at night. Making his supper and having no one to talk to. Mick always said no one could make his cocoa like she could. Sheila felt very lonely as she lay wide-eyed looking at the flickering red light that shone under the picture of the Sacred Heart on the opposite wall. Mick was getting on like herself. She worried about him. If anything happened to him in the middle of the night he'd be there all alone with no one to help him.

"O Sacred Heart of Jesus, I put Mick in Your tender loving care. Free from all harm and danger. Amen," she whispered as she reached out to her locker to get her Rosary beads. She might as well say the Rosary. She'd offer it up for Mick and for Ellen.

Ellen was opening her cafe tomorrow. She was going to miss that too. Sheila really had mixed feelings about it all. If it came to nothing, Ellen would be terribly disappointed. She and Miriam had invested a tidy amount of money in the venture. It was a heavy responsibility they had burdened themselves with. The young women of this generation were very unsettled in themselves, Sheila mused as she tried to find a more comfortable position. Her pillows were crumpled but it was too awkward to try and fix them with one hand. It was a vexation having her other one in plaster.

Miriam had come to visit and at least had had the manners to apologise for her ungracious behaviour, which was more than that other little madam, Emma, had. That girl was an ungrateful biddy. All the kindness that Sheila had shown her and she hadn't even stuck her nose around the corner of the door to wish Sheila well. Vincent claimed she had a tummy bug and didn't want to spread it around. A likely story, Sheila sniffed as she kissed the crucifix and began the first decade of the Sorrowful Mysteries.

Chapter Fourteen

Ellen hadn't slept well. She'd been far too nervous and excited. By seven-thirty, she was dressed and downstairs in The Deli's spotless kitchen, peeling potatoes and carrots and chopping up onions for the soup. Stephanie was fast asleep and she kept the adjoining door open so she could listen out for her. It was a dark frosty cold morning. The sky was clear, for which Ellen was very grateful. It had been windy and showery last night but that had passed away.

Miriam arrived at eight-thirty and Denise soon after. The three of them worked feverishly, baking scones and breads and icing the cakes and sponges they'd already made.

By ten-fifteen there was a queue outside as a horde of excited children, accompanied by resigned parents, eagerly awaited the arrival of Santa. Glenree was busier than normal for a Saturday morning. But it was only a few weeks to Christmas and people were stocking up and buying presents. There was a great buzz about. The weather was bright and cold. Had it been raining, there wouldn't have been half as many people outside, looking forward to something different in the life of their small town. It wasn't often a new place opened and curiosity was rife. All the hammering and banging and building had intrigued the locals, who were dying to see just what Ellen Munroe and her pals had done to the old cafe.

There were times when nosiness was a bonus, Ellen grinned as she saw curious faces peering in through the windows. Miriam was in Ellen's sitting-room helping Doug into his Santa outfit. Denise was putting the finishing touches to a big platter of sandwiches which were to be served with cocktail sausages and cheese snacks, free of charge, for the first hour of opening. The breads and scones were baked, the soup simmering in the big pot, vol-au-vents were cooling on baking trays awaiting their chicken and mushroom filling. Rows of stuffed rashers sat neatly on foil-covered trays. The kitchen was humming with activity.

The deli counter was a mouth-watering eyeful of colourful salads, baked hams, turkey and selections of other cold meats. At the other end, sponges, tarts, cream cakes, brown breads, soda breads, jams and preserves and big dishes of fresh cream were a calorie-counter's nightmare. A selection of iced Christmas cakes and puddings reposed on a display decorated with red ribbons and boughs of fresh holly.

"Ellen."

"Mam, quick!"

Ellen heard Miriam and Stephanie call her simultaneously.

"I'm coming," she called back as she struck a match and watched the flames catch the rolled-up papers and logs and turf in the big fireplace. They had turned on the central heating earlier, and The Deli was warm already. They could switch it off if the fire made it too hot. She raced upstairs, dying to see Doug.

"Oh! *Oh!*" she breathed. Doug stood, rounded and plump, in his red suit, white-bearded, eyes twinkling, carrying a bulging sack full of presents. He was the most realistic Santa she'd ever seen.

"How did you make him so *fat!*" Ellen couldn't believe her eyes.

"Pardon me," Doug said indignantly, his voice muffled from the depths of his cotton-wool beard.

Miriam laughed. "I stuffed acres of quilting padding into him."

"Mam, Mam, isn't this brill! Doug said I could be his helper. I'm going to wear my frilly dress that's great for twirls."

"And I've made her a little crown and wand," Miriam said fondly. "Quick, hurry and get into your dress. We'll be opening soon."

Stephanie was so excited she flew on winged feet into her bedroom, pigtails flying.

"Thanks, Miriam. She'll be chuffed!" Ellen hugged her sister-in-law gratefully.

"Sure it's her big day too. It's great, isn't it?" Miriam was as bad as Stephanie. "It's a bit like a wedding or something."

"Well, if I thought Ellen would marry me, I'd ask her," Doug interjected. "Just imagine the publicity you'd get. *Santa weds in Irish deli. Christmas cancelled due to honeymoon.*"

"Stop it, you. And behave yourself today."

"I might! How about *Santa, overcome by heat, runs amok and strips naked in Irish deli?*"

"Doug, I'm warning you," Ellen giggled.

"Get down to your pots, woman. Just remember you owe me for this. What did you say? Steak and kidney pud whenever I wanted it?" Doug's eyes glinted beneath his cotton-wool eyebrows.

Ellen smiled back happily. A spark of joy touched her. There was no one she'd prefer to share this day with than Doug.

"Well. I suppose this is it." Doug reached out and squeezed her hand. "Good luck, love. Let's go." He picked up his sack of goodies. "Is my Fairy Helper ready?" he called out.

"Here I am." Stephanie raced in breathlessly. "Mammy, will you zip up my dress? Auntie Miriam, where's my crown?"

"Stay calm," Ellen instructed although she understood exactly how Stephanie was feeling. She zipped up the dress, placed the gold foil-covered crown on her daughter's head and handed her the wand. "You're a beautiful fairy."

"And you're a beautiful mammy. Come on, let's go."

"We'll go out the side door and come up on the crowd from

behind. And then you be ready to open the door. Right?" Doug ordered.

"I forgot to mention, Doug, we've put a red ribbon across the door. You have to cut it and make a little speech," Ellen said airily.

"You never said anything to me about any speech or cutting any ribbons," Doug exclaimed, aghast.

"All you have to say is something like . . . I now declare The Deli open, good luck to all who eat in her, or whatever you like, and then turn the sign to open," Ellen soothed.

"If you're not careful, I'll tell them not to set foot inside the place if they don't want an episode of the galloping trots. Are you really sure you want me to say something?"

"Yes," Ellen said firmly. "Just act the part of Santa and say 'Ho, ho, ho' or 'Season's greetings'. You'll be fine."

"Ho, ho, ho, my hat!" Doug grumbled as he led the way downstairs, followed by a sniggering Ellen and Miriam. He walked out the back door carrying his sack, followed by Stephanie, who was twirling her wand most professionally.

Ellen and Miriam hastily divested themselves of their aprons, gave their hair a quick brush and went into The Deli, ready for the big moment.

"Come on, Denise," Miriam called. As they positioned themselves at the door a ripple of excitement spread through the crowd of curious onlookers. Ellen could see Ben, Vincent and Emma in the middle of the group. She was half-surprised to see Vincent and Emma. They usually went to Dublin on Saturday mornings and then had lunch out somewhere. Emma's curiosity must have got the better of her, Ellen thought uncharitably. She hadn't seen her sister-in-law since the disaster of Andrew's christening. Mick came out of the butcher's and joined them. He gave Ellen the thumbs-up when he saw her, a look of pride on his ruddy face. She wanted to go out and hug him. It was thanks to Mick and his belief in her that she was here today on the brink of a whole new life.

Screams of excitement erupted from the assembled children when they saw Santa striding along with his sack of goodies.

"Ho, ho, ho, children! Season's greetings!" Ellen heard Doug call, very convincingly. He really was a pet, she thought affectionately.

She turned the key in the lock and opened the door.

"Ho, ho, ho, Ellen, Miriam and Denise! I've come all the way from the North Pole to meet the good children of Glenree and to open this lovely new deli. I hope you've got some pudding for me and some carrots for Rudolph," Santa boomed heartily.

"Hi, Santa," Ellen beamed, handing him the scissors. "Will you cut the ribbon?"

"I'll need some help." Santa stroked his beard. "Where's my Fairy Helper?"

"Here I am!" Stephanie was pink with delight.

"Right, you take the scissors and we'll cut it together." He placed his strong tanned hand over Stephanie's dainty little one and they stood poised to cut.

"Ladies and gentlemen, it gives me great pleasure to open this magnificent new deli. I happen to know there's lovely food waiting for all of us. And if you haven't made your Christmas cake or pudding to leave out for me on Christmas Eve, you'll be able to buy them here. And you all know how much I love pudding and cake."

Loud yells and cheers greeted this pronouncement.

"I now pronounce this deli open. May all who eat in it enjoy their grub and not put on an ounce." Laughter and applause echoed along the street as Stephanie and Doug cut the ribbon, and turned the sign to open. Doug led the way, switched on the Christmas tree lights to loud applause and sat at the table specially prepared for him. There was a mad scramble of children trying to get close to him.

"Line up, please," Ellen instructed as she and Miriam organised a queue.

"Ben, take over, we've got to serve," Miriam ordered, as a crowd of friends, neighbours and shoppers surged through the door eager to see what the girls had done to the place.

"Queue up now, one at a time." Ben took over crowd control as Doug, assisted by Stephanie, began to dole out the presents.

"Mummy, I want to be a Fairy Helper too." Julie Ann broke away from Emma and came to stand directly in front of Santa, who glowered at her in a most un-Santa-like manner.

"You can't, Julie Ann. This is *my* cafe and I'm Santa's helper," Stephanie said indignantly, standing her ground for once.

"Julie Ann, behave yourself," Vincent said sternly.

"But I want to be a fairy," Julie Ann insisted.

"Well, you can't be. Now that's enough."

"It's not fair. Stephanie gets *everything*! She's got a Mary Poppins bedroom in the roof and now she's got a cafe, and she's a Fairy Helper. And I get nothing. It's really mean." Julie Ann was red in the face with temper and frustration. *"I want to be a fairy! Now!"* Her screech echoed around the cafe.

Santa sat, mesmerised by her tantrum, the likes of which he'd never seen. He looked helplessly at Ellen. Seeing the horror in his eyes, she got a fit of the giggles and had to turn away. This was one of Julie Ann's best.

Emma was mortified.

"Vincent, take her outside and do something with her," she hissed.

Vincent, furious, scooped Julie Ann, kicking and screaming, in his arms and carried her out the door.

"I hate you, Daddy," she wailed as they left The Deli.

Andrew started to howl in his mother's arms.

Emma got utterly flustered.

"I'm really sorry about this, Ellen. Good luck with the new business. I'd better go," she clipped.

"Don't worry about it, Emma. Kids will be kids," Ellen murmured.

"Julie Ann gets more like her father every day," Emma said pointedly. "Let's hope Andrew has *my* temperament." She threw her eyes up to heaven and swept out.

Ellen's jaw dropped. The cheek of her to blame that sort of behaviour on Julie Ann's Munroe genes. She really could be a snippy little madam, she thought crossly, raging that she hadn't come up with some equally cutting retort.

"Rise above it," Santa twinkled, amused.

"I bet you won't come to her on Christmas Eve," Rebecca interjected solemnly, fascinated that her cousin had dared misbehave in front of Santa.

"Hello, little girl. What's your name?"

"Rebecca Catherine Munroe," Rebecca said shyly.

"And I happen to know that you're a very good little girl. Fairy Helper, have you got a present for this good little girl?"

"That's my cousin," Stephanie said proudly as she delved into the sack and handed Santa a wrapped parcel. She'd been sworn to secrecy about Santa's identity.

"I know," said Santa as he handed the gift to Rebecca. "And so are that young lady and young man." He pointed to Connie and Daniel.

"How did you know that?" Rebecca was amazed.

"Santa knows everything. He knows that this little boy here," Doug drew a timid little chap to his side, "lives on Red Barn's Road and he helps his granny with her shopping."

The little fellow was puffed with pride as he gazed trustingly at the awe-inspiring figure in front of him. "An' I've stopped pickin' my nose too," he confided, much to the amusement of the adults.

"You're a great boy," Santa said kindly as he handed him his parcel.

Doug really had a way with kids, Ellen thought admiringly as she watched how he had a word for all of them.

The next hour passed in a blur of mad activity. People dropped in and bought cakes and cold meats and side salads to take away and enjoyed the finger-food the girls were serving. There was much praise for the decor and Ellen felt extremely optimistic that the business would provide the three of them with a good income. Santa and his helper were kept busy until every child had got a present and it was with great relief that he stood up at midday having acquitted himself with flying colours.

The girls had planned to serve lunches from twelve until two. Now that the official opening was over, they were ready to get down to business.

Doug hastened gratefully through the front door cheered by the few remaining children. He was baked alive in his red suit. He couldn't wait to be rid of it. He had the key to Ellen's back door and, when he got in to the safety of the flat, he flopped onto the sofa.

He was sitting there, minus his cotton-wool beard, opening the buttons of his suit when Ellen rushed in. He stood up to greet her.

"Doug, I can't stay a minute. I just wanted to say thanks very much for what you did." She threw her arms around his neck and hugged him tightly.

"Whist, woman, you're welcome." Doug hugged her back. Then he lowered his head and kissed her fiercely.

"Oh!" Ellen looked into his hazel eyes, surprised by how much she'd enjoyed it.

"Oh what?" Doug smiled down at her.

"Just oh!" She actually felt shy.

"I got carried away," he teased.

"I'd better go, in case we've got a real customer," she murmured.

"You'd better. Miriam and Denise mightn't be able to dish out a bowl of soup on their own. How about if I get carried away just once more, seeing it's the day. that's in it?" Doug stroked her cheek.

She drew his head down and kissed him ardently. It was a long deep French kiss.

"You're beautiful," Doug whispered huskily.

"So are you," she whispered back, burying her face in his neck.

"What a day you pick to kiss me like that," he said ruefully as they heard Stephanie running upstairs and drew apart.

"It's a new beginning day. The best sort of day." Ellen squeezed his hand.

"And it's only starting," Doug smiled down at her.

She wanted to throw herself at him again. "I'm very happy, Doug. Thank you for all you've done for me."

"So am I, love. I wish it was closing time and I could have you all to myself."

"It'll be something to look forward to," Ellen promised.

"Hi, Mam. Hi, Doug." Stephanie danced into the room twirling her wand. "Uncle Ben said can I go to the Botanic Gardens with them? We're going to see the squirrels."

"That's very kind of Uncle Ben – of course you can go," Ellen agreed.

"Mammy, would you say the real Santa's fairies saw Julie Ann being so bold?" Stephanie inquired.

"Maybe they did. Who knows where they are, so close to Christmas?"

"Just say she didn't get any toys this year. She might even get a sack of ashes," Stephanie said happily, anticipating the disaster of disasters that might, hopefully, befall her cousin.

"You don't worry about Julie Ann, you just worry about being a good girl yourself," Ellen said as she tucked Stephanie's pigtails into her bonnet. "Be a good girl for Uncle Ben."

"I will. I don't want to get a sack of ashes, Mam," Stephanie said fervently as she hurried out the door.

"A sack of ashes would be too good for that other little demon of hell," Doug observed as he struggled out of his red jacket.

"She's only a child, Doug," Ellen reprimanded.

"Ellen, no other child of my acquaintance behaves like Julie Ann. She's a law unto herself. She's spoilt rotten. But don't worry, my good woman, I won't let her Munroe genes put me off wooing you." He grinned.

"You rotter." Ellen gave him a puck in the shoulder. "I'll see you later."

"I hope you're run off your feet with customers."

"Thanks, Doug. I'd better get going."

"One more kiss?"

"Doug, I won't be able to concentrate on what I'm doing. I'll probably put too much pepper in the soup or something."

"Coward!"

"Yeah, I am," Ellen agreed and fled. She knew she'd lowered the emotional barrier that she'd erected around herself because of Chris. She'd crossed that bridge for the first time with Doug today and it made her feel very happy.

Half the tables were occupied when she got downstairs and Miriam flashed her a look of relief from behind the counter. "I think Denise could do with some help in the kitchen."

"I'm on my way."

It was a hectic day. She hardly had time to think about the lovely interlude with Doug. But now and again when she had a minute to herself she'd remember and feel a warm secret glow.

Local curiosity and a busy shopping day ensured that they had customers all day and by the time they closed at six-thirty the girls were shattered. They had sold out of all their home baking and were going to have to spend the next day at their stoves.

"We're going to have to get some suppliers if this keeps up," Miriam remarked as she scrubbed the soup pot.

"I'd say things will even out," Denise yawned as she washed down the worktops.

"It was a great day, all the same, girls. If we even did a third of what we did today, we'd be doing well." Ellen collected all the dirty table napkins, dishcloths and tea towels for washing. It took them another half-hour before they were ready to leave. They were bushed by the time they locked the door behind them.

Ellen drove Miriam home and collected Stephanie. Then they called in to see Mick, to find out how Sheila was. Mick was delighted to see them. He wanted to hear all about the day's events and he insisted they stay for supper. By the time she and Stephanie got home it was almost nine. Stephanie was yawning her head off. Ellen bundled her upstairs to bed. She was asleep in minutes.

She'd just made herself a cup of coffee when the phone rang. It was Doug.

"I thought you'd be here by now. The kettle's boiled. I kept you a gooey cake. Stephanie's fast asleep and if you don't get here soon, I'll be too." Ellen tried to stifle a yawn.

"I'm not going to be able to make it, Ellen." Doug sounded glum.

"Ah Doug! I was looking forward to telling you all about it. Why can't you come over?" She was hugely disappointed. Concern washed over her. Doug would have been looking forward to the evening as much as she was. "What's wrong?"

"A fellow over in Swords rang me. His chimney collapsed and there's a crack in the gable wall. He was really stuck. I'm here now, helping him out. The chancers who built this place should be shot. Talk about sloppy work. He's lucky the whole place didn't collapse around his head. I'm sorry, Ellen. I'd love to be with you, tonight of all nights, but I couldn't leave this chap in the lurch, sure I couldn't?"

"Of course you couldn't. That's because you're such a nice Doug," Ellen smiled down the phone. "It's awfully cold tonight, have you got your heavy jacket on?"

"I have, and thank you for asking."

"Will you have to work very late?"

"I'm just putting some supports up tonight. I'll see what I can do for him tomorrow."

"Will you be able to come over at all tomorrow? Can you come for your dinner?"

"Ellen," Doug said patiently, "Remember I told you I was giving my brother-in-law a hand with his extension. I can't let him down. I promised to have it finished before Christmas. It'll be another late night. I told you that last week."

"I know you did. Sorry, I forgot. That means I'm not going to see you over the weekend, and Monday I'll be working," she said ruefully.

"Don't mind me, woman, I'm just playing hard to get," Doug teased. "I'll call into The Deli on Monday." He lowered his voice.

"I can't really talk, Ellen. I just wanted to say, today was lovely and I wish I was there with you now."

"I wish you were too, Doug," Ellen said wistfully. "I'll see you Monday." She hung up reluctantly. Typical! Now that she'd finally let herself feel attracted to Doug, and just when she'd have liked a lovely kissing and cuddling session, a chance to be intimate and close, she was going to have to wait. Couldn't the gods smile on her just once? She took her coffee into the bathroom, ran a hot bath, perfumed the water with bath salts and lavender bubble bath and sank into it wearily.

Today had been almost perfect. If Doug had been with her now it would have been the icing on the cake. The realisation hit her with a little shock. She wanted to be with Doug. Chris wasn't in her head any more. She'd hardly given him a passing thought in the last week.

Did that mean she didn't love him any more? She frowned and blew away a soap bubble. If you stopped loving someone, did that mean that what had gone before hadn't really been love? Had it just been an illusion of love? She'd read in *The Messenger* once that real love was unconditional. Pure unselfish love made no demands. Had her love for Chris been conditional on his loving her in return? Because he didn't she'd stopped loving him. What did that say about her? That she'd only loved him because she was needy and lonely? Ellen shied away from the thought. It wasn't something she cared to admit to. Who liked to face their weaknesses? It was very late and she was too tired to start analysing her relationship with Chris. Anyway she'd given him enough time and energy.

It wasn't Chris's love you were scrutinising, it was your own and now you're running away from it. Coward! Her inner voice would not be banished so summarily.

But how could you love someone and not expect something back from them? Was it possible? she argued with herself as she soaped herself with Lux soap. Mick loved Sheila warts and all. If she'd really loved Chris, she'd have been able to come to terms with his selfishness and his cheating, lying ways. Was that what unconditional love meant?

Doug cared very much for her, she knew that. And for a long time she hadn't been able to give anything back other than friendship. And he'd accepted that and put no pressure on her. Was that unconditional love?

But she'd put no pressure on Chris. She'd always been reluctant to make demands, probably because she'd been terrified that he'd leave. If that wasn't being needy, what was? Ellen thought wryly as she took a sip of coffee. She'd hoped that he'd marry her when she got pregnant but she hadn't demanded it. She'd let him make up his own mind. When they'd got back together again she'd never asked him to leave his wife for her. That was something she'd vowed she'd never do. That was a decision Chris would have to make on his own. And one Ellen knew he'd never make, no matter what promises he made. In some ways he was utterly gutless. With Chris it was always the easy option. He didn't want to accept any responsibility for his actions.

Once, he'd told her she was too soft for him. She'd known he was comparing her and Suzy. He'd made it sound as though her softness was a flaw in her character. Suzy, from what he told her, was bossy enough. She wouldn't let him away with things. When he'd accused her of being too soft, Ellen had been so tempted to tell him that it wasn't a question of being soft, it was a question of treating him like an adult and letting him make his own choices and decisions. How typical of him to turn it back on her and make it seem as if she was at fault.

Doug had great backbone, Chris had none. It was his great loss really, Ellen thought sadly. The good sides of him, the sense of fun, the enthusiasm for his work, his ambition, his charm and boyishness drew people to him like magnets. But behind it all there was nothing of substance.

Maybe she'd had to realise that before she could truly value Doug. Chris hadn't it in him to be faithful. Suzy hadn't got such a great deal after all, Ellen reflected. Wisdom did come with age. Seven years ago she'd envied Suzy Wallace with all her heart.

Ellen stepped out of the bath and wrapped a bath towel around her. Even the central heating couldn't disguise how bitterly cold it had turned. Doug would be freezing. If Chris had phoned her to say he wasn't coming to see her, Ellen would have immediately suspected a lie. Doug she trusted implicitly.

Suzy was Chris's wife, with the big house, big car, affluent lifestyle, plenty of money, but, there and then, Ellen knew she wouldn't swap all that for one second of the peace of mind she had with Doug.

She got into her snug, passion-killer, flannelette nightdress, remembering how, when she'd been sleeping with Chris, she'd shivered in flimsy baby-dolls. Ellen smiled as she snuggled down under the sheets. Right this minute she was content, serene . . . and warm. She was asleep before she knew it.

Doug shivered as he hammered a nail into a wooden support. Of all the nights for this to happen. You'd think it was for spite, he thought irritably. Just when his relationship with Ellen was finally going in the direction he'd longed for. At last she was beginning to return his feelings. He'd waited long and patiently for this. It had been hard sometimes. Often he'd wanted to shake her and say, "Forget that bastard, he's not worth a second of your time." Especially when she'd taken him back in the summer. That had been a low point. He'd wanted to break Chris Wallace's pretty-boy jaw so badly. He'd wanted to tell him to butt out of Ellen's and Stephanie's lives and stop toying with them. But he knew that would have got him nowhere. Ellen could be very stubborn. She was prickly about other people criticising her precious ex. Besides, she had to come to the realisation that Chris Wallace wasn't good for her, herself, if it was to mean anything. And if *their* relationship was to mean anything and not be a one-sided affair, she had to come to him of her own accord.

Today had been that first real step. Doug smiled at the memory of her kisses. They had been very precious. He'd been dying to see her tonight. He wanted to make sure that he hadn't been reading too much into the kisses. He'd wanted to have time alone with her when she was relaxed and at ease. He had no intentions of putting her under any pressure in any way though. He'd never do that to Ellen. She could dictate the pace. He was happy just to be with her.

But tonight he wouldn't be and he missed her. He sighed regretfully as he hammered away. Nor would he get to see her tomorrow. Talk about Murphy's Law! Still she'd sounded really disappointed when he'd spoken to her on the phone earlier so that could only be good news.

Doug was ever the optimist. The thought cheered him because it looked like being a long night. He yawned as he secured the first support beam against the gable wall and cursed the builders who'd mucked up his night.

"You've what!" Suzy couldn't believe her ears.

"We've moved to an apartment near Herbert Park in case you phone the old flat and get a stranger on the line. I'm just letting you know in case you need to contact me in an emergency," Chris said coldly. "Get a pen and I'll give you the number."

"Fine," Suzy said through gritted teeth. She laid the receiver on the hallstand and took a deep breath. She was *deeply* shocked. She could hardly breathe she was so angry. That fucker had just moved into a new apartment with Alexandra. Obviously the relationship was far stronger than she'd realised. She was wounded to the core. It was horrible. She felt as though she'd just been kicked in the stomach. Hard. Chris and Alexandra were serious about each other. They were a unit. She and the children were just irritations. Nuisances. Suzy was so distressed by this thunderbolt she started to shake. But not for one instant would she let Chris know how upsetting the news was to her. Oh no! She wouldn't give the bastard that satisfaction. She took a deep breath to steady herself.

"Give me the address and number." Her tone dripped icicles.

Chris was equally cold as he gave her the details. Her pen shook as she took them down, her writing spidery and uneven. It was hard to concentrate on what he was saying. It was very unsettling to think that her husband was phoning her from the home that he shared with his lover. Her ex-best friend. It was vulgar. Agonising. It took every ounce of self-control that she possessed to keep her voice from quivering. Only pride got her through it.

"Thank you. And I'd prefer if you didn't phone quite so late at night in future," Suzy snapped and hung up. Her heart was thumping. She'd never expected this. All right, so maybe she'd told him he wasn't to come back home, but she'd expected him to get a place of his own, not move into a new apartment with that fucking husband-stealing cow.

"I hate you, you lying poxy bastard," she raged as she walked back into the lounge and poured herself a stiff vodka. She was so angry she wanted to knife Chris and Alexandra. Her hands shook as she raised the glass to her lips. How could Chris do this to her? Cancel her and their past out as if it counted for nothing? Didn't he have one ounce of remorse for what he'd done to her and the kids? How could he treat people so callously? Was this the way he'd treated that woman in Glenree? And countless women before and since? Had he no humanity in him at all?

Suzy shook her head unable to fathom the man she'd been married to for all these years.

And Alexandra! Didn't she feel any guilt? Couldn't she see that Chris had responsibilities to his children, whatever about Suzy? Didn't that trouble her? Didn't she miss their friendship at all? Had it meant nothing? Had Alexandra just used her all these years? Was it true that like attracted like? Well, if it was, they were well suited. But they wouldn't get the better of her. She wouldn't let those shits grind her down.

Suzy took a gulp of her drink. It burned the back of her throat but she welcomed the fiery shock. She needed it. No wonder there'd been no response to her postcard. Alexandra was obviously too busy moving into her new pad. It was still waiting for her at work. Suzy had been on tenterhooks all week waiting for Alexandra's phone call. When it hadn't come, she'd phoned Stuart and Stuart's with the intention of hanging up when Alexandra came on the line, but she'd been told that Alexandra was out of the office for a few days. Now she knew why.

Had the card arrived? There was no reason that it shouldn't have. Surely it would have been seen by several people. The gossip and speculation would be rife. Even better, Suzy thought savagely. The more people who knew exactly what a devious bitch Alexandra was, the better. Now that word was filtering out and people were commiserating with her she found she was exaggerating Chris and Alexandra's affair wildly. She didn't care. For all she knew it had been going on through their entire marriage. She wouldn't put it past either of them. She wasn't going to protect them in any way. She was going to say the very worst about them. She wanted their friends and acquaintances to *think* the very worst of them.

Suzy had been invited to a make-up party by Madeleine Conway, the wife of Victor Conway, a very successful businessman they knew through their set. Stuart and Stuart's acted for him. He was Alexandra's client. Victor, a white-haired ageing Lothario, was well known for his roving eye and Madeleine was famous for the tight rein she kept on him and the purse-strings. Madeleine's money had financed the business at the beginning. She came from a rich background. She held a large amount of the company shares.

A timely warning to Madeleine about Alexandra's husband-stealing antics was next on Suzy's agenda. Madeleine would get so paranoid she'd freak. Heaven knew what consternation she'd cause.

Suzy poured herself another drink. What you sow, you reap was the old saying. And come hell or high water, Alexandra Johnston was going to reap the harvest of her duplicity.

Chapter Fifteen

Alexandra drove into the office car park, delighted to be back at work. She was on top of the world. She *loved* her new apartment. Yesterday she'd discovered that one of her neighbours was Martyn Whelen, an absolutely dishy hunk who was a well-known media personality. He was never out of the society pages. The most eligible bachelor in the country was living in the penthouse in her apartment block. Unfortunately he was just a *little* too young for her. She'd be accused of cradle-snatching if she made a play for him. Nevertheless the social cachet of having him as a near neighbour was an unexpected coup.

Last night, Chris had been extremely cranky after he'd phoned Suzy to tell her about their move. He'd gone all sulky and morose. But she'd soon sorted him out. She'd gone to the bedroom, taken all her clothes off, put on her thigh-high patent leather boots, draped a long, see-through black chiffon scarf around her and vamped it into the lounge. That had cured his cough for him.

Alexandra smiled at the memory. She loved making a man want her and then, when he was putty in her hands, taking control of him. What a challenge Marcus Lynn would be. She must schedule a meeting with him soon, she decided as she hurried up the steps to the office. Great sheets of sleety snow whipped around the building. She shivered. It would be a good day to get her head down and catch up on the backlog. Two weeks was a long time to be out of the office. Alexandra breezed through the revolving doors, full of energy.

Peggy, the receptionist, wearing the most ghastly long orange sleeveless cardigan over a blue maxi-skirt and a black skinny-rib, was gossiping with several typists. It irritated Alexandra. What sort of impression would that make on clients? It was unprofessional. They all turned to stare at her. Peggy gave a nervous titter. Alexandra eyed them coldly.

"Isn't it time everyone was at their desks?" she said crisply. Lax office efficiency simply would not do. Reluctantly the typists moved towards the typing pool. They kept turning around to look at her. It was most unusual. Maybe they were impressed with her new Burberry coat. It was fashionably smart and businesslike. Perfect for this weather.

"Peggy, kindly hold all my calls for half an hour. I want to deal with my post. Is there much?" Alexandra pulled off her black kid gloves and untied her Hermès scarf.

Peggy blushed puce. "Oh, there's plenty of post, Miss Johnston. It's *all* on your desk."

Alexandra looked at her curiously. What on earth was wrong with the girl? She was extremely jittery. "Thank you, Peggy. And remember. No calls for the next half-hour." Alexandra strode over to the lift. Something would have to be done about the front-desk personnel, she reflected crossly. She couldn't be sure, but she thought she heard giggling. What was wrong with them all this morning? They were decidedly giddy. The lift was in use and she waited impatiently for it to descend. Moments later, the doors whooshed apart and Ron Evans, the accountant, stepped out.

"Well good morning, Alexandra." He smirked at her. "And how are *you*?"

Not the better for seeing you, you baldy little weed, she was tempted to retort. Ron Evans was not her favourite person. In fact he gave her the creeps. He was a tight-fisted, penny-pinching, small-minded, skinny little fart of a man who had a puffed-up sense of his own importance. She wouldn't trust him as far as she could throw him. It was well known in the office that Ron, who was thoroughly devious, was a master of sharp practice in his business dealings. He was universally disliked by the staff.

Each month when Alexandra handed in her expenses she could be sure of a visit from him, questioning each and every item. It drove her mad. What did he expect her to do? Bring her clients to Woolworth's for sausage and beans? She was successful with her clients because she made them feel important. Nothing but the best for them. In the long run, it paid. Clients who were happy, and made to feel they were valued, stayed put and often brought in new clients. But Ron with his suspicious accountant's mentality couldn't see beyond his nose and his precious profit-and-loss columns. The man had no long-term vision.

He was the bane of Alexandra's life and she wondered why he was being so overly friendly this morning. He knew she was well able for him. He was wary of her sharp tongue, especially after a particularly vicious exchange when she'd told him he was a Mickey Mouse accountant with the business sense of a gnat. He'd never forgiven her for that. Usually he stuck his sharp pointy beak in the air and pretended not to see her. Today, though, his beady little eyes were practically leering at her from behind his spectacles.

How are you indeed? What was it to him, the slimy little worm?

"I'm fine, Ron." Alexandra swept past him into the lift and pressed the control panel. That horrible little toad in his ill-fitting pin-striped suit and lemon nylon shirt was enough to put anyone off their work first thing on a Monday morning.

The lift glided silently upwards. Alexandra liked this building. It was modern and with-it. Their old offices had had antiques for lifts. You'd be quicker walking upstairs. It was thanks to her that they'd relocated to a more modern building. The old offices off Wicklow Street were ancient and drab and totally unsuitable for the image they needed to portray. Malachy MacDonald, the MD, and, of course, tight-wad Evans hadn't wanted to move. It had taken months to persuade them.

That was the trouble with cheapskates, Alexandra sighed. They hindered expansion.

Her office was beside the lift. None of the partners was in yet.

The car park had been almost empty. She was just as glad. She wanted to get stuck in straight away. She'd see them for coffee at eleven.

Peggy hadn't lied about the post, she thought idly when she saw the pile on her desk. It was enormous. She went over to the window and pulled the cord of the Venetian blinds. The leaden sleety sky offered little natural light so she switched on the strip light. She took her coat off, hung it up and went over to the oval mirror on the wall. She looked fine, she thought with satisfaction. All her bruises were gone. Her green eyes, outlined with Mary Quant black kohl pencil, were bright and alluring. Her chignon hadn't a black hair out of place. Her *Coral Dawn* lipstick was lusciously inviting on her full mouth. No wonder she drove men mad with lust, she thought in amusement. She could almost fancy herself.

"Right, to work, Johnston," she said aloud as she sat into her black leather chair eager to begin opening her mail. Who knew what new clients wanted her to work her magic for them.

Oh! she thought in surprise as she picked up a pop-art postcard that was lying on top of all the brown and white assorted envelopes. She didn't know of anyone who was on holidays at this time of the year, she mused as she turned it over and began to read.

"Oh my God!" she muttered, horrified, as her eyes scanned the bold clear writing. She thought she was going to have a heart attack as she read:

Dear Slut Johnston,
It's bad enough when men abuse women. But when women abuse women . . . they are the lowest of the low. And when a so-called friend steals a woman's husband like you've stolen mine, she is beneath contempt. You've seduced my husband and deprived my children of a father, but you're welcome to him. Because he's no better than you. You contaminate decent people with your deceit. So keep Chris tied to your bedstead, the way he was the last time I saw him. I wouldn't have him back if he was the last man on earth. He's all yours, seeing as you couldn't even manage to get a man of your own.

You pretended to be my friend all these years, and then you lured my husband away from me. Some friend! I wish you the joy of him. He's a lying, cheating, moody, selfish shit who doesn't give a damn about anyone. He's found his perfect match.
Suzy Wallace.

She's crazy. She's a crazy fucking stupid malicious bitch. Alexandra's hands flew to her flaming cheeks. No wonder they'd all been looking at her so strangely, giggling and tittering at her behind her back. No wonder that beady-eyed little bollix had been leering at her. He was probably having a wonderful time fantasising about being tied to her bedstead.

Alexandra felt ill. She picked up the card between her finger and thumb and scrutinised the postmark with a sinking heart. It had been here for days. Probably floating around the office from person to person while they all made distasteful jokes at her expense.

She'd worked so damned hard to get where she was. To earn a reputation as the best in a man's world. And to have it ruined by *this*! She tore the card into tiny bits in swift savage movements.

The revenge of a woman scorned. God! It froze her soul to think of the damage to her reputation. And all because she'd allowed her hormones to lead her astray in a moment of crazy madness. Chris Wallace wasn't worth her reputation.

Alexandra lit a cigarette. She really *had* underestimated Suzy. She'd always been fairly malleable in the past but the worm had certainly turned. What was wrong with the silly bitch anyway? Everything Suzy'd written about Chris in that card was true. Why the hell was she so upset about their fling? He'd been cheating on her with someone before Alexandra. Probably that woman in Glenree. Would Suzy have made such a fuss over *her*? These things went on all the time. People got over affairs without making the huge song and dance Suzy was making about it. Alexandra felt a tinge of unease. If her erstwhile friend could do this, what more was she capable of?

She was certainly on the horns of a dilemma now, she thought agitatedly as she paced the beige-carpeted floor. She couldn't turf Chris out because she couldn't afford the rent on her own. Otherwise she'd kick his ass out so quick he'd see stars. What a damned mess. And the worst thing was, she was the author of her own misfortune.

"Shit! Shit! Shit!" she cursed aloud. What the hell was she going to do?

The first thing she was going to do was give Suzy a piece of her mind. She dialled the number with venom.

"Hello?" Suzy sounded as if butter wouldn't melt in her mouth.

"How dare you, you silly little cow. Have you any idea – "

Click.

Alexandra stared impotently at the dead receiver. The bitch had hung up. She felt like flinging the phone out the window. She took some calming breaths. This situation *had* to be handled properly.

She wasn't going to go around the office with her head hanging. The only thing to do was to brazen it out. She wasn't going to have any silly little typist tittering at her. And Ron Evans could dream on – it was probably the nearest he'd ever get to any action anyway, she thought nastily as she ripped open the first letter in her mountain of post.

At eleven promptly, make-up immaculate, wafting *Chanel No 5* behind her, Alexandra swanned into the office canteen. The hum of Monday-morning gossip died away as every pair of eyes turned to look at her.

"Morning all," Alexandra drawled coolly. "I missed you all dreadfully . . . it's a joy to be back. Mrs Walsh, I'll have a cup of black coffee and a Marietta." She smiled at the canteen lady. Head high she strode between the tables to the one reserved for directors. Malachy MacDonald eyed her warily. He knew all about the card.

"Morning, Malachy, I need a light." She placed a filter tip between her coral lips and arched an eyebrow at him.

"Oh . . . oh yes of course." Malachy, taken aback by her aplomb, fumbled for his lighter and clicked it. Alexandra inclined her head to the flame and drew on her cigarette. Exhaling a long thin plume of smoke she turned to her MD and smiled silkily.

"Well, Mal, I've been gone for two weeks. I'm sure there's been lots happening. Do tell."

The rest of the staff watched in fascinated admiration as Alexandra sat, cool as a cucumber, talking to the MD as though she hadn't a care in the world.

Ron Evans sipped his sweet milky tea and dreamed of being tied to Alexandra Johnston's bedstead. Some men had all the luck!

The nerve of her to phone. Even though she'd been expecting it, Suzy's mouth had dried and her palms had turned sweaty when she'd heard Alexandra begin her tirade of abuse on the phone. Hanging up had given her a great sense of power.

So the card had arrived, she thought with immense satisfaction as she sat staring out at the back garden, battered by whistling winds and relentless driving sleet. Her garden looked the way she felt. Ravaged, neglected, stripped bare, withered away. Even the sweetness of revenge couldn't lift her depression. Christmas was coming. The time of cheer and goodwill to men. Well, she was all out of goodwill. She hoped Alexandra and Chris rotted in hell and that their lives were riven by misery. Forgive and forget was not her motto. An eye for an eye was the very least that pair of snakes deserved.

"Mummy, my Dinky is broken. I wish Daddy was here 'cos he'd fix it for me. When is Daddy coming back to live in our house? Why does he have to be away all the time? I want Daddy." Adam trotted into the kitchen holding up his favourite little red car.

Suzy's heart sank. Adam really missed his father. He wasn't eating and he was fretting at night. Christina had gone to the other extreme and was becoming impossibly naughty. Surely Chris must have known, when he embarked on his sordid little fling, that it would have repercussions on his children if he was found out. Even that hadn't stopped him, she thought bitterly. His kids weren't as important to him as his own selfish needs.

"We'll ask Santa Claus for a new car." Suzy deftly changed the subject.

"Will Daddy be home for Christmas?" Her son's blue eyes were raised trustingly to hers.

Oh Adam, please be quiet, she begged silently.

"Will he, Mum? Will he buy us a turkey?"

"We'll have a turkey, don't worry. We'll have the biggest fattest turkey in the world."

"But will Daddy be here to eat it with us? Will his work be all done on Christmas Day?"

"I don't know, pet. Maybe." Suzy knelt down and hugged her son tightly. Her eyes brimmed with tears. *Fuck you, Chris,* she swore silently. She might want him out of her life for good. But his children in all their innocence loved him and missed him. Even a shitty, selfish, uninterested daddy was better than none, it seemed.

Emma's nose wrinkled in distaste. She *hated* the smell of hospitals. Her high heels tapped noisily down the long drab corridor that led to Sheila's ward. Julie Ann trotted along expectantly beside her. All her cousins had been to visit Sheila. She'd been really worried that she wasn't going to be brought to see her nannie and she'd pestered her and Vincent. After the episode on Saturday at Ellen's, Emma was reluctant to bring Julie Ann anywhere. The mortification of it still stung. Emma cringed at the memory.

She saw the sign for Sheila's ward and drew to a halt. She hunkered down and glared at her daughter. "Now I'm warning you today, Julie Ann. If you make a holy show of me you'll be very sorry. There'll be no Christmas tree, no presents and no panto. Do you hear me?"

Julie Ann tossed her pigtails and scowled.

"Do you hear me, Julie Ann?"

"Yes, Mummy. Now come on. I want to give Nannie her card,"

her daughter said dismissively. Emma knew her warning had gone in one ear and out the other. The older she got, the naughtier she got. She practically ignored Emma. Sometimes she openly defied Vincent. Julie Ann's wilfulness was something she just couldn't handle, Emma reflected, as they continued their progress down the corridor. Imagine what she was going to be like at the teenage stage. It was a daunting prospect.

The nearer she got to the ward the lower her heart sank. Now she was going to have to eat humble pie with Old Bat Munroe, and apologise for the incident at the christening *and* invite her to stay with them. She'd promised all of this to Vincent. She couldn't get out of it.

She turned into Sheila's ward. Her mother-in-law's bed was down near the window. Sheila was sitting up, wearing a pink knitted bed-jacket over her brushed-cotton nightie. She was reading. She looked pale and tired, Emma thought, a little shocked. Sheila was usually so healthy and sturdy. Julie Ann raced towards her.

"Nannie, Nannie. I've made you a card. And I've brought you a big box of chocolates with a ribbon on it." She thrust the chocolates at her grandmother.

"Hello, dear." Sheila's face lit up. She glanced up at Emma expectantly.

"Er . . . I was sorry to hear about your accident, Mrs Munroe. I hope you're feeling better. Em . . . I'm sorry about what happened at the christening. I didn't mean what I said. I hope you'll let bygones be bygones." She was practically babbling.

"Certainly, Emma. I don't hold grudges. I know you were upset." Sheila was magnanimous now that the apology had been made. "I'm glad to see you're up and about. Vincent told me you had a tummy upset. Now do sit down, dear, and have a chocolate. I'm not really partial to dark ones myself so eat as many as you like." She held out an opened box of chocolates. Emma smarted. She'd brought a box of dark chocolates. Trust Sheila not to like them. And how rude of her to make it known.

"I *love* dark chocolate," she said tightly, taking one.

"Me too, can I have some?" Julie Ann asked eagerly, fingers poised.

"You can have two but that's all," Sheila instructed firmly. "You won't eat your tea otherwise."

"Yes I will. I *always* eat my tea," Julie Ann argued as she dived on the chocolates. "Don't I, Mummy? I could even eat the whole box and still eat my tea," she added defiantly.

Oh Lord! Emma's heart sank. If Julie Ann started her shenanigans it would be mortifying.

"Can I have two more, Mummy?" Julie Ann demanded through a mouthful of toffee.

"What did Nannie say?" Emma said weakly.

"But tell her I will eat my tea. Tell her I'm allowed."

"Now, now, don't be cheeky, like a good girl." Sheila asserted her authority resolutely.

Julie Ann glowered at her grandmother. "I'm not cheeky, Nannie. Don't say that!"

"Julie Ann," Emma hissed. "What did I say to you about Christmas trees and presents and the panto?"

"But Mummy," Julie Ann wailed, "it's just not fair. Andrew gets *everything* and I get nothing. I bet if he was here Nannie would give him loads of sweets."

"Don't be silly, Julie Ann," Sheila interjected. "Andrew has no teeth. He can't eat sweets."

"He has so teeth." Julie Ann sulked. "He's always screeching crying 'cos there's one growing."

"Ah, and how is the little dote?" Sheila turned to Emma.

"A bit cross, unfortunately. He has his first tooth coming. He's starting early." Emma tried to ignore her daughter, who was kicking the leg of the bed.

"Stop that, Julie Ann." Sheila grimaced as the bed jarred.

Julie Ann, mutinously, kept kicking.

Emma flushed. "Do what your nannie tells you, immediately. Or I'm going to take you home this minute." She had a brainwave. "And you're not coming to Ellen's cafe to play with your cousins."

Julie Ann stopped in mid-kick. "Now? This afternoon?"

"Not if you're naughty." Emma felt a wave of relief as she regained control of her wayward daughter.

"But I'm not naughty, Mummy. I'm a very good girl. I don't even want any more chocolates." Julie Ann was all sweetness and light. In spite of herself, Emma felt a flicker of amusement. There were times when Julie Ann reminded her of herself when she was a child. It was like looking in a mirror.

"And what do you make of the cafe, Emma?" Sheila asked. "I believe the opening day was a great success."

"It looked like it," Emma agreed. "They've done a lovely job on it."

"I suppose I won't see sight nor sign of Ellen and Miriam now that they're *entrepreneurs*." Sheila sniffed.

"They'll be busy all right," Emma murmured, aware that this was her opening to ask her mother-in-law to come to her house to convalesce.

"I hope they haven't bitten off more than they can chew."

"I hope not." Emma was polite. "But as the girls are so busy, Vincent and I were wondering if you'd care to spend a few days with us after you come out of hospital. Just until you get on your feet."

"Oh! Well now." Sheila was taken aback.

"You'd be most welcome," Emma said dutifully, thinking of how pleased Vincent would be with her.

"Well, that's very, very kind of you, Emma." Sheila's tone was much more cordial. "I'll have a chat with Mick. He should be in any minute."

"Oh, we'll go now, then," Emma said hastily.

"To visit our cousins," Julie Ann piped up.

"No rush. Sure Mick would be delighted to see you." Sheila settled back against the pillows.

"No . . . no . . . we don't want to tire you out. Besides I don't like to leave Andrew too long," she fibbed.

"Of course you don't. The little pet," Sheila agreed. "I'll let you know then. And thank you for your kind offer."

"You're welcome." Emma smiled weakly. Her heart was in her boots. She'd been hoping against hope that her mother-in-law would reject the offer out of hand. Instead she seemed quite taken with the idea. And, if that wasn't enough, she was going to have to go into that stupid deli so that Julie Ann could see her cousins. It wasn't her day. And the way things were going, much worse was to come.

"Come along, you." She scowled at her daughter but Julie Ann was oblivious to her bad humour, anticipating the treat in store.

"We'll see you, Mrs Munroe. Get well soon."

"I will indeed, and give your mother my regards." Sheila waved graciously.

"She's a judge's daughter, you know," Emma heard her mother-in-law say proudly to the woman in the next bed.

Too blooming good for you, Emma thought sourly as she followed her excited daughter out of the ward.

Sheila lay back against the pillows and waited for her tea to come. The clickity-clack of the tea trolleys being wheeled along the corridor sent a frisson of anticipation through the ward. Mick had brought her a tea brack. She was looking forward to a slice. All the visitors were gone and it was as if the ward had exhaled a deep breath and contracted back to normal. Visitors were tiring, if well intentioned. Mick was fine, he didn't need to be entertained, but she'd found Emma and Julie Ann's visit wearing.

She was pleased to see Emma though. That unpleasantness at Andrew's christening had distressed her. It was good that it was all over. And her daughter-in-law's invitation to stay with them was most surprising.

It was certainly more than Ellen and Miriam had offered, she thought crossly. Now that they had more important concerns on their minds.

Maybe she just might go and stay with Emma for a day or two. That would give them something to think about. Ellen had shown scant consideration for her. She who had given her daughter a roof over her head when many mothers would have put her out of the

house for coming home pregnant. Some people had short
memories. Madam Miriam was another one who forgot kindnesses
received. She *would* go to Emma's and show that pair up, Sheila
decided as she sat up for her tea.

"Your wife's a fucking malicious cow, and I want to know what
you're going to do about it, Chris!" Alexandra was livid, her voice
shrill and demanding down the phone. "I've a good mind to sue
her for defamation of character!"

"What can I do about it? It's too bloody late now," Chris
growled. He couldn't believe his ears when Alexandra had read the
card aloud to him. Suzy'd really flipped. She was dangerous.

"Go and tell her you'll cut her off without a penny if she doesn't
behave," Alexandra demanded.

"Leave it with me. I'll deal with it. I'll see you tonight."

"No you won't. I'm going to the theatre and I'll be late home,"
Alexandra snapped. "Bye."

Chris glared at the receiver. It was as bad as being bloody
married to her. It was all right for Alexandra to tell him to cut
Suzy off without a penny. She didn't know about his tax evasion.
She didn't know about the sword of Damocles that was waiting to
chop his head off. Suzy held all the cards whether he liked it or
not.

Hell, if she could send a card like that to Alexandra's work she
was capable of anything. He wasn't going to go stirring it up. He
sighed deeply. Now he had two viragos on his back. What he
wouldn't give for a night in Ellen's arms. He badly needed some
tender loving care. Alexandra couldn't be tender if she tried. Suzy
was too eaten up by bitterness to forgive and forget. Ellen was so
different to both of them.

What was she doing now? he wondered as he stared out the
window. She must think about him sometimes. She'd worshipped
him. He knew that. It had always made him feel very good to
know that there was someone there who he could be sure of, come

hell or high water. It had been the greatest shock of his life when Ellen had ended their relationship.

Maybe she was missing him too, he thought hopefully. She must still have feelings for him. They'd shared such precious times. Surely she couldn't blot out the memories just like that.

He'd really thought she was his for life when they'd resumed their relationship. Seven years apart had made their second time around much more passionate and intense. How could Ellen settle for that beardy jerk? They had nothing in common, Chris was sure of it. And after all, Chris was Stephanie's father. That had to mean something. Chris gazed dejectedly at his reflection in the small mirror on the window sill and felt very sorry for himself. He looked strained and harassed. He had bags under his eyes. He was going very grey at the temples, he noted with dismay. A man under pressure. Maybe if Ellen saw him she might feel pity for him and have a change of heart. He'd always been able to depend on her compassion. Christmas was the time of year for ending quarrels and bad feeling.

Speaking of Christmas, he'd have to discuss arrangements with Suzy. She'd need extra money for the kids' toys. And where was *he* going to spend Christmas? Alexandra was going off to stay with friends in London. He was like a homeless waif. He might as well be on the streets.

Chapter Sixteen

Ellen snuggled up on the sofa, in the crook of Doug's arm. A howling gale raged outside and the rain battered the window panes relentlessly. The fire blazed brightly. Flaming pine logs crackled, scattering showers of golden sparks up into the sooty dark chimney. The lamplit room was snug and warm. A haven after her hectic week.

"Imagine it's a week since we opened. It seems like yesterday." She smiled up at Doug.

"It seems like a year to me. This is the first time I've had you to myself." Doug stroked her cheek.

"Our timing's terrible." Ellen sighed. "You're up to your eyes at work, I'm up to my eyes in The Deli, I'm beginning to wonder what I've let myself in for."

"It'll even out. It's still a novelty. You're bound to be busy."

"But it's crazy, Doug. We can't keep up. We keep running out of food. Everyone wanted soup today. I suppose because it was so cold. I had to go shopping for potatoes and carrots twice. And then the bloody fire went out three times. And getting the napkins and towels dry in this weather is a nightmare. The kids fought all day today. I swear to God, I nearly swung for Connie with her impudence, she almost put Julie Ann to shame. That's most unlike her. Maybe she resents Miriam working. I don't know. And then of course . . . there's Mother!" Ellen threw her eyes up to heaven.

"She's queening it over in Emma's and doing her best to make me feel bad."

"Dear oh dear. We are feeling sorry for ourselves," Doug teased. "Think of the noughts adding up in your bank account – that will fix you."

Ellen laughed. "Yeah, that was good. Denise was so chuffed. I suppose I've always been used to having my own money. She has to practically crawl on her knees to get anything from Jimmy. It must be horrible to be married to someone you detest and to have to be dependent on them for money. I'd die! I'm really, really glad that she's got her own money now."

"So am I, she deserves it. And you deserve every penny you earn. You've worked damn hard for it." Doug bent down and kissed her soundly. Her arms tightened around his neck as she kissed him back, tasting, exploring, soft butterfly kisses that became more insistent.

Breathless, they drew apart. "I really missed you," Doug said huskily. "All I wanted to do was to be with you."

"I wanted to be with you too. I love being with you, Doug. I love the way we talk for hours. I'm always dying to see you to tell you things."

"Me too." Doug hugged her tightly. "We've been close friends for more than a year now. It's been one of the nicest times of my life, thanks to you."

"Oh Doug! That's a lovely thing to say. Thank you."

"I mean it. You're very important to me, Ellen. And so is Stephanie."

"I know that," she said quietly. "And you've never pushed or been impatient with me. You'll never know how much I appreciate that."

Doug grimaced. "I wanted to, Ellen, many times. I wanted you to feel for me what you felt for him. But I know you have to come to me yourself. Not out of a sense of obligation or because you feel you owe it to me, but because you want to. I really want you to come to me because you *want* to," he said emphatically.

"I know that, Doug. I want to come to you because I want to, too," Ellen said shyly.

"Do you still think about him?" he asked, tentatively.

"Not as much as I used to," Ellen answered truthfully. "Before, he'd be on my mind from the minute I woke up until the time I went to sleep. But now he just drifts in and out now and again. And I ask myself, did I mean anything at all to him or was it just lust? And then there are other times when I think that he *did* need me. And that he did love me in his own selfish way. At least I like to pretend that to myself. It helps me to feel it wasn't all a total failure."

"He was a fool to let you go, Ellen. And for that, alone, I feel sorry for him. But he made his choices and he has to live with them. And you have to move on. If you want me to travel by your side, you know I will." He stared into her eyes, his hazel eyes earnest and unwavering. If it was true that the eyes were the mirror of the soul, Doug had a good soul, Ellen thought humbly as she met his gaze and saw the truth of what he said and the love he had for her mirrored there.

"I think you deserve better than me, Doug," she whispered.

"Don't say that, Ellen," he said sternly.

"But how can you love a woman who's been as stupid and gullible and self-deceiving as I've been?" she blurted. "Don't you ever think that I deserved everything I got for being such a woefully bad judge of character, not once but twice. What's the old saying? Fool me once, shame on you. Fool me twice, shame on me! How can you have respect for me when there are times I hardly respect myself for being so easily taken in? And for still believing that somewhere there has to be a spark of decency in Chris? Even now I can't accept that he's totally without good. That's because I can't love what he is. I can only love what I want him to be. So that's not much of a love, is it? Maybe I just can't love anyone warts and all."

"For God's sake, Ellen, don't be so harsh on yourself." Doug was shocked by her words.

"I'm sorry, Doug, I need to say these things to you. They're things I think to myself. After what I went through with Chris, I find it hard to believe that anyone really does love me. And I find myself questioning my love for him, and I wonder have I wasted all those years on an illusion." She started to cry as the relief of saying what she'd been bottling up for so long became too much for her.

"Aw, Ellen, shush." Doug rocked her gently. "Of course you loved him, there's no question of that. Much more than he deserved," he added grimly. "But he abused your love and you were deceived by a master. There's no shame in that for you. And I know what I'm talking about, Ellen, I went through it too with Geena, don't forget. Women do it to men too, you know. I asked myself those questions too. You don't have the monopoly on being gullible and self-deceiving."

"Yeah, I know." Ellen wiped her eyes. "Geena was an idiot, if you don't mind my saying so. Actually I think she was crazy."

Doug smiled. "Thank you. Right now I'm glad we didn't marry, believe me." He cupped her chin in his hand. "Isn't it strange how we both went through the same sort of thing? But they say there's a reason for everything. And maybe our reasons were that we'd really appreciate each other when it was time for us to be together. I believe in fate, love. I believe we were meant to go through what we went through before we came together. You're a very, very special woman, Ellen, and it's an honour to love you."

"Oh Doug. I don't know what to say." Ellen was overwhelmed.

"You don't have to say anything. I just want you to know that. And I'm really glad that you shared all those things with me. The more we talk and share the better it will be." He held her tight and she felt a bond of closeness to him that was almost tangible.

As she lay in bed that night, she mulled over what Doug had said. Never in a million years would Chris have been able to talk to her like that. He hadn't the depth. Much as he liked to think of himself as a deep and complex man, the truth was that Chris was truly shallow. If she'd never known him, she'd never have been able to appreciate what she'd found with Doug. Maybe there was something to this fate thing, after all, she thought drowsily. Wasn't it said that to know joy you had to know sadness? She'd certainly known plenty of sadness. Her heart lifted on butterfly wings. Maybe her time for joy had come at last.

Miriam yawned and nearly gave herself lockjaw. She was whacked and there was still a pile of ironing to do. Ben was working a late shift. She'd only seen him for about twenty minutes today.

Her gaze moved to the old toby jug on the mantelpiece. A wad of pound notes and ten-shilling notes, all wrapped in an elastic band, nestled in the black-capped top. Miriam felt a surge of pride. Her first pay-day, yesterday. It was worth the weariness. She knew exactly what she was going to do with it. To hell with the new Electrolux and the rest. She was going to buy Ben a lovely leather jacket for Christmas. He'd never owned one and she'd remembered him admiring a black one that Vincent wore. Ben would look dead sexy in a leather jacket, Miriam thought happily as she unplugged the iron.

Enough was enough. She'd catch up on the ironing on Monday. She had to steep the peas for Sunday dinner and get out clean clothes for the children. Daniel had polished the shoes and they lay neatly shining in a row on the fender, reflecting the dull red glow of the dying embers. One thing Miriam was very particular about was making sure the children were turned out spotlessly for Sunday Mass. Polishing the shoes on a Saturday night was a ritual that had been followed in her mother's house and in her grandmother's house before that.

Miriam liked Saturday night. She liked preparing for the Sabbath. The routine never varied. Once *The Late Late* was over, the peas were steeped, the potatoes parboiled, and two different-coloured jellies cooled slowly in white bowls. The table was set for breakfast, and a freshly baked brown loaf and white soda scone were placed on the wire tray to cool. The aroma of fresh bread and sweet jelly and the tang from the steeping peas was special to Saturday night. Miriam liked it.

Then it was time for her bath and then the glorious moment when she would sink into her downy bed. How she longed for sleep, Miriam thought yearningly as she poured the boiling water onto the greengage jelly, the children's favourite. Since she'd started working in The Deli, sleep had become a precious jewel. She wouldn't linger in her bath tonight. Bed called to her too enticingly. And poor Ben! No nuptials tonight either, she thought ruefully. She knew she'd be asleep before her head hit the pillow. It had been the same every night of this mad, exciting, exhausting week.

They wouldn't have to get up too early in the morning. She'd make it up to him then, she promised herself as she stirred the jelly impatiently, waiting for it to melt.

Thirty-five minutes later, after a dip in the bath, Miriam slid into her big comfortable double bed and pulled the patchwork quilt up around her ears, before tucking her hot-water bottle against her tummy. She was in that delicious state between drowsiness and sleep when the door opened. Rebecca came and stood by the bed.

"Mammy," she said plaintively. "I've got an earache. Will you put some drops in it?"

Struggling to open her eyes, Miriam sat up heavily.

"I'm sorry, Mammy. It just hurts."

"It's all right, pet. Get into my bed here until I go and get some hot water." She pulled the blankets up over her daughter. Wearily she rooted under the bed for her slippers and shivered as the cold air nipped at her warm skin. She pulled on her quilted dressing-gown and padded down to the kitchen.

She was so tired she ached to her bones. But poor Rebecca needed her attention and some mothering. She couldn't stint on that, no matter how tired she was. She'd made that promise to herself when she started working and she wasn't going to break it. Mrs Munroe would never be able to throw that at her, Miriam thought resentfully, as she remembered her mother-in-law's most recent dig at her, when she'd called in to visit her in Emma's.

Sheila was a bitter old pill to be sure. But for all her talk, she wasn't exactly the world's greatest mother herself. Mrs Munroe and Ellen didn't have a close relationship despite *her* staying at home and giving all her time to her family.

"So put that in your pipe and smoke it, Sheila Munroe," she

muttered as she got ear-drops and warm water and went to attend her daughter.

⁓⚬⁓

Denise McMahon looked at the housekeeping money her husband Jimmy had just handed her. It was five pounds short.

"Why am I short?" she asked, perplexed.

"I told you when you started earning your own money you could pay your own way," he growled.

Denise stared at him, and hated him.

"You're a callous bastard, Jimmy McMahon. A mean-spirited, malicious slug. Why don't you just get the hell out of here and go and live with your mistress? I'm sick of you. And so are the kids."

Jimmy stabbed a finger in her face. "Listen, you! This is *my* house. If you and the kids want to move out, *you* go. Otherwise shut the fuck up."

Denise stared at him in impotent fury. She wanted to smash his glasses into his face and pull handfuls of his lank hair from his head. She wanted to scrab her nails down his face so viciously that blood would flow. Her anger was so strong she could feel it in a tight hard knot in her breastbone, like a malignant growth that was taking her over. He was the winner every time. He held all the cards. She was a slave in bondage to her husband. He owned the house. He controlled the purse-strings. He held the power. She had none.

She'd been so delighted with her first week's wages. It seemed at last that there was light at the end of the tunnel. Now he'd even taken that away from her. She'd have to make up the deficit. Five precious pounds she wouldn't be able to save. Now the tunnel seemed never-ending and she didn't have the energy to even try and keep her spirits up. She burst into tears and cried bitterly as Jimmy, unmoved by her distress, picked up his paper and turned to the sports page.

"I need a shirt ironed for Mass tomorrow." He eyed her coldly.

215

Denise knew he was enjoying every moment of her torment. He was in control and that was just the way he liked it.

What a hypocrite he was. Parading up to the front of the church every Sunday. A pillar of the community. If only they knew. She turned away and picked up her daughter's cardigan to sew back a button that was loose, but her fingers trembled so much, and her eyes were so blurred with tears, she couldn't thread the needle. She was in a nightmare. Trapped in a marriage that was full of cruelty and there was no way out.

Sheila lay in bed in her daughter-in-law's guest room and yawned prodigiously. She had spent three days recuperating in Emma and Vincent's and she'd quite enjoyed it.

She was the centre of attention. All the family had called to visit. She'd gone out of her way to praise Emma to high heaven in front of Ellen and Miriam. Just to let them know that it wouldn't have killed them to be a bit more attentive. The neighbours and members of the guild had dropped in to see her and she'd had a most enjoyable time, sitting up in her sumptuous peach and cream bedroom, listening to her visitors oohing and aahing about the luxury of Emma and Vincent's house. It was all very satisfactory and she was sleeping like a log at night, undisturbed by snores and cucks, and rackety windows.

Mick had told her to stay as long as she liked, so she might stay until the following week, certainly until Tuesday or Wednesday, she decided, giving a little stretch in the comfortable bed. It was nice being waited on hand and foot. And she had a perfect excuse for not having to make cakes and puddings for the guild for Christmas. It was unfortunate that it had happened the year she was president. But there was nothing she could do about it now, so she'd just have to lie back and enjoy it. She'd make a pudding and cake for Mick, of course. No one else's would do for him. He'd been eating her cakes and puddings for more than forty years and she wouldn't fail him this time. Nonetheless, it was a rare treat to be pampered and looked after. After all, she'd been through a dreadful ordeal. She was lucky to be alive. Her eyelids drooped. She was tired after all the visitors. She hadn't said her third Rosary yet, but maybe, seeing as she was still recuperating, the Almighty and His Holy Mother would overlook it this once if she went to sleep instead.

Emma gritted her teeth as she listened to her mother-in-law's earth-shattering snores from the bedroom next door. She'd never heard anything like it. Vincent lay asleep beside her, his arm around her. He'd sleep through an earthquake, she thought resentfully.

Her nerves were in shreds. Mrs Munroe had taken over her house and its routine. It was worse than Paddington Station. Everyone from Glenree seemed to have come visiting and the absolutely infuriating thing was that Mrs Munroe *expected* as a matter of course that they would all be offered tea and biscuits. It was exhausting. Poor Mrs Murdock was run off her feet. And Emma had the stress of seeing all these yokels from the village trooping through her house . . . and the nightmare of it all was . . . it looked as though her mother-in-law was planning to stay indefinitely. Emma knew she'd never survive another week of this carry on. It was enough to induce a blood pressure attack!

Andrew started squalling. That was the last straw.

"Vincent!" She tapped his shoulder. He snored on serenely. She elbowed him in the ribs.

"Wha!" He shot up, bleary-eyed and dishevelled.

"Andrew's crying. Will you go and see to him? I've got a blinding headache. I just hope it isn't my blood pressure again," she moaned.

Vincent staggered out of bed.

"I might go to the doctor on Monday for a check-up. These headaches are always a bad sign." If he thought she was stressed and that her blood pressure was up, maybe he'd ask his mother to go home. It would be a perfect excuse and she would still be seen to have done her duty.

"I'm sure there's nothing to worry about, pet," Vincent said reassuringly as he tied the belt of his dressing-gown. "After all, you're on blood pressure tablets now. It's probably just an ordinary old headache. I'll bring you two aspirin when I've settled Andrew." He padded quietly from the room leaving his wife fuming.

It was *not* an "ordinary old headache" by any manner of means. He could rid himself of that notion. He was out of the house all day. He didn't have to put up with Her Ladyship Munroe milking it for all it was worth. Well, tomorrow, like it or lump it, she was going to visit her parents, alone, and he could cope with Julie Ann, Andrew, and his precious mother and her never-ending visitors. See what kind of a headache he'd have after a day of it, she thought maliciously as she buried her head under the pillows in an effort to drown out the ear-splitting rumbles emanating from next door.

"Madeleine, it was a lovely make-up party. Thank you so much for inviting me. It was just what I needed to get me out of the house. I was getting terribly depressed." Suzy gave the older woman a brave smile.

"You poor lamb. I can't tell you how horrified and upset I was to hear about . . . er . . . to hear of your troubles," Madeleine said tactfully.

"It's been agonising." Suzy's lower lip quivered.

"Oh, sweetheart, don't cry," Madeleine urged in dismay. "Come and sit down for a minute. Now that all the others have gone you can tell me anything you want. You know I won't breathe a word to anyone." Madeleine was *dying* to hear all the gory details of the affair between Chris and Alexandra Johnston.

That Chris Wallace was having an affair was not in itself surprising. He'd always had a reputation as a womaniser before he married and a leopard never, but never, changed his spots. The absolutely shocking element was that he was having the affair with

Alexandra Johnston, Suzy's best friend. *That* was truly contemptible. And even more amazing considering all the derogatory things he used to say about Alexandra.

"I could have coped with a woman I didn't know, Madeleine," Suzy wept. "But to have an affair with Alexandra. I still can't believe it. She was my bridesmaid, you know. It's such a betrayal." Suzy was sobbing with gusto now.

"I know, darling, I know," Madeleine soothed as she poured a stiff brandy for them both. Nothing like a brandy to loosen the tongue.

"How did you find out about it, sweetheart?"

Suzy hiccuped. "It was horrible, horrible."

"Here, drink up, pet," Madeleine encouraged, oozing sympathy. "Did someone tell you?"

"No." Suzy shook her head and took another gulp of brandy. "I caught them."

"Darling! How devastating for you. Where did you catch them?"

"In Alexandra's apartment. She had Chris tied to her bedstead. They were making love."

"I don't *believe* it!" Madeleine exclaimed in thrilled horror. Wow! This *was* juicy. "And what happened?"

Between hiccups and sobs, Suzy told Madeleine the sorry saga.

"My poor little lamb." Madeleine patted Suzy's arm in sympathy. She was dying to ring up Ciara Doolan, her best friend and comrade-in-gossip. This was above rubies. Now that Suzy had spilled the beans, she couldn't wait to get her out of the house.

"You know, Madeleine, I never really realised until now that Alexandra is man-mad. And it doesn't matter whether they're married or not. I mean, look at the amount of relationships she's had. Once she conquers, she moves on. Chris might think he's got her for life, but from her track record I can tell you she'll dump him and move on to someone else eventually. She's like a praying mantis."

"Hmm, it's dreadful behaviour all right. And she's not getting any younger either. Look, pet, you're distraught, shall I call a taxi? You can leave your car here."

"No, no, I'll go home in my own car. I'll be fine. Thanks for a delightful evening. And thank you for being so sympathetic. It did me a world of good. You're so lucky with Victor, he's such a pet. I know he'd never cheat on you. Mind," Suzy gave a mirthless laugh, "you'd want to make sure *Miss-Man-Eater-Extraordinaire* doesn't get her claws into him. She does his advertising campaigns, doesn't she? Just watch her, Madeleine. I wouldn't trust her as far as I could throw her."

Madeleine's jaw sagged.

That took the wind out of your sails, Maddy dearest, Suzy thought spitefully. She knew full well that Madeleine would be on the phone to her crony, Ciara Doolan, as soon as Suzy was out the door.

Suzy didn't give a hoot. *That* was exactly what she wanted. She wanted everyone to know about Chris and his tart. And she wanted to put the wind up Madeleine. Victor Conway was notoriously susceptible to a pretty face. Not that he had it in him to do anything about it, Suzy thought scornfully as she looked at a framed photo of Victor on the sideboard with his white hair combed carefully over his bald patch and his silly little dicky bow, screaming against his loud check jacket. A ladies' man in his own mind, but that was all. Men were such vain idiots when they got to his age.

If Alexandra flashed a bit of leg at Victor, he'd probably have a coronary. It was no harm planting the seed in Madeleine's mind though. See how long Alexandra would be working for him then.

Flushed with triumph, and brandy, Suzy drove the short distance home.

Tonight had seen another nail in the coffin of Miss Alexandra Johnston's career. By the time Suzy was finished with her, her name would be mud.

Chapter Seventeen

"**B**ut Madeleine, she's a damn good PR woman," Victor Conway blustered as he buttered his toast and spread a generous helping of marmalade on top. His wife had just informed him that he was to get rid of Alexandra Johnston as his PR woman and give his business to one of the male partners in Stuart and Stuart's. None of them could touch Alexandra for talent and brains and get-up-and-go. He liked Alexandra. She was a bright, sexy woman with a lot of spark and she knew her stuff. She'd a great ass too, he thought longingly, staring across the table at his spouse, who did not look a million dollars first thing in the morning. In fact Madeleine had never looked a million dollars. She'd been a handsome woman in her prime, yes. But that wasn't today or yesterday. Sexy . . . never. Victor thought of Alexandra sitting opposite him in a black lacy negligee and almost choked on his toast. Chris Wallace was a damn lucky blighter.

"Don't be ridiculous, Victor. There are plenty of good advertising people around. But our continued association with her is tantamount to endorsing . . . even condoning, her despicable behaviour. I will not allow that."

"Madeleine, these things happen all the time. It's none of our business. She does a good job and that's all I care about. Now are we meeting the Kavanaghs for dinner on Wednesday?"

"Don't change the subject, Victor. If you don't switch to

221

someone else, I'm going to phone Mona MacDonald and insist that she tell Malachy to get rid of her. In fact I think I just might do that anyway. That old fool only employs her so he can ogle her legs."

Victor threw his eyes up to heaven. Madeleine was off and there was no stopping her. She had a bee in her bonnet about Alexandra Johnston. But then again his wife knew Chris Wallace's wife. And it was obvious she was taking sides.

Trust women! In his view no man cheated on his wife without good reason. It was a long time since *he'd* had the opportunity of cheating, he thought regretfully as he speared a sausage and doused it liberally with tomato ketchup.

He could argue as much as he liked – he knew from experience that the moment Madeleine had fixed her gimlet eye on the divine Alexandra, her fate was sealed.

"Miss Johnston, Mr MacDonald would like to see you in his office. He'll be free at eleven." Peggy Kinsella gave Alexandra a saccharine smile. Even first thing on Monday mornings, Peggy always managed her "professional" smile.

"Fine, Peggy." Alexandra hid her irritation. After all, Malachy was the big cheese, she couldn't very well let a junior member of staff think she was anything but in awe of him.

Damn! Alexandra thought as she swept into the lift. Usually when Malachy wanted to see her, he had some grandiose scheme that was invariably way off beam and she'd have to spend valuable time humouring him, massaging his ego and deflecting his nonsense when she could be doing her own, far more important work.

Really it was time the old buzzard retired. He'd been around since Noah. Advertising was a hell of a lot different from when he'd started out. Getting him to move with the times was like banging her head off a stone wall.

Why he was kept on as chairman and MD at his age amazed

Alexandra. Something about shares, she'd heard on the grapevine.

Malachy's avuncular geniality belied a sharp brain. And when it came to his own survival he was ruthless. The rumour was that years ago he'd persuaded a trusting, gullible spinster aunt of the Stuarts to sell him her shares at a less than fair price. Combined with his own, the shares had given him control of the company. There was consternation when it happened. The Stuarts had threatened legal action. But Malachy was a devious operator and had made sure that his back was covered. He'd promptly married the aunt – despite the fact that she was forty and ten years older than him – and shut them all up. The company was well and truly under his thumb. And the Stuarts, father and son, had to bite the bullet and get on with it.

Life was not all a bed of roses for Malachy, however. The aunt, once the novelty of having a gold ring on her finger and being a "Mrs" had worn off, cast off her mantle of *Sweet-Timid-Little-Woman-who-Deferred-to-Big-Strong-Men* and turned into a nagging, iron-willed termagant. Malachy might be a devious, back-stabbing, sharky operator in the business world, but he'd well and truly lost the battle at home. He was firmly under the rule of thumb. Mona's thumb.

Alexandra had met Mona MacDonald once. A very tall, thin rake of a woman who exuded an air of dissatisfaction and gloom. Privately Alexandra christened her Hatchet-Face.

"I don't approve of women working," she'd declared coldly when Malachy introduced her. "It's unladylike. But Malachy seems to be very impressed with you . . . for some reason." The unspoken *But I'm not* . . . hung in the air between them.

"Malachy's got good taste." Alexandra had tried a joke.

"That's a matter of debate," Mona had retorted cuttingly. Her nostrils had flared with distaste and she'd eyed Alexandra up and down.

Alexandra had instantly realised that Mona saw her as a threat. Malachy liked to think of himself as a suave, sophisticated ladies' man. It was all in his own mind, however. Certainly in her case. Malachy was the last man on earth she'd think of in those terms.

"Some of us have to work," she'd responded evenly. "We don't have husbands to keep us."

"I'm sure you'd have no trouble getting a husband." Mona had sniffed.

"Sometimes it's easier said than done." Alexandra had smiled sweetly. *If it wasn't for your shares, you wouldn't have got one,* she'd longed to retort. But she'd restrained herself. Mona MacDonald could block her way up the ladder of success.

Today, though, she wasn't in the humour for Malachy. She had a hell of a hangover and she was up to her eyes preparing a presentation for Marcus Lynn. It had to be perfect. She was going to make her move on him soon. Chris was getting on her nerves. She'd had enough of him. Once she was sure of Marcus she was going to send Chris packing. He could go back to Suzy. It might stop the woman doing crazy childish stunts like posting abusive cards.

Alexandra was still as mad as hell about that. It had really made her position at work extremely uncomfortable. She found it hard to believe that Suzy was capable of such spite. She'd always deferred to Alexandra when they were friends. Alexandra had been the leader, Suzy the follower. This new, vicious Suzy was unsettling.

The only thing that kept Alexandra going was the hope that Marcus would fall for her. That and her trip to London for Christmas. She was going to stay for the sales and she was going to have a ball shopping. Buying in the sales made good economic sense. She invariably got designer labels reduced to a fraction of their full price. She always bought the basics of her wardrobe each year at the sales. Maybe the day would come when she'd be able to pay the full price instead of scrimping. If she became Mrs Marcus Lynn, that would certainly be the case. Maybe Marcus might set her up in her own agency. Wouldn't that be a thought?

Her eyes sparkled at the idea. Just imagine telling that suspicious little tight-arse, Ron Evans, where he could stick his expenses. On second thoughts, no . . . that might give him some pleasure, Alexandra thought nastily. She really loathed that furtive slug. If she ever had her own agency she'd make sure to employ an accountant who didn't have a devious mind and who was competitive, with-it and had *some* business sense.

She spent the next twenty minutes imagining that Marcus had made a takeover bid for Stuart and Stuart's and she was experiencing the enormous pleasure of sacking Ron, Malachy and half the typing pool. It was such a satisfying fantasy she was still smiling when she rapped briskly on the boss's door for her eleven a.m. appointment.

"Alexandra, my dear," Malachy greeted her effusively. "Come in, like a good girl."

Alexandra gritted her teeth. Malachy was a dreadful chauvinist. Good girl, indeed. She hated it when he addressed her so.

"You're looking ravishing today."

"You look pretty dishy yourself, Mal." She returned the compliment as indeed he fully expected her to. It was always quid pro quo with Malachy.

Malachy simpered and fiddled with the carnation he always wore in his lapel. One of his many little affectations. "That's very kind of you, Alexandra. At my age one doesn't expect compliments."

Oh get on with it, you vain old goat, Alexandra urged silently.

"Malachy, you have the get-up-and-go of a man half your age. Don't give me that nonsense," she retorted briskly. He loved it when she spoke to him like that.

Malachy gave an amused chuckle and gave her a pat on the arm. "Oh to be young and single again," he twinkled.

Thank God you're not. Alexandra tried not to shudder. *It must be a real bummer of a plan if he's this geed up,* she reflected. The more crazy and unworkable the plan, generally, the more manic Malachy tended to be.

"Make yourself comfortable, my dear." Malachy indicated the chair opposite his desk. "I'm afraid I have something to tell you that you may not like."

"Oh!" Alexandra frowned.

"Well, no point in beating about the bush. Victor Conway phoned me this morning. He'd like Thomas Scully to take over his account – "

"I don't believe it! The ungrateful old twit!" Alexandra exploded.

Malachy held up a restraining hand. "Let me finish, Alexandra. It seems that Madeleine, his wife, is a friend of . . . er," he paused. "I believe she's friends with a lady called Suzy Wallace . . . "

Alexandra stared at him in horror as the blood drained from her face.

"Oh! Oh I see."

"There's no need for me to continue then," Malachy said silkily. "Other than to say that Victor asked me to tell you that he was very happy with the work you did for him and he wishes you continued success."

Alexandra stood up. "Well, if that's all, Malachy, I'll get back to work," she said calmly.

"Fine, fine," Malachy agreed.

Alexandra walked gracefully to the door.

Great carriage, magnificent chassis, Malachy thought admiringly as he held the door open for her. He liked a woman with good carriage. Most young women today had no idea how to carry themselves. Clumping around in those dreadful platform shoes. He wondered if he could ban them as unsuitable office wear.

"Good morning, Malachy." Alexandra walked out, head held high. Inwardly, she was in turmoil.

That sly bitch had gone whingeing to Madeleine-Interfering-Cow-Conway. Alexandra still couldn't quite believe that her former friend was capable of such vindictiveness. That was low. Worse than the card. She was stunned and very much unnerved. What else was Suzy going to do to get revenge? The sooner Alexandra kicked Chris out of her life, the better. It was imperative that she get to work on Marcus Lynn as soon as possible.

She saw Thomas Scully emerge from Ron Evans's office. He gave her a smug smile. Alexandra wanted to kick him in the goolies. She gave him a saccharine smile back. Not for diamonds would she let on that she was ruffled.

"Can't wait to get my hands on the Conway account." Thomas didn't even have the cop-on to pretend he was cool about the whole affair. He was like a little boy.

Alexandra laughed. "Darling," she drawled in her most condescending tone, "you're welcome to it. It'll be something for you to cut your teeth on. We all need to start somewhere."

Thomas reddened. "Yeah, well some of us are on the up and others are definitely on the slippery slopes."

Alexandra eyed him laconically. "You know something, Tommy? You'll make a good PR some day . . . when you grow up. A tip while you're growing . . . gauche behaviour is not on. Develop some equipoise. And if you don't know what that means, look it up in a dictionary."

"Sarky bitch," Thomas sneered. But he was raging with himself for letting her see how delighted he was to have snaffled the Conway account from under her nose.

Alexandra smiled sweetly and carried on to her own office. Once inside, her own composure crumbled. What a bloody way to start a week. She rooted in her bag agitatedly. She needed a cigarette. Her fingers shook as she lit up and drew deeply, inhaling down into her lungs. Victor Conway's account was a prestigious one and she'd worked damn hard on it. Now it was snatched from her and given into The Boy Scully's sweaty, grasping little palms. It was sickening.

What business had Madeleine Conway got sticking her big prudy nose into Alexandra's business and making judgements about her. It wasn't a one-sided affair, yet Chris wasn't being punished. It really was a man's world. Well, she wasn't finished with them all yet. Not by a long chalk. She picked up Marcus Lynn's file and dialled his number with one immaculately manicured finger that still trembled slightly. His secretary answered the phone.

"Good morning, Maggie, it's Alexandra Johnston, can you put me through to Mr Lynn, please?"

"Just one moment, Miss Johnston, I'll tell him you're on the line," the younger woman said. For some reason it made her feel old. Maggie had always called her Miss Johnston and Alexandra had taken it as a sign of deference. Now, she wasn't so sure.

She pulled open her desk drawer and pulled out the ornate

antique hand-mirror that Suzy had given her as a gift one Christmas, years ago. How ironic that it was Suzy's gift. She studied her reflection in the mirror. Horror of horrors, there were several grey hairs in her gleaming tresses, and the signs of ageing around her eyes were a cause for grave concern. The lines that ran between her nose and mouth were deeper than she cared to admit. She'd be a facelift case soon, she decided, depressed by the image that was reflected back at her.

"So, Alexandra. How's it going?" Marcus's sexy voice shook her from her reverie. She loved his voice. It had a deep rasping timbre, a bit like Leonard Cohen's, her favourite singer of all time. She'd listen to Marcus talk for hours. The thought of that sensual voice whispering sweet nothings in her ear was highly erotic. Usually she was sure of men. She could read them like a book. Marcus was an enigma.

"Marcus, good to hear you. Listen, I've come up with an idea I'd like you to check out. How are you for lunch any day this week?"

"Um . . . let's see. I'm in London tomorrow. Wednesday's good."

"Not for me, I'm afraid." Always let them think you've someone or something more important than them. Another of her golden rules. "How's Thursday?"

"I do have a meeting scheduled at one-thirty. Hold on a second, Alexandra, and I'll speak to my secretary to see if she can do some juggling." Alexandra heard a murmured conversation down the line.

"I've rescheduled that one for twelve-fifteen. How does one-thirty in the Burlington suit?"

"One-thirty's fine. The Burlington . . . " She made a face. "I was there three times last week. Will you trust me to pick somewhere nice and I'll phone Maggie with the arrangements?"

"Sounds good to me. We can catch up on all the news and gossip. Looking forward to it, Alexandra." She could sense that he was smiling.

"Me too, Marcus. See you then." Alexandra smiled back and hung up. Always hang up first was her motto. If all went to plan, it would be more than lunch she'd be having with Marcus Lynn. In time it might even be breakfast, dinner and tea!

Chapter Eighteen

"It was the least I could do, Suzy," Madeleine's voice came crisply down the telephone wires. "I don't like that kind of behaviour. Victor was more than happy to tell Malachy he wanted someone new. I must have a word with Eleanor O'Shea. She's a friend of mine. Her husband is a client of Madam Johnston's. I'll give her a little word of warning. We women must stick together. You and I must have lunch some day soon, to get you out of the house. I'll call again, sweetheart. Bye."

"Bye, Madeleine. Thanks." Suzy smiled as she hung up the receiver. She punched her fist in the air. So Madeleine had taken the warning to heart. Victor's virtue was now safe and Alexandra was off the case, so to speak.

How awkward it must be for her at work now. She'd have no credibility left. First the postcard and now this. Suzy smiled grimly. Good enough for her. Suzy knew how hard she'd worked to get where she was. Alexandra had moaned about it often enough in the past. Just as she'd moaned about all the shits she had to work with. She had no time for them. They were holding her back, she felt. But she was just using them to get as high up the ladder of success as she could before moving on. She'd confided to Suzy, that she intended to build up a big list of clients before going out on her own.

That's what she thought, Suzy thought vindictively. Victor

229

Conway was well and truly off her list. The first to go. If that friend of Madeleine's persuaded her husband to drop Alexandra, that would be two down. If Alexandra kept losing clients she'd be out of Stuart and Stuart's so fast her head would spin. One thing Chris used to say over and over was, there was no loyalty in business. Everyone was looking out for themselves. Even Alexandra's famous sex appeal wouldn't help her if she wasn't bringing in the dosh.

The phone rang. It was Chris.

"What do you want?" she demanded.

"Look, Suzy, I think you should cut out the crap with Alexandra. Enough is enough. If she loses her job, I won't be supporting her and I'll have to come back home. I know you don't want that. So give it a rest, OK?" he said wearily.

"I don't know what you're talking about, Chris. I couldn't care less about Alexandra and her job, or whether she loses it or whether she keeps it. But one thing I do know is that you won't be coming home here so forget it," she said snootily, furious that he'd phoned her to plead his precious Alexandra's cause.

"For heaven's sake, Suzy, we've two kids to think about. At least let me come home for Christmas and make a family thing of it for the children," he appealed.

"We won't be here for Christmas. So get lost, Chris. If you were so worried about our kids, like you pretend you are, you'd never have betrayed us the way you did, so cut the sanctimonious crap and fuck off, you lying skunk." Suzy slammed down the phone.

What a hypocrite he was. Pretending he had the kids' interests at heart. For some reason he wanted to come home for Christmas. Alexandra was probably going to London. She usually went for Christmas. Well, he needn't think he was going to use her. He could go and spend Christmas on his own. Or with his toffee-nosed mother. She was damned if he was going to slither back just because it suited him.

She picked up the phone. She'd told Chris she wasn't going to be at home for Christmas. That had just popped out. But now that she'd said it, she'd better do something about it. Her friend

Niamh in Wicklow had suggested she spend Christmas with her and her two children. That was precisely what she was going to do, Suzy decided. Chris could like it or lump it. She wasn't going to let him manipulate her ever again.

Chris sat doodling at his desk. Suzy was downright vicious. She hadn't softened her line at all. He had to admit she'd surprised him. He'd been sure that she'd never stick being in the house alone with the kids. He'd expected that after a while, when she'd got over the shock of it, when she'd got some of the anger out of her system, she'd cool down and consider letting him come home. Instead she seemed to be coping, and to heap coals on the fire she was even going away for Christmas.

Everyone was going away, he scowled, feeling immensely sorry for himself. No one wanted to be with him. He stared out the window. It was snowing. Great swirling white flakes blotting out the view.

This had been the worst year of his life. Why had he got involved with Alexandra in the first place? It was too close to home and he was paying the price for it now. It was all Ellen's fault. If she hadn't rejected him, he'd never have turned to Alexandra and he wouldn't be in this god-awful mess. Things looked as if they weren't going to get any better. What a way to start a new decade. He flung down his pen and picked up his diary. One of his clients, Jilly Fleming, was a sexy-looking bird with legs that went on and on. She fancied him too. She was always giving him come-hither looks and making suggestive remarks. She was married to a much older man. Chris got the impression he wasn't too effective in the sack. Maybe she was free for lunch. He needed cheering up. Jilly would do fine. Chris picked up the phone and dialled the number.

It was a beautiful dress. Black, slinky, with a square neckline that suggested just the tiniest bit of cleavage. Alexandra didn't believe in being obvious. Plunging necklines were not her style. A hint of bosom was far more erotic than acres of flesh. Mystery, teasing and tantalising were what it was all about. She was an expert, Alexandra thought confidently as she surveyed her reflection in the full-length mirror in her bedroom.

She'd left the office early to come home and change. She was going to tell Marcus she had a cocktail party to go to later in the evening . . . if he made any comment about her dress. Slowly she eased a sheer silk black stocking up her shapely leg and fastened her suspender. If all went well, Marcus would unfasten it and stroke his tanned fingers along the inside of her thigh. She shivered at the thought of it. Her nipples hardened. She was aroused just thinking about it.

She smiled languidly at herself in the mirror. Her hair fell in loose soft curls around her face. Her make-up was subtle. Her peach lipstick made her mouth look very kissable. Would he be able to resist her?

She didn't think so.

Her life was going to change completely. She'd wipe the dust of Stuart and Stuart's off her feet so fast it would leave them breathless. She'd be rich and envied, and she'd be having the most fantastic sex of her entire life. She just knew it. She slid her fur coat around her shoulders, picked up her handbag and set out on the seduction of Marcus Lynn.

"Luigi's? I don't know it, do you?" Marcus Lynn slapped some aftershave on his jaws, combed his hair and emerged from the washroom into his large airy office overlooking Stephen's Green. Maggie, his secretary, shook her head.

"Miss Johnston said it's new. It's Italian but it's only a five-minute walk for you. That was one of the reasons she chose it."

"That was thoughtful. I'm hungry." He grinned wolfishly.

"You always are," Maggie retorted. "If it's nice, you can bring me there for my Christmas lunch."

"You're on. Be good! See you later." Marcus raised a hand in farewell as he strode out of the office in his usual panther-like way. He liked Alexandra Johnston. She was forthright, intelligent and highly entertaining. Alexandra had the saltiest tongue of any woman he knew. She didn't hold back. Her acerbic comments made him laugh. No one was safe. But she was excellent at her job. She'd a real eye for marketing and knowing what was in fashion. Marcus valued her judgement. He was looking forward to seeing this new plan she'd come up with. *And* he was looking forward to lunch.

"This was a surprise, Chris," Jilly murmured as Chris filled her wineglass for the third time.

"I generally bring valued clients to lunch around Christmastime. I'm sorry for the short notice. I've been up to my eyes but I really wanted to do this and today is one of the few days I have free." Chris held her gaze.

"Lucky I was free too." Jilly stared seductively back.

"How's Louis?" Chris asked. Louis was the unsatisfactory husband.

"You know Louis, always whingeing about something. He's away on business." Jilly slid her hand across the table and rested it lightly on his.

"When will he be back?"

"The weekend." Jilly slipped her foot out of her shoe and slid it along his calf and then up along his inner thigh until it reached his crotch. She pressed gently until she felt him harden.

"Let's give ourselves a Christmas treat," Chris whispered huskily as he stroked her foot with his hand and pressed it against him even closer.

"Oohh yesss, let's," Jilly breathed. The thought of doing it with a virile attractive man was nearly enough to make her come there and then.

With indecent haste, Chris paid the bill, ushered Jilly out to his car, and drove at speed to her luxury detached house in Ballsbridge. Minutes later they were wrapped around each other on the cream shag-pile carpet of Jilly's luxurious lounge.

"Do it to me, do it to me," Jilly groaned with pleasure at this rare treat. Louis usually disintegrated after ten seconds. Chris considerately obliged.

The skies darkened. The snow fell silently as they enjoyed every second of their Christmas bonus.

"I've ordered for both of us," Alexandra announced coolly.

"Have you now?" Marcus grinned.

"I know you of old, Lynn. You're still a peasant at heart. Left to your own devices you'd have bacon and cabbage every day."

"I happen to like bacon and cabbage. I was reared on it, I'll have you know."

"Just for once in your life, do what you're told and trust me." Alexandra smiled into her companion's dark eyes. Marcus looked as dishy as ever. He didn't even realise how sexy he was. That made him all the more attractive.

"I'm all yours. What have you ordered?" He held out his hand for the menu.

"Parma ham, olives and grissini. Minestrone soup. Piccata alla milanese with risotto. And zabaglione for dessert if you're a good boy." Alexandra grinned.

"It's far from zabaglione I was reared." Marcus sat back in his chair and looked at her.

"You're all dressed up. You look very posh."

"I've something else on later. I hope you don't mind."

"You could dress up in a sack and you'd look good in it, Alexandra. Of course I don't mind. Now, tell me all the news . . . "

They talked and laughed and exchanged ideas over a thoroughly enjoyable meal and when it was over Marcus raised his glass to her approvingly. "That was delicious, Alexandra. The veal was melt-in-the-mouth. And that mushroom and cream sauce . . . "

"See! I was right. Trust me. I know what's best for you. I'm glad you enjoyed it, Marcus. I thought this would be handy for you. And it's nice and cosy. The Burlington is so . . . so business-lunchy," Alexandra said lightly. "Come on now, do have a brandy. I insist."

"Good Lord, woman! I've a stack of work to do when I get back to the office," Marcus laughed.

Alexandra laughed back at him. The man was so sexy. The way he said "woman" in that deep delicious voice made her quiver. She loved his accent. A West of Ireland lilt that years in the city hadn't erased. It was divine and he was drop-dead gorgeous.

"Marcus, never turn down a brandy when Stuart and Stuart's are paying. Just think of the pleasure you're giving Ron Evans," she said wickedly.

Marcus grinned, baring even white teeth. "In that case I'd love one. Far be it from me to deprive Ron of his pleasure."

"You know," she said slowly, "it's so frustrating having someone like Ron stepping on your toes every time you try and introduce something new. Malachy and he are so cautious. I'd really love to set up on my own. I'd like to hire my own team. I know I could make a go of it," she confided, her eyes wide and guileless.

"You'd make a great job of it, Alexandra. You're terrific at what you do. That plan you've come up with is pretty slick."

"Thank you, Marcus." Alexandra let her hand rest lightly on his hand. "I really appreciate that."

"It's true. You're good." Marcus shrugged. In the dim light of the small intimate restaurant his brown eyes glittered almost black.

"I'm the best." Alexandra arched an eyebrow.

This was it, she decided. She was sure he was receptive. They'd had a delightful lunch. The best ever. They clicked so well and always had. He had to like her as much as she liked him.

"Marcus, work isn't the only thing I'm good at," she murmured, leaning closer so that she was staring into his eyes. "Do you know what I'm saying?"

Marcus looked at her in shock and eased away. "Alexandra, I think we'll forgo the brandy. Maybe we should get back to work." She froze. She'd misjudged the signals he was sending. This was a disaster.

"Are you sure?" she asked in amazement.

"Alexandra, let me put it like this, so there's no mistake," Marcus said quietly, a troubled expression darkening his eyes. "I like you a lot but I'm in a relationship as you know. And I'm committed to the woman I love. I don't two-time."

"I see. Pardon me, Marcus, I made a bad judgement." Alexandra's voice shook with humiliation.

"Thanks for lunch, I'll be in touch." He stood up and nodded down at her, his expression unreadable.

She smiled weakly. "Fine." She watched him leave and wanted to weep. All her dreams went out the door with him. She'd made a dreadful fool of herself. She was losing her touch. And she'd never be able to look him in the eye again.

Heavy-hearted, she paid the bill and hailed a taxi. To hell with the office. She wasn't going back there. It was snowing heavily and it was bitterly cold. She had the beginnings of a thumping headache. The only place she was going was to bed, alone. It was one of the lowest moments of her life.

Later that evening Chris phoned to say he was going to a Christmas booze-up and was staying in a friend's house. Alexandra was just as glad. She wanted to be alone to wallow in her depression.

The following morning she dragged herself into work. But she really didn't want to be there. Marcus's humiliating rejection of her stung. She'd been awake all night thinking about it. What a fool she'd made of herself. No man had ever flatly turned her down as he had. Was she really losing it? Was her sex appeal letting her down? That was the most frightening thought she'd ever entertained. Suddenly her options seemed to be shrinking rapidly.

Don't think about it! Alexandra nibbled the tip of her pen as she read through a marketing strategy she'd prepared for a new client. It was hard to concentrate. And that was most unlike her. Usually she was very focused on whatever project she was working on.

At ten-forty-five Peggy phoned. "Mr MacDonald would like to see you at eleven in his office," she said crisply.

"Very well," Alexandra snapped. What did *he* want? She really wasn't in the mood for Malachy. He was getting short shrift from her today whether he liked it or not.

At ten-fifty-five she left her office and walked along the carpeted corridor towards Malachy's room. As she passed the accounts department, Ron poked his head out first as he usually did when emerging from his office. He reminded her of a snake the way he slithered around the offices. Alexandra eyed him coldly. His face broke into a sly knowing grin when he saw her.

"Aahh, Alexandra, off to see the boss? Well, good luck."

"Sorry?" she clipped. Why was the little weasel wishing her good luck?

"Aahh! You don't know, then. I'm sure Malachy will tell you all about it." He smiled insincerely but his reptilian little eyes were hard and cold.

What the hell was he talking about? He obviously knew something that she didn't. But snowballs would roast in hell before she'd ask him. Alexandra felt a tremor of unease. Ron enjoyed power games. He liked bossing the clerical staff around. He could get away with that but it was unusual for him to try it on with her. He was extremely wary of her. Alexandra despised him. At heart he was a coward. He practically had a shit attack if Malachy said boo to him.

"Ron," she said crisply, "I don't have time to stand here yapping. I've a lot of work to do, if you don't. Excuse me." She swept past.

Ron's air of self-importance deflated.

"Bitch," he muttered. How he'd love to be a fly on the wall at the meeting between her and Malachy. That stuck-up cow wouldn't be so stuck-up very shortly, if only she knew it.

Alexandra, a little thrown by the encounter, rapped smartly on Malachy's door.

"Come in," her boss invited.

Alexandra opened the door and marched into the office. "Malachy, I'm really up to my eyes," she insisted as she shut the door and came to stand in front of his mahogany desk.

Malachy studied her from behind his silver-rimmed glasses. He was looking particularly natty today, Alexandra thought in wry amusement as she noted the red carnation in the buttonhole of his cream jacket and the burgundy handkerchief decorating his breast pocket. Dressed to impress! Obviously he was taking a woman to lunch. Malachy always dressed to the nines on such occasions. He loved playing his role of powerful business executive to the hilt.

"Sit down, Alexandra. This is rather difficult." Malachy's watery blue eyes were less than friendly. The avuncular, good-humoured facade he usually sported, gone.

Alexandra sat down feeling suddenly shaky. What was all this about? She'd seen Malachy turn on people many times. Especially at strategy meetings when he'd eff and blind and rant and rave if he wasn't getting his own way. He was an outrageous bully. But it had never been directed at her. Malachy steepled his fingers and rested his chin on their tips. He had a weak chin. She'd never noticed that before, she thought a little wildly.

Alexandra took a deep breath. It was always best to be in control.

"What's the problem, Malachy?"

"I'm afraid, my dear, you are." The coldness in his voice chilled her. Malachy had never been anything other than charming to her until now.

"I beg your pardon!"

"I'm sorry but I must ask for your resignation. Marcus Lynn has asked that someone else handle his account. And, on top of the same request from Victor Conway, I really feel that – unfortunately – the time has come for us to part company. I cannot take the risk of losing clients." He slid an envelope across the table to her.

"An excellent reference and a more than generous cheque to keep you going until you find another position," he said smoothly.

Alexandra picked up the envelope and stared at it. "You're joking!"

"Indeed, anything but. I'm sorry, Alexandra. You're very good at your job but we expect a certain standard from our employees. And discretion in their private lives. I can't keep you on. It's too high a price to pay."

Too high a price to pay! She couldn't believe her ears. She was being sacked. He could say he was asking for her resignation but the reality was that she was getting the boot.

She jumped to her feet.

"You can't do this to me, Malachy. You *owe* me. I brought big clients with me when I moved from Weldon's. I raised your profile out there, buster. And don't you *dare* speak to me about standards, you gutless little creep. You wouldn't know what a standard was if it slapped you in your smug mush. You, who haven't an ounce of honour or integrity, talk about standards. Ha! You that people don't have a good word for. You that rip people off left, right and centre . . . Don't make me sick, Malachy MacDonald. Your hypocrisy stinks! Standards indeed. That's the best one I've heard in years. Let me tell you something." She pointed a finger aggressively under his nose. "This was a Mickey Mouse company for years because you and that miser, Ron Evans, were making a balls of it. The sloppiness, the inefficiency, the lack of vision . . . I could go on and on. You haven't got a clue – "

"I resent this. I deeply object to your accusations," Malachy blustered, banging his hand on the desk. "This is a reputable company, and my business ethics are above reproach. I think you'd better go."

"Business ethics!" Alexandra snorted "You're hilarious, Malachy. You can kid yourself all you like but you know, and I know, that no one out there respects you. The things I've heard said about you would curl your hair if you had enough of it," she added insultingly. "And I won't be playing happy families, believe me. I gave you my loyalty but you showed me none. I'm just a commodity to you. Well, let me tell you, you miserable little shit, I'll bad-mouth you every chance I get. You're going to get everything you deserve and more. And you know something?" She glared at him, her eyes dripping scorn. "That carnation makes you look an even bigger idiot than you are."

Malachy's jaw dropped in horror. His vanity was enormous. That last slur was even more offensive than the one to his business reputation. *That* one hurt.

Alexandra didn't wait to hear his reply. She marched out the door and practically took it off the hinges, she slammed it so hard.

Ron slunk out of his office. He'd heard the raised voices. He gave a leery grin, but before he could say anything Alexandra turned on him.

"You can take that smirk of your pimply little face, Ron Evans. You're a sleazy two-faced little git and I won't be sorry to see the back of you. Go back to adding up your sums – it's all you're good for."

"Got the sack, did you?" Ron sneered. "Good enough for you."

"Oh, you're brave now, aren't you, Ron?" Alexandra advanced two paces towards him. Ron paled and stepped back.

"You're not worth my time, you little turd," she spat. "Do you know your problem . . . Ronnie? You've got no balls!"

The accounts clerk sniggered. Alexandra was delighted she'd heard the remark, as she was meant to. It would be around the office like wildfire. Ron went various shades of red and purple as Alexandra strode down the corridor to her office. Once inside, she leaned her forehead against the cold plane of the door, and took a deep breath.

The sack! How ignominious. It was so brutal. So unexpected. What the hell was she going to do? With trembling fingers she opened the envelope that contained the cheque and her reference. She scanned it quickly. Glowing. An excellent reference. The hypocrite. Just as well she'd got that before she lost her temper and let fly. She'd never have got it after she'd told Judas MacDonald exactly what she thought of him.

Her eyes widened. There was nothing to stop him cancelling the cheque though. She wouldn't put it past him. She'd better cash it immediately. Fortunately her bank was just two doors down. Alexandra grabbed her bag and coat and hurried to the elevator. Five minutes later she stood in front of the cashier and handed him the cheque. He counted two hundred pounds into her hand. It was a pretty mean pay-off for all the work she'd done for them but it was better in her hands than theirs. She'd need it to tide her over until she got a new job. If she didn't get one soon, she'd never be able to keep up the rent on the apartment. It looked as if she was going to be stuck with Chris whether she liked it or not.

"Fuck you, Marcus," she muttered as she hurried back to the office. She'd read him all wrong. He could at least have had the decency to tell her that he didn't want to work with her any more instead of going to Malachy behind her back. The elevator was in use when she got back to the office so she ran upstairs, intent on clearing out her desk as quickly as she could. She wasn't going to spend one minute more than was necessary in that hell-hole.

Malachy MacDonald was sizzling. No one had ever insulted him the way Alexandra Johnston had ten minutes ago. Such impudence. Such language. How dare she? That was the thanks he'd got for taking her on and teaching her everything he knew about the advertising business. She'd been his special protégée. He'd enjoyed her success. It reflected on his training. She had a superb client list. Nevertheless losing two big clients could start a domino effect. The business was cut-throat. Those clients could leave the firm. That danger had to be averted. She had to go. But instead of going gracefully, she'd gone spitting like a she-cat, issuing insults that were outrageous. Slanderous! He'd sue her. Malachy paced the office floor in a temper. For two pins he'd take her to court but, then, she knew enough about his business practice to get him into trouble. Unfortunately. The papers would have a field day. It wouldn't do to have every Tom, Dick and Harry reading about how Stuart and Stuart's conducted their business. Image was everything.

If only he hadn't written her that reference. He couldn't very well get it back. She'd refuse to give it. Alexandra was as hard-nosed as they come. A thought struck him. He picked up the phone and dialled an extension.

"Ron, get your ass in here, I want you to do something fast," he barked. Madam Johnston would be sorry she hadn't held her tongue when she went to cash her cheque.

"Oh . . . oh I see. Right, thanks." Ron Evans couldn't hide his disappointment. He'd thought all his Christmases had come together when Malachy had called him into his office and told him to cancel Alexandra Johnston's pay-off cheque.

Had it been left to him, he'd have just given her her two weeks salary, all she was entitled to. He certainly wouldn't have given her a golden handshake. But Malachy had insisted. Now he was bitterly regretting it. Ron had done his best to earwig when Alexandra had gone into the boss's office but unfortunately he hadn't been able to catch what was said. Obviously Alexandra had given Malachy the sharp edge of her tongue. He was certainly regretting his generosity. And rightly so. But it was too late, Alexandra was no fool! The cheque was well and truly cashed.

"I demand that you return that money and your reference." Malachy, red-faced with anger, pounded his fist on Alexandra's desk.

"Go whistle." She was ice-cool.

"You have no principles, Miss," he thundered.

"Ah yes. This is *Mister-Honesty-and-Integrity* speaking," Alexandra sneered. "It does my heart good to see it."

"You are an . . . an ingrate. I warn you there won't be a company in the city that will employ you when I've finished."

"I'm trembling in my boots, Malachy. Go away and stop bothering me. I'm trying to clear my desk."

"This is the thanks I get. This is the thanks." He was like a turkey, his Adam's apple bobbing up and down at a rate of knots.

"No, Malachy, you've got it the wrong way around. You owe *me* the thanks. Instead you've given me a slap in the face. I won't forget that. So *you* take care. I've seen you and Ron in action. And it's not a pretty picture. You've a very selective memory when it suits you. But I know the stunts you pull. You sail close to the wind, Malachy. Very, very close. I've attended business meetings here, don't forget. So don't you threaten me."

Unable to deny the truth of her words, knowing that he had made a very powerful foe, Malachy was speechless. His professional standing was extremely important to him. He was, after all, the grand old man of advertising in the city. Loose talk in the right ears could damage his reputation beyond repair. Knowing he'd met his match, Malachy withdrew with as much dignity as he could muster.

Alexandra watched him go with slitted eyes. If Malachy wanted to tangle with her, he'd find her a worthy adversary. How right she'd been to cash the cheque immediately. Her instincts had been absolutely spot on. It was such a pity they'd let her down about Marcus. Otherwise she wouldn't be sitting here, jobless.

She packed her bulging address book, her most precious possession, into her bag. It represented everything she'd worked for. All those contacts, all those clients. She'd have to write to her clients and tell them of her departure from Stuart and Stuart's. Hopefully most of them would come with her.

She packed her hand-mirror carefully. She didn't want to break that and risk seven years' bad luck. She was having enough bad luck as it was.

Still, she could start afresh somewhere else. Nineteen-seventy was edging closer. A new decade and a new step forward in her career, she decided briskly as she walked out of her office without a backward glance.

"Bye, Alexandra," Ron peered out of his office and jeered.

"Crawl back into the hole you crawled out of, Ron." Her tone dripped contempt. She was so tempted to give him a smack in the chops but knowing the type he was, she knew he'd sue her for assault. If he thought there was money in it for him, he'd sue a gnat for landing on his nose. Money was Ron Evans's god.

His prissy little mouth tightened. He'd never been able to get the better of her. Even now, when he had the upper hand, she was able to reduce him to the level of a schoolboy. Quick responses were not his forte.

"You're not so big for your boots now," he managed. But Alexandra was gone, wafting *Chanel No 5* in her magnificent wake.

"You've been sacked!" Chris was aghast. "But how? Why?"

"Thanks to Suzy and her nasty little tricks." Alexandra sipped a glass of red wine, apparently unmoved.

"How can you sit there and be so cool about it?" Chris demanded. "How are you going to pay your rent?"

"Is that all you're worried about, darling? Silly old me. I thought you might be a *tad* upset for me. I thought you might be the teeniest bit concerned for me. That's twice in one day that my worth has been measured in terms of money. Ain't life a bitch!"

"I am upset for you. It's terrible," Chris backtracked.

"Well then stop worrying about things like rent. I'll get a job soon enough," Alexandra said tiredly. "Now, if you'll excuse me, it's been a hell of a day. I'm off to bed."

She marched out of the room with her glass of wine, leaving Chris staring after her in dismay.

He needed this bombshell like a hole in the head. Alexandra needn't think he was paying for this place by himself. If she didn't get a job soon, he was going to have to examine his options.

The time had come to rethink his relationship with Alexandra, he mused. She was no use to him if she couldn't pay her way. Maybe their affair had run its course.

Chapter Nineteen

Katherine Wallace pushed her way through the throngs of Christmas shoppers that surged into Switzer's. Organised as ever, she'd just finished buying the last of her Christmas presents. The sharp northerly breeze reddened her cheeks as she hurried along Grafton Street. Afternoon tea in the Shelbourne was just what she needed to revive her, she decided as she dropped a silver sixpence into a carol singer's box.

Twenty minutes later she was sipping Earl Grey from fine bone china and eating a scone topped with jam and fresh cream. It was pleasant to sit in the big armchair by the window and watch the to-ing and fro-ing outside. She stretched her legs. This cold weather made her bones ache. She was starting to feel old.

She took an elegant leather-bound notebook out of her bag and flicked it open. She scanned the neatly written names on her Christmas shopping list. Yes . . . everyone covered, she thought with satisfaction. It had taken three separate trips into town. Today she'd been buying for her grandchildren. The large bulky box of Lego that she'd bought for Adam rested against the side of the chair. Christina's nurse's outfit, complete with watch and stethoscope, looked most impressive. And her other grandchildren were well looked after too. But something niggled. And no matter how hard she tried, Katherine simply could not banish the image that came every time she'd picked up a toy in the toy department.

A memory of blue, blue eyes and dark hair and a perfect little rosebud mouth. How earnestly those eyes had gazed into her own. Stephanie Munroe was one of the most beautiful children she had ever seen. Stephanie Munroe was her grandchild as much as Adam and Christina and the others.

Would Ellen be annoyed if Katherine bought Stephanie a present? Would it be too much of an intrusion? She felt so strongly that she must do right by that little girl. Chris had disowned her without a thought. To have reared a son with no moral code must be an indictment of her. She had gone wrong somewhere, Katherine decided unhappily. She felt an obligation towards that child to try to right the wrongs somehow.

She'd seen a beautiful china doll's tea set in willow pattern. It had a sugar bowl, milk jug and teapot all in miniature. Stephanie had cousins. She could entertain them to tea.

Even though she was tired and her arms ached from carrying parcels, Katherine finished her tea and retraced her steps along the Green, back to Grafton Street. She bought the tea set and, on impulse, selected a soft angora scarf in palest pink. It would go very well with Ellen's colouring. It would be a little gesture from one woman who'd known heartache to another. In that respect at least, they were kindred spirits.

The afternoon lull had settled on The Deli. Lunchtime had been satisfyingly busy but, once two o'clock came, things usually quietened down until around five when the people coming home from work would drop in to buy something for their tea, or perhaps have tea as a treat.

The bus to and from town stopped two doors away from them. It was excellent for passing trade. Teenagers from the secondary school liked eating upstairs. They happily munched goodies and skittered and giggled and flirted away there for an hour or two after school. As long as they didn't get too boisterous, the girls were happy to have them as regular customers.

At quiet times, they arranged between themselves, according to their needs, who would have time off to go home and do chores or whatever needed to be done. Mealtimes were very handy. They and the children got whatever was on the menu and Miriam took home a dinner for Ben.

Denise had stopped cooking for Jimmy. He could go and be fed by his mistress, she'd told the girls. She was damned if she was cooking a meal for him, especially after his meanness in docking her housekeeping money.

Now that they had settled into a routine, it wasn't quite so hectic. Stephanie, Rebecca and Denise's two little girls were perfectly happy to play away together after their homework was finished. Connie and Daniel, Miriam's older children, were allowed out on the green to play with their friends if it was fine. If not they watched TV.

The Deli closed at six-thirty and if Ben was on shift and not there to collect Miriam and the children, Ellen usually dropped them home.

"Do you want to go and do some Christmas shopping?" Miriam asked Ellen as they cleaned out the kitchen.

"I was thinking I might pop over to Ma. I feel a bit guilty," Ellen confessed. "I'm sure Emma thinks we're hard-hearted wagons."

"For God's sake, Ellen, it's the first time she's ever put herself out for the family. Look at all the times I've taken Julie Ann off her hands. Look at all the times you've let her stay here playing with Stephanie and she puts no pass on it. Let her look after your mother. And let Vincent do it too. He's not great for putting himself out either. He'll do it for Pamela and the Judge, but he doesn't kill himself doing anything out of the ordinary for your mam and dad like you and Ben do. Ben told him he was whitewashing the farmhouse last spring, hoping he might offer to help. Some hope," Miriam retorted.

Ellen smiled wryly. "The pair of them will think that they've done their duty for the next five years. And the annoying thing is, Ma will think so too. You and I will have 'How good Emma and

Vincent were to me' shoved down our necks for ever and a day. What you and I do is taken for granted. You'd never get a word of thanks. Well, you would from Dad," she amended.

"I wonder will our kids talk about us like this some day?" Miriam said slowly. "I wonder, if Ben or I are sick, will there be arguments about who'll look after us? It's a bit daunting to think about, isn't it?"

"Miriam, don't get me wrong. I don't mind in the least mucking in and helping out at home. My parents have been very good to me and Stephanie. It's Emma and Vincent that bug me. Just because they did something to put themselves out, for once, they think we should all be on our bended knees giving thanks," Ellen remarked crossly. "Did I tell you that I met Vincent at Mass on Sunday and he told me that 'poor Emma' was getting bad headaches again and he was worried about her blood pressure? She'd gone to spend the day with her parents. He was trying to make me feel guilty. I know it. They'd make you sick. And isn't it convenient to be able to get blood pressure when it suits you?"

"You nasty little cat," Miriam grinned.

"Yeah, well a saint I ain't," Ellen admitted ruefully. "Anyway, I'll ask Ma if she wants me to do any of her Christmas shopping for her. And I'm going to ask her if she and Dad would come and stay with me for Christmas."

"I bet she'll want to stay at home."

Ellen sighed. "I know. It would make life much easier if she'd come and stay with me. I'd like Stephanie to spend Christmas in her own home. You know, I think she's got a lot more confidence in herself since we moved into our own place. She loves her bedroom and inviting her friends in to play. She always had to be so careful not to break anything when we lived at Mam's. It really was the best move I ever made."

"Well then, you just tell your mother that you *insist* that she spend Christmas with you." Miriam scrubbed a worktop with extra vigour to add emphasis to her words.

"You're a hoot, Miriam," Ellen laughed. "*You* telling *me* to *insist*. And you the biggest softie of all."

"Oh stop it." Miriam went pink. "You know what I mean."

"Anyway, I'll go over there and be as nice as pie to darling Ems and see what Mother has to say for herself." Ellen drew a deep breath and squared her shoulders. "Wish me luck."

"I think you'd better take off your apron first," Miriam murmured, untying the strings behind her sister-in-law's back.

"Good thinking. Emma might make me use the tradesman's entrance." Ellen ran her fingers through her hair. "Where's my bag and I'll stick a bit of lipstick on. You know her, she's always done up to the nines."

Twenty minutes later, she stood on her sister-in-law's doorstep and rang the bell.

Mrs Murdock, holding a bawling Andrew, answered.

"How are you, Mrs Murdock, what's wrong with him?" Ellen held out her arms for the baby.

"He has a cold, the poor little fellow."

"You poor little pet," Ellen crooned. He was such a gorgeous baby with his big eyes and dark silky eyelashes that any woman would give her eye-teeth for. Andrew's lips quivered, as he gazed up at her. "Aahh don't cry, there's a good boy." Ellen cuddled him. She loved babies. It was a huge regret for her that Stephanie was an only child. She would have liked a little companion for her. Although her daughter was blessed to have cousins so close to her in age.

"You have the knack, Ellen," Mrs Murdock approved as Andrew's lips stopped quivering and his downy little head settled against her shoulder.

"Is Emma at home?"

"She's lying down . . . not feeling the best." Mrs Murdock was tactful.

"I see. Well, I'll just pop up and see Mam for a minute. Where's Julie Ann?"

Mrs Murdock threw her eyes up to heaven. "She's gone to a birthday party with some friends of Mrs Munroe's."

"Oh yes . . . the one the magician was going to be at." Ellen nodded. Stephanie and Rebecca had been listening to their cousin's boasts all week.

"The very one." Mrs Murdock reached out for Andrew. "So it's a peaceful house today." There was a ghost of a smile on her lips. "Would you like a cup of tea, Ellen?"

"Not at all, Mrs Murdock. You carry on. I'll just run upstairs to Mam."

Her mother was saying her Rosary when Ellen went into the bedroom.

"I'm nearly finished," she said querulously. Sheila hated to be interrupted in the middle of her Rosary.

Ellen nodded silently and went over and sat in the window seat. The view was very beautiful. She could see Glenree, down in the valley, between the winter treetops. Dusk was deepening and the sky, deep blue, almost indigo, was tinged with pinks and mauves. The smoke, curling up from the chimneys, shimmered into the sky giving a dim foggy effect. Lamps shone invitingly in house windows.

A horse whinnied. She could hear the faint clop-clop of hooves. It was a nice day for riding, the breeze bracing and invigorating. So many of the families who lived in the area owned horses. North County Dublin was horse-riding country and the sound of galloping hooves across the fields was as familiar to Ellen as the sound of car horns in the city. Some day she would buy Stephanie a pony, she vowed. It was her daughter's dearest wish.

The church steeple peeping from behind the trees was comfortingly familiar, silhouetted against the darkening sky, as it had for fifty years and would for another fifty and more to come. A little to the right, between the bare branches of a majestic oak, she could see the tip of Stephanie's window and a glimmer of the new red-tiled roof that Doug had put in when he'd renovated the flat. It made her feel so safe to have her own place. That awful insecurity that had haunted her for so long after Stephanie was born had ebbed away. Her father had sided with her when Sheila objected to her moving out with Stephanie. It was time they had a home of their own.

This was her place, her roots were here. She'd been through the best of times and the worst of times and now she felt content. It was a peaceful moment.

"I wasn't expecting to see you," Sheila's voice intruded. She sounded petulant. "You being such a busy woman these days."

Rise above it. Ellen ignored the dig and the acerbic tone.

"How are you feeling, Mam?"

Sheila put on her weak-as-a-kitten voice. "I'm getting along, I suppose. But I'm not sleeping at all. The pain gets to me. And it always seems to be worse at night."

"I came over to see was there any Christmas shopping you'd like me to do for you?" Ellen decided against offering sympathy. Otherwise the litany would go on and on.

"Oh!" Sheila hadn't expected this. "Well, now that you mention it, I've been here worrying about how I was going to get presents for everyone and you know this year I think everyone will have to make do with money in their Christmas card. I won't be doing any Christmas shopping."

"An excellent idea, Mam. Everyone will understand." Ellen couldn't believe that she was getting off so lightly.

"Of course I couldn't very well give money to Emma and Vincent, after them being so kind to me. I'll have to get something for them. Besides they have so much money, the little token I'd give them wouldn't mean anything," Sheila declared.

Ellen swallowed her irritation. Typical.

"And of course I'd have to get something for your father. And a little gift for Tilly Doyle, she's been very good to me too. Keeping me up to date on what's going on in the guild. I'll be wanting a couple of boxes of Christmas cards. Get me the holy ones. And I'll be needing stamps. Here, get me a pen and I'll give you a list." Sheila sat up, all businesslike. She was looking much better, Ellen observed as she handed her mother a pen and a page from her note pad.

Sheila wrote furiously. "There!" she said, five minutes later, as she handed Ellen a list as long as her arm. "And I'll be wanting some wrapping-paper, now that I remember. Put that down."

"Yes, Mother," Ellen said dryly. For someone who wasn't going to do any Christmas shopping, it was a long list. Now that they were on the subject of Christmas, she might as well mention her plans for Christmas Day.

"Mam, I was hoping you and Dad would come and stay with me for Christmas. I think it would be the best plan. I'd be able to look after you. It would give you a break and you wouldn't have to be worrying about cooking for Christmas," she said firmly.

Sheila looked at her in surprise. "But now, Ellen, you know how your father likes his own fireside. And I've neglected him long enough. I think it would be much better if you and Stephanie came to us. You could cook dinner, certainly. That would be most kind of you. Now would you do me another favour if you wouldn't mind. I have some nightdresses and underwear that need washing and I don't want to be a trouble to Emma – "

A knock on the door interrupted the conversation. It was Tilly Doyle from the guild. Sheila's demeanour changed immediately.

"Tilly, come in. How are you? How did the bring-and-buy go last night? Ellen, on your way out would you ask Mrs Murdock to bring Tilly a cup of tea? My washing's in the bag at the bottom of the wardrobe." Ellen was briskly dismissed.

"Hello, Ellen," Tilly smiled. "How's the cafe going?"

"Very well, thanks, Mrs Doyle," Ellen said politely.

"Do you know what we were saying at the meeting the other night? Some of us think the guild should have their Christmas lunch in your new cafe to give you a bit of support."

"Thanks very much indeed, Mrs Doyle." Ellen smiled. She wasn't sure if having the guild for lunch was worth all the hassle she'd get from Sheila or the snide remarks from Bonnie Daly and her cronies. That "some of us" wasn't lost on her.

"You never told me that, Tilly." Sheila sat up straight.

"It went right out of my head, Sheila, when I popped in the other day. I was so intent on telling you about Nora Kelly."

Nora Kelly, in her fifties and a widow of just two months, had scandalised the guild by going to a dinner dance with Johnny

Sheridan, a separated man and a notorious rake. Nora had also had her hair dyed ash-blonde. It was the talk of Glenree.

"I take it then that those not in favour of a lunch in Ellen's deli included Bonnie and her minions?" Sheila was all business.

"Well, of course Bonnie *is* making the most of your absence," Tilly remarked discreetly. She was firmly in Sheila's camp but it didn't do to be seen to take sides.

"I'd say she is!" Sheila's lips thinned. "I'm sure it's a sad day for her that I'm not in my coffin. But she'd better make the most of it. I'll be at the next meeting, Tilly, and let me tell you . . . "

Ellen slipped away, grinning. Nothing was guaranteed more to get Sheila out of her sick bed than the thought of Bonnie getting away with murder in the guild.

Sheila was herself, for sure. Emma and Vincent were ready for canonisation, just as she and Miriam had predicted. And how typical of her to put the blame on Mick, because she didn't want to come and stay at Ellen's for Christmas. Mick was the most easygoing soul. He'd eat his Christmas dinner in a tent if he had to. Ellen made a face. Despite her best efforts it looked as though she was going to spend Christmas at her mother's.

Emma lay rigid with suppressed fury. She could hear the murmur of voices in the adjoining guest room. Her house was like a hotel with people trotting up and down the stairs in a steady stream to her mother-in-law's bedroom. She felt like a prisoner in her own home. She'd heard Ellen's voice earlier and now she could hear that nosy old trout, Tilly Doyle. She'd been in and out to visit Sheila like a yo-yo. Prying and poking. She'd actually followed Mrs Murdock into the lounge, once, so that she could have a good look around. It was sheer impertinence. If Sheila didn't go back home soon, Emma was going to insist that Vincent tell her to leave. Enough was enough. She'd done her duty.

A chortle of laughter from next door set Emma's teeth on edge. Sheila knew very well that Emma was resting. You'd think she'd at least have the consideration not to make such a racket. An answering cackle sent her diving under the pillows as she did her best to drown out the sounds of her unwelcome guests.

Alexandra lit a cigarette and stared moodily out of the window. Time hung heavy on her hands. Once Chris had gone to work, she'd turned over and tried to go back asleep but, infuriatingly, sleep would not oblige. Her thoughts kept rampaging through her mind. She'd never been in a situation like this before. She'd always been in control. The apartment block seemed so dead and empty once the clatter of doors and the starting of car engines died away after the early-morning rush to work. They all had jobs to go to. She faced a day that stretched out endlessly with nothing to focus on.

She could imagine the gossip running riot in the canteen today. They'd all know by now that there'd been a mighty row and that she was gone. At least they'd all have heard by now that Ron Evans had no balls. Alexandra smiled vindictively as she remembered her parting shot to the devious accountant.

She got dressed and went out to buy the papers and then had croissants and coffee in a cafe in Ballsbridge while she eagerly scanned the job advertisements. Nothing jumped out at her. No positions that suited her skills. Friday was the best day, she comforted herself. Friday's papers always had pages of job adverts. She decided to go into town and get her hair done in Peter Mark's and came home feeling a bit more optimistic.

She made herself a cup of coffee and sat down to revamp her CV. That kept her going for most of the afternoon and she was feeling reasonably confident and cheerful until she started listing the names of her clients. Her pen hovered over the page as she went to write down Marcus Lynn's.

He'd really done the dirty on her. Why didn't he have the guts to tell her he was going to another PR? Instead he'd gone scuttling to Malachy behind her back. What did he think she was going to do the next time she saw him . . . *ravish* him! What a major let-down he'd been. Men! Who'd be bothered with them? Alexandra flung down her pen. She was really mad with Marcus. They'd always got on so well. She glanced at her watch. Four-thirty. On impulse she picked up the phone and dialled a number.

"Marcus Lynn, please," she said to the secretary. "It's Alexandra Johnston." Maybe he wouldn't take the call. Maybe he was a coward.

"Alexandra?" Marcus's baritone came down the line.

Alexandra took a deep breath. "Marcus, I would very much have appreciated it if you'd apprised me of the fact that you intended replacing me as your PR instead of going to Malachy behind my back. I worked hard for you. You owed me that much."

There was silence for a moment. It was obvious he was taken aback.

"I made a mistake, Marcus. I misread the situation. But I think the punishment was severe."

"Alexandra, whether you believe it or not, I was thinking of you as well as myself when I made the decision to replace you. I thought it might be embarrassing and uncomfortable for you to have to deal with me again. I thought it was the easiest thing to deal directly with Malachy. I didn't discuss the situation with him. I just said we'd had a difference of opinion about marketing strategy. It happens all the time," Marcus said firmly. "I'm sorry if you're upset."

"Not only am I upset, Marcus. I'm unemployed. Thanks to you."

"*What!* I don't believe it!" Marcus sounded genuinely shocked. "That's ridiculous. I didn't make a big deal of it. I'll speak to Malachy straight away. That's far too drastic. Nothing could have been further from my intentions. You must believe me, Alexandra."

"Well, I've burned my bridges there. Whether you phone Malachy or not, I won't be going back after what I said to that egotistical old coot. So don't bother. I expected better of you, Marcus, and that's the truth."

Alexandra put the phone down abruptly. She felt much better for getting that off her chest. Since she was burning bridges left, right and centre, she might as well burn one more. She rubbed her eyes tiredly. She'd had enough of writing her CV. She'd continue tomorrow. After all, what else had she to do?

The phone rang. Alexandra picked it up, expecting it to be Marcus with more abject apologies.

"Yes?" she said curtly.

Silence. But someone was at the other end. She could hear breathing.

"Yes?" she repeated.

The line went dead. A silent phone call. She'd been getting them ever since Chris had given Suzy the telephone number.

It had to be her. It was the type of neurotic, unpredictable behaviour she'd come to expect from her former friend.

"You're a fucking idiot, Suzy," she snarled as she slammed down the receiver. She felt like getting into her car and racing over to Suzy's and really letting her have it. It was bad enough getting the sack from work without having to put up with cowardly malicious phone calls as well.

She marched into the bathroom and ran a bath. Although he didn't know it yet, Chris was going to take her out somewhere posh for dinner. And he was paying. She was saving her pennies for a rainy day. And somehow she felt that day was coming sooner than she'd ever expected.

Chapter Twenty

"And they didn't look happy? Good. Were they arguing?" Suzy quizzed her informant keenly. This was music to her ears. A friend of hers, Lindsey Keating, had seen Chris and Alexandra having dinner together in a smart Italian restaurant the previous evening and had phoned Suzy first thing, to divulge the news.

"I couldn't hear, unfortunately," Lindsey was sorry that she couldn't be a bit more detailed in her reporting. "Alexandra hardly ate her food, she just kept pushing it around her plate."

"Hell! Maybe she's pregnant." Suzy felt sick with fear.

"Could you imagine Alexandra Johnston pregnant? Now that would be something. Imagine her two stone overweight and looking like a beached whale. Imagine her having to clean poohy botties and wash dirty nappies. Oh joy!" Lindsey was missing the point completely.

"I don't want her to be pregnant, Lindsey. That would mean they'd have a lifelong bond no matter what. I don't want that. I want them to split. I want them to detest each other again." She burst into tears.

"Oh dear," Lindsey murmured. She'd just put her size sevens right into it. "Well, if it's any comfort, Chris had a face like a funeral director. And they weren't lovey-dovey or anything," she added hastily.

"Were they holding hands?"

"Absolutely not. I was a bit surprised actually. I mean it's still early days for them as a couple. I would have thought they'd have been more affectionate."

"Lindsey, who's to say it's early days? They've known each other since before we were married. Alexandra was like a third partner in our marriage. Always interfering. Always trying to stir up trouble between me and Chris. Maybe she had her eye on him then. Maybe she's always had her eye on him. I don't know how long they've been messing about together."

"True. True. They're well suited, Suzy. Rotten liars, the pair of them. She was no friend to you and you deserve much better than Chris," Lindsey consoled. It was hard to know what was the right thing to say. Eggshell-walking was always difficult. Still, a bit of abuse directed at the errant partner and his mistress always went down well in these situations.

"What was she wearing?" Suzy sniffed, wiping her eyes on her sleeve.

"Oh it was – " Lindsey had been just about to describe Alexandra's black maxi-skirt and jade mandarin blouse in glowing terms – but it might not be what Suzy wanted to hear in the circumstances, so she toned down her description to suit the occasion – "it wasn't anything spectacular. Just a black maxi and a blouse."

"A maxi would look brilliant on her, she's so tall. I suppose it clung to every inch, knowing Alexandra. Has she put on weight or anything?"

"Nah, she's still the same."

"Did they see you?"

"Yep. Chris gave a half-hearted wave. He didn't come over. He'd know better, I'd say. He wouldn't get a friendly reception from me. I didn't wave back."

"Thanks, Lindsey." Her friend's support lifted Suzy's forlorn spirits.

"Well, I think he's a rat! If you're going to have an affair, at least don't have one with your wife's best friend. That's the lowest of the low. That's real sly." Lindsey couldn't hide her distaste.

"And you say he didn't look happy?"

"He definitely wasn't his usual effervescent self. He had his hangdog look. You know, *The-Weight-of-the-World-is-on-my-Shoulders* expression. I don't think she's good for him. When we were leaving, they were in the little bar at the front and I heard her telling him that his hair was too long and that he was to get it cut. She's very bossy, isn't she? You'd think she was his mother."

"Chris would enjoy that. He likes women telling him what to do. It means all their attention is focused on him. I used to have to do it all the time. He's like a child. And of course Alexandra adores telling people what to do."

"If I spoke to Michael like that, I'd be told where to get off pretty quickly, I can tell you. In fact, if I told my husband to get his hair cut, he'd freak," Lindsey observed.

"Yeah, well you're married to a *real* man, Lindsey, someone who can think for himself. Not a wimpy little Peter Pan who's never grown up." Suzy was bitter.

Lindsey burst out laughing.

"It's not funny, Lindsey."

"Sorry. Sorry, Suzy. It's just I have this vision of Chris, dressed in green tights and a little hat, prancing around the place. Peter Pan Wallace. I could imagine him in panto."

"And I could imagine Alexandra Johnston with warts on her nose flying her broomstick," Suzy snapped. "Anyway, Lindsey, thanks for phoning. I have to meet my darling husband at lunchtime to buy the children's Christmas presents. I haven't told him I'm spending Christmas at Niamh's. I'm not telling him where we're going. He walked out on us so he can just bugger off."

"It's tough on the kids though," Lindsey murmured.

"Well, life's tough, unfortunately, I'll let you know how things go."

"OK, pet. Talk to you soon."

Suzy replaced the receiver and hurried upstairs. Today she was going to look . . . *stunning* . . .

Emma was on top of the world. Mrs Munroe had upped and gone home. Whatever Tilly Doyle had said to her yesterday, she'd been like a cat on a griddle for the rest of the day. Then last night, she'd announced that she was going home in the morning. Mick was given his instructions to have the fire lit and to collect her after breakfast.

She was free again. She'd wanted to sing the Hallelujah chorus as Sheila departed, bag and baggage. She'd done her duty and been a good wife to Vincent. The ordeal was over. Now she could start enjoying the Christmas season. She was having lunch with the girls in town. She wouldn't have to feel guilty now, knowing that her mother-in-law would be waiting for her like a spider when she got back. There'd be no reproachful glances and murmurings that "Poor Andrew was fretting for you." It was like being out of jail.

Two hours later, dressed to kill, in a suede mini, matching fringed jacket over a black polo and black leather boots, she was sipping a pre-lunch Martini with the girls.

Gillian, Diana Mackenzie and Rhona Ryan were in great form. The gossip was flying.

"Did you see Belinda Power at Harriet Kennedy's hen-party? She was poured into the most hideous pink jersey mini. Her spare tyres would have kept Michelin in business for a year and talk about here's me bust and me arse is coming. I never saw anything like it. It was revolting. And Belinda actually thought she was the height of fashion. That girl thinks she's Sophia Loren. Doesn't she ever look in the mirror?" Rhona remarked bitingly.

She and Belinda didn't speak, after Belinda had made insulting remarks about Rhona's wedding, to someone who'd immediately repeated them back. Their friendship had ended and a feud had been born.

"Of course she does. She's so vain she used to have a mirror hidden in her maths book. That's why she got an F in her Leaving Cert. She was too busy studying herself. Pythagoras never got a look-in. *Mirror Mirror on the wall, who's the fairest one of all* . . . Certainly not Thunder-Thighs-Power," Emma declared.

The others laughed at this delicious piece of bitchery. Belinda Power was a wagon of the highest order. She'd been an awful lick at school, always toadying up to the nuns. She'd married a solicitor who was a big high-flyer and the competition between her and her classmates was fierce. The "outdoing stakes" were very high where Belinda was concerned.

Rhona turned to Emma. "Speaking of Harriet Kennedy, Emma. I believe she asked Suzy and Chris to the wedding and Suzy said they wouldn't be going, because Chris has left her and is living with Alexandra Johnston. Is it true?"

"*What!*" Diana and Gillian chorused.

Emma shifted uncomfortably in her chair. Rhona Ryan was a Nosy Parker. Trust her to bring up the subject of Chris.

"It's true," she admitted.

"You never told us," Gillian said indignantly. "He's having an affair with Alexandra Johnston. I thought she was Suzy's best friend. How horrible! Poor Suzy. How long has it been going on?"

"A while."

"But I didn't think they liked each other. They were always sparking off each other." Gillian was puzzled.

"I'd never mind that," Diana remarked. "Obviously a facade to throw people off the track. Mind, Chris used to be quite scathing about Alexandra. He'd go quite close to the bone sometimes."

"Is Suzy in bits?" Rhona asked sympathetically.

"I haven't really been talking to her," Emma murmured.

"And imagine he's moved in with Alexandra! That's very final, isn't it?"

"Hmm." Emma wished heartily that they'd change the subject.

"Did you hear that Anna McManus has split up with Gerard Butler? The engagement's all off," Diana announced obligingly.

"*What!*" More consternation.

The McManus-Butler wedding was to have been the event of the season.

Diana looked smug. She drew breath waiting to drop her next bombshell.

"Apparently she called unexpectedly one evening – she has a key to his flat – and found him dressed in ladies' underwear."

"I don't believe it!"

"You're not serious!"

"Cripes!"

This was a revelation to beat all revelations. They stared at Diana, stunned.

"But Gerard is six-foot four and he weighs at least sixteen stone. Have you ever seen him lumbering around the courts in his tennis shorts? Where would he get ladies' underwear to fit him? Was it bloomers?" Gillian was agog.

"No, it was suspenders and stockings and frilly panties and a bra, according to Anna," Diana explained helpfully.

"Uggg!" Emma winced. "What a horrible sight. Those white legs in stockings and suspenders. How revolting!" She gave a little shudder.

"He mustn't have a very big you-know-what, if he could fit into frilly knickers," Gillian observed as she took a slug of Campari. "Maybe Anna was saved from a life of frustration."

"Gillian!" Emma giggled.

"Oh dear, I'll never be able to look him in the eye again," Rhona snorted.

"He never looks people in the eye anyway. He's a bit shifty if you ask me. I wonder does he take a D cup or a C cup? He was probably Madam Nora's best customer," Diana grinned.

They all guffawed as they followed Gillian into the dining-room.

"It would have been a good wedding though," Emma remarked lightly. Now that the talk had turned away from Chris, she was enjoying herself immensely. But maybe, since the hotel wasn't far from his office, she might pop in before she went home and arrange a private lunch for the two of them before Christmas.

Suzy sipped a cup of coffee in Le Savoir Faire downstairs in Switzer's, where she'd arranged to meet Chris to do the Christmas shopping. She'd taken great care to look her best. A friend was minding the twins, so she'd had time to get her hair cut and highlighted. Her make-up was heavier than she normally wore but she'd needed to disguise the dark circles under her eyes. She'd lost weight in the past few weeks, but the smart, well-cut, cream and gold wool suit looked superb on her. She wasn't going to look like a wreck any more, she'd decided.

If Chris was wining and dining his mistress in public, it was obvious he didn't care who saw them. He was telling the world that he was with Alexandra. So with Alexandra he could stay. It was *really* rubbing her nose in it. He wasn't even trying to be discreet. Not like the Malones, a couple they knew who'd split up two years ago. Terry Malone lived with his mistress, but he was paranoid about anyone at work knowing. He carried on a ridiculous charade, pretending that he was still living with his wife and children. Anyway, Vivienne Malone was mad to put up with it, Suzy scowled. She even went to his office party with him so that they wouldn't guess at work. Suzy wouldn't be so facilitating, if Chris ever asked her to accompany him to a function. That was why she'd told Harriet Kennedy out straight that they wouldn't be going to her wedding. And she'd told a shocked Harriet the reason why. Chris had left her. He could take the consequences. She wasn't going to pretend everything was hunky-dory when it patently wasn't.

"Howya." A sullen voice intruded on her thoughts.

"Oh it's you, Chris," Suzy said tartly as she drained her cup and stood up. She slipped her sheepskin coat over her shoulders.

"I haven't had my lunch yet. I'm starving. What's the rush?" Chris sat down opposite her and looked around for a waitress.

"I'm in a hurry, Chris. I'm meeting someone later. I want to get the presents bought."

"Who are you meeting?" he asked grumpily.

"You don't know him," Suzy retorted snootily as she swept past him.

Chris's mouth opened and shut like a codfish.

"What do you mean, I don't know him?" he demanded.

"Chris, I don't have time to stand here discussing my personal life with you. Let's get the presents and get out of here." Suzy didn't wait for his response but walked on, head high.

Deal with that, buster, she thought triumphantly. The only way to handle Chris was to beat him at his own game. If he thought she was seeing someone else, he'd go mad. He'd have to know who it was. He couldn't bear the thought that she might get over him.

"Wait a minute, Suzy." Chris grabbed her arm. "Are you seeing someone?"

"Chris, I have no intention of discussing my private life with you. Just as I have no intention of sitting at home pining for you. I wouldn't have you back if you crawled on your hands and knees to me. Alexandra is welcome to you. I'm well rid of you. Now let's go and shop."

"Well, if you're seeing someone let him pay your bills, Suzy. And go and live with him." Chris was hopping mad.

"Nice try, Chris. But I'm staying put in my own home. And *you* will continue to support me, or I'll be taking that little trip to the tax inspectors."

"You're a vindictive bitch," Chris barked.

"No, *darling,* just fed up being a doormat," Suzy snarled. They entered the toy department in stony silence. Suzy led the way to the train sets. Adam had dictated his letter to Santa the previous evening and a train set was top of his list.

"You pick, you're the expert," Suzy ordered.

"Look, the least you can do is tell me where you're spending Christmas. Surely I can come and see the kids on Christmas Day," Chris raged.

"Absolutely not," Suzy said icily. "You made your choice, now live with the consequences. We won't be at home."

"You're depriving the children of a father, Suzy. You have no right to do that. You're putting your feelings before theirs. You're the one who's being totally selfish."

"Don't you dare lecture me, you shit. Don't you dare accuse me of being selfish," Suzy hissed, incensed. "You were never a father at the best of times anyway. I could count on the fingers of one hand the times you read them a bedtime story. When did you ever bring them to the park unless I nagged you? If they weren't in bed when you got home from work, you threw a mickey fit and moaned about their toys messing up the place. You didn't even come home for their birthday party, you were too busy entertaining a client. Or screwing Alexandra. So go fuck yourself, Chris, and stop being such an almighty hypocrite."

"Shut up! People are looking at us." Chris's face darkened with fury. He walked away. Suzy was shaking with rage. All her good intentions of staying cool, calm and collected had evaporated. She wanted to batter him. Only that she needed Chris to carry the heavy parcels to where her car was parked, she would have walked out and left him there.

She walked over to the rocking-horses and selected one of the more expensive models. Her kids might be deprived of a father but they were damn well going to have a decent Christmas present, she fumed.

Chris was reading the details on a train set when she went back to the display. "This one seems the best," he muttered.

"Fine. I've picked the rocking-horse, let's pay and get out of here."

"I hope *you're* paying, Suzy. God knows I'm giving you a big enough allowance as it is," Chris said indignantly.

"Oh, don't be such a cheapskate, Chris. If there's one thing I really detest in a man, it's meanness. I bet you'll be buying Alexandra something tasty from Weir's," Suzy spat. "So you can damn well pay for your kids' Christmas presents. Remember, you won't have to buy me one this year. That will save you a fiver at least."

"Oh yeah! They're my kids when it suits you. Well, if I'm paying for their Christmas presents I want to see them opening them."

"You can piss off, Chris. I'll pay for them myself."

"Right! I will. If that's the way you want it." Rigid with fury, Chris stalked out of the shop.

Suzy, bursting with hatred, watched him go. How typical of him to use his children as a weapon. How typical of him to kid himself that he was a kind and caring father. And then when she didn't submit to his blackmail, to drop the whole pretence and leave her to pay for the presents. Well, whatever chance he'd had of seeing them over Christmas, he'd none after this. And if one more person stuck their noses in and said the kids shouldn't be deprived of their father, and that she should put them first, she'd swing for them.

"Do you think it's fair, Emma? I mean they *are* my kids. I'm their father." Chris's blue eyes flashed with anger. He was sitting in his office with Emma. Her unexpected arrival had found him pacing up and down in a fury. She'd made him sit down and tell her what was wrong. It had all erupted out of him. "She can't dictate to me like that. I'm *entitled* to see them, Emma. They're my flesh and blood too."

"I know they are," Emma soothed. "It's just I'd imagine that Suzy's feeling a bit raw at the moment. You have to give these things time."

"Yes but it's Christmas. And she's behaving like a spiteful cat. You wouldn't believe it, Emma. You wouldn't believe what she's capable of."

"What on earth did you have to get involved with Alexandra Johnston for? Of all people? Honestly, Chris, you couldn't have picked anyone worse if you'd tried. Are you happy with her?"

"She's OK," Chris said sulkily. "But she lost clients at work because Suzy's been such a bitch. And now they've given her the boot. I can't afford to support her *and* Suzy. My life is an absolute mess."

"Oh Lord! What's she going to do?"

"I don't know. But she better do something quick. That apartment costs a bomb. Why the hell couldn't Suzy keep her big mouth shut? It's nobody's business except ours."

"So what are you going to do for Christmas?" Emma asked sympathetically.

"Damned if I know. I suppose I'll be stuck in the apartment with Alexandra. She'll hardly go to London now. She won't be able to afford it." He thought of something. "Emma, listen," he said urgently. "How about if you phoned Suzy and had a girlie talk with her. She's seeing someone else. I want to find out who it is. And you could find out where she's going for Christmas for me. She wouldn't tell me."

"She's seeing someone else? How do you know that?" Emma was amazed.

"She told me! How do you like that? She told me she was in a hurry because she was meeting someone. A man. And she has the cheek to lecture me. Will you phone her?"

Emma made a face. "I don't think she'd tell me anything. She knows we're pals, Chris. I wonder who she's seeing?"

"Yeah! It's sickening, isn't it? If you hear anything let me know."

"Well, you should know that it's all over town about you and Alexandra – and it wasn't me gossiping."

"I couldn't care less, Emma. To hell with the lot of them. The stories I could tell you about who's having affairs. Everyone's at it. I just got caught."

"Did you hear about Anna McManus and Gerard Butler?"

"That moron. He chickened out of a deal with me. Lost his nerve. He'd have made a packet too. He's all talk and no action. What's he up to?" Chris scowled.

"He likes dressing up in suspenders and bras and frilly knickers. The engagement's off."

"You're *kidding*!"

"Nope! Sad but true!" Emma grinned.

"Well, that will knock me and Alexandra off the number one gossip spot," Chris said dryly. "I wonder if he wears them to the rugby matches. He's such a big bloke. The mind boggles, doesn't it? That's his reputation down the Swanee. He'll lose clients quicker than Alexandra did, when that gets around. Poor sod. He won't have much of a Christmas either."

"I'm sorry for you, Chris, I really am." Emma reached out and squeezed his hand.

"How's Ellen?" Chris asked.

"She's fine. Her cafe's doing a roaring trade," Emma said lightly.

"Is she still seeing that bearded bogman?"

"Chris! Don't be like that. He's a decent chap. He's done an awful lot of work for Ellen."

"Well, she must be hard up. That's all I can say."

"Look, how about if I take you to a slap-up lunch some day over Christmas?" Emma changed the subject.

"Thanks, Ems. You're my only pal," Chris said gratefully. "I'd like that."

"Well, I'll phone you and we'll arrange it. OK?"

"OK. Where are you off to now?"

"I'm meeting Vincent. We're going Christmas shopping together. Then we're going to the pictures. Then we're going to have dinner in the Russell," Emma said happily.

"You're a lucky little sod, you know. Haven't you *ever* been tempted to have a fling? Haven't you ever fancied another bloke?" Chris was curious.

Emma shook her head. "No. Vincent's all I ever wanted. I love him."

"No one's ever really loved me," Chris said sadly. "I'm an outcast."

"Darling, stop feeling sorry for yourself. It's all your own doing. Now be a good boy and eat your greens and I'll talk to you soon." Emma kissed him lightly on the forehead, waved and sashayed out of the office in high spirits.

Chris watched her go and couldn't help but smile. Emma was one of a kind. And she'd always had a soft spot for him. He sighed. It was depressing listening to everyone making plans for Christmas. Suzy had really taken the wind out of his sails today. She'd looked extremely well. Much better than the last few times he'd seen her, when she'd looked very haggard. The new hairstyle took years off her. Who the hell was she seeing? It was a bit bloody much all the same. It hadn't taken her long to get over him, he thought sulkily.

He was in a right pickle now. Suzy had a new suitor and he was stuck with Alexandra. His whole life had gone belly-up. And there wasn't a damn thing he could do about it.

<hr />

"Of course I'm going to London for Christmas, Chris. I always do. I need a break. I'm damned if I'm going to stay here in Dublin and have little ninnies pointing their fingers at me as if I was some horned Jezebel or something." Alexandra lay sprawled on the sofa sipping gin.

"But what about me?" Chris demanded. "I don't want to stay here by myself."

"Darling, we all have our problems, you'll just have to cope."

"But how the hell can you afford to go to London? You haven't got a job."

"Thanks to your spiteful cow of a wife. Look, Chris, I'm not staying here. I've had enough of Dublin and its petty busybody gossips to last me a lifetime. I'm going to London for Christmas. It's arranged. And then I'm going to come back and get a job. By God, I'll show those bastards that I'm the best in the business. So for once, my egotistical darling, this is not about your feelings and needs, it's about mine and if you don't like it, tough!" Alexandra glared at him.

"You call *me* egotistical. You could give master classes. Women! You're all the bloody same," Chris snarled as he slammed the door after him and went to bed.

Alexandra watched him go. She was really getting fed up with him. Why she'd ever been mad enough to start a fling with him, she'd never understand. If only she didn't need his rent money. God, she was really looking forward to London. She'd decided to stick to her original plans even though it would eat into her nest-egg. She couldn't face the idea of having all the movers and shakers around town knowing that she'd been given the boot from Stuart and Stuart's. If only she could get a backer to set her up in her own company. But who?

Maybe she'd find someone in London. She was going to go to as many smart parties as she possibly could while she was there. Fortunately her friends were well connected. It was too good a chance to miss. Chris could go stuff himself. He wasn't being a bit supportive. She should have known better than to expect anything more of him. Suzy was welcome to him. Alexandra had other concerns. She had her future to worry about.

Chapter Twenty-One

"Welcome back, Sheila. We certainly weren't expecting to see you at the meeting tonight. Are you sure you're up to it?" Bridget Curran greeted Sheila warmly.

"I've been away too long, Bridget. I feel very bad about it. But I'm back now, thank God." Sheila took her place at the top of the table. In the president's chair.

"You gave us an awful fright," Molly Ryan remarked.

"I gave myself an awful fright," Sheila retorted crisply. It was nice to be back in her rightful position. Just as it had been very nice last night to sleep in her own comfortable bed with Mick's arm around her. There really was no place like home.

She noted that Bonnie Daly looked quite miffed to see her. It gave her immense satisfaction to be back in control of the guild. Madam Bonnie could take a back seat again.

"And how are the ribs and the wrist and the bruises?" Bridget inquired kindly.

"Well, as you can see, my wrist is still bandaged for support, you know. The ribs are healing slowly but surely. I stayed with Emma and Vincent for a few days to recuperate. They all wanted me to stay with them of course. I've been blessed with good children, but with Ellen and Miriam tied up with the cafe, I decided to go to Vincent and Emma. And I was treated like a

271

queen." This was said loudly enough for Bonnie to hear. Bonnie's children were not the support they should be to her in her old age.

"Was Tilly telling you that some of us thought it might be a good idea to have our guild lunch in Ellen's cafe this year, rather than in the Glenree Arms?" said Bridget. "It would be a nice gesture of goodwill."

"It's very kind of you. I know they're run off their feet." Sheila wasn't going to have the guild thinking that Ellen was on her bended knees waiting for their custom. "We can certainly discuss it at the meeting and if it's a majority decision I can ask Ellen to book us in."

"I don't think it's actually on the agenda for discussion tonight. Just let me check," Bonnie piped up sweetly. As secretary, she controlled the agenda. She scanned her notepad. "No, no, we have five items for discussion. The Christmas lunch isn't one of them."

"For goodness sake, Bonnie! If we don't decide where to go tonight it will be too late. And when, may I ask, have we ever put it officially on the agenda? Stop your nonsense," Bridget said briskly.

"Well now, Bridget, I don't care for your tone. We have to keep some control over what's discussed or, as you well know, we'd get nothing done. And if you don't like the way *I'm* running the meetings, you go for secretary next year," Bonnie bristled.

Sheila's lips thinned. Who did Bonnie Daly think she was, to be talking about *running* the meetings? As secretary, she was answerable to the president, Sheila. It was the president who ran the whole organisation. Responsibility for running the guild rested on her capable shoulders and no one else's, for this term.

"I think, Madam Secretary, I'll call this meeting to order. Time is getting on. We'll discuss the matter of our Christmas lunch after all *official* business has been discussed. If you'd kindly say the opening prayer and read out last week's minutes." Sheila gave Bonnie her sweetest smile.

Bonnie, raging, smiled back, equally insincerely. "Certainly, Madam President. Our prayers for your full recovery must have been granted. Obviously Saint Peter felt heaven wasn't ready for you yet. He blessed *us* with your presence instead."

"Indeed he did, Bonnie. What a kind thing to say." Sheila pretended that the sly and very sarcastic dig had gone completely over her head. "Now let's get down to business or, as you'd say yourself, we'll get nothing done."

That will teach you to try and get the better of me, she thought grimly as Bonnie, utterly discomfited, stood up and called on the Lord to bless the Women's Guild of Glenree.

"Ellen, you know full well I'd be very happy to come over to you for Christmas. But you know your mother. She's funny about these things," Mick explained.

Ellen polished the candlestick she was holding with extra vigour. She'd slipped over after work to clean the silver and the brasses and to dust the ornaments that lay in the big glass-fronted unit in Sheila's parlour. Miriam was minding Stephanie for her. She hadn't realised that her mother had gone to a meeting.

"But sure, Ellen, I can look after everything here. Don't you worry. I know you'd like to spend Christmas in your own place," Mick added kindly.

"Dad! I'm not leaving you to cook a Christmas dinner on your own. Stephanie and I'll come over on Christmas Eve and stay until the day after Stephen's Day."

"I'd be lost without you, Ellen." Mick smiled at her.

"And I'd be lost without you." She patted her father companionably on the arm. "I was surprised Mam went off to the meeting. I didn't think she'd be up to it."

"I'm delighted she went." Mick puffed contentedly on his pipe. "If your mother didn't go to her meetings then I'd be worried. Seemingly Bonnie was getting notions above her station. Your mother'll be nipping that firmly in the bud."

Ellen grinned. "I'd say it will be a lively meeting. There'll be skin and hair flying – in the nicest possible way of course. Mother, being president, will win hands down."

"Oh, Bonnie won't go down without a fight. I'll be getting an earful tonight no doubt." Mick chuckled. "I'll tell you what, I'll stick the kettle on and we'll have a nice cup of tea for ourselves."

"Good thinking," Ellen approved as she gave the candlestick a final rub. If there was one thing she hated, it was doing the brasses and silverware. But her mother wasn't able to manage and Ellen knew she liked to give the house a thorough cleaning before Christmas. She'd do the net curtains for her tomorrow, and that would be that much done.

She was tired though. When she was finished in Sheila's she had a pile of table napkins to iron at home and a batch of stuffing to prepare for the stuffed rashers, one of the most popular dishes on their menu. Her own flat would have to do with a lick and a polish for Christmas, she thought ruefully. Still, she was looking forward to the weekend. Doug was bringing a Christmas tree and she and Stephanie were going to help decorate it. Stephanie was bursting with anticipation.

The days were really flying. Running a deli was hard work. But very satisfying. She and Miriam and Denise got on extremely well. They were a good team.

An hour later, the glass doors of the china cabinet sparkled, displaying an array of gleaming silver, brasses and china. Even Sheila wouldn't be able to find fault with them.

Ellen took the net curtains down from the windows and folded them neatly. She could wash them first thing in the morning, before The Deli opened, and pop over with them in the afternoon. She went from room to room collecting the curtains. Fortunately Sheila, being the extremely efficient housewife that she was, had a small stitch of different-coloured thread sewn on to the top corner of each curtain, so there'd be no mix-up. She must do the same with her own sometime, Ellen decided.

"Right, Dad! I'm off. What time are you collecting Mam?"

"I'll give her another half-hour. You know the way they all like to chat after the business is over." Mick lifted his head from the basin of cranberries he was preparing. Sheila liked to make her own cranberry sauce for Christmas. Because of her wrist, he'd decided to get them ready as a little surprise for her.

"I'll see you tomorrow, then." Ellen gave him a kiss. Sometimes she wondered if Sheila realised how lucky she was to have a husband like Mick. Out of the blue, Chris came to mind. Was he up to his eyes in Christmas preparations at home with his children? She couldn't quite imagine him decorating a Christmas tree or hanging up chains and balloons. When they'd been together he rarely spoke about his children. Sometimes she sensed that it wouldn't have mattered to him at all if he'd never had any. One thing was for sure, he'd never be caught dead at a kitchen sink preparing cranberries to help his wife.

But Doug would. She smiled to herself. There were a lot of similarities between Doug and Mick. It was funny, she'd never realised that until now. "See ya, Dad."

She looked at her father, standing in his slippers, his pipe sticking out of the corner of his old cardigan pocket as he topped and tailed the cranberries, and felt a huge rush of affection for him. His quiet, unwavering support had been the one constant in her life. God had blessed her with the father she'd been given. She sent up a little prayer of thanks and entreaty that he'd have many happy fruitful years ahead of him. If anything ever happened to Mick, she'd be lost.

Katherine neatly wrapped shiny Santa paper around the box containing Stephanie's tea set. She took a strip of sellotape and sealed the sharply pointed ends. Katherine took pride in wrapping her parcels. Untidy wrapping was anathema to her. Her presents were noted for crisp expensive wrapping-paper and starched ribbons. Not for her the wafer-thin paper sold in sheets by the street sellers.

She surveyed the large colourful parcel with pleasure. The more she thought about it, the more she knew she'd done the right thing, buying her newly acquired granddaughter a Christmas present. Stephanie's father might have disowned her, her grandmother wouldn't.

She hoped that Ellen wouldn't mind. She would perfectly understand if the younger woman wanted to keep her distance. But somehow, after that brief but highly charged meeting at the christening, Katherine felt at ease with Ellen. She didn't think her gesture would be rejected. She lifted up the phone and dialled Emma's number.

"Hello?" Her niece's pert tones made Katherine smile. Emma was such a consequence.

"Emma," she said briskly. "Aunt Katherine. I need Ellen Munroe's telephone number. I have a Christmas present for Stephanie. I'd like to make the arrangements to give it to her."

"Oh!" Katherine heard the surprise in Emma's voice. Let Emma and anyone else be surprised, shocked or dismayed, if they cared to. This was something she had to do.

"Just a minute, Aunt Katherine." Katherine could hear the flicking of pages. Emma called out the number. Katherine took it down in her elegant neat script.

"Thank you, dear. I hope you're all keeping well. No doubt we'll see you over the Christmas with the children. I'll be having a family get-together as usual. I'll be in touch to make arrangements."

"Right. Thanks. Thanks very much, Aunt Katherine." Emma was polite. Katherine smiled wryly as she hung up. That had certainly taken the wind out of her niece's sails. But she didn't care any more. She'd spent far too long hiding behind a facade. From now on she was going to do what felt right for her and if people didn't like it that was their problem. Katherine squared her shoulders. It was a good feeling to think that she was coming to a stage in her life when she didn't care what people thought. She'd lived under that cloud for so long, burying all her resentment and anger at Jeffrey's womanising. Holding her head up among friends and acquaintances, pretending to the world that everything was all right. Denying her true feelings. She might have protected Jeffrey and the family name but she'd been very cruel to herself, she thought fiercely.

No more. Her feelings were as important as anyone else's. It had been a long hard lesson. But she was learning. And somehow she knew that her little grandchild was going to be very important to her. They would teach each other.

"Hello?" Ellen tried to stifle a yawn. It was after ten. She'd already spoken to Doug. She wondered who this could be.

"Ellen. It's Katherine Wallace. I hope you don't think I'm taking a liberty. I phoned Emma for your number. My dear, I bought a little gift for Stephanie for Christmas. I was hoping you might come over for tea some afternoon over Christmas. Of course if you would prefer not to, I quite understand."

"Oh!" Ellen's eyes widened.

"Well, maybe you might prefer to keep your distance." Katherine sounded surprisingly disappointed.

"Not at all, Mrs Wallace. It's very kind of you. I know Stephanie would be delighted."

"Would she?" The older woman sounded as though she was smiling. Ellen's heart softened. Poor Katherine. She'd had her troubles too. It was Ellen's impression from their brief encounter that she was quite lonely, despite the busy social life she led. It was thoughtful of her to buy a present for Stephanie. She wasn't going to deprive Chris's mother of the pleasure of giving a present.

"She's actually making a card for you in school at the moment. They're all doing them for their parents and grandparents."

"How lovely," Katherine sounded genuinely pleased. "Well, instead of posting it, get her to hand-deliver it. Shall I phone next week to make arrangements?"

"That would be really nice, Mrs Wallace. If you're sure you want to."

"I am, dear. Very sure. What's her favourite food?"

Ellen laughed. "Sausage and chips."

"Sausage and chips it is, then. I'd rather fancy them myself. It's a long time since I cooked chips. I'll look forward to it. I'd like to give you my number."

"I have a pen." Ellen took the number down.

"Thank you, Ellen. You're very kind."

"You're welcome, Mrs Wallace," Ellen said warmly. "Take care." She replaced the receiver, smiling. What a nice thing to happen! Stephanie would be thrilled. She'd gone to a lot of trouble making her Christmas cards and she'd confided that the one she was making for "the new nannie" had to be extra-special because it was the first card she'd ever done for her. She was one up on Rebecca and Connie because they only had one nana and now she had two.

Katherine had seemed to genuinely want to have her and Stephanie visit. Ellen didn't mind. Having met her at the christening, Ellen was not in awe of her. Ironic though it was, they had much in common. It would be good for Stephanie to have some contact with her father's side of the family. It might help to lessen the sense of abandonment she'd feel when she was older. When she realised that her father had let her down.

Perhaps she might have some contact with Chris, through Katherine. If that was what she wanted. Ellen picked up the iron and pressed it against a creased napkin. Who would have thought that Chris's mother would want to stay in contact? What would Chris think of that? Ellen wondered curiously. Or would he ever know?

"You've invited them to visit? And Ellen agreed to come?" Chris was stunned. He'd called in to his mother's to explain that Suzy was taking the children away for Christmas, so if she wanted to see them, she'd need to arrange it soon. He'd idly picked up a large parcel that was lying on the sofa and seen that it was addressed to Stephanie. Then Katherine had dropped her bombshell. She'd invited Ellen and Stephanie to tea.

"She was rather sweet about it, actually, Christopher," Katherine remarked as she snipped the end of a length of ribbon.

"But why on earth do you want to bring them here?" Chris muttered.

Katherine fixed her son with a piercing stare. "The child is my granddaughter. I want to get to know her. I won't turn my back on her, like you did."

"You should let sleeping dogs lie," he argued.

"I did that for far too long, Christopher. And it made me a very unhappy woman," his mother retorted. "This time I'm doing what *I* want to do. I think Stephanie and I will both benefit from getting to know each other."

"Don't you think it might be awkward for me?" Chris was most perturbed to think that his feelings hadn't even been considered.

"I might have had second thoughts if you were still with Suzy. And I would have been more concerned about her feelings than yours, quite frankly. But the truth is, I don't care any more if it's awkward for you. You have to handle that. And besides it's not as though I'm inviting *you* to tea. It's just Stephanie, Ellen and myself. So really I can't see why you're making all this fuss."

"No one gives a toss about my feelings," Chris exploded. "Suzy's taking the kids away. Alexandra's going to London. You're having Ellen to tea. What about me? Who gives a damn about me?"

"Don't use vile language, Christopher. I can certainly understand how Suzy feels. I wish I had been as strong when I was in her position. I've no sympathy for you there at all. And as for that Johnston hussy, I hope she stays in London. She'll certainly never set foot in my house – "

"But don't you understand my feelings at all, Mother?" he interrupted angrily. "I've been deserted by everyone."

"Christopher, you brought it all on yourself. When you treat people badly, you can expect to be treated badly. You ran away from your responsibilities towards Ellen and Stephanie. You ran away from your responsibilities towards Suzy and the twins – "

"I'm sick of this. I didn't come here for a lecture. And it's a bit late now to be telling me about my faults and failings. If you'd been a better mother, all this mightn't have happened. If you'd made my father happy, he'd have stayed at home. So don't *you* tell me about *my* shortcomings." Chris picked up his car keys and marched to the lounge door. He didn't care if his harsh words hurt his mother. She'd hurt him!

Katherine looked at him sadly. "They say the truth always hurts, Christopher. You and I have to live with that."

"I'll be talking to you," he growled and closed the door behind him, sorry that he'd called.

He drove off in a temper. He didn't want to go back to the apartment. Alexandra was like an antichrist. She was coming up to her period. He'd get no good out of her for the next few days. There was no point in going home. Suzy wouldn't want to see him. Where could he go? Who could he turn to who would understand his unhappiness?

He thought of Ellen. How he longed to drive to Glenree and feel her arms wrapped around him in welcome! What comfort she had always given him! What love and warmth and joy! But what if he called and she shut the door in his face? What if he called and the Neanderthal was there? He couldn't depend on Ellen any more either.

He drove towards Donnybrook. He'd stop in Kiely's and have a pint.

The place was packed. Standing room only. Bad move, he thought glumly as he queued for a drink.

"Chris? How are you?" a familiar voice roared in his ear.

Chris's heart sank. Not Big-Deal-O'Hara.

"Wait until I tell you about the deal I've just closed. The biggest deal ever," Lorcan O'Hara boasted. "Here, let me buy you a brandy. It's a night for celebration. You'll never hear tell of a better deal than this."

For the next hour Chris listened, bored out of his skull, as Lorcan told him in minute detail of a deal he'd just concluded, selling tape recorders. Lorcan hadn't earned the title *Big Deal* for nothing. Because when Lorcan did business, everyone knew about it.

"I think you should consider upping your life insurance," Chris interjected wearily as Big Deal paused for breath. He figured he might as well try and sell a bit of insurance while he was stuck here.

"Ah! I could be dead in the morning. Why would I leave the old bag a bigger fortune than what she's got?" Lorcan laughed.

"Well, apart from your pension, just say you were in an accident. Say you had a stroke and you were disabled. You'd want to have a lifestyle comparable to the one you have now," Chris urged.

"Well now, I'll think about it," Lorcan promised.

"You said that the last time we met. You know, Lorcan, now's the time to be saving for the rainy day. Now, when the money's coming in."

"You know, you'd sell ice to the Eskimos, Chris. No wonder they say you're one of the best in town. Raise my premiums by another one per cent. I'll sign the papers the next time I'm in your neck of the woods."

"Two per cent," Chris pressed.

"Go away out of that. If I was to up my premiums by two per cent, I'd have no standard of life *now*."

Chris laughed. He knew there was no point in arguing. Better one per cent than none.

He drove back to the apartment hoping that Alexandra had gone to bed. All he wanted to do was flop.

His mistress was out. Her car wasn't in the car park and there were no lights on in the apartment. She hadn't even told him that she was going out, he scowled, as he let himself into the dark hallway.

He shrugged out of his coat and stood, undecided whether to sit and watch some TV or go to bed. It was after half eleven and he was tired. Bed was his best option tonight. Ten minutes later he lay in his cold lonely bed. There was no point staying awake for Alexandra. He couldn't get into her bed just for a cuddle. She wasn't the cuddly sort. He remembered how nice it had been snuggling up with Ellen. Sadness swept over him. He missed her. Imagine his mother inviting her to tea. Obviously she liked Ellen. She must do or she'd never invite her to the house.

A thought struck him and his eyes opened wide in the dark. Of course . . . The answer to all his problems . . . Who said life didn't have happy endings? Chris smiled. What a brainwave. It was so simple. So perfect. It was time to put his misery behind him. He knew *exactly* what he was going to do.

Chapter Twenty-Two

"Now, Ellen, don't let me down. There's twenty of us coming next Monday, not eighteen as originally planned. And remember, Bonnie will be looking for something to moan about. Don't give her the opportunity," Sheila instructed down the phone.

Ellen gritted her teeth. "Mam, if you'd prefer to go to the Glenree Arms it's quite all right with me."

"No! No! We want to come. It was a fair vote. Most of the committee were in favour. And I, to remain impartial, abstained. So Madam Daly can't say it was my vote that swung it. Now will I get your father to make the brandy butter? You know there's no one like him for making brandy butter. And then we can keep some of it for ourselves."

"Right, Mam."

"I've told your father to give you the best turkey and ham in the shop for the luncheon. It *will* be Miriam who's cooking it, won't it? You know the way you're inclined to let things overcook, although you're not bad at making the stuffing."

"Mother, I have to go. I need to get organised. The teachers are coming in after school for a Christmas dinner," Ellen said impatiently.

"Oh, we're not the only group having a Christmas do then?" Sheila sounded surprised.

"No, Mother, you're not. I'll start organising yours now." She clattered the phone down. She was fit to be tied. It was the Friday before Christmas week. They were up to their eyes, and the guild lunch was causing more trouble than it was worth. This was the third phone call she'd had from Sheila about it. There'd be more. She was half-sorry the guild hadn't voted for the Glenree Arms. Ellen could understand her mother's anxiety. Bonnie Daly and her friends would never let it pass if anything went wrong with the meal.

She was getting a headache thinking about the damned thing.

"You've to cook the turkey. Mother's instructions. I overcook things, if you don't mind," she informed Miriam.

Miriam laughed. "Stay calm, Ellen. There's three of us. We'll be fine."

"I think we need someone to help out," Ellen fretted. "Or should we just close for the duration of the lunch?"

"I don't think so," Denise chipped in. "If we put them all out of harm's way upstairs, we can keep downstairs free for our regulars. We could get Maria Walsh in to clear tables and wash the dishes."

"Right. What will we give them for starters?"

"Melon?" Miriam suggested.

"Bit boring."

"Prawn cocktail?" Denise ventured.

"Oh yeah. That always looks good. And it's nice and light."

"What soup?" Miriam asked.

"Pepper and garlic." Ellen grinned. "That would shut them up. Our cream of potato and carrot will do fine. Then turkey, ham, roast and cream potatoes, carrots, peas, celery and Brussels sprouts, with cranberry sauce and gravy."

"I'm hungry already." Denise popped a piece of raw carrot into her mouth and crunched on it.

"Plum pudding and brandy butter or trifle for dessert," Miriam rounded off the menu. "You'd better go shopping, Ellen."

"I could get a dozen bottles of wine, I suppose, in case any of them want it. You know how Lizzie Regan likes her drop. We could give it to them on the house. And a sherry before lunch," Ellen mused.

"We'll have Bonnie singing her silly little head off before she knows it." Denise's eyes gleamed with anticipation.

"That's that arranged then." Ellen gave a sigh of relief and went off to write out a shopping-list.

The minute he saw it, Doug knew it was the Christmas present he wanted to buy Ellen. It was a gold filigree chain with an exquisite cross hanging from it. The cross was set with tiny diamonds, which sparkled under the spotlight in the jeweller's display cabinet.

"I'll take that one, please." He pointed it out to the assistant. He watched as the young girl carefully laid it on a bed of black velvet in a long slender box. He was delighted with himself. Every time he came into town he'd been on the lookout for something special. Now he'd found it.

A small gold bracelet with a single charm caught his eye. The charm was a tiny kitten. Stephanie would love that, he thought. He could buy her a new charm every Christmas. It would be a special thing between them.

He'd already bought her a set of Spirograph. Stephanie was very creative and artistic. She spent hours colouring and drawing. He had the cards to prove it. She'd enjoy experimenting with all the designs.

He asked the assistant to wrap the bracelet for him and paid for his purchases with a happy heart. It would be a great Christmas. They were going to decorate the tree in Ellen's flat tomorrow night. He was really looking forward to it.

It was almost like having a family of his own. Maybe soon, they *would* be his family. He was going to ask Ellen to marry him. It was what he wanted more than anything. He was going to ask her on New Year's Eve. The beginning of the new decade. And the beginning of a new life for them. And he wasn't going to entertain any negative thoughts that she'd say no. They were meant to be together. He was certain of that.

He studied the engagement rings. Some of them were beauties. They'd look lovely on Ellen's slender finger. He was tempted to buy one there and then, but he hesitated. Just say she didn't like the one he picked? She was going to have to wear it for the rest of her life. She should be the one to choose. They could choose it together. Whistling, Doug strode down Grafton Street. New Year's Eve couldn't come soon enough for him.

"Alexandra!" Marcus Lynn's unmistakable deep voice at the other end of the phone gave Alexandra a start.

"Yes, Marcus?" She didn't let on she was surprised to hear from him. How on earth had he got her number?

"I insisted Malachy give me your number. He was most reluctant to." Marcus must have known what she was thinking. He sounded wryly amused. "I gather you left poor Mal with a rather large flea in his ear."

"Huh!" Alexandra snorted. "He can dish it out but he can't take it. And they're the worst sort, believe me. Now, Marcus, I'm sure you're not phoning me to discuss that conceited old windbag. I'm busy," she said curtly.

"I'm sure you are." Marcus cleared his throat. "Look, I feel bad about you getting the boot. I didn't think there'd be repercussions like that."

"Well, there were, and there's nothing you can do about it now," Alexandra retorted with an edge to her voice. What the hell was Marcus annoying her for? He was hardly going to ask her for a *date*!

"Well, actually there is something that I can and have done, if you don't mind my taking the liberty."

"Oh!" Her voice took on a friendlier tone.

"You know Arthur Reynolds, the property tycoon?"

"Yes," Alexandra said cautiously. Arthur Reynolds was a multi-millionaire who led a jet-setting lifestyle. He'd been the number one client at Weldon's, her former company. He had a finger in plenty of pies. Property, supermarkets, magazine publishing. He was only forty *and* he was unmarried. *And* he was even better-looking than Marcus.

"He's a friend of mine."

He would be, Alexandra thought ruefully.

"So?"

"He's leaving Weldon's. They sent him a bill that was way over the top just because of who he is. He wasn't impressed. They backed down immediately, once he queried it, and they couldn't have been nicer but they picked the wrong man to try and screw. That's why Arthur's a multi-millionaire. He doesn't let people take advantage."

"The bloody idiots," Alexandra snorted. "They get so greedy and start ripping people off. There are some people you can rip off, Marcus, and some you can't. The secret is knowing who to do it to. They should have kept him so sweet. They'll never get a client as big as that again."

"Malachy's got wind of it. He's sniffing around."

"Oh, he would. He's got a nose like a bloodhound. He looks a bit like a bloodhound too, actually, with those hanging jowls," Alexandra said viciously. She would never forgive Malachy for being so spineless. "I bet Stingy-Arse-Evans is wetting himself with excitement at the thoughts of nabbing Big-Cheese-Reynolds."

"That's what I like about you, Alexandra," Marcus laughed. "You have such a *unique* way of putting things."

"Why are you telling me all of this, Marcus?" Alexandra asked tetchily.

"I'm telling you because he's considering taking on a PR to work exclusively for him as another option."

Alexandra sat bolt upright in the armchair she'd been lounging in.

"He's looking for a PR?"

"As I say, it's one of the options he's considering. Are you interested?"

"Don't ask daft questions, Marcus!"

"Right. I'll get on to his secretary and get her to call you right away to arrange a meeting. He's impressed with what you've done for me. I told him you'd left Stuart and Stuart's because of professional differences. I implied that they wouldn't give you a decent budget. That will cover the reasons for your leaving."

"You didn't have to do any of this. So why did you?" Alexandra was curious.

"No, I didn't have to do it. But I didn't mean you to get the sack. Professionally you're a great PR. There's just one thing I should warn you about." Marcus hesitated.

"Spit it out, Marcus. Is he in a committed relationship? Is that what you're trying to say?" she asked dryly. "Don't worry. I've learned my lesson there."

"Actually you're barking up the wrong tree. Despite public appearances, Arthur is . . . er . . . let me put it this way, he's not really a ladies' man."

"What do you mean?" Alexandra was mystified.

"Oh, Alexandra, use your intelligence. All those flashy blondes. Relationships that never last. All those pictures in the society pages. Lives at home alone . . . do I have to spell it out?"

"Good heavens." Alexandra's eyes widened. "But he's so gorgeous-looking. He's a fine thing. Are you certain?"

"Alexandra, you'll be wasting your time, so don't even consider it. And keep it strictly to yourself. This is completely off the record. Now will I get his secretary to call you or not?"

"Why not?" Alexandra didn't give a hoot if Arthur liked to dance around his mansion in pink tutus waving an umbrella. His personal life was his own business. As long as he kept it out of the papers. But he was one of the last men in the world she would have thought homosexual. She had no problem with that. To each his own was Alexandra's motto.

Her eyes sparkled. Just think of the money she'd have to spend. Ron Evans would go into a decline at the thought of it. And imagine snaffling a client of Arthur Reynolds's calibre from under

Malachy's greedy little snout. How delicious! How absolutely divine!

"Good luck then. No hard feelings?" Marcus was as straight as a die.

"None! Thanks, Marcus." Alexandra hung up first. She stood up out of the chair and did a twirl. This was the biggest opportunity that had ever presented itself to her. She had to get the job, she just *had* to.

She waited by the phone, willing it to ring, and when it did she almost jumped out of her skin.

"Miss Johnston? Arthur Reynolds's secretary. Mr Reynolds would like to arrange a business meeting with you before he goes skiing for New Year. How does the twenty-ninth of December suit?"

"Just a moment." Alexandra pretended to check through her diary. Normally she'd make them change the date. No point in letting them think she was too eager. But if Arthur was going skiing, she wanted to be in the ring good and early. Malachy would be like a terrier with a bone if he thought there was a chance of nabbing Arthur Reynolds. Over her dead body. Malachy thought she was on the floor. Ha! She'd show those shits. She'd go from success to success. Leaving that Mickey Mouse cheapskate company would be the best thing that ever happened to her. She gave her diary pages another little flick.

"That's fine," she cooed.

"Ten-thirty, then, in Reynolds House, Baggot Street." The secretary was brisk and businesslike.

"Ten-thirty," Alexandra agreed and hung up. She'd have to come home early from London. She'd miss the sales but she didn't care. This was the most important interview of her career. If she got this job the sky was the limit and Malachy MacDonald and Ron Evans could weep into their plum pudding.

"Oh Mammy, this is the best day of my life," Stephanie exclaimed breathlessly as she followed Doug upstairs, reaching out to touch the prickly tip of the huge Christmas tree he was hauling up behind him. The rich pine scent filled the hallway. Stephanie inhaled with pleasure.

She and Doug had gone shopping in Dublin early that morning while her mother was busy in The Deli. Just the two of them. And he'd let her buy loads of stuff. They'd bought Christmas tree lights. *Three* boxes and zillions of shiny baubles and tinsel and paper chains. And little robins and tinkling bells and fat Santas that spun around. She couldn't wait to put them on the tree.

Then they'd gone into Roches Stores and she'd bought her mammy some *Apple Blossom* perfume. Grandad Mick had given her loads of money to do her Christmas shopping. She'd bought him some pipe cleaners and a tobacco pouch. She'd bought Nannie Sheila a set of white hankies with little pink roses and the letter S embroidered on the corner. They were *gorgeous*. She'd bought Doug some aftershave, one day when she was shopping with her mammy. Even though he had a beard, Ellen said he used it to make him smell nice. Stephanie gave a little smile. She loved giving people surprises. After she'd finished all her shopping, Doug had taken her to Woolworth's where she'd had the biggest plate of sausage and chips she'd ever seen. The sausages were really fat. She'd been *stuffed* after them. Then they'd gone to look at all the toy shop windows. And then they'd driven to a place Doug knew and picked the biggest, fattest Christmas tree they could find.

Now it was time to decorate it and she just couldn't wait. Julie Ann had had her tree up for ages. She kept boasting about it. Stephanie had been a bit worried that Christmas was getting nearer and nearer and there was no sign of hers going up. But now the day had come and she felt like bursting, she was so glad about it.

"And a partridge in a pear tree," she hummed as Doug pushed the tree into the sitting-room and lifted it into the silver bucket that was waiting in the middle of the room.

"Now we have to make sure it doesn't tilt over," Doug explained. "Ellen, will you hold it until I prop it up with some logs?"

"I'll hold it too," Stephanie offered. She watched Doug, on his hands and knees under the big bushy tree, as he stuck logs in the bucket and pulled them out and stuck them in again at the other side.

"It's too big, Doug," Ellen said.

"It's not, Mam, it's not." Stephanie looked worriedly at her mother. Maybe she might decide to get a smaller tree. Stephanie wanted her tree to be as big as Julie Ann's. Julie Ann's tree only had red and gold baubles. They had all different-coloured baubles. And Julie Ann's tree had no tinsel on it, because Auntie Emma didn't like tinsel.

"It's in. Stop panicking, Ellen." Doug winked at Stephanie and she felt fine again.

"Mothers don't know much about Christmas trees," she whispered in his ear.

"You're right," he whispered back. "Just as well you were with me to pick it."

"Stop whispering, you two," Ellen said in her pretend cross voice but Stephanie knew she was happy because she kept smiling and giving her little hugs.

"Doug, you'll have to lop off a few branches at the bottom."

"Do I tell you how to make your steak and kidney pie, woman?"

"Stop it, Doug. This is ridiculous. It takes up the whole room. It'll never fit in the corner."

"Do you hear your mother, Stephanie? She has no faith. I think she should go out to the kitchen to make us a cup of tea and leave the experts to it."

"Yes, Mammy. Don't worry, me and Doug know *exactly* what we're doin'. You make the tea."

"All right then. Make a mess of it," Ellen said. But Stephanie knew she was only joking.

When she was gone, Doug got the saw. "I'll just take a few little branches off the bottom but don't tell her."

"I won't," Stephanie promised. He showed her how to saw the branches and then how to tie them to the upper part of the tree with catgut so there'd be no bare bits. By the time Ellen came into the sitting-room with the tea it was all ready to be decorated.

The most exciting part was when Doug had arranged all the lights and told her to switch off the lamps. Then, in the dark, he put the plug in and Stephanie gazed at the twinkling lights on the tree and knew she'd never seen anything so *beautiful.* She just couldn't stop smiling. "I bet no one has a tree as nice as this one anywhere." She slipped her hand into Ellen's.

"I'd say not." Her mother smiled down at her.

"I bet my Guardian Angel is really glad she lives here." Stephanie patted her shoulder where her beloved Angel sat, morning, noon and night.

"I bet she is. And I bet she's a real happy Angel because she's got such a good little girl to look after."

"I'd say Julie Ann's gets a right headache sometimes," Stephanie observed sympathetically.

Ellen and Doug laughed. Stephanie looked at them in surprise. She hadn't meant to be funny. She sometimes felt very sorry for her cousin's unfortunate Angel.

"Why are you laughing?"

"No why. Just because we're having fun and this is nice." Ellen tweaked her ponytail.

"I love you, Mammy."

"I love you too," Ellen hugged her tightly. Stephanie looked at Doug. He was smiling at them. She hurried over to him and flung her arms around him. She didn't want to leave him out. "I love you too, Doug."

He lifted her up in his arms and swung her in the air and she squealed. Then he rubbed his beard against her cheek and she squealed again. It was prickly and furry at the same time.

"And I love you, Stephanie. You're a great girl," he praised. It made her feel very happy. She was just the same as Rebecca and

Julie Ann. Having Doug was like having a daddy. She must ask him about giving her mammy some of his seeds for a new baby. That would be *brill*. But she'd better wait until Christmas was over. She didn't want Ellen to have to go into hospital to get the baby and miss her Christmas dinner.

They had their tea and mince pies in front of the fire with only the Christmas tree lights on and it was like being in fairyland. Then they put the baubles on the tree. She put on all the robins and Santas. Ellen arranged the tinsel. It just kept getting more beautiful, Stephanie decided.

When the tree was finished and Doug had wrapped shining tinfoil around the bucket to make it look pretty, they had more tea and mince pies. Then it was time to put up the chains and holly. The chains kept falling on Doug's head and once he said a bad word and had to say "Excuse me," and her mammy made a face at him. Stephanie didn't mind. The boys at school were always saying bad words.

Then the very last thing . . . the crib. Doug had put a little red light in it for them, right over Baby Jesus's head, and her mammy put trailing ivy along the roof, and some of the Christmas tree branches behind it, so that it looked like the crib was in a forest. Doug hung a gold star from the ceiling and it twinkled like a real one, spilling its light onto the crib. Julie Ann's crib had no ivy and branches or even straw. Stephanie just knew she'd be dead jealous when she saw hers.

It was one of her latest nights ever, she thought happily as she lay in bed looking at the stars. Almost midnight. She thought she saw something flashing across the sky. Stephanie closed her eyes tightly shut and pretended to be asleep. Just in case it was one of Santa's fairies. She really wished it was morning so she could see her beautiful tree and crib again.

Suzy stepped back from the Christmas tree she was decorating and surveyed it critically. There were gaps between the lights. She was making a hames of it, she thought dispiritedly. It was Sunday morning and all she wanted to do was to snuggle up in front of the fire with the Sunday papers, a cup of coffee and a cigarette. But she had to make some sort of effort for Christmas, for the children's sake, even though it was the last thing she wanted to do. The twins were arguing loudly over a little china reindeer. They'd been like two little briars all morning.

"Stop it, the pair of you, or I won't bother finishing this tree," she snapped, at the end of her tether. She heard a smash and turned around to find the decoration in bits on the floor. Christina started howling.

"It's all your fault," Adam gave his twin a shove and she overbalanced into the box of decorations. Christina screeched in fury and indignation.

"*Stop it!*" Suzy yelled. She walloped Adam on the legs and he started bawling. "Jesus, Mary and Joseph, I'm sick of the pair of you. Get out of my sight into the hall until I clean up this mess."

"It's all his fault," Christina bellowed, red-faced with temper as she clambered up from the box.

"*Out!*" Suzy gave her a rough push. Christina cried even more loudly. "I'm here trying to decorate for Christmas on my own and you won't even behave for me. Get out. Get out! Get up to your room." Suzy bundled the twins into the hall and slammed the door shut. If they weren't careful she'd go mad and leather them.

She was angry at everything. Angry at the unfairness of her situation. She'd done nothing wrong. Yet she was the one who was paying for Chris's atrocious behaviour. She was the one left looking after the kids. She was the one lying in bed unable to sleep at night, tormented. She was the one who was expected to swallow her own anger and put the children first. It wasn't fair! It just wasn't fair!

A friend of hers, Joanna Rogers, had gone so far as to suggest that she was being selfish by not letting Chris come to see the kids at Christmas. Why should he be allowed to swan in and out of their lives as it suited him? Why should she be made to feel that she was being vindictive and mean? She was a damn good mother. But that wasn't enough. She was expected to behave like a goddamn saint and pretend nothing had happened. Forgive and forget and let Chris pretend he was the world's greatest father.

Was there no one, not one fair-minded soul, to stand up for her and say to Chris on her behalf,

You did wrong.

You treated this woman shamefully.

You are beneath contempt.

Chris had people to make excuses for him. The twins had her to protect their best interests. She had no one. Not one single person understood her anger, her heartache and her ferocious, unquenchable resentment.

The phone rang. She grimaced as she walked out to the hall to answer it. Who the hell was this?

"Yes!" she snarled.

"Suzy, it's Katherine Wallace. I – "

"I suppose you're going to tell me I'm being a selfish mother too and that your darling son has a right to see his children. Well, don't bother. I'm sick of it!" she exploded.

"I think you're very brave, Suzy. I wish I'd had the guts to stand up for myself and my feelings as you're doing," Katherine said quietly. "I wish I'd been true to myself."

"What?" Suzy wasn't sure if she'd heard right. Was her snooty mother-in-law sticking up for her?

"I said I think you're very brave. And strong. I admire you," Katherine reiterated.

"Oh, Mrs Wallace." Suzy burst into tears. "Oh, Mrs Wallace." She sobbed.

"Oh dear. Are you on your own?"

"Yes." Suzy wept.

"Look, I'm not very good at this. But how about if I come over? I wanted to give the children their presents before they go away and I wasn't sure when you were going."

"If you want to." Suzy tried to compose herself but she couldn't.

"I'll be over in half an hour. Put the kettle on and we'll have coffee and a little chat," Katherine instructed briskly.

Suzy went back into the lounge tears streaming down her face. Who would have thought that her only supporter would be her cold distant mother-in-law?

She cried, great gulping sobs that shook her thin frame. It had all got too much for her. She couldn't take it any more. She wanted to run away and hide somewhere and pretend all this wasn't happening. It was a living nightmare. These horrible feelings of rage and hatred and deep, deep hurt were making her feel ill. Her head felt as if it was going to explode. She had a permanent knot in her chest, and what felt like a weight that could not be lifted. Every morning when she woke up, her shoulders ached with tension. How *could* people expect her to be civil to Chris? He was the cause of all of this. Eventually her sobbing subsided and she took several deep breaths. She couldn't indulge in the luxury of falling to pieces, she had responsibilities. If she cracked up who'd take care of the twins?

She opened the door into the hall and saw that the twins had come down from their bedroom and were sitting on the end of the stairs. Adam had one arm protectively around Christina. They were sucking their thumbs. Their eyes wide and frightened. The thumb-sucking disturbed her. Adam had always sucked his. But Christina had grown out of it. All of this was having a very bad effect on them. They were only three. Their lives shouldn't be full of anxiety and fear. Guilt enveloped her. It wasn't their fault, the poor little things. God only knew what terrifying thoughts were running through their minds. They had enough uncertainties to cope with because of Chris's absence without her lashing out at them.

She rushed over to them and knelt down and put her arms around them.

"I'm sorry. Mummy's really sorry she lost her temper. We'll get another reindeer. Don't worry."

"You hit me very hard, Mummy. Look, my leg's all red," Adam accused, sticking his leg up to be inspected.

The imprint of her hand showed against his white skin. Suzy felt sick.

"Darling, I'm sorry." Her lip quivered. "I'm terribly sorry."

"It's all right, Mummy, don't cry." His reproachful expression became anxious.

Suzy swallowed, hard. She couldn't lose control again. It was too frightening for the children.

"Guess what? Gran Wallace is coming over and she's got presents for you. Quick, let's tidy up so we'll be all ready," she urged.

"Christmas presents?" Christina perked up.

"Yes. Isn't that exciting?"

"Have we got one for her?"

"Oh God!" Suzy's hand shot to her mouth. She'd been feeling so angry and bitter when she'd been doing her Christmas shopping, she'd told Chris he could buy his own present for his mother.

She had an unopened bottle of *Evening in Paris* upstairs on her dressing-table. Or maybe she might give Katherine the Max Factor gift set she'd bought for Lindsey. Perfume was such a personal choice – maybe *Evening in Paris* would not be to her mother-in-law's taste. She could buy Lindsey something later in the week.

"Quick, we have to wrap it!" Suzy jumped to her feet. The twins, diverted from their trauma, rushed upstairs ahead of her. Suzy directed them into their bedroom. "I'll bring it in to your room. Don't move."

She didn't want them to see the stocking fillers that were at the bottom of her wardrobe with the rest of her Christmas shopping. The train set and rocking horse were in the attic.

Galvanised, she had the present wrapped and under the tree, the smashed figurine hoovered up and the kettle boiling when Katherine arrived.

"Hello, Mrs Wallace," she said awkwardly when she opened the door.

"Hello, dear." Katherine smiled and stepped inside. She was looking as chic as ever in her smart camel-hair coat and brown leather boots.

"Have you got a present for us, Gran?" Adam didn't beat about the bush.

"*Adam!*" Suzy remonstrated.

"It's all right, Suzy. They're only toddlers. Presents are most important at that age." Katherine was understanding.

"Do you want to see our tree, Gran? We're decorating it." Christina took her grandmother's hand.

"Of course I do," Katherine said enthusiastically.

"Let me take your coat, Mrs Wallace, and then I'll make the coffee." Suzy was flustered. She'd never seen this side of Katherine before. The other woman was making a huge effort. It was rather endearing.

She made coffee and took out her best china and set a tray with cups and saucers and sugar and milk. She put a doily on the biscuit plate. Katherine was a stickler for such niceties when she was entertaining.

She pushed open the lounge door and came to a full stop. Katherine was on her hands and knees beside the twins, helping them to fix shiny balls onto the branches of the Christmas tree.

"It's much better fun when you've got small helpers," she announced from the floor. "Much less lonely than doing it by oneself. And see, I've been given a lovely present." She held up the Max Factor gift set. "That was kind of you. I know you've so much else on your mind."

Suzy felt a stab of guilt. Her mother-in-law had turned out to be a bit of a brick. No one else had taken her side as she had.

"Now, my dears. I'm going to go out to the car to get your presents and you can open them now as a special treat. And then Mummy and I are going to have a cup of coffee in the kitchen, while you're playing. How about that?" Katherine rose elegantly from the floor and took her car keys from her handbag. The twins scurried ahead of her, all excited.

Five minutes later there wasn't a peep out of them as they played happily with their eagerly unwrapped Christmas presents.

"Now we can talk," Katherine murmured as she took the tray of coffee and ushered Suzy into the kitchen.

"I'm sorry for blubbing on the phone and for being so rude, things just got the better of me," Suzy said miserably.

"Suzy, believe me. I know *exactly* what you're going through. I went through it myself. I just didn't have the courage to kick Jeffrey out. I was too concerned about what people might say. I was afraid that people would think that I had failed as a wife in some way. Especially afraid that they would think that I hadn't satisfied him . . . you know, maritally . . . I was afraid of being on my own. I was *too* damn afraid," Katherine said emphatically as she stirred her coffee. She looked at Suzy, her blue eyes angry.

Suzy had never heard her mother-in-law swear before. It was rather shocking coming from her.

Katherine grimaced. "Because of that fear, Suzy, I lived a lie all my married life. And no one knew how deeply miserable and angry and frustrated and resentful I felt. I never honoured my feelings or myself the way you're doing. I never stood up for myself. You've every right to be mad and hurt. You've every right to be upset. It's like a bereavement, my dear. Only with a bereavement you can finally let go. With a betrayal, it's there always. *Haunting* you!"

The bitterness behind the words stunned Suzy. Poor Katherine. She wasn't cold and detached at all. She'd suffered as much as Suzy. Only she didn't show it to the world.

"I'm sorry for what you had to endure, Mrs Wallace. I never realised . . . " Suzy's voice trailed off. She didn't know what to say.

"It's all right, dear. We're all given our crosses to bear. It's the way we bear them that matters. I made myself a martyr. Because I accepted what he did to me, my husband never had to face up to the consequences of his selfish, irresponsible behaviour. By appearing to condone his unfaithfulness, by allowing him to continue to have affairs and by giving him the easy option of staying at home, I did us all a great disservice. Jeffrey included. My children grew up thinking infidelity was acceptable. Christopher has been unfaithful to you. He sees no great wrong in it. If I had taken a different path and made his father leave, he wouldn't have seen the pattern continue. He would have learned the hard way that such behaviour is unacceptable. Things might have been different for him and you." Katherine looked very sad.

Suzy reached out and patted her hand awkwardly.

Katherine gripped her hand tightly. "Suzy, don't follow my path," she urged fiercely. "Do this for yourself. If you don't, you won't be any good to them." She indicated the lounge where the twins were. "Because of what Jeffrey did to me, I shut down all my feelings. I buried all my anger. I looked after my children, certainly. But I didn't nurture them. Because I couldn't. There was no room for nurturing. No room for softness in my heart. How could there be when it was filled with rage? I was a bad mother, Suzy, and there's nothing I can do about it now except try to help you learn from my mistakes," Katherine said vehemently.

"Because Chris is your son, I thought you'd take his side." Suzy sighed. "It's such a relief to hear this."

"Christopher is my son, yes. And perhaps he turned out the way he did because of the way I reared him. Because of what he saw happen between Jeffrey and me. I can't deny that. But I don't condone his behaviour. He's my son. I love him. But I don't like him – if you can understand that."

"I know he's the twins' father and he should be with them but I can't stand even to be in the same room as him. I feel so . . . so revolted!" Suzy burst out. "If it had been anyone but Alexandra. She was supposed to be my best friend."

"That's a double betrayal. At least I never suffered that. I'm very sorry for you, Suzy. I'm very sorry that a son of mine could stoop so low." Pink stained Katherine's cheeks.

"It's not your fault, Mrs Wallace." Suzy bit her lip to try and prevent herself from crying. "It's just everyone keeps saying he should be with the children for Christmas and I really don't want him here."

"Of course you don't! People find it very easy to pontificate. They can never understand until they've gone through it. Then it's a different kettle of fish," Katherine declared crossly. A glint came into her eye.

"This is just a suggestion, dear. Maybe you might mull it over.

Instead of Christopher spending time here, maybe the twins could go and spend some time with him."

"Oh, Alexandra'd have a fit. She's not good with children. They drive her mad." Suzy shook her head regretfully.

"All the better. Exactly what she needs," Katherine said calmly.

Suzy's eyes widened.

"Oh! I hadn't thought of that."

"I had to go into hospital once when the children were young. I was there for a month. Jeffrey had to look after them. His lady friend of the time wasn't at all pleased. She couldn't stand children. It was the end of *that* great romance. Of course he had more affairs. But I felt *immense* satisfaction when that particular liaison ended," Katherine admitted. "You go away and have a few nice days of peace and quiet for yourself and let Christopher and Madam Johnston get on with it. That's my advice if you want it. Now I really must go. I'm going to a cocktail party later on and I haven't even decided what to wear yet." She leaned over and gave Suzy a quick peck on the cheek. "I won't wish you a happy Christmas, Suzy, that would be insensitive. Just do the best you can, dear. You have my number."

"Mrs Wallace, thank you very, very much." Suzy was overwhelmed.

"For what?" the older woman asked wryly. "For advice that I never followed myself? Hold your head high, dear. And be true to yourself." Katherine walked out of the kitchen and peeped into the lounge.

"Goodbye, twins. When you come back from your holidays I'll get Mummy to bring you over to my house for tea."

"Thanks, Gran," Christina rushed over and gave Katherine a hug. Adam stood with his finger in his mouth. He wasn't as affectionate as his sibling. In fact Suzy was lucky to get a hug from him herself.

"Thanks, Gran. I might give you a kiss the next time I see you. Sometimes I don't give hugs. 'Cos I'm a boy," he explained.

"Is this a Wallace speaking?" Katherine remarked, eyebrows arched, as she made for the door.

Suzy laughed in spite of herself.

She stood watching her mother-in-law drive off. Who would have believed that toffee-nosed Katherine Wallace had such humanity in her? And to come up with that brilliant brainwave of landing the twins on Alexandra. That was out of this world, it was so clever.

Alexandra would go spare.

Suzy took a deep breath. She felt renewed. She had an ally. Someone who had made her feel it was all right to be angry. It was as though Katherine had given her permission to be herself. She wasn't a bad mother. She didn't have to pretend. She wasn't going to suffer any more than she had to, because of Chris's behaviour. And the icing on the cake, Alexandra was going to have a miserable few days with two lively toddlers under her feet. Suzy hoped against hope that she'd be home from her trip to London. Today was turning out far better than it had started out.

"Twins? How would you like to go on two holidays? One with Mummy and one with Daddy?"

"A holiday. Two of them. Yippee!" Christina was delighted.

Adam nodded cautiously.

"Daddy will bring you to the zoo and the circus. And the panto," Suzy encouraged. "Wouldn't you like that?"

"Yes, please, Mummy."

"Let's go ring him then." Smiling, she picked up the phone to tell Chris the good news.

"What?" Chris couldn't believe his ears. Suzy was backing down. She'd just said he was right after all. It was important that he spend time with the children over Christmas. A broad grin creased his face. He knew she'd come to her senses. Now he'd have two options to choose from. Just in case his plan didn't work out with Ellen. What a relief, life was starting to look rosy again.

"I'll come home Christmas Eve." He stretched out on the sofa and took a slug of his whiskey and soda.

"No, no, we're going away, Chris. I told you that," Suzy said calmly. "You can have the kids on the twenty-seventh. I'll drop them over. You can have them for a week."

Chris shot up from the sofa almost spilling his drink. "What do you mean you'll drop them over? They can't stay here," he protested, aghast. This wasn't going to plan at all.

"But I thought you wanted to be with them?" Suzy said innocently. "They're looking forward to spending time with Daddy. I've told them they're going on two holidays. One with you and one with me. They're dying to talk to you," Suzy said sweetly.

He wanted to throttle her. She must be going for a few days away with her new lover. That was why she was dumping the kids on him. What other reason was there?

"Listen . . . I'm not having that," he blustered.

"Hello, Daddy." Christina was on the other end, bubbling with excitement. "We're coming to stay with you. Mummy says you're going to bring us to the panto and the zoo and the circus. An' Daddy, can I bring my dolly? An' can – "

"It's my go."

Chris could hear the twins arguing. What was all this about zoos and pantos and circuses?

"Hello, Daddy? Daddy, I miss you."

Chris's heart softened at Adam's forlorn tone.

"I miss you too."

"Well, I'll send us over for our holidays soon. And I'll bring my dumper truck to show you," Adam promised.

"Good boy," Chris said weakly. "Put me on to Mummy."

"Now listen, Suzy. I can't land two kids on Alexandra – "

"Not only are you taking them for a few days after Christmas, *darling*. But come the New Year you can take them every second weekend. You're absolutely right. They need their father. And it's selfish of me not to accept that. Alexandra will just have to get used to it. But I'm sure that won't be a problem if she really loves you," Suzy pointed out reasonably. "Bye, Chris. I'll be in touch."

Chris was speechless. He'd made such a song and dance about

his right to see the kids that he couldn't very well backtrack without losing face. She'd been really cunning, telling them first that they were going to stay with him. Obviously they were looking forward to it. How on earth could he get out of it?

Alexandra would freak! She didn't like children. They irritated her. If he announced the twins were coming to stay there'd be murder. Tough! He was paying half the rent on the apartment, he was *entitled* to have his kids to stay.

He wanted to strangle Suzy. He felt utterly out of control. Impotent. She was calling all the shots! He was thoroughly sick of her. How could he get her out of his life? And he'd noted her sly little dig at the end about how, if Alexandra really loved him, she'd put up with the children.

Well, the day was coming when Suzy'd really suffer. Now she'd never get him back no matter how hard she tried. She was going to end up a bitter, vindictive, lonely woman and he'd be as happy as Larry. She'd be sorry. He'd a plan up his sleeve that would pull the rug right from under her feet.

Chapter Twenty-Three

"What do you bet that's Mother!" Ellen scowled as the phone rang in The Deli. Sheila was driving her nuts. It was the Monday before Christmas, the day of the guild lunch and she'd phoned her twice already.

"Hello, The Deli." Her tone had an edge.

"Ellen, I just wanted to check one thing." Sheila sounded agitated. Ellen threw her eyes up to heaven and made a ferocious face. Denise and Miriam started giggling.

"Yes, Mam. You know I'm really up to my eyes."

"I know that. I was just wondering whether you put plenty of sherry in the trifle. The last day-trip we were on, *The Gourmet Daly*," Sheila's voice dripped scorn, "ordered trifle for dessert and when she tasted it she said at the top of her voice, if you don't mind, 'They must have stood in the next room when they were pouring the sherry!' Can you credit that? I don't want her to have any excuse for that sort of smart-alec talk today. And make sure all your salt and pepper pots are full. She got one that was empty and we had to listen to her moaning for the duration of the meal. Oh and one other thing – when you're making the gravy add in some sherry for extra flavour."

"Yes, Mam. It will all be taken care of. Now I'm going. I'm needed in the kitchen. Goodbye." She hung up and turned to the girls. "For crying out loud!!!"

"What's wrong now?"

"Bonnie bleedin' Daly will be the death of me. I'm to make sure there's enough sherry in the trifle so she won't make disparaging remarks about how far away I was when I poured it in. And I'm to make sure the pepper pots and salt cellars are all full! And I'm to add some sherry to the gravy for extra flavour." Ellen was fit to be tied.

"Just think of all the new customers we'll get," Denise soothed.

"It's not worth it," Ellen moaned. "I'll never make old age. I'll be dead of stress before I'm forty! But I'll tell you one thing, girls. If I go I'm taking Bonnie Daly with me. If she says one word out of place I'll tell her to stuff the parson's nose where it hurts. And then I'll crown her. That's if I don't take to the sherry first myself."

"No, let's get her pissed," Denise said wickedly. "We'll pour extra sherry into her portion of trifle and keep topping up her glass. Imagine if she had to be carried out."

"Well, you know she hasn't got a head for alcohol at all – one glass and she's singing. Do you remember that party of Mam's, Miriam, when I was expecting Stephanie? She and Mam were still friends. Will you ever forget her singing *This is my Happy Day?* And that was after one glass of sherry." Ellen laughed.

"Ah now, Ellen, she's elderly," Miriam demurred.

"That doesn't excuse bad manners," Ellen riposted.

"I'd love to hear Bonnie Daly singing *This is my Happy Day.*" Denise was game.

"And you will, my dear. You will," Ellen retorted. Elderly or not, Bonnie had been a thorn in her side for too long.

The next few hours were hectic as the trio prepared lunch and attended to normal business. At half eleven, Miriam and Ellen went upstairs to set the tables. They pulled the tables from the banquettes and made one long table along the windows. They had seasonal red and green mats and napkins. Denise had arranged floral displays which looked very pretty. Red candles added a festive touch. Ellen had bought a box of twenty-four crackers in

Arnott's, in red, green and gold, and they complemented the colours on the table. It looked very elegant when they were finished.

"Definitely as nice as the Glenree Arms." Ellen straightened a soup spoon.

"Nicer!" Miriam declared. "The Arms could do with a coat of paint inside. It's gone a bit shabby. Come on, we'd better get a move on. We've to do the prawn cocktails."

The prawn cocktails, with their dusting of paprika, were in place when Sheila arrived to inspect.

"Very nice, very nice indeed," she proclaimed as she surveyed the table. Sheila was dressed in her new mauve twinset and navy pleated skirt. Her hair had been permed for the occasion and she wore her best pearls.

"Now, Ellen, I've bought a big box of chocolates for afterwards. Mick has them next door. And I've a little book of tickets. We'll have the draw for the president's prize after the meal. It's a bottle of whiskey, a turkey and a ham. Would you get the chocolates and whiskey from Mick, like a good girl?"

"Right, Mam." Ellen bit down her irritation. She had enough to be doing without running last-minute errands. She hurried downstairs and out of The Deli. Her father chuckled when he saw her.

"You look harassed. Has the ordeal started?"

"You could say that," Ellen said wryly. "I've to collect the chocolates and the whiskey. She'll be lucky if I don't drink it first."

"Stay calm, Ellen. You'll be grand. If the smell is anything to go by. My mouth is watering every time I go out the back. How is it cooking? It should be a nice bird. I picked it specially. It was a twenty-four-pounder."

"It's cooking fine. I'll plate you up a dinner and you can have it upstairs in the flat if you like," Ellen offered.

"You're a peach, Ellen. I'd love it. I'm dying for a bit of turkey. Would you give me a wing and a slice of the leg?" Mick rubbed his hands.

"I'll give you half a leg and a wing and a sliver of breast if I can spare it. And I'll give you some crispy streaky rashers off the top."

"Don't say anything to your mother, though. She made up a meatloaf for me at home," Mick warned.

"I won't say a word," Ellen promised.

"What kept you?" Sheila asked tartly when Ellen returned five minutes later. Her mother had taken up a stand at the door.

"Dad was busy."

"I'd like you to greet everyone when they arrive."

"Mam, I have to help out in the kitchen. I can't stand at the door for the next half-hour."

"Well, it would be good manners!" Sheila retorted huffily. "Ah, Tilly, welcome." She turned on her presidential smile as the first guest arrived.

"Hello, Mrs Doyle," Ellen said politely.

"Something smells nice," Tilly Doyle sniffed appreciatively.

"I hope so. Would you like a glass of sherry, Mrs Doyle? On the house."

"That's very kind of you, Ellen. I'd love one."

"Mam?"

"Well, seeing as it's the occasion that it is, I'll partake." Sheila was gracious.

"Excuse me a minute. If you'd like to go on upstairs I'll bring them up to you."

Three more ladies arrived just then and they were all agreeable to a glass of sherry. Ellen hastened to do the honours. She filled a tray with sherry glasses and poured in the amber liquid, hoping she wouldn't slop them. Bonnie was just arriving.

"Ah, Bonnie." Sheila was regal. "A glass of sherry?"

"Well, maybe I'll just have a mineral," Bonnie said stiffly. She was done up to the nines in a Paisley print dress. She wore her best hat for the occasion.

"For goodness sake, Bonnie, have a sherry and stop your

nonsense. A mineral indeed!" Lizzie Regan snorted, as they all went upstairs.

"Let me take your coat, Mrs Daly," Ellen murmured, as she laid the drinks on a table.

"Thank you, Ellen." Bonnie was not at all impressed with Lizzie.

"Here, get that into you," Lizzie proffered a glass.

"If you insist," Bonnie clipped, but she took the glass and took a dainty sip.

Ellen hurried downstairs with the coats.

"Ellen, get in here quick," Denise poked her head out of the kitchen.

"What's wrong?" Ellen's heart sank at the look of dismay on her friend's face.

"The arse fell out of the turkey when we were trying to get it out of the roasting-dish. There was too much stuffing in it," Denise whispered.

"Oh crikey," Ellen groaned. It had all been going too smoothly to be true.

There was stuffing everywhere. The underside of the turkey was stuck to the parchment paper.

Miriam was spooning stuffing onto a dish. "Don't panic. What they don't know about they won't worry about," she muttered, flushed from the heat. "Just don't let your mother into the kitchen."

"She's upstairs doing her presidential bit." Ellen picked a skelp of turkey out of the roasting-dish and tasted it. "It's nice," she announced through bulging cheeks.

"Stop eating it," Denise remonstrated. "I'll carve it and see how we get on. We can disguise these bits." She indicated the sorry-looking portion in the roasting-dish. "We'll just pour gravy over them if we have to."

"Right. Give them another ten minutes to get sloshed and I'll tell them to sit down. How's the soup?"

"Fine. Oh cripes, turn those potatoes off, they're going into mush," Miriam gave a squawk of dismay as she lifted the lid off the potatoes.

"How are the roasties doing?"

"They won't be long." Denise peered into the oven. "I think they should begin eating their starters soon. We don't want the roast potatoes overdone."

"I'll go up and see how many more have arrived." Ellen was utterly flustered.

Everyone had arrived by the time she went back upstairs.

"I see you don't use tablecloths," Bonnie remarked pointedly.

"Hardly, with pine tables, Bonnie," Sheila interjected quickly.

"Oh but there's something classy about a linen tablecloth." Bonnie smiled sweetly.

"Ah yes, dear, but The Deli is rather avant-garde, as they say." Sheila was snooty. "Linen would be out of place."

Bonnie, who hadn't a clue what avant-garde meant, glared at Sheila.

"Well, you can't beat a bit of class, I think. But then I was reared to it."

Sheila went deep puce with fury. "Indeed, Bonnie, but you'd never guess it," she declared frostily.

"I think the table is delightful," Stella Dwyer cut in diplomatically. "And the prawn cocktail looks delicious."

"If everyone is here maybe you'd like to start," Ellen suggested. There were murmurs of agreement as the ladies took their places. Ellen poured the wine and soon the members of the guild were eating and drinking with relish. Bonnie and Sheila were seated as far away from each other as possible, she noted with relief. For a minute or two it looked as if there was going to be a full-scale row!

For the next two hours the girls were rushed off their feet, plating up, serving, pouring drinks. Sheila had Ellen running up and down like a yo-yo.

"Does she think I've jets up me arse?" she growled to the girls as she made yet another trip to the kitchen. The main course was ready to be served. Fortunately the earlier catastrophes went unnoticed. The roast potatoes were done to a T. The turkey was moist and tender. No one noticed that the potatoes were slightly mushy. Denise creamed and seasoned them perfectly. The sherried gravy came in for lavish praise. Judging by the empty plates, the meal had gone down a treat.

The sherry and wine loosened tongues and every so often guffaws and chuckles would resound through The Deli, as the twenty guild members thoroughly enjoyed their Christmas lunch. Bonnie, on her second glass of red wine, tucked into her sherry trifle with gusto. True to her word, Denise had added an extra measure to her dessert. She'd also topped up Bonnie's sherry glass at every opportunity.

Ellen hid a smile as Bonnie's eyes watered, but she finished every scrap and gave a delicate little hiccup. Her cheeks were flushed, her beady little eyes bright as buttons. Lizzie Regan poured herself another glass of wine and added some into Bonnie's glass. "Get that into ya, Cynthia," she urged.

"Oh tee hee hee," Bonnie giggled. "Oh dear, dear, dear, ha ha. Ha ha ha," she chuckled mirthfully. She was as drunk as a skunk.

Lizzie started singing. *"Poor old Dicey Reilly, she has taken to the sup . . . "*

"This is my happy day," warbled Bonnie.

Denise and Miriam, grinning from ear to ear, stood at the kitchen door enjoying the goings-on upstairs.

"Ladies, ladies!" Sheila frowned. Things were getting out of hand. There was too much hysterical hilarity.

"Let's pull the crackers," Tilly suggested. There was great merriment as crackers were noisily pulled and paper hats placed on heads.

Bonnie, her red hat dangling lopsidedly over her eye, giggled again. *"In my Easter Bonnet with all my eggs upon it,"* she slurred. Sheila was affronted. She glared at her sworn enemy. "Behave yourself, Bonnie."

"You behave yourself, *yourself*," Bonnie retorted tipsily.

"We're having a party, Sheila. This isn't a committee meeting," Lizzie remonstrated, not at all impressed by her president's school-marmish tone.

"I believe for every drop of rain that flows a flower grows . . . "
Bonnie's thin soprano floated through The Deli. Ellen snorted
into her handkerchief. Miriam and Denise were in kinks. Tilly
Doyle was openly guffawing, as were half of the assembled
guests.

"I think it's time to serve the coffee." Ellen hastened downstairs.

"Denise, I think you overdid the sherry," she said, half-shocked
now at the state they'd got Bonnie into. "She's absolutely
fluthered."

"Yeah, well she ratted on me once to my mother when she
caught me smoking and I was kept in for a month. Revenge is a dish
best served cold . . . or in a sherry glass." She smirked unrepentantly.
"She'll never live this one down. What's she singing now?"

They cocked their ears.

"Hail redeemer, king divine. Priest and lamb the throne is Thine!"
wafted downstairs.

"She's on the hymns now," Miriam laughed.

"Oh, Denise McMahon, may God forgive you!" Ellen shook
her head. "I think one of us better bring her home."

"Don't be such a spoilsport. She might do a striptease yet and
really liven up the joint." Denise was incorrigible.

"I'll take her," Miriam offered.

"I'm not going up there by myself. Denise, you can come with
me to pour the tea. I'll take the coffee-pot." Ellen was starting to
fret. Sheila would probably blame her if the guild lunch was
ruined.

"Coward," teased Denise, who was enjoying herself hugely.
When they arrived back upstairs Bonnie was in full flow.

"Angels, saints and nations sing . . . "
Sheila was hopping mad.

Miriam came up and caught Tilly's eye. "Will we take her
home?" she whispered.

"I think so," Tilly agreed. "Get her coat."

"Lord of life, earth, sky and sea. King of love on Calvaryyyyyy."
Bonnie's thin voice cracked.

"Good woman yourself, Bonnie," Lizzie applauded.

"It was a great party, Bonnie. It's time to go now," Tilly said firmly.

"Oh but I haven't sung *South of the Border* yet," Bonnie declared indignantly. "*South of the border down Mexico way. That's where I –* "

"Now, Bonnie, Ellen has to clear up here. We'll all be leaving in a minute." Tilly slid the older woman's coat on.

"Just when I was starting to en . . . en . . . joy myself," Bonnie slurred irritably.

"We've another party next week," Tilly soothed. She led Bonnie downstairs, watched by the ladies of the guild. Miriam followed. A buzz of conversation broke out upstairs.

"*Disgraceful.*" (Sheila)

"*At her age –* "

"*She was only having a bit of fun.*"

"*Never could hold her drink.*"

"*I bet this won't be recorded in the minutes.*"

"*So much for class! Ha! Ha!*"

Ellen kept her face straight as she continued to pour the coffee. Sheila was on her high horse. Bonnie had disgraced the guild. Ellen needn't have worried – this had made her mother's day. Bonnie had lost quite a lot of the high moral ground she relished. The guild Christmas lunch had turned out to be a lively affair. A triumph for Sheila in terms of her feud with Bonnie. All in all a great success, Ellen decided with satisfaction as she handed around the after-dinner mints. They'd be closing The Deli for Christmas. She was looking forward to the break.

"But it's not fair, Mummy. Stephanie has loads of tinsel on her Christmas tree. Why can't we have tinsel?" Julie Ann demanded.

"I've told you before, Julie Ann. Tinsel is tacky. I don't like it. Now stop annoying me," Emma said through gritted teeth. She was changing Andrew's nappy. A chore she detested. Mrs Murdock had the flu. It was most inconvenient. Julie Ann was on her school holidays and she was driving Emma mad.

"You're a mean mummy."

"Julie Ann! Cut it out."

"Won't!"

"That's it. Up to your room, madam."

"No!" screeched Julie Ann.

"This minute!" yelled Emma. Andrew started howling.

The phone rang. "Crumbs!" She laid Andrew in his pram and hurried to answer it. It was Chris.

"Hello, Emma. What do you think of this? Suzy wants me to take the kids for a week. She wants me to keep them in the apartment. I don't think that's very fair. Do you? I think I should be entitled to spend time with them at home."

Typical Chris. Not a word about how was she or any such niceties.

"It's very difficult, Chris. I understand how Suzy feels." She tried to keep the irritation out of her tone.

"You women, you always stick together," Chris moaned. "Does no one understand how *I* feel? I can't have the kids here. Alexandra's not into children at all."

"Maybe you could stay with your mother for a few days and have them visit there," Emma suggested helpfully.

"Are you mad! Do you know what she's done? She's gone and bought Stephanie a Christmas present. It's a bit much, Emma. It really is."

"I know, she rang me looking for Ellen's number." Emma studied her reflection in the mirror over the phone-stand. She could do with a facial, she decided.

"*You* gave it to her!" Chris roared down the phone.

Emma jumped. "Don't yell! You nearly deafened me," she snapped.

"How could you?" Chris was fuming.

"Don't be ridiculous. How could I not?"

"Do you think she told Ellen about me and Alexandra?" he asked agitatedly.

"How would I know, Chris? I'm not psychic, for God's sake. Look, I have to go, Andrew's crying." Emma had had enough of her cousin's dramas. She had plenty of her own.

"Right, bye." Chris hung up ungraciously.

"Bugger you, Chris," Emma muttered. Families were a pain in the butt sometimes. She went into the lounge. Julie Ann stuck out her tongue at her. At her wit's end, she did the only thing she could think of . . . she stuck out her tongue right back! The look of shock and horror on her daughter's face gave Emma a modicum of satisfaction as she picked up her son and tried her best to soothe him.

Chris dialled his mother's number. He was seething. If Katherine opened her big mouth to Ellen she could ruin everything. He had to nip it in the bud and fast.

"Hello?" His mother's cultured tones made him even more irate.

"Mother, it's me."

"Yes, Christopher." Katherine was cool.

"I just want you to know that when you're having tea with Ellen and Stephanie, I'd prefer if you didn't discuss me or my personal problems. Er . . . have you said anything to Ellen about them? Have you told her I'm not living at home?" He just had to know. His palms sweated as he waited for his mother's response.

"Christopher, hard as it may be to accept, your name never came up once in our conversation. Nor do I expect it to. I wouldn't be so insensitive as to discuss you with Ellen, you may rest assured," Katherine retorted tartly.

"I see. Well, thanks," Chris muttered. He felt like a six-year-old who'd been put in his place.

"What are you doing for Christmas Day, Christopher?" Katherine inquired.

"I don't know."

"That woman you're . . . co-habiting with is going away, isn't she?"

"Yeah," Chris said forlornly.

"Very well, then. You'd better come and have lunch with me," Katherine said briskly.

"Right, thanks." Chris felt a vague sense of relief. He'd dreaded spending Christmas Day alone. At least he'd get some decent nosh in his mother's.

"I'll be having mulled wine and mince pies on Christmas Eve as usual but you can give that a miss if you like, in view of your situation," Katherine instructed. "I'll see you for lunch on Christmas Day at one-thirty. Don't come any earlier. I'll have the neighbours in. See you then." She hung up smartly.

Chris felt like a pariah. He dropped his head in his hands. At least Ellen didn't know about Alexandra. Or that he wasn't living at home. It was crucial that she didn't hear about it from anyone other than him.

At least Katherine seemed to have taken a real shine to Ellen. That would make his plans much, much easier. For that, at least, he was grateful.

"Suzy! Did you hear the news? Alexandra got the boot from Stuart and Stuart's." Lindsey's excited voice trilled down the phone.

"What? How? Who told you?" Suzy's eyes widened in amazement. A sense of elation suffused her.

"Malachy MacDonald was at a sherry reception that Michael was at and the things he was saying about Alexandra had to be heard to be believed. He said he'd given her the sack for gross incompetence and for dragging the reputation of Stuart and Stuart's in the mud because of her disreputable private life. Mind, that's a bit much to take coming from him. You know the way he conned that silly woman into marrying him. If that's not being disreputable, I don't know what is."

"Oh, who gives a hoot about Malachy MacDonald, whoever he is. Tell me more about Alexandra," Suzy urged.

"Well, that's all I know," Lindsey said petulantly. "She's out on her ear. Michael said it was the talk of the night."

"Has she got another job?"

"I don't know."

"But she's been sacked."

"She's definitely been sacked," Lindsey confirmed.

"Oh Lindsey, you'll probably think I'm an awful bitch. But that's the best news I've heard in ages. That's made my day."

"I thought it would. I couldn't wait to tell you." Lindsey grinned at the other end.

"Oh, I'd love to have been there when she was getting the bullet."

"Me too."

"I'll tell you what. I'll give Madeleine Conway a buzz, to see if she knows anything, and I'll get back to you later, OK?"

"Good idea. Ring her now. I'm dying to know all about it."

"Right, bye." Suzy replaced the receiver and beamed. She felt on top of the world. Alexandra had got the chop. How ignominious. She must be mortified. Her reputation in tatters. Well, that would teach her to mess with other men's wives, Suzy thought exultantly.

Only one other thing would give her as much satisfaction and that was if Chris kicked her out. She didn't want him back . . . definitely not. Especially after her talk with her mother-in-law. But she wanted that relationship ended. More than anything else in the world she wanted Chris to leave Alexandra. She didn't care who else Alexandra shacked up with as long as she and Chris split. The thought of them living happily ever after was too much to endure. Every day they spent together in that posh apartment was a thorn in her heart. It grieved her to think of them as a couple, living in domestic bliss.

Well, Alexandra's unemployment could only put a strain on

the relationship. Chris would never be able to afford the rent of the apartment on his own. He wouldn't be able to support her *and* his family. There and then, Suzy resolved to ask for an increase in her housekeeping money in the New Year. She might as well keep the thumbscrews on and really add to their misery.

She hummed happily as she dialled Madeleine's number. The other woman answered almost immediately. Suzy grinned. The phone was like an extension of Maddy's arm.

"Madeleine, hi. It's Suzy. I'm just ringing to wish you a happy Christmas. I'm going to stay with a friend so I won't be around for a while. Thanks for all the support."

"No trouble, sweetheart. I'm glad to be of assistance. And have a lovely time with your friend. How are you anyway, lamb?" Madeleine asked kindly.

"Well, it's a difficult time. I find it very rough emotionally. You know what Christmas is like. With all the memories and so on. I just have to put on a brave face for the children."

"Of course you do, pet. I'm sure it's very hard. The only small comfort I can give you is that Miss Johnston won't be having too jolly a Christmas either. You did hear the news that she's been let go from S & S's?"

"Hmm, I did hear something in passing. I don't know any of the details." Suzy was deliberately offhand.

"Well, from what I can gather," Madeleine confided knowingly, "Malachy made a pass at her and she rejected him. Obviously she must have been leading him on. All that flirting. You know the way she carries on. Mona MacDonald was always extremely unhappy about it. She doesn't trust Malachy an inch. Not that she's really got anything to worry about, I'd say," Madeleine scoffed. "Who'd look twice at that little popinjay? But apparently Malachy, who thinks he's Ireland's answer to Cary Grant, propositioned Alexandra. He's actually supposed to have *groped* her in the office. Can you believe it? Well, of course there's no nooky with Mona and never has been . . . he welched on that, according to Victor. Poor Mona will die wondering. Maybe he was overcome with lust or something. Alexandra seems to have that effect on men," Madeleine sighed.

"But who told you all this?" Suzy was gobsmacked.

"One of the girls in the typing pool knows Laura Henderson's daughter. She told the daughter, the daughter told Laura and Laura told me. I don't know how true it all is. But it doesn't surprise me in the least."

"How sleazy," Suzy wrinkled her nose in distaste.

"Well, as you know to your cost, dear, she's a temptress. Only this time she tempted a silly old man who thought he was on to a good thing. So between the jigs and the reels she got the sack and Malachy's going around like a demon, according to Victor. It must be a *crushing* blow to his vanity. Malachy has an ego the size of Everest."

"I don't know him," Suzy murmured. It was hard to get a word in edgeways when Madeleine was in full flow.

"That's no loss, sweetheart. He's not a very nice person. A bit devious, to say the least and still remain charitable. So all is probably not well in paradise. And aren't we cheering?"

"Thanks, Madeleine," Suzy said warmly. Maddy might be a right old gossip but her heart was in the right place.

"We'll get together in the New Year, lamb, and we'll have a nice lunch – my treat."

"That's a date," Suzy agreed. "Take care. And Happy Christmas."

She walked into the kitchen and plugged in the kettle. She was dying for a cup of coffee. She'd phone Lindsey later. Suddenly for the first time in ages she was ravenous. She opened the fridge. It was pretty bare. There were eggs and cheese. She felt like an omelette. That's what she'd cook.

She was on such a high. Alexandra was jobless. That would drive her crazy. Suzy wanted to sing and dance with exhilaration. She felt alive again. She knew it was wrong to revel in someone's bad luck, but she didn't care. She couldn't help it. The more disasters Alexandra Johnston had in her life, the better. And she'd gloat over every one of them, Suzy vowed as she whipped the eggs and added the seasoning.

It was the first meal she'd enjoyed since the night she'd discovered her husband tied naked to Alexandra's bedstead. Things were looking up.

Chapter Twenty-Four

"Oh Doug! It's beautiful!". Ellen breathed as she gazed at the delicate chain and cross nestling in its velvet bed. It was Christmas Eve, and they were exchanging presents under the Christmas tree before Ellen and Stephanie left to go and stay at Sheila's.

"Let me put it on." Doug smiled. She smiled back and touched his cheek.

"Thank you, Doug. For everything."

"I think you better get me a piece of mistletoe, Stephanie." Doug winked. "I feel a kiss coming on."

"Don't be long, I'm dying for my present." Stephanie wasn't at all interested in the romance of the moment. She was far too anxious to unwrap the two gaily wrapped presents Doug had put under the tree for her.

Doug laughed as he secured the chain around Ellen's neck.

"Here." Stephanie held out a branch of mistletoe she'd taken from the mantelpiece.

Doug took the berried spray and held it over his and Ellen's heads. Gently, lightly he kissed her lips. "That chain comes with all my love," he murmured. "I want you to wear it for ever."

Ellen looked into his hazel eyes and saw the love mirrored there.

"I will," she said simply and hugged him tightly to her.

"Now can I open mine?" Stephanie urged.

"Yes, go on." Ellen stood in the shelter of Doug's arms and watched happily as her daughter dived under the Christmas tree and hauled out the big rectangular box. She tore the wrappings impatiently, her eyes bright with anticipation.

"Ooohhh, Doug. Mammy, look, it's Spirograph. Brillo! Thanks, Doug." She launched herself at him, the precious gift tucked under one arm.

Doug hugged her tight. "I'll want loads of pictures. Really artistic ones."

"You'll get them. Can I start one now?"

"No, pet, we'll have to go soon but you can bring it over to Nannie's and do one this evening," Ellen said.

Stephanie's eyes lit up. "I know, I'll do one for Santa this evening before I go to bed. Just think of the surprise he'll get."

"There's another surprise for you under the tree," Doug reminded her.

"Oh yeah!" Stephanie burrowed under the tree again and came out clasping the small square box. "Two presents. Mammy, I'm dead lucky," she declared earnestly as her fingers struggled with the well-sellotaped gift. "Oh look," her eyes widened. "It's in a box like yours. *Oooohhh!*" she gasped in delight. "Mammy, it's a charm bracelet. Look at the little kitten. It's like Sooty when she was a kitten." Sooty was Stephanie's much loved cat. She presented the box to Ellen for inspection.

"Doug, it's beautiful." Ellen lifted the bracelet from its soft paper. "Here, let me put it on."

"No, Mam, Doug has to put it on, like he put your chain on," Stephanie insisted.

"Of course he has to." Ellen handed the bracelet to Doug.

Doug knelt down in front of Stephanie. "For the second lady in my life." He smiled at her as he fastened the clasp.

"And have I to wear mine for ever?" Stephanie asked solemnly.

"You do." Doug nodded.

"And is it with all your love, too?"

"It is. Ellen, can I have the mistletoe, please?"

Ellen wordlessly handed him the mistletoe. She had a lump as big as a football stuck in her throat.

Doug held the mistletoe over Stephanie's head. Trustingly she raised her face for his kiss.

Tears brimmed in Ellen's eyes as she watched Doug softly kiss Stephanie's pink cheek.

"With all my love, Stephanie."

Stephanie flung her arms tight around his neck. "Thank you for my two presents. Especially my bracelet. Even Julie Ann doesn't have a bracelet like this. No one in my class has one," she confided.

"Next year, I'll give you another charm," Doug promised.

"Mammy, why are you crying?" Stephanie spotted her mother's tears.

Doug looked up at Ellen and grinned. "Stephanie, your mother's a great big softie. One night I took her to the pictures and she drenched me from crying at the sad bits."

"But this is a happy bit." Stephanie was confused.

"Oh, she cries at them too," Doug said matter-of-factly.

"Do you, Mam?"

"Yes," Ellen sniffled.

"Here, woman, have a good blow. I brought one specially for the occasion." Doug handed her a freshly laundered white handkerchief.

Ellen gulped and laughed at the same time. She felt a fool but watching Doug with Stephanie had made her feel so emotional. His thoughtfulness was immensely touching. His kindness so genuine. Ellen, who'd been sadly lacking in receiving kindness in her relationship with Chris, still found herself overwhelmed by Doug's care. Secretly she didn't feel she deserved such love.

Doug put his arm around her.

"Come on, woman, pull yourself together. You promised me a piece of pudding and brandy butter."

"But wait, Doug. You've to open *your* presents." Stephanie hauled out a large parcel from under the tree.

"Mammy, you have to give him this one. This is Mammy's. Wait until you see it, Doug! You'll *love* it," Stephanie assured him.

"I hope you like it, Doug." Ellen handed it to him.

Doug was even more impatient than Stephanie as he tried to unwrap his parcel. But Ellen had bound it tightly.

"That's cruelty," he exclaimed as he struggled with yards of sellotape.

Stephanie squealed with excitement and clapped her hands. "Can you not wait, Doug?"

"No, I can't. Your mother's an awful woman for keeping me in suspense like this."

"Take it slowly," Ellen said firmly, enjoying his boyish eagerness.

"Oh Ellen!" His face was a study when he unwrapped his gift. "It's beautiful." He sighed. "A real stunner."

Ellen laughed. "I don't know how you can call a fishing-rod beautiful."

"It's an *Abu*! The best of swag. She's a beauty, Ellen. How did you know which one to pick?" Doug studied his new prize proudly.

"Dad helped," Ellen admitted.

"There's something else." Stephanie, sporting a melon-slice grin, handed him another box. "That's to go with that one. It's from Mammy, too."

Doug eyed Ellen sternly. "Two presents. One was more than enough."

"Well, this one complements the other one," Ellen explained, chuffed with his reaction.

"Ahh, Ellen!" He looked so happy when he opened the box of flies that she'd bought to go with the rod that she almost started crying again.

He fingered the feathery fronds lovingly. "The trout'll go mad for these," he murmured.

Ellen laughed. Mick was exactly the same about flies. He had a huge collection and he was always driving Sheila mad, looking for the feathers on her hats.

"Thanks very much, Ellen." Doug enveloped her in a bear-hug. She hugged him back, unable to speak.

"Now you've to open mine." Stephanie thrust her gift at him.

"Have you tied yours as tightly as your mad mother's?" Doug demanded.

"Yes," Stephanie giggled.

"Lord above! I've two mad women in my life." He struggled again to untie the ungainly parcel.

"Ah! Stephanie!" He was delighted when he saw the photo of her and Ellen in a home-made varnished ice-lolly-stick frame.

"I made it myself," she said proudly.

"That makes it all the more special. I'll put this beside my bed. I'll see the two of you first thing in the morning. And last thing at night." He studied the photo with pleasure.

"And there's something else," Stephanie pointed out.

"My goodness!" Doug delved deeper. "Wow! *Bay Rum* aftershave. I'll have to fight the women off. Thank you very much, Stephanie. I'm a lucky man."

"That's 'cos you're always kind to us. We wanted to buy you really, really nice presents. Mammy said she wished she had a *fortune* to spend on you," Stephanie divulged innocently.

"Did she?" Doug glanced at Ellen, who blushed.

"Yep, she did. 'Cos she really likes you. 'Cos you make her laugh," Stephanie remarked airily as she petted her kitten charm. "You know what I was thinking?" she said seriously, her blue eyes earnest.

"What were you thinking?" Doug tried to keep his face straight. Ellen bit her lip wondering what indiscretion her daughter was going to come out with next.

"I was thinking that when Christmas Day is over, could you put one of your seeds in Mammy's belly button so she could get a new baby? Julie Ann says it's dead easy. That's how Andrew came. And can we watch 'cos Auntie Emma and Uncle Vincent won't let her see how they do it. I told her, I bet Doug wouldn't mind. He even showed me how to grow peas in a glass." Stephanie was completely oblivious to the consternation she was causing.

Doug and Ellen stared at each other.

"Mmm . . . Stephanie – " Ellen paused. She'd been just about to say that people had to be married before they could make babies, when she remembered her own circumstances. She didn't really want to get into any convoluted explanations.

"Stephanie . . . making babies is kind of private. It's only for grown-ups. And that's why Julie Ann's not allowed watch. And it's really up to Holy God if he sends a baby or not," she said weakly, chickening out.

"Well, I'll ask him in my special intentions." Stephanie was full of confidence.

"Right! But don't talk to Julie Ann about it. Or anyone else. Those kind of things are private."

"When I'm big, Doug, can you give me some seeds too? If I can grow peas, I'm sure I could grow babies. Mammy, can I go down to Grandad Mick and show him my bracelet?"

"Oh very good idea." Ellen nodded vigorously. "Tell him we'll be going home to Nannie soon and that I'll collect the turkey and ham from him."

"OK." Stephanie skipped happily out of the room, her arm held up in front of her, admiring her jewellery.

"God bless her innocence," Doug laughed. "Great idea though."

"I'll have to talk to her. Julie Ann would wilt you. She's as precocious!" Ellen groaned.

"But look, she's forgotten about it now. They get an idea in their heads, they air it and move on to something else."

"I know but just say she came out with that in front of Mam. Could you imagine the reaction?" Ellen sighed. "I hope she doesn't say anything like that when we go to visit Mrs Wallace. I'll have to warn her."

Doug looked at her in surprise. "Mrs Wallace? Is she something to do with that other bastard?" He was scowling.

"Oh Doug, don't be like that," Ellen remonstrated. "Chris's mother rang me a while back. She's bought Stephanie a Christmas present. And she invited us to tea."

"You never told me," he said quietly.

"*Doug!*" Ellen was dismayed by his tone. "I forgot all about it. Things have been so mad. That guild dinner was a nightmare. I would have said it to you. I'm only going to the woman's house for tea. It's got nothing to do with Chris."

"I wish you weren't. I can't help how I feel," Doug growled.

"Look, Doug. *She* rang *me*. And she's very nice actually. She feels bad that Chris deserted Stephanie. I think she wants to try and make up for it in some way. And she is Stephanie's grandmother. I'm glad she's acknowledging that for Stephanie's sake. I think it will be good for Stephanie to have some contact with her father's family. Maybe she won't feel so rejected when she starts to reason these things out for herself. And another thing I can't ignore is the fact that she has a half brother and sister. There may be meetings with them in the future. I don't know. I'll just have to play it by ear. It's not an easy situation. But I can't deny Stephanie access to her relatives just because it makes my life easier. That wouldn't be fair, Doug," Ellen pointed out.

"I know. You're right. It doesn't mean I have to like it though," Doug retorted grimly.

"You have a choice in all of this, Doug. I don't," Ellen said quietly.

They stared at each other. Doug stony-faced and angry. Ellen resolute.

"Fuck that bastard!" Doug exploded. "He's even managed to ruin the loveliest Christmas Eve I've ever had."

"That's only because you're letting him. And he's not going to ruin mine." Ellen put her arms around Doug and raised her lips to his.

"Thank you for my beautiful present. Thank you for your kindness to Stephanie. Thank you for being the nicest man I've ever met." She kissed him lovingly, passionately, wantonly.

He kissed her back fiercely, holding her tightly to him.

She was breathless when they drew apart.

"We'd better stop," Doug said huskily. "Stephanie might come up and get a lesson in the facts of life that would have Julie Ann's eyes out on stalks."

Ellen giggled in spite of herself.

"Oh, Doug, Doug, Doug." She buried her face in his shoulder.

"Ellen, soon it will be a new year and a new decade. You're going to have to make some decisions about where we're going. You can't run away from it for ever," Doug murmured into her hair.

"I know," she whispered.

"I only want to make you happy," he said earnestly.

"You do make me happy, Doug," Ellen looked into his eyes. "I never had a nicer Christmas Eve either. Not with anyone," she added emphatically.

"Could you keep New Year's Eve free for me?"

"Why? What are we doing?"

"You'll see," he promised. "Will you be able to get a babysitter?"

"I'm sure Mam and Dad wouldn't mind looking after Stephanie. Mam doesn't like New Year's Eve. She never goes out that night."

"Right. Well, wear your poshest frock. And leave the rest to me," Doug instructed.

"OK," Ellen agreed happily. And kissed him again for good measure.

❦

"Here you go, darling, don't drink it all at the one go." Alexandra held out a wrapped bottle to Chris.

"Oh! Thanks. Hold on, I'll go and get yours." Chris put the bottle down on the sofa without unwrapping it and walked out of the room.

Alexandra glanced impatiently at her watch. Chris had offered to drop her to the airport but time was getting on and she didn't want to be late. She wanted to have plenty of time to wander around the Duty Free.

He might at least have opened his present, she thought crossly. That bottle of Hennessy had cost an arm and a leg, considering her circumstances. Brandy was too bloody good for him. She should have bought him a bottle of plonk. She'd deliberated about buying him a present at all, but decided reluctantly that she couldn't burn her bridges with him until her new job was in the bag. It was best to keep him sweet just in case.

Alexandra sighed. If she didn't get the job with Arthur Reynolds, she might very well slit her wrists. She'd met Karen Finlay, a PR she'd been friendly with in Stuart and Stuart's, and they'd gone for a drink. Karen, who couldn't stand Ron Evans and who wasn't too enamoured of Malachy, had told Alexandra that Malachy was bad-mouthing her to anyone who would listen. And Ron Evans had told one of the typists that, if she didn't pull up her socks, *he'd* give her the sack the same way he'd given Alexandra Johnston the boot. She was being held up as an example.

Alexandra was furious. Typical of that lying toe-rag. She was so mad she seriously considered ratting on Ron to the tax people about all the nixers he did. If he had the taxman down on him for tax evasion that would soon wipe the self-satisfied smirk off his pimply mush.

As for Malachy, if he was going to play dirty, she was going to play twice as dirty. He had a few skeletons in his closet that she knew about, regarding his practice of ripping clients off. She knew about the padded bills and false accounting.

That evening she sat down and sent him a note, short and to the point.

Malachy,
If I hear one more squeak out of you about me, I'll be writing to the Dillon Group, Victor Conway and Ganley Inc. I'm sure they'd be very interested to find out about the way their bills were beefed up! The choice is yours. So bugger off and shut up . . . or else.
Yours sincerely,
Alexandra Johnston.
PS The same goes for Ron Evans.

If Malachy MacDonald thought for one second that he could trash her professional reputation and get away with it, he had another think coming. If he'd said anything derogatory about her to Arthur Reynolds she'd wipe the floor with him.

Another five days to her interview. It couldn't come soon enough. She wished Christmas was well and truly over. She glanced at the scrawny artificial Christmas tree that stood in front of the balcony doors. It was a sad-looking affair. Chris had arrived home with it the previous day and insisted on putting it up. She thought he was mad. Maybe he was trying to cheer himself up because he would be on his own for Christmas. He was going to his mother's for lunch – other than that he'd no plans, he'd informed her.

Alexandra hadn't told him she was coming home early. She didn't want him to know about her interview, in case she didn't get the job. She'd tell him she'd come home early to save money. She was also curious to know if she would find him entertaining another woman. Knowing Chris, she wouldn't put it past him. No! Surprise was the name of the game and she'd certainly surprise him.

"Come on, Chris," she yelled. "I don't have all day."

"What's the rush? Here, Happy Christmas." Chris handed her a rectangular package. He gave her a peck on the cheek.

Alexandra unwrapped it briskly. *Chanel No 5*. How predictable. He certainly hadn't sat down and racked his brains to think of something special. No more than she had for him, she acknowledged.

"Thank you, darling. *Very* thoughtful." The sarcasm in her tone went completely over his head.

"I know it's your favourite, Alexandra." Chris smiled ingratiatingly.

"You certainly know how to pamper a woman," Alexandra said dryly.

"A sensual perfume for a sensual woman. That perfume was invented with you in mind." Chris kissed her hand gallantly.

"You charmer." Alexandra laughed in spite of herself. "Come on, take my bag out to the car. I might buy a sexy nightie when I'm in London. And you can slide it off me inch by inch, when I get home."

"Hmmm," Chris murmured as he nuzzled her ear. "Have we time for a dress rehearsal?"

"No, we don't. You'll have to save it all up for me." Alexandra gave him a sultry stare.

"You're cruel." Chris pressed himself against her. He was aroused.

"But you like it when I'm cruel, don't you?" Alexandra caressed him.

"Come on, Alexandra, let's do it before you go away," Chris breathed, as he slid his hand inside her blouse.

"Ah ah!" Alexandra slapped him lightly. "All good things come to those who wait. Just think what a stallion you'll be when I get back."

"Please, Alexandra," Chris urged frantically.

She slipped out of his embrace. She wouldn't have actually minded a quickie, but this way was better. He'd have her on his mind while she was away. Keep them with their tongues hanging out was her motto. Rule number one. Tempt and tease.

"Do I have to phone for a taxi?" she purred.

"You're a witch, Alexandra." Chris growled.

"Yeah. That's me, wild and wicked. Think dirty thoughts when I'm gone and if you're good . . . we'll have a night of carnal lust, baby." She smiled seductively.

"Promises, promises," Chris said dryly.

"We'll see, now drive me to the airport or I'll miss my flight!" Alexandra slipped her fur coat over her shoulders and sashayed out the door. She had Chris where she wanted him . . . right in the palm of her hand.

Chris watched Alexandra disappear through the departure gate. She was something else. When she put her mind to it, she could really turn him on. But it was just a game to her. She had no real feelings for him. And he had none for her. It was lust, plain and simple. He was under no illusion that she wanted him living with her because she was crazy about him. She needed him to pay the rent. Nothing more, nothing less. Well, he wouldn't be a pawn in her little game for much longer. If things went to plan he'd be in the arms of a truly loving woman. Ellen would never turn him on and leave him dangling the way Alexandra just had. That was a mean thing to do. But Alexandra wouldn't be so smart when he packed his bags and walked out of her life for good. Alexandra Johnston had picked the wrong man to mess around with, as she would find out to her cost. It would be her tough luck if she had to leave that apartment. He'd have no qualms about that at all.

It all depended on Ellen. Life was strange, he thought despondently, as he walked to his car. Once upon a time, Ellen had been desperate for him to be a part of her life. Now he was desperate for her to take him back. If only he could persuade her. All his problems would be over. He could live with her and Stephanie. His mother would feel he was taking some responsibility for past deeds. She liked Ellen, that was a huge plus. He'd have a roof over his head that wouldn't cost him anything. A loving woman to take care of him. And Suzy and Alexandra could go whistle.

If he told Ellen that he'd left Suzy because he didn't love her and that he was living in a flat – he needn't say with whom – she'd surely feel sorry for him. She had such a soft heart. And she did love him very much. He'd always known that. If he told her that he couldn't get her out of his head and that she haunted him night and day, and that he only wanted to be with her and be a father to Stephanie, she'd have to take him back.

It was what she'd always wanted. This time he'd make a commitment to her. Once Ellen realised he was serious about making a fresh start with her, she'd dump that builder bloke out on his ass where he belonged.

Ellen loved *him*. Always had and always would, he assured himself once more. And he loved her. Of all the women he'd ever been with, Ellen was the one he truly loved. Once she realised that, they'd be together for ever. Chris was full of confidence as he started the ignition and drove off into the night.

Chapter Twenty-Five

"Well, there he goes." Mick rubbed his hands. "He's left the North Pole and heading for Iceland. Time to get ready for bed, I think."

"How long will it take him to get here?" Stephanie asked anxiously. She and Mick had been listening to Santa on the radio, reading out names and getting presents packed onto his sleigh, ready for his long trek.

"Maybe three or four hours. Look where I showed you on the atlas. Where's Ireland?"

Stephanie proudly pointed it out.

"And the North Pole?"

Stephanie jabbed her thumb on the spot.

"Excellent," her grandfather praised. Ellen hid a smile. Mick had gone through the same routine when she'd been a child. And he still made it all sound like the most exciting adventure ever.

"Will the reindeers be very tired?" There was a trace of anxiety in Stephanie's tone. Ireland looked a long way away from the North Pole.

"Oh, they're powerful reindeers. They've been training for this night all year long, never you fear. They'll be landing on this very roof in a few hours' time," Mick assured her.

"I just hope Santa remembers that I'm here and not in my own house," Stephanie fretted.

"Stephanie, you saw me putting the note up the chimney to remind him. You saw it was gone the next morning. He won't forget," Ellen said firmly.

"I think it's time to light the candle." Sheila bustled into the kitchen.

"Can I do it, Nannie?" Stephanie jumped up from the table.

"Yes, but be careful," Sheila said fondly. She handed Stephanie the long red candle and led the way into the parlour. Mick and Ellen smiled at each other and followed. Sheila parted the heavy drapes on the window and pulled aside the net curtains.

"Now place it in the holder and make sure it's straight," she instructed.

Stephanie did as she was bid.

"Now, Mick, switch off the light." Sheila smiled at her husband. Mick smiled back. They'd been through this ceremony every Christmas of their married life.

Ellen's resentment faded. Even though she'd wanted to spend Christmas in her own home, she was happy to share this little ceremony with them. And both her parents were as pleased as Punch to have Stephanie staying with them. Her childish excitement and anticipation brought back happy memories. Ellen would have been churlish to begrudge her parents a night of joy.

Sheila struck a match and handed it to her granddaughter. Solemnly, eyes as wide as saucers, Stephanie lit the wick and watched the candle flicker into light.

"Dear Jesus, let our candle light Your way into the world this blessed night," Sheila prayed.

"Amen," Mick, Ellen and Stephanie responded. They stood silently in the dark watching the candle flame brightly. In other windows across the valley candles shone like beacons. All over the country thousands of flickering lights sent their beams of welcome to the heavens.

Ellen clasped Stephanie's hand. In two days time it would be her precious child's birthday. Stephanie would be seven. How frightened and betrayed and distraught she'd been, awaiting the birth all those years ago. Miriam had been so kind to her that Christmas. And Chris, who'd never contacted her once, after he'd discovered she was pregnant, had got engaged without a care in the world. Seven years ago there'd been no light at the end of the tunnel. And yet here she was, a strong woman who'd come through it all. A woman who was at ease with herself.

Thank you, God. Somehow, on this special night, the silent prayer of thanks Ellen sent up seemed appropriate.

"Right, Stephanie, let's go and find the biggest stocking in my sock drawer. It's time we hung it up!" Mick decreed.

"Ooohhh yes, grandad!" Stephanie skipped out of the room and up the stairs on the trail of the soon-to-be-filled Christmas stocking, her eyes dancing with excitement.

Mick winked at Ellen. "I got your mother to knit a huge one. Wait until she sees it."

"He's worse than any child," Sheila declared but she was smiling.

⚬⚬⚬

Denise McMahon looked at the bulky rectangular box plonked inside the door of her shed and felt unbridled rage engulf her. It was a brand new Hoover. With six attachments. She'd watched her husband unloading it from his car the previous night. Denise knew it wasn't for her. She had a vacuum. Why on earth would he buy her a new one? Especially now that he'd got so mean with his money and the atmosphere in the house was taut with tension.

It was a Christmas present for that scabby little cow he was screwing. Esther Dowling was reaping the benefits of Jimmy's wage packet and their children were going short because of it. The money Jimmy'd given her to spend for Christmas was derisory. She'd had to dip into her precious earnings yet again. Every time she needed something new for the kids now, it was a battle.

"Don't be annoying me about bloody money, you're always the

same," Jimmy roared at her when she'd said she needed more than he'd given her to buy the girls Christmas clothes and toys.

He obviously hadn't batted an eyelid when he'd been shelling out her housekeeping money for that Specky Spinster's Christmas present. Esther had bought a new house in Swords and Jimmy was certainly helping her to furnish it. Doing the big fella with money he should be spending on his own family.

He was upstairs now, doing himself up. Denise had got the whiff of aftershave wafting out of the bathroom. He'd grunted that he was going out for a few hours. Denise knew where he was going. He was going over to Swords to throw his white skinny leg over that simpering little bitch with her wide innocent eyes and her *Helpless-Little-Me* ways.

Imagine, he couldn't even spend Christmas Eve with his children. Denise clenched her fists in anger as she stood in the cold, dimly lit shed trying to compose herself. His two daughters were just a nuisance to him. She'd been Christmas shopping last week and she'd got delayed in Dublin. Then she'd missed the bus and had had to wait another hour for the next one. It was almost half seven when she got home.

Jimmy was waiting for her, face like a thundercloud. "Don't you bloody think you're landing me with them just because you're working now and you haven't time to be gadding about during the week," he'd ranted wrathfully. "Don't pull any of your smart stunts on me."

"They're your children too, Jimmy," Denise insisted.

"You wanted 'em. You look after 'em," was the response she'd got. He didn't even care if Lisa and Michelle overheard him. His daughters' feelings meant nothing to him. He'd stormed out and hadn't come home until cockcrow.

Denise filled her basin with potatoes from the sack. She was preparing the Christmas dinner and needed potatoes to parboil them for the morning. The more she'd prepared in advance, the better. He'd be at home for his Christmas dinner, the two-faced hypocrite. She scowled. And he'd be at Mass in the front seat, ready to do the collection. Everyone would think he was a great man. Ready to help out where he was asked. A real street angel and house devil. That's what she was married to.

No one would believe that fine, upstanding, honest, hard-working Jimmy McMahon was capable of the lies, deviousness and emotional cruelty that he meted out to his wife and family. No one would believe her. She had to put on a facade of normality when visiting his relatives and hers. She was part of the lie because she hadn't the guts to walk away from him and fend for herself.

She looked at the brown box that Esther would open with little squeals of delight. Did she ever see the dark side of him? Denise wondered. Or was he always charming to her? Did she ever see the moody, aggressive, abusive, threatening side of Jimmy or was that reserved solely for her and the girls. Probably. Her husband was sly. He could switch the charm on and off as required.

Tiredly she switched off the light and walked down the garden path to the back door. Jimmy was in the kitchen when she stepped inside. He was polishing his glasses. His hair was washed, his jaw smooth, shaved of its five-o'clock shadow. He smelt nice. He used to take care of himself and keep himself groomed when he was courting her but that had all worn off, once he'd got the ring on her finger and felt he was entitled to have sex whenever he wanted. Not that he'd been great in bed either. He was lazy and selfish, only concerned with his own pleasure. Her marital life had been a big disappointment. And now, because she couldn't bear to be near him, she slept in her daughters' room. Deprived of love and warmth and companionship and sex, all the things she'd expected when she'd said "I do." Her fairytale had had a very bitter ending. But he was having the life of Reilly.

"I'll need a white shirt ironed for Mass tomorrow," he grunted, his slitty brown eyes cold and hostile.

"I ironed a white shirt for you," Denise snapped.

"I'm wearing it."

Denise put the basin of potatoes in the sink. She felt herself start to shake.

"Listen you, if you want a white shirt ironed for Mass get your lazy little tart to iron it for you. I'm sure she'll be delighted to do it for you when you give her her brand new Hoover. And the next time I see her, I'm going to ask her how she can live with herself knowing that the money you're spending on her should be spent on your daughters and their home."

"By Christ, I'll break your bloody neck!" Jimmy advanced menacingly on her. His eyes were black with fury. Denise felt a sudden fear. He was six-foot four and he had his fists clenched. He was vicious. She shrank back.

"You listen to me, ya poxy bitch," he roared, jabbing his finger into her face, "if you ever say anything like that to me again and if you ever go near Esther, I'll punch you so hard in the face, I'll break every tooth in your head. I'll knock you into kingdom come. Do you hear me?"

"Daddy! Stop it." Lisa and Michelle stood in the doorway, crying.

"Do you hear me?" Jimmy yelled, ignoring their distress.

"Jimmy, stop it." Denise was horrified as well as petrified. How could he do this in front of the girls?

"Just you remember," he warned and stabbed his finger hard into her shoulder. It hurt and she winced.

"There's more where that came from," he threatened. He barged past Denise, out the back door, slamming it hard behind him. The sobbing little girls ran to her.

"Mammy, I hate Daddy," Michelle sobbed.

"Sshhh, sshhh, it's all right." Denise hugged them close. "Don't worry, it's all right." She felt faint. Jimmy had come very close to striking her. Would that be the next step? A battering! She couldn't think about it now. She had to reassure her daughters and create a semblance of normality.

"We better put a glass of milk and some mince pies out for Santa," she said lightly, although her voice had a quiver in it.

"Daddy told us there was no Santa. He said *he* bought the toys with his money," Michelle hiccuped.

"What? When did he say that?" Denise couldn't believe her

ears. How typically spiteful of Jimmy to take it out on the kids.

"He said it the day he was minding us."

"Why didn't you tell me?" Denise asked weakly.

"'Cos he told us not to. He told us we wouldn't get any toys if we didn't behave ourselves."

"You will get toys, pet. Don't worry," Denise promised.

"Is there no Santa, Mammy?"

Denise saw two pairs of doubtful brown eyes raised to hers.

What was she supposed to say?

"What do you think?" she asked gently, testing the water.

The younger one, Michelle, said solemnly, "I think there is one, 'cos a girl in my class saw his sleigh and heard bells in the sky last year."

"I think she's absolutely right," Denise agreed. "Why don't you go and get your stocking? And we'll hang it up."

"Daddy's not going to get anything 'cos he was really bad. And I wish he'd go away and never come back." Michelle marched out of the room, a very angry and confused little girl.

"There's no Santa, Mam, sure there isn't?" Lisa said flatly. "I know there isn't."

Wordlessly Denise held out her arms to her. Lisa slipped into her mother's embrace and Denise stroked her head. "Don't let on though to Michelle or Rebecca or Stephanie. We have to pretend."

"I hate pretending. And I hate pretending that I like Daddy. And if he ever pokes you with his finger again I'll stab him with a knife."

"Stop, pet. Don't say things like that. He won't do it again. He just lost his temper, that's all," Denise lied.

Tears spilled down her cheeks as she held her elder daughter tightly. Tonight they'd lost their childhood. From now on they'd worry every time they heard Jimmy's voice raised in anger. Christmas Eve should have been a night of carefree anticipation and innocent delight, instead it had turned into a night of fear. Denise would never forgive Jimmy for that.

Julie Ann knelt on her window seat peering out into the darkness. She wished her mummy and daddy were at home. They'd gone to a party and she had a new babysitter. It wasn't even Mrs Murdock. Some girl from the village that she didn't know was downstairs eating *loads* of *her* chocolates and drinking *loads* of her lemonade. When Julie Ann had told her she wasn't going to bed until her mummy came home, that girl had said, "Get up those stairs or I'll give you a clip in the ear." No one had ever spoken to her like that before. Julie Ann stuck her tongue out and the girl chased her upstairs and told her that she'd wallop her. Andrew had cried for ages and she just left him in his cot crying. She wasn't at all like Mrs Murdock and Julie Ann didn't like her one little bit.

She climbed down off the window seat and picked up the big red sock that was lying across the bottom of her bed. She was the only one who had a big red sock. Stephanie and Rebecca always had grey socks that men wore and they weren't as big as hers, she comforted herself. Santa would have to give her loads of presents to fill *her* sock.

She'd asked for a new bike with stabilisers. And a new Barbie and a cash register and shop set. She'd have the best toys in the school. She heard a noise outside and her heart leaped to her mouth. She flew over to the window. Maybe it was Santa coming. She wanted to see *everything*. She peered eagerly into the starry sky. But it was still the same as before. Just stars and the moon. She listened intently. Was that the sound of tinkling bells?

Just say her mummy and daddy came home just as Santa was landing on the roof. They might frighten the reindeers away. Everyone knew reindeers didn't like to be seen. It was very upsetting indeed, Julie Ann fretted. No other mummies and daddies that she knew went out on Christmas Eve. Auntie Miriam and Auntie Ellen were getting their food ready for Christmas. Uncle Ben was helping Auntie Miriam. They were all staying in because Santa was coming. Even Mrs Murdock was staying in her own house with Mr Murdock.

Why couldn't her mummy and daddy stay at home on such an important night? Julie Ann thought crossly. Why did they always have to be going to parties?

⸙

"Nice little vinegar," Emma murmured to Gillian as she sipped a glass of white wine at Diana Mackenzie's supper party.

Gillian spluttered. "Bitch!" She grinned.

"Well, I ask you, Gillian. How cheap can you get? It's pure plonk. You and I serve the best wine and champagne when we're having a bash. Diana's always the same. She guzzles it down and then serves us rubbish. Has she no shame? Or that cheapskate husband of hers?"

"Don't be silly, Emma," Gillian derided, "Nick would drink methylated spirits and think it tasted good."

"True," Emma agreed.

"Look, there's Anna McManus. She looks a bit miserable. I wonder is Gerard Butler dressing up in his frills tonight?" Gillian bit into a smoked salmon vol au vent.

"It's just as well she found out before the wedding. Think of the disaster it would have been if she'd found out afterwards." Emma stared at the object of their pity, curiously. Gillian was right, poor Anna looked drawn and haggard. Just when she thought she'd been set for life this awful thing had happened to her and she was back to square one, looking for a man.

"She's no spring chicken either." Gillian followed her friend's gaze. "Poor thing!"

"Oh no, here's that crashing bore, Philippa Devine." Emma fixed a false smile in place. "Philippa, nice to see you," she fibbed.

"And you, darlings." Philippa air-kissed Emma's and Gillian's cheeks. "So how's life in the sticks, Emma? As my father would say." Philippa gave a hearty guffaw. She was known as Philippa *"As-my-Father-Would-Say"* Devine, because of her irritating habit of constantly quoting her equally annoying father, a less than scintillating so-called "personality". Philippa hero-worshipped him.

"Don't be ridiculous, Philippa. If you'd any sense of geography you'd hardly call North County Dublin the sticks. They don't build airports in the sticks, you know. And we live only ten minutes from the airport." Irritation got the better of Emma.

"Oh, my father maintains that a mile north of Trinity is the sticks," Philippa volunteered. She took a slug of her red wine. She had a fondness for the grape.

"And how is Daddy?" Gillian asked sweetly.

"Marvellous! Marvellous! He's starting a new series on RTÉ soon. Very intellectual, very thought-provoking. He's researching it at the moment." Philippa's grey eyes sparkled with enthusiasm. She'd gained entry to many a party on her father's coat-tails.

"How's Dennis?" Emma inquired.

Dennis was Philippa's long-suffering husband. He too was "an intellectual", as Philippa was prone to point out. He was a sub-editor on an evening paper and if Philippa was fond of the grape, Dennis was even fonder of it. Emma could see him, pissed as a newt in the corner.

"Couldn't be better," Philippa said stoutly. "I say, Emma, is it true that Suzy and Chris have split up?"

"Unfortunately yes." Emma sighed. She was heartily sick of being asked about Chris, Suzy and Alexandra Johnston.

"But it's Alexandra Johnston he's involved with? Isn't it?" Philippa asked. Her grey eyes bulged earnestly behind her bottle-top glasses.

"I believe so," Emma said tightly.

"How extremely *peculiar*, as my father would say. I saw him in a restaurant with Jilly Fleming and they looked most . . . er . . . rather intimate. That's why I thought I was mistaken when I heard it was Alexandra Johnston he'd left Suzy for."

"I really don't know, Philippa. You'd have to speak to Chris about it," Emma said through gritted teeth.

"Oh gosh . . . no. Couldn't do that. None of your ruddy business, my father would say. I was just curious, that's all."

Philippa drained her glass and raised it aloft. "Must top up." She beamed. "'Scuse me."

"She'll be four sheets to the wind before the evening's out. I saw her taking a slug out of that little bottle of vodka she carries in her bag," Gillian observed. She eyed Emma cautiously. "I wouldn't be a bit surprised if she did see Chris with Jilly Fleming. She's man-mad. She told me Louis's a real dead duck in bed."

"I wouldn't believe a word out of Philippa Devine's mouth, Gillian. She's permanently pissed," Emma retorted crossly.

"Hmm," Gillian murmured non-committally.

Emma frowned. She was highly annoyed with Chris. What the hell was he playing at? Privately she was quite sure Philippa hadn't been mistaken about Chris and Jilly. He was getting a real name for himself. And she was absolutely fed up having to answer questions about his private life. If this party was any indication of what the season was going to be like she was going to rusticate in the goddamn sticks. Emma scowled as she sought Vincent in the high-spirited throng.

"Cheer up!" Vincent reached out an arm and drew her close. "Guess what?" he whispered.

"What?"

"Did you see me talking to Ray McLean?"

Emma nodded.

"He's selling a property in the city centre and he wants me to look after it for him. It's going to be a very lucrative deal. I think I feel a skiing-trip coming on."

"Oh Vincent," Emma squealed. "When?"

"The end of January. Early February. We'll see what Mrs Murdock says. What do you think?"

"Oh darling, a whole week of you all to myself. Bliss!" Emma sighed, cuddling in close.

"Let's see if there's any mistletoe at this party." Vincent led her out of the crowded room. They slipped into a small drawing-room off the hall. It was empty. Vincent closed the door and drew her close.

"Mrs Munroe, did I tell you that you look stunning tonight?" he murmured against her ear.

"Yes, you did, but you can tell me again," Emma sighed happily, all thoughts of Chris and his *ménage à trois* banished as she kissed her husband passionately without a piece of mistletoe in sight.

Suzy sat sipping brandy in the firelight while her friend Niamh put the children to bed. David, Niamh's husband, had taken his father for a drink and the two girls were just going to flop after the frenzy of the day. Niamh was extremely organised. All the preparations were made for the Christmas dinner. The big oval table in the dining-room was set. The rest of the night was theirs. She had insisted that Suzy relax while she bathed her own two daughters and the twins. She'd been too exhausted to argue. It must be the country air, she thought wearily. She was yawning her head off.

It was such a cosy room, Suzy reflected as she snuggled into a corner of the old plump sofa, which stood at a right angle to the huge log fire. Niamh hadn't pulled the curtains and Suzy could see the lights of houses in the distance, scattered over the hillsides, like fireflies against black velvet. Now and then the lights of a car travelling along the mountainy winding roads would flicker and shimmer before disappearing into inky darkness. The stars sparkled far, far brighter than she'd ever seen them in the city. A golden wedge of moon hung low between the hilltops.

It was a peaceful scene but it made Suzy feel immensely sad. Tears brimmed in her eyes. How had Chris spent Christmas Eve? Had Alexandra left him alone and gone to London? She hoped she had. That would have to mean they weren't as crazy about each other as they seemed. After all, she reasoned, if you were nuts about someone, wouldn't you want to be with them morning, noon and night? Especially at Christmas.

That hadn't really occurred to her when Chris had asked her to allow him to come home for Christmas. She'd been too mad to think straight. But as she thought about it now, a forlorn hope glimmered on the horizon. Maybe the love affair wasn't running too smoothly. Why hadn't Chris gone to London with Alexandra? Had she not asked him to go? Or had she asked him and he'd said no? Surely she would have wanted to stay with him. Surely they'd want to spend their first Christmas together.

If Alexandra had got the sack, perhaps she wouldn't have been able to go to London. Maybe she and Chris were cuddling in front of the fire right this minute.

It was the not knowing that got to Suzy. She'd dialled Alexandra's number earlier but there'd been no answer. Were her husband and best friend together or apart?

"Please let them split up, please," she prayed. How she *willed* that affair to break up. It was the one thing she wanted most in the world. She wouldn't care if he shacked up with another woman. Anyone as long as it wasn't Alexandra. The hatred she felt for her former friend could not be described. Its malevolence increased with each passing day. There was no respite. She was riven with misery picturing them together, going to cocktail parties as a couple while she was banished from her rightful place at Chris's side. The humiliation and shame of having people know that he preferred to be with Alexandra than with her was unbearable. What had Alexandra ever given him that she hadn't? Was it the sex? Was it because Chris thought she wasn't good in bed? She'd never tied him up and played erotic games with him. And yet, she'd always felt she'd satisfied him.

Suzy swallowed hard. She wouldn't cry any more. But it was difficult, very, very difficult. She hadn't imagined how painful Christmas would be. Hard as she tried she couldn't stop thinking about them, such was her obsession.

It had been particularly bad the past few days. Mrs Wallace's support seemed to have brought her anger bubbling to the surface. She was a woman alone, with two young children to think of, and her selfish slug of a husband was having a wonderful time living like a bachelor. Life was so damned unfair. She'd never have thought her life would end up in tatters the way it had. She'd been riding high. When Chris had proposed to her, seven years ago, just after Christmas, there was no happier woman. And Alexandra had pretended to be delighted for her. Her so-called best friend.

Well at least that bitch had got the sack. And her name was mud in their set. Suzy was making sure of that. And she was keeping tabs on just who entertained them as a couple. Anyone who did was dead in her book. She'd cut them. Just like that. Katherine had given her backbone. Her mother-in-law had told her to hold her head high. By God she would. She wouldn't lie down and die under this disaster. This was a war she was determined to win.

Suzy took another sip of brandy. It burned her throat. She heard the high jinks upstairs and gave a tight smile. Alexandra and Chris would have their hands full in another few days and she wished them the joy of it. See how long they'd last together when Alexandra found out that she was going to have two lively children staying every second weekend.

"So, are you looking forward to Christmas?" Chris leaned forward and gave the blonde beauty beside him the full benefit of his most intimate stare.

"No! I loathe it," she said frankly.

"Why?" Chris pretended to be shocked.

"It's so boring. Mummy and Pops will have friends in for drinks and then it's time for lunch. And after that there's nothing to do."

"So you live at home?" Chris was disappointed.

"Yaw. I'm a secretary in RTÉ. I live in Blackrock. It suits me for the time being until I find a place of my own." The blonde took a sip of her drink.

"Let me get you another," Chris offered. "Dubonnet and white, wasn't it?"

"You've a good memory." The blonde smiled.

"And *you* have a beautiful smile," Chris said huskily, giving her his best come-hither look.

He made his way through the multitudes swarming the bar. Kiely's on Christmas Eve was jam-packed. The smell of sweat and alcohol and cigarette and cigar smoke mingled with the delicate scents of women's perfume. The festive air of gaiety and good humour lifted his spirits. Sod Alexandra and Suzy, he hadn't lost his touch. That blonde bird, Alison, that he'd just pulled was a cracker. He was in with a chance. He wasn't going to end up sleeping alone, tonight of all nights. His wedding-ring was in his breast pocket. It was time he took it off for good anyway, he decided defiantly as he ordered another round of drinks.

"So, Chris, you're in insurance?" Alison turned limpid brown eyes on him as he sat down beside her again and poured the white lemonade into her Dubonnet.

"I have my own insurance company. Business is good," he confided.

"And where do you live?"

"Myself and a friend share one of those new apartments near Herbert Park." He kept his answer deliberately evasive.

"Wow!" Alison was clearly impressed. "They're fabulous."

"Come back for coffee, and you can see for yourself," Chris invited casually. "Or have you another party to go to?"

"Well, some of the girls," she indicated a group of giggly young women, "felt like going for a meal. I haven't eaten anything much today, I thought I'd go with them."

"As a matter of fact I haven't eaten much either. Look, I know this superb little Italian place that does magnificent pasta dishes, how about coming for a meal with me? I can drop you home later," Chris suggested.

"Have you nothing else on?" she asked in surprise. "I thought you business types would have lots of cocktail parties to go to."

Chris gave her his best world-weary gaze. "Alison, I could spend all night dropping into cocktail parties and suppers but they get so boring. Let's be mad and do something different. Let's have a meal and then go and drink champagne on the top of Killiney Hill." He brought his light-hearted boyishness into play.

"Won't it be cold on top of Killiney Hill?"

"I can keep you warm." He darkened his eyes seductively.

Alison met his gaze squarely. "Sounds good to me." She stroked his hand. "Then we can go home to your place for coffee."

Yes! Chris silently acknowledged his expertise with birds. Alison would certainly be a very happy woman by the time he was finished with her. He could always see her again if he wanted to. Or not. The choice was his.

Alexandra was living it up in London. Suzy was with another man. Ellen was with that hairy ape. He'd feared being on his own tonight. But it wasn't going to happen. So stuff them all, he thought triumphantly as he let his hand slide seductively along Alison's thigh.

Chapter Twenty-Six

"**C**ome in, dear. Make yourself at home. You found the address all right?" Katherine opened the door wide to admit Ellen and Stephanie. It was the Sunday after Christmas. The day they'd decided upon as the most convenient for tea.

"Thank you, Mrs Wallace. We got here fine. Your directions were spot on." Ellen smiled as she handed the other woman a gift tin of shortbread.

"Ellen, there was no need," Katherine reproved.

"It's just a small token, Mrs Wallace," Ellen assured her. "The shortbread is home-made. One of my partners has a very rich recipe that's five hundred years old. Her Scottish grandmother gave it to her and she makes it for The Deli. I hope you like it."

"What a lovely thought. I'm sure I shall." Katherine was charmed. "Hello, Stephanie." She smiled down at her granddaughter.

"Hello." Stephanie smiled back and thrust a box of chocolates at her. "This is for you too."

"Dear, dear, two presents. I'm very lucky today. Thank you very much."

"Your hair is nice." Stephanie studied her grandmother with approval. She didn't look at all like a grandmother.

"Is it?" Katherine patted her ash-blonde bob. "I had it done specially yesterday, you see. For my very special guests."

"Who are they?" Stephanie inquired innocently.

"Why, you and Mummy, of course."

"Oh!" Stephanie's eyes lit up. She hadn't thought of herself as a Very Special Guest. "What will I call you?" she asked as she unbuttoned her smart red coat.

"Well, I'm your grandmother. How about Gran?"

"Gran, guess what?" Stephanie hadn't a hint of shyness about her as she gazed up at her new grandmother.

"What, dear?"

"It was my birthday on Saint Stephen's Day. 'Cos that's why I'm called Stephanie. And I was seven. And guess what?"

"You'll have to tell me." Katherine smiled.

"We had a party. But it wasn't really for grown-ups. And do you know what Julie Ann did?"

"What did she do?"

"She saw my Spirograph and she wanted it and she broke one of my special Spirograph pens."

"Tsk, tsk! What a shame," Katherine tutted, entranced by her granddaughter's direct air.

"An' then you know what?" Stephanie's eyes were wide. "She ate *all* the chocolate biscuits and gave herself a pain in her tummy and then she went blah all over the floor. And Auntie Emma was really cross."

"I bet she was," Katherine chuckled. "Now let's not stand in the hall. I have a lovely big fire lighting in the lounge. It's nice and cosy there. Let me take your coat, Ellen."

Ellen handed her coat to the older woman, who hung it in a neat cloakroom off the hall. The hallway was extremely elegant, Ellen thought in admiration as she looked around her.

Striped cream and green embossed paper lined the top half of the walls, complemented by a deep green silky paper below the dado rail. A richly hued carpet of greens and creams covered the stairs and hallway. The pile was so deep, Ellen could feel it soft beneath her shoes. A gleaming gold ornate mirror hung on one wall. Beneath it, an antique table, on which reposed a Belleek china rose bowl, filled with winter roses. On a matching table, between two of the cream doors that lined the hallway, an urn of holly sprays and red and white carnations made a beautiful festive display. A cream and green lamp stood on a small stand beside the front door.

"You have lovely taste, Mrs Wallace," Ellen complimented her hostess.

"When the boys left home and my husband died I was tempted to sell, I must admit," Katherine confessed as she led the way into the lounge, "but I've lived here all my married life. And I do rather love my gardens. So I completely redecorated. It won't have to be done again in my lifetime. Now, dear, can I get you a drink before we have tea? I'm sure Stephanie would like lemonade."

"Yes, please," Stephanie piped up.

"A sherry, gin and tonic, vodka and tonic, Dubonnet, white wine?"

"A Dubonnet would be lovely." Ellen sank down into a deep sofa.

"Maybe Stephanie might come and help me," Katherine suggested.

"Of course I will, Gran," Stephanie agreed eagerly. She'd been warned to be on her best behaviour.

Ellen felt more relaxed as she watched the duo depart hand in hand. She'd been a little apprehensive about coming to Mrs Wallace's for tea. Just say they had nothing to talk about. Ellen felt she wasn't great at polite conversation. That was more Emma's forte. But the older woman seemed genuinely pleased to see them and Stephanie was chuffed to have another grandmother.

It was a beautiful room. Ellen gazed around with interest. Katherine had exquisite taste. Wide expensive pale blue and gold rugs covered the highly polished floor. Pale blue drapes, tied back with gold tasselled cords, hung from the windows. The frilled pelmets were trimmed with gold edging.

Great bowls of massed fresh flowers stood on the ornate tables that dotted the large room. Alongside the flowers, framed photos, china figurines – Ellen thought they were Lladro, but she wasn't sure – and Waterford crystal stood elegantly, in nonchalant display. So different from her mother's regimented *Best China* cabinet in the parlour.

The sofas, arranged in front of the fireplace, were covered in blue and gold chintz. A small coffee table held magazines and a selection of Sunday papers. Blue and gold lamps were everywhere. But they weren't needed yet even though an early dusk was beginning to mute the vivid sunset.

A perfectly shaped fir Nobilis, strung with white lights and blue and gold decorations, stood in front of the long window, casting sparkling prisms of light into the room. Boughs of holly and long slender red candles were the only other Christmas decoration. Elegant and understated, just like Katherine.

Ellen smiled wryly, thinking of her own jolly, gaudy adornments. Even though it was a big wide room, there was a comfortable snug feel to it. A very nice room to relax in, she thought, as she flicked idly through a magazine.

"Here we are." Katherine handed her a long slim glass of ruby liquid that was cool to the touch. Stephanie solemnly offered a bowl of peanuts.

"Mammy, I'm having sausages and chips for tea. But you and Gran are having something different."

"Mrs Wallace, I hope you aren't going to any trouble," Ellen remonstrated.

"None at all, my dear. I got two T-bone steaks to go with the chips. This is a rare treat for me, you know. I'd never cook myself chips normally," Katherine said briskly.

"Now, Stephanie, if you go over to the Christmas tree you'll find two parcels underneath it. Would you be so kind as to bring them over to me, please." Katherine's eyes twinkled.

Stephanie needed no second urging. She sped across the room on winged feet, her pigtails flying. Moments later she was back, her arms full.

"The big box is yours and the small soft one is for your

mummy." Katherine settled back and prepared to enjoy the unwrapping.

"Mrs Wallace, you shouldn't have," Ellen murmured in embarrassment as Stephanie dumped the parcel into her lap.

"It's just something small and I hope it suits." Katherine sipped her sherry.

Ellen unfolded the soft pink angora scarf from beneath the layers of tissue paper it was wrapped in.

"Oh, it's lovely," she exclaimed in delight, rubbing it against her cheek. "Thanks very much."

"My pleasure, Ellen." Katherine was gracious.

"Mammy, look!" Stephanie chirped excitedly as she gazed in awe at the magnificent tea set unveiled from its crisp wrapping.

"Oh, Stephanie, what do you say to your gran? It's gorgeous." Ellen got down on her knees beside her daughter and fingered one of the delicate cups. "It's really beautiful." She smiled up at Katherine.

"I thought it was rather special. A special present for a special girl," Katherine said quietly.

Stephanie jumped to her feet and threw her arms around her surprised grandmother.

"Thanks very, very much, Gran," she exclaimed, her face alight with pleasure. "It's brill!"

Katherine, unused to such displays of childish affection, returned the hug warmly, her face wreathed in smiles.

"So some day you can have a tea party and I'll come and visit you, if Mummy won't mind?" She glanced at Ellen.

"I'd be delighted, Mrs Wallace. I really would," Ellen said, and meant it.

"Mind that, Adam." Chris snatched Alexandra's sandalwood pen box from his curious son's grasp. This was a nightmare, an absolute nightmare. Christina had already broken one of Alexandra's prized handcrafted wine goblets. There was going to be hell to pay because of it.

True to her word, Suzy had arrived yesterday at midday with the twins. She'd insisted he come down to the foyer. She had no intention of setting foot inside the building, she told him snootily over the intercom. She kissed the twins, handed him a case of clothes and toys, and announced that he could drop them home the following weekend. "And they're to go to Toby Collins's birthday party tomorrow afternoon. His card and present are in the case."

"But I have to go to work," he protested. "I can't close the office for a full week."

"You've done it before when you lived with me. Just left your secretary to open up. Anyway Alexandra can look after them – I hear she's unemployed," Suzy retorted tartly.

"She's in London," Chris growled.

"Well, they're all yours then. You've got them all to yourself. Just what you wanted. Bye, darlings." She blew the twins a kiss and departed without a backward glance.

He'd forgotten exactly how much attention small children needed. He'd forgotten their curiosity and their short attention span. He'd forgotten that bottoms needed wiping, and sometimes accidents happened. He'd forgotten squabbles and temper tantrums. And as for cooking for them and feeding them, or rather watching them feed themselves, that was a complete and utter trial to him. And now they were wrecking Alexandra's prized possessions.

"Don't touch anything again, Adam." Chris tried to keep his irritation in check.

"I want to play with it," Adam protested.

"Well, you can't," Chris barked.

Adam's mouth opened wider than Galway Bay and he started to howl. "I want Mummy," he bawled.

"Adam, stop crying for heaven's sake. Get your Dinkies and we'll play cars."

"Don't want to play with you," Adam pouted. "You're too cross."

"I'm sorry. C'mere. Give Daddy a big hug." Chris scooped his son up and started to tickle him. Adam squealed with pleasure. Chris winced. He'd made inroads into Alexandra's brandy gift to him the previous night and he was desperately hungover.

"Right, let's get shipshape, we're going to visit Gran today," he declared.

"But you said we could sail our boats and feed the ducks," Christina insisted.

"Yes, we'll do that first." Chris picked up a mug of milk that was in danger of being knocked over.

"What's for dinner, Daddy? I'm hungry," Adam whined. "Why have you got no turkey?"

"I've got nice steak and potatoes though," Chris said heartily. He'd bought steak because he could fling it on the pan and it was handy. Mashed potatoes and gravy and tinned peas would do fine with it.

"We'll go to the park first and then I'll get dinner." The twins scurried to get their coats.

Herbert Park was a godsend, he thought gratefully as twenty minutes later his children happily fed the ducks and sailed their little sailboats along the edge of the pond. This was a singular treat for them and he'd been able to quell any misbehaviour by threatening not to allow them feed the ducks.

At least the weather was fine, if a bit chilly. He blew on his hands and rubbed them together watching his breath freeze in the icy air.

All in all, Christmas hadn't been the disaster he'd dreaded. Alison had stayed on Christmas Eve. She'd phoned her parents and fibbed that she was going to a party and was staying overnight with friends. He'd dropped her home in time for lunch on Christmas morning and then made his way to his mother's. She'd cooked a superb lunch for them both. He couldn't fault her there. He'd spent the rest of the day lounging around in her house and then on Saint Stephen's night he'd enjoyed another night of sex with Alison who seemed to be totally enamoured of him. He'd been a tad worried that she might realise that the flatmate was a woman but he'd made sure to lock Alexandra's bedroom door and pocket the key. She had an en suite and he had his own bathroom so there were no tell-tale signs there. Alison hadn't seemed to notice anything untoward. He knew she thought he was a good, eligible catch. He'd let her down gently when the time came. That might come sooner than she'd expect if all went to plan with Ellen.

Today was the day everything could change. He was sure it was today that his mother had invited her to tea. Anyway, whether it was today or not, he was going to drive past his mother's house every day until he saw Ellen's car parked in the drive.

He rubbed his hand over his stubbly jaw. He'd shower, shave and change when he got home. He looked a sight.

A thought struck him. On second thoughts, maybe he wouldn't tidy himself up. If he looked a wreck Ellen might have more sympathy for him. He'd better let them have their tea though. Katherine would not be at all pleased if he gatecrashed their meal.

He was dying to see Ellen. He did miss her. She was a beautiful, loving woman and she belonged with him. Chris felt quite cheerful as he called his children and set off for the apartment to cook dinner.

"That was delicious, Mrs Wallace. It's a treat to have a meal cooked for me." Ellen wiped her mouth with the beautiful cream linen napkin that matched the elegant tablecloth.

"I'm glad you enjoyed it. Did you enjoy it, Stephanie?"

"Oh, I'm stuffed," Stephanie responded earnestly.

"Let's have our coffee in the lounge," Katherine suggested.

"Well, let me clear away the dishes," Ellen offered.

"Not at all, Ellen. Leave them. It won't take me long."

"Are you sure?"

"Absolutely sure," Katherine said firmly.

They were ensconced by the fire, sipping their coffee, chatting about various menus Ellen could try out in The Deli when they heard the front door open. Childish voices called out. A look of dismay crossed Katherine's face. Before she could say anything the door burst open and two small children rushed into the room.

"Hi Gran, we were feeding the ducks today," the little boy said.

"Ellen, I'm sorry about this," Katherine said agitatedly as Chris walked into the room.

Ellen's heart did a flip-flop.

"Oh! Oh! Hello, Ellen," he said, before turning to his mother. "I'm terribly sorry, Mother, I didn't realise you were having guests."

"Well, I have as you can see, Christopher," Katherine said tightly.

"Gran, can we have lemonade?" the little girl asked as she watched Stephanie sipping hers through a straw.

"Gran's got visitors, we can't stay." Chris ran a hand wearily over his jaw.

Ellen felt as though she were holding her breath. It all seemed a little unreal. He looked very tired, she thought, shocked by his ungroomed appearance.

"It's OK, Chris, it's time we were going." Ellen placed her coffee cup on the table and stood up. She had to get out of here.

"Christopher can bring the children tomorrow." Katherine directed an icy stare at her son. "Please finish your coffee, Ellen."

"Are you my daddy Christopher?" Stephanie got up and walked over to him. She stood looking at him curiously. Chris was clearly abashed. He glanced at Ellen. He needed her permission. Their eyes met. She nodded imperceptibly.

"Yes, I am, Stephanie." He smiled into her serious blue eyes.

"Are you trying to grow a beard like Doug?"

Chris was taken aback by her childish directness. "Er . . . no . . . I just didn't shave."

"Oh!" Stephanie eyed him sternly. "My grandad shaves every morning. Sometimes he lets me put the frothy stuff on his face."

"Does he?"

"Yes, he does. He's tidy." The rebuke was pointed.

Good for you, Stephanie, Ellen approved.

"Why are you her daddy too? Are you everybody's daddy?" Christina demanded truculently. She didn't like her daddy being another girl's daddy. "Do you live with her now?"

"No, he doesn't," Stephanie said dismissively.

Katherine was horrified.

"Really, Christopher – "

"Gran, please can we have some lemonade? I'm parched," Adam whined.

"I'll help you get it," Stephanie offered.

"Is that your tea set?" Christina asked curiously.

"Yes. Would you like to drink your lemonade out of one of the cups? I'll let you if you like," Stephanie volunteered magnanimously.

"Ooohh yes. Can I? What's your name?"

"Stephanie. What's yours?"

"Christina an' his name is Adam. We're twins," she declared importantly.

"Did the two of them fit in the mammy's tummy?" Stephanie was agog as she turned to Ellen.

Oh Lord! Ellen nodded. "Yes, now why don't you set out two cups for Christina and Adam," she encouraged hastily. She felt sick. Stephanie was here in her grandmother's house playing with her half brother and sister while her father looked on. She'd never envisaged a scene like this in her wildest dreams. She was in turmoil. Seeing Chris again was a shock. It always was when she hadn't seen him for a while.

"I'll tell you what. I'll fill a jug with lemonade and we can pour it into the cups," Katherine said briskly. "And then Christopher must take the twins home because it's getting near their bedtime."

"Oh, Daddy lets us stay up late," Christina said airily as she followed her grandmother and Stephanie out to the kitchen. Adam hurried after them, afraid he'd miss something.

"I *am* sorry, Ellen," Chris said contritely. "Mother never said."

Ellen said nothing. She sat down slowly on the sofa.

"So, how have you been? You look great." Chris eased himself down beside her.

"I'm fine." She stared straight ahead, unwilling to meet his gaze.

"How's the new business going?"

"Fine."

"Ellen, please don't be short with me. I can't bear it."

"I wish you hadn't come."

"Why? Does that mean you still care about me?" he asked hopefully.

"No!" She was emphatic.

"What does it matter then?" he muttered.

"It's not fair on your mother!"

Chris sighed. "True. I didn't know you were going to be here. I only have the kids for a week and I wanted to bring them to see her. Again I can only apologise."

"What do you mean you only have the children for a week?" Ellen was confused.

"Suzy and I've split up. Our marriage is over. I moved out of home. I live in a flat now," Chris said wearily.

"You've split up from Suzy? Why?" Ellen was shocked.

"You wouldn't believe me if I told you," he challenged.

"What are you talking about, Chris?"

"My marriage is over because I don't love Suzy. I never have. There's only one woman I've ever loved and that's you, Ellen. I tried to tell you that the last time we were together. I told you I'd leave Suzy for you. But you didn't want me." He hung his head dejectedly.

"But I thought you were only saying it, the way you always say things. You know what you're like . . . promises, promises." Ellen was flabbergasted.

"Well, I wasn't. I meant it. Anyway, one way or another, Suzy and I are through."

"I'm sorry, Chris," Ellen said miserably. This was deeply shocking news. And he was saying he loved her. Still! He must be sincere. It stunned her. She couldn't take it in. He looked so forlorn her heart went out to him. He had dark rings around his eyes and a greyness to his skin that she'd never seen before.

"Ellen, I love you. I really do. I only want to be with you," he pleaded.

"Please, Chris, *don't*!"

"We could live together. I'd be a father to Stephanie. I'd do my utmost to make you happy. Couldn't you even think about it?"

He heard Katherine coming out of the kitchen.

"Please let me phone you, Ellen. Please meet me and talk it over. Please say yes before Mother comes in."

Ellen didn't know what to say. Chris and Suzy had separated. He still loved her. He wanted to live with her. What was she to think?

"Please, baby," he said huskily.

It was the old endearment that did it. "All right," she whispered as Stephanie, carrying a plate of biscuits, marched into the room followed by the twins and their grandmother. The surprise appearance of her father hadn't knocked a feather out of her, Ellen thought in relief.

"Time for tea," she announced, blithely unaware of the tension between the adults. "It's pretend tea, it's really lemonade," she informed Chris.

"It sounds delicious. I'd love a cup." His eyes crinkled as he smiled. Ellen's heart gave a little twist. His smile had always disarmed her.

Katherine, in silence, poured the lemonade into the small cups. Ellen could see she was angry with Chris. It made her feel embarrassed.

Stephanie busied herself handing out the cups. "Isn't this fun, Mammy?" She handed Ellen her cup.

"Yes, love, it is."

"Mammies get theirs first," she explained to Chris as she handed him his. "Then daddies." She studied him intently. "Are you rich?"

"Stephanie!" Ellen spluttered. "That's rude."

"Why do you ask?" Chris asked curiously.

"Julie Ann's daddy is very rich. She has a pony. I was just wondering."

"Would you like a pony?"

"Yep." Stephanie handed Christina a cup and saucer. "My mammy's going to buy me one," she added confidently. "'Cos she's going to get rich, 'cos she's got a deli."

"I see." Chris sipped his lemonade thoughtfully. "You're lucky to have such a kind mammy."

Stephanie turned her baby-blue eyes on him. "Yes, I am," she declared as she offered around the biscuits. "And I've got a Doug too. He's even better than a daddy. He built me a Mary Poppins bedroom."

So put that in your pipe and smoke it, Ellen thought fiercely. She hoped that last remark made Chris feel well and truly ashamed of himself.

"Oh," Chris said, deflated. "Well, we really must be off, Mother."

"We don't want to go. We want to stay and play with the girl," Christina protested.

"It's time for us to go too," Ellen said firmly. "Tidy up, Stephanie, and say goodnight to your gran."

"Can I wash the tea cups, Gran?"

"Of course, dear." Katherine gave a strained smile. "We'll do them now." She gathered up the small cups.

"I'll help." Christina skipped out of the lounge.

"Me too." Adam followed.

"Look, I *am* sorry that I barged in. I didn't know that you were here. But I'm not sorry to see you, Ellen. You look beautiful. Will you be at home or at work tomorrow?"

"At home. I've closed for the week."

"I'll call you then."

"I don't know." She was having second thoughts.

"Just one call. What harm is there in that?"

"It's over, Chris."

"It will never be over between us and you know it." Chris reached out and cupped her face in his hands.

Ellen nearly jumped out of her skin at his touch, it was so unexpected.

"I love you." He stared into her eyes.

"Stop it, Chris," Ellen hissed, petrified Katherine would walk in.

"I love you," he repeated and let her go. He walked out of the room calling to the twins. Ellen, dry-mouthed, heard the sounds of voices in the hall, and then the opening of the front door. Moments later, she heard the car start then Katherine closed the door.

"Ellen, I'm truly sorry about that. It was most unexpected. I had no idea Christopher was going to call." Katherine swept into the room, apologising profusely.

"Don't worry about it, Mrs Wallace. These things happen." Ellen tried to reassure the clearly distressed woman.

"It was unforgivable. I never intended for you to feel uncomfortable in my home."

"Honestly, Mrs Wallace, I'm fine. And I had a lovely time."

"So did I, Ellen. I hope it's the first of many visits."

"It is," Ellen assured her. "Where's Stephanie?"

"She's drying the dishes." Katherine smiled. "She's a lovely child. A credit to you."

"She's a good little girl," Ellen agreed proudly. Stephanie had taken her father's arrival in her stride and even put him in his place.

Between them they packed up the tea set and when Stephanie had her coat on she reached up to Katherine for a kiss.

"Thanks, Gran. Will you come and visit us soon?"

"Of course I will, dear." Katherine held her tightly.

"We'll make the arrangement," Ellen promised. Impulsively she leaned across and kissed Mrs Wallace on the cheek. "Thank you."

"And you, dear, and you," Katherine patted Ellen on the arm.

She waved after them until they edged out of the long drive into the traffic. Ellen gave a sigh of relief as she drove towards the city. "Did you have fun?" She glanced at Stephanie in the mirror. Her daughter was curled up under the tartan rug.

"It was brill, Mam." Stephanie yawned. It had been a long day.

"And what did you think of . . . em . . . Christopher?" Ellen asked curiously.

"He's got very white hands," Stephanie remarked.

"Oh!" Ellen hadn't expected that.

"Not like Doug's. Doug's got real brown hands, Mammy, 'cos he works outside an' he's very strong," Stephanie explained patiently.

"I see. Would you like to see Christopher again?"

"I don't mind, Mammy. Can I play with the boy and girl again? Can I go to see that gran again?"

"I'm sure you can," Ellen said non-committally.

"Can I play with my tea set when we get home?" Stephanie was more concerned with her new present than she was about meeting her father.

"Of course you can." Ellen smiled. It was no big deal for her. Chris meant nothing to her. Perhaps it was just as well. Ellen sighed deeply. Why had he come into her life again? What unseen hand was guiding their destiny? Giving her a choice, just when she didn't want one? Life was so unfair. Why couldn't he have wanted to be a part of her life when she'd really wanted and needed him? A year ago she would have been deliriously happy had he told her he'd left Suzy and wanted them to live together. It would have been a dream come true.

There was going to be no easy way out of this. She was going to have to make a decision between Doug and Chris. And this time it would be final.

Katherine was furious with her son. He'd spoiled the little tea party she'd been enjoying so much with her enchanting new granddaughter. He should have phoned her to see if it was all right to visit. And to come visiting looking such a sight. Terribly bad manners! The state of him. Unshaven, bleary-eyed. She'd never seen him look so bad. Poor Ellen had been most ill at ease. You could have cut the tension with a knife.

She was a very nice woman, Katherine reflected as she cleared away the tea dishes. Very different from Suzy. Much warmer. Suzy was more brittle. Suzy was more like her, Katherine admitted. Chris should have stood by Ellen and married her. He regretted it. That was obvious from the way he'd looked at her. And Ellen still had feelings for him. Katherine could see that. Even after all he'd done to her.

Women were such fools! she thought crossly as she folded her linen tablecloth neatly, ready for the laundry basket. And if Ellen didn't put Chris behind her and stay with that good man she'd spoken of so highly, she was the biggest fool of all.

Alison Guilfoyle lit another cigarette from the butt of the one she'd just finished. He'd promised he'd phone but she hadn't heard from Chris. It was now late on Sunday evening and the phone remained stubbornly silent. She checked it once more as she had a dozen times that day. It sounded fine.

Why didn't he phone? They'd got on like a house on fire the twice they'd been together. The sex had been pretty good too. And he'd seemed to really like her. He'd told her she was like a breath of fresh air. Vibrant and refreshing. She could hardly believe her luck, finding a handsome, suave, sophisticated, successful, *eligible* man on Christmas Eve of all nights.

He'd be a great catch! She'd be the envy of her girlfriends if she swanned up the aisle on his arm. She wondered what his flatmate was like. Chris hadn't volunteered much information and his bedroom door was locked. She'd tried it on her way to the loo. Just to have a peep. The flatmate's room had an en suite, Chris had told her when he'd been giving her the guided tour. She'd wondered if he paid more rent than Chris. He was abroad for Christmas.

"Phone me, phone me," she muttered as she stared at the phone, willing it to ring. Her parents were out. She could have gone to a party herself but she'd been too afraid she'd miss Chris's phone call.

Alison slouched into the lounge and flung herself into her father's easy chair. A box of chocolates lay unopened on a side table. Impatiently, she tore the wrapping off and took a couple. She hardly tasted them. A tear trickled down her cheek. Why was it that men always said they'd phone and then they never did?

"*When I fall in love, it will be for ever,*" Chris crooned as he tidied away Dinky cars and dolls' clothes. The children were asleep in his double bed. He was sleeping in Alexandra's room. She'd be home a day after the twins went back to Suzy. If all went as he dearly hoped it would, he'd be moving into Ellen's place. Alexandra would just have to get a new lodger to pay the rent.

Ellen had got a shock when she'd seen him and a bigger shock when she'd heard about him and Suzy. It had all gone perfectly to plan, he congratulated himself as he got a cloth to wipe the melted chocolate off the fireplace. Katherine was annoyed. Chris was well aware of that. He didn't care. He had to see Ellen and he'd seen her. And she still had feelings for him.

She couldn't hide it. That was the best bit. He'd work a bit of his old Black Magic on her and they'd be fine again. Life would be good.

He was on his hands and knees rubbing the stains out of the tiled fireplace when he heard a key jiggle in the front door and the familiar clip-clop of high heels along the hall. He knelt, frozen, as Alexandra flung open the door.

"What the fuck's going on here?"

Chapter Twenty-Seven

"What the bloody hell are you doing here?" Chris blustered.

"I *live* here, remember? What are all those toys doing out in the hall? Who owns those coats?" Alexandra snapped.

"I have the kids staying over for a few days," Chris muttered.

"*What!*" Alexandra was horrified. "They can't stay here." She'd been half-expecting to catch Chris with a woman. It was a rich irony to find him cleaning up after his two kids instead.

"Suzy dumped them on me," Chris whined. "It's not my fault."

"Well, you'll have to take them back to her tomorrow. And that's all there is to it," Alexandra ordered.

"I think she's away, so I have to look after them. And besides you weren't due home for ages."

"I decided to come back early," Alexandra said curtly. "But I certainly wasn't expecting *this*! They have to go, Chris. Tell Suzy to get her ass back home fast."

"I don't know where the hell she is," Chris exploded. "And anyway, Alexandra, I pay half the rent here. I can have who I like to stay. They're sleeping in *my* room. So shut the fuck up."

"And where are you sleeping?"

"Er . . . I was sleeping in your room."

"Well, you can forget that! Sleep on the settee tonight, Chris." Alexandra swept out of the room and slammed the door hard.

How the hell was she expected to prepare for a most important interview with kids in the house? It didn't matter that he didn't know about it. They still shouldn't be here. The nerve of him smuggling them into her apartment behind her back. For two pins she'd been tempted to chuck him out there and then. But her future was too uncertain. She needed to know she had that job before she tossed Chris out on his ear.

She hefted her case onto the bed and carefully unpacked the new beige suit she'd bought in London, for the interview. She'd bought a pair of Italian leather tan shoes and a matching tan handbag to go with it. It was extremely businesslike and smart. Perfect for the image she wanted to portray. She'd only need to run the iron lightly over it. Although it wasn't badly creased at all, she observed with satisfaction. It would be good for travelling.

Alexandra unpacked, neatly and methodically. A hesitant knock on the door made her scowl.

"Yes?" She opened it slightly.

Chris stood outside with two glasses of brandy.

"A welcome home drink," he smarmed.

"Thank you," Alexandra said frostily, took the proffered glass and closed the door firmly in his face.

"So! How did the tea party go?" Doug handed Ellen a mug of tea and sat down beside her on the settee. Stephanie was fast asleep in bed and he'd lit the fire for Ellen so they could snuggle up in front of it.

"It was nice, Doug. Mrs Wallace went to a lot of trouble." Ellen tried to keep her tone light and non-committal. She took a sip of the hot sweet tea and put the mug down on the floor.

"He was there, wasn't he?"

Ellen didn't answer for a moment. Doug stared at her. She couldn't meet his gaze.

"Why do you say that?" she asked eventually, fiddling with a tassel on a cushion.

"I know by you, dammit. The minute I looked at you this evening I knew. I can see it in your eyes, I can see the unhappiness. And only one person in the world puts that there," he said bitterly. "So what did he have to say?"

"He's left Suzy. Their marriage is over. He's living in a flat."

"Is he now? Poor, poor Chris," Doug derided.

"Don't be like that," Ellen snapped.

"Why? What should I be like? Thrilled that you met one of the greatest shits going?"

"Oh shut up, Doug!" Ellen had had enough.

"You knew he was going to be there, didn't you?" he accused.

"I did *not*," Ellen protested indignantly.

"It was all a big set-up – "

"It wasn't. I knew nothing about it. I didn't know his marriage had broken up either." Ellen was furious. How could he think it was a set-up? What did he take her for?

"Does he want to see you?" Doug demanded.

Ellen stayed stubbornly mute.

"I *thought* so." Doug jumped to his feet. His face was suffused with anger, the muscle in his jaw jerking, the veins in his neck corded. "I thought so. And I suppose you agreed. Well, I'm sick of this, Ellen. How can you even consider meeting him after the way he's behaved? Are you crazy, woman? Can't you see him for what he is? A user. A manipulator. He's a self-serving bastard! He comes first and you never will. Or Stephanie. And still you're prepared to put up with it. Well, you're a fool. I don't understand you. I never will. He says jump – you say how high? And that's always the way it will be." His eyes were like flints.

"That's not true, Doug," Ellen protested heatedly. "You've no business saying that!"

"Haven't I? Obviously not. All I know is I'm not putting up with it any more. It's like beating my head off a brick wall."

"Who's *asking* you to put up with it?" Ellen jumped up, incensed by the disgust in his voice and the contempt in his eyes. "You've no business talking to me like that."

"No! You're right, I don't," Doug snapped. "You can have him. You're welcome to him. Goodbye, Ellen."

He picked up his leather jacket, strode across the room and left without a backward glance. She heard him go downstairs. And then the front door closed and there was silence.

She sat down in frustration and fury. Just who the hell did he think he was, talking to her as if she was a *child*? How dare he judge her? How dare he call her a fool? She could make her own decisions without any help from him. They were all the same. Men! Right now she wanted nothing to do with any of them.

Doug started the car and gunned the engine. He was as mad as hell. What was wrong with the woman? Couldn't she see what was in front of her nose? Was she so cracked about Chris that nothing else mattered? It seemed so.

He was sick of it. He couldn't take any more of it. Ellen knew how he felt about her. It didn't seem to matter. He'd thought he was getting places with her. He'd felt confident enough to plan on asking her to marry him. But after this he was back to square one. Well and truly.

"Cut your losses before it gets any worse, you fool," he muttered as he swung the car around and headed home. What a lousy way to end the best year of his life. It was time to admit that Ellen would never be his.

Alexandra had hardly slept a wink all night. She'd have to disguise the dark shadows under her eyes, she fretted. She peered anxiously at her reflection in the mirror in her en suite. At least she had an en suite. She wouldn't have to share a bathroom with those brats of Chris's.

She sighed. What a way to be going for an interview. She'd never been so nervous in her life. Everything was riding on this job. Her career and reputation were on the line. So was her apartment. It was *crucial* that she do a brilliant interview. There was no room for nerves. She had to be totally in control.

Alexandra switched on the shower and stood beneath the bracing spray. She could hear the twins running up and down the hall. She gritted her teeth in irritation. What did Chris think this was, some kind of a crèche, for God's sake? The sooner she was financially secure again the better.

At ten-thirty precisely, she was sitting in front of Arthur Reynolds's large teak desk answering the questions he fired at her. Outwardly she looked as cool as a cucumber. Sophisticated, articulate, in control. Inwardly, she quaked. So much was at stake. But she did look the bee's knees, she silently reassured herself, trying to picture how Arthur Reynolds was perceiving her. The suit was extremely chic and her make-up and elegant chignon flawless. The questions and answers flew across the table like a ping-pong ball. Eventually, Arthur leaned back in his chair and narrowed his eyes.

"Why exactly did you leave Stuart and Stuart's, Alexandra? There's a lot of gossip doing the rounds."

Alexandra's heart sank. The question she'd been dreading.

"I'm sure there is, Arthur" – he'd asked her to call him Arthur – "as you know, Dublin is a small city and the advertising world is notorious for gossip and Chinese whispers. I have no intentions of bad-mouthing my former employers. I think it's a duty of an employee or an ex employee to be loyal. I left for professional reasons. Their vision and mine did not coincide. I don't approve of sloppy incompetence. I found the budgetary restrictions frustrating. The accounting left something to be desired. And I'm afraid that's all I'm going to say on the matter," she said crisply.

"I see," Arthur said non-committally, his expression inscrutable. "You know Malachy MacDonald has made approaches to me?"

"So I've heard," Alexandra replied evenly. She wasn't going to let him see that she was rattled.

"What do you think I should do?"

Alexandra gave him a cool stare. "That's entirely up to you, Arthur. You must make up your own mind."

"Hmm. Well, it's not too difficult." He smiled. "How soon can you start? And I think a salary commensurate with your position is appropriate." He named a sum that was almost twice her old salary. "I'll expect miracles for that," he added humorously.

"You'll get them," Alexandra grinned. "I can start as soon as you need me."

"First thing tomorrow. Come along, I'll show you your office. Now you'll need to get a secretary and an assistant. I can promote in-house or if there's anyone you'd like to recommend?"

"I have an excellent young woman I could recommend as my assistant. She'd have to be employed on the same salary she's on at least." Alexandra was brisk. "I know a good secretary with PR experience also."

"Fine. I'm sure we could go a little higher with both salaries. I want you to get a good team around you. One that you're happy with. And I want the best profile possible."

"You may rest assured, Arthur, your life is going to change," Alexandra promised her new boss.

She wasn't joking. Into women or not, he'd need a wife to entertain his corporate clients and keep him moving up the ladder of success. *She* was going to make herself indispensable to Arthur Reynolds and when the time was right she was going to suggest an alliance that would suit him and her. Marriage, in other words. Lovers could come and go, his and hers. She'd have his name, a ring on her finger, and power and money. It would suit her just fine. Alexandra drew a deep breath. What a *magnificent* way to start the new decade.

"Jane, I'm really in a pickle. I have the kids. Suzy's dumped them on me and she's taken off. Don't ask me where. And I have to meet a client this afternoon. I'm stuck, could you mind them for me?" Chris begged his sister-in-law. "I'll make it up to you."

"Go on," Jane said dryly. "What time do you want me to take them?"

"Can I get back to you? Won't be long. Thanks a million, Jane. You're a doll." Chris hung up, pleased with himself. So far so good.

Now for the difficult part. He dialled Ellen's number. Please let her be in, he willed, as the phone rang and rang, unanswered. He was just about to hang up despondently when she picked it up.

"It's me," he said.

"Oh! Hello, Chris," Ellen sounded flat. Depressed.

"What's wrong?"

"Nothing."

"You said I could ring you," he reminded her quickly. He heard her sigh at the other end of the line.

"Yes, I know what I said."

"Ellen, can we meet? Are you free this afternoon?"

There was silence for a long time.

Then to his great joy she said, "Where?"

"You pick." He could afford to be magnanimous.

"Your flat," Ellen suggested.

Chris put on his best hard-done-by voice. "It's a bit of a kip, Ellen. It does me. All I need is a bed and a cooker. But I'd really rather take you somewhere nicer."

Good touch, the bed and the cooker bit. It added just the right note of pathos, he applauded himself silently.

"I don't really want to go to a pub or a hotel," Ellen said slowly.

"No, just somewhere where we can be by ourselves," Chris agreed. "Where? A walk on Howth, or Killiney?" He named two of their old haunts.

There was silence while she pondered the question. "How about the Botanic Gardens? I could meet you at the Addison Lodge."

"Perfect," Chris approved. "What time?"

"Two o'clock?"

"OK, love. I'll see you then." He replaced the receiver quickly, afraid she'd change her mind. He dialled his sister-in-law's number and told her he'd drop the children over to her at quarter past one. Everything was working out just the way he wanted it.

He made himself a mug of coffee. The twins were playing noisily in the hall.

He'd had a hell of a shock when Alexandra'd walked in last night. That had been totally unexpected. And then she'd gone out this morning, dressed to kill, and wouldn't tell him where she was going. She'd been in a real snit with him. Something was up. He felt uneasy about it. She was behaving very mysteriously indeed.

It was imperative that he persuade Ellen to take him back. If he didn't he was up shit creek without a paddle. Alexandra didn't want him. Suzy didn't want him. Ellen had to. She'd never let him down yet. This time he'd go all out to woo her, he vowed as he stared out the window at a robin nestling in the bare-branched tree outside the kitchen window. This time they'd be together for good.

Ellen nibbled on a corner of toast. She wasn't really hungry. When the phone had rung, she'd half-hoped it was Doug. Instead it was Chris. She was so annoyed that it wasn't Doug, ringing to apologise, that she'd agreed on the spur of the moment to meet Chris.

Ben and Miriam had collected Stephanie twenty minutes earlier to take her into Dublin to see the moving crib with her cousins. They were making a day of it. They were going to a matinee in the afternoon. Ellen had the day to herself. She didn't want to sit staring at the four walls, so now she had a date with her ex-lover, she thought wryly.

She couldn't believe that Chris had ended up in a flat. It sounded horrible. A bed and a cooker. What a lonely way to live! She didn't want to meet him in Howth. Doug and she often walked the pier there. Killiney was too far away. The Botanic Gardens had been an inspired idea.

She wondered would he kiss her. For a long time after they'd split up she'd dreamed of him kissing her and making love to her. But he wasn't in her head like that at all now, she reflected ruefully. Now it was Doug's arms she imagined around her.

She'd never seen Doug as angry as she'd seen him last night. Ellen sighed. Now that her temper had abated a little she admitted that there was only so much he could take. She'd pushed him over the edge.

But still, he'd been very rude and pass-remarkable. He'd called her a fool. It was up to him to ring and make up. She set her jaw stubbornly, cleared away the breakfast dishes and headed for the bathroom. She was going to have a nice long soak and decide what she'd wear this afternoon. She wanted to look her best. Chris always had that effect on her.

She arrived at the Addison at ten past two, dressed in her Christmas outfit. A suede midi-skirt and a black polo-neck jumper. It was extremely slimming and her long black boots and black wool jacket were elegant yet casual. It was like an outfit Emma might wear. Ellen was very pleased with the sophisticated effect. Her hair, washed and blow-dried, lay silky and feathery at the nape of her neck. She'd taken extra care with her make-up.

Ellen had deliberately come ten minutes late. She wouldn't give Chris the satisfaction of thinking she was dying to see him. He was waiting for her. His face lit up when he saw her. In spite of herself she softened. He looked older, tired, defeated. With little of the brash confidence that she'd known. When he held out his arms to her, she slipped into them and hugged him back.

"Hiya, Chris."

"It's great to see you, baby," he said quietly, "Would you like a drink or will we go for our walk?"

She shook her head. "I don't want a drink, thanks, Chris."

"OK, come on." He took her hand and they walked outside into the dull gloomy afternoon. They crossed over Botanic Road and walked hand in hand through the high green gates of the Botanic Gardens.

"What way do you want to go?"

"Let's take the long way around to the Rose Garden. We'll do the Cemetery Walk," Ellen suggested. There were few other people around. Only the chirruping of the birds, the rustle of the wind in the foliage and the crunch of their shoes on the path broke the silence.

"I thought you might have had something on," Chris ventured.

"No. I was free this afternoon," Ellen said. It was strange talking to him like an acquaintance rather than someone she loved passionately. There was a barrier that had never been between them before. "Are you not working?"

"It's my chance to be with the twins for a couple of days. They're going to my-sister-in-law's tomorrow so I'll go in to the office for a few hours in the afternoon to let my secretary know that I'm still on the planet and just to keep things up to date."

"Couldn't you patch things up with Suzy?" Ellen asked hesitantly.

"Nah!" Chris shook his head. "It's over. Nothing's going to change that. I made a mistake and now I'm paying for it." He plucked a berry off one of the snowberry shrubs and flicked it in the air.

"I'm sorry," Ellen murmured.

"Not half as sorry as I am." Chris squeezed her hand. They walked past a row of lime trees underneath which grew masses of mistletoe.

"Look at the mistletoe." Chris broke off a sprig and dangled it over her head.

"Don't do that," Ellen protested. "We'll be thrown out if you're caught." She evaded his embrace and walked on.

"Who's going to catch us on a miserable day like today? There isn't a sinner around," Chris said in exasperation. Clearly she was in no humour to be kissed. He threw the berried spray away in disgust. They walked close to the black iron boundary railings that separated the Gardens from Glasnevin cemetery. It was eerie. A mist seemed to hang from the branches of the trees which feathered the top of the tombstones, enveloping them in shadowy wreaths. A bird hopped out of a holly bush, startling Ellen.

"God! What was that?" she exclaimed.

"It's only a bird," Chris laughed. "A feathered one. What did you think it was? A ghost . . ."

"Come on, let's walk quicker past this place." She speeded up her pace.

"Scaredy-cat," Chris teased, throwing an acorn at her.

Ellen laughed, the smile curling around her lips, brightening her eyes. He was incorrigible.

"Oh Ellen, it's great to be with you again. We had fun sometimes, didn't we?" His tone was wistful. He stopped and drew her close to him.

"Yeah, we did," Ellen said sadly, laying her head on his shoulder. They held each other tightly.

A man, shoulders hunched, hands shoved into his greatcoat pockets, walked past them, breaking the moment. They resumed their walk around the gardens. Eventually they came to Socrates' statue. Chris struck a pose.

"Stop it, you idiot," Ellen laughed in spite of herself and then exclaimed in delight at a bed of bachelor's buttons, their little buds peeping out. It was an uplifting sight. Small hints of spring were everywhere. They'd watched a squirrel gambolling under the trees and Ellen had seen the tips of daffodils bursting through the earth. Her own were coming out at home. It cheered her up.

They strolled along the riverbank on the path that led to the Rose Garden. The rolling grounds of the Holy Faith Convent bordered the river on the other side, and in the lowering dull afternoon the great red-bricked convent on top of the hill made Ellen think of Rebecca's Manderley or Scarlett's Tara or some such place.

"The views from the windows up there would be nice, wouldn't they?" Ellen remarked.

"Not half as nice as the view from where I'm standing," Chris averred.

Ellen threw her eyes up to heaven. "You're as flowery as ever, Wallace."

"I was just paying you a compliment, *Munroe*," Chris retorted sulkily. They came to the green iron bridge that crossed the sludgy dank Tolka to the Rose Garden. Ellen picked up a twig, threw it into the river and leaned over the bridge to watch its progress.

"It's a pity the sun's not shining. We could figure out the time on the sundial. That was always one of our treats when we were kids." She smiled, watching her twig float out from under the bridge and over the little waterfall.

"Fuck the sundial, Ellen." Chris twisted her around to face him. "Look, we have to talk properly," he pleaded. "This walking on eggshells and polite conversation about views and sundials is driving me nuts."

"There's nothing to talk about, Chris. It's over," she said heatedly.

"If it was over you wouldn't be here." Chris stared at her hard.

There was a grain of truth in what he said, Ellen privately admitted. She could have turned him down outright. Why had she come? Why had she put herself in this position? Why was she letting him into her head when she'd promised herself she never would again? And why . . . the biggest why of all . . . had she jeopardised what she had with Doug? He was right. She *was* a fool.

"Look, Chris, I shouldn't have come. I don't really know why I did. I'm going home."

"Ellen, please . . . please don't go until you've heard what I have to say. You owe me that much at least."

"I owe you *nothing*," she said sharply.

"All right then. You owe me nothing. I treated you like dirt, I admit it. *Please*. Just listen to what I have to say." He guided her into the sheltered little circular shrubbery opposite the bridge and led her to the wrought-iron seat. The camellias had buds on them already, Ellen noted disconnectedly, trying to keep her wits about her.

Chris sat down beside her and took one of her hands in his. He stared at her earnestly.

"Ellen, look, I know I have no right to ask but I have to. You're on my mind night and day. All I want is for us to be together.

Could you give me one last chance to make it up to you? I'll spend the rest of my life trying to make you happy. I swear it. I'll be a father to Stephanie. We'll be a family. You could come and work with me. We'd be a great team. You were always so interested in my work. You're the only woman who ever showed any interest. Suzy hasn't got a bull's clue, nor has Ale . . . er . . . any of the others," he caught himself just in time. "You could be the office administrator. Just think how good it would be. Working together, living together. Ellen, it would be so good."

"But I've got my own business," Ellen murmured, stunned at his vehement pleading.

"You could get someone to run it for you. Ellen, we were meant to be together!"

"It's too late, Chris," Ellen said gently. "There's someone else in my life."

"Oh, Ellen, please don't say that," Chris muttered. To her immense dismay, his eyes filled with tears and he buried his face in her shoulder. "I love you. I really do love you. Please don't desert me." His body shook with sobs and Ellen, horrified, felt tears brim in her own eyes. She had no idea that he felt so strongly for her. None at all. She'd never in a million years have believed this of Chris.

"Please, Chris, please. Don't," she whispered in distress, wrapping her arms around him. This was awful. She hated to see him so tormented. It made her feel a heel.

"Tell me you still love me," he urged. "Tell me you still have feelings for me."

"I do love you. I'll always love you. There'll always be that bond between us. But it's different now."

"It's not, it's not. Let me show you." He raised red-rimmed eyes to hers and then kissed her wildly, passionately.

"I love you," he muttered. "I love you. I want you. You must want me."

"Chris, stop," Ellen tried to disengage herself from him.

"Jesus, Ellen, don't do this to me!" There was actual panic in his eyes. "Think about it. Promise me you'll think about it."

"All right, Chris. I'll think about it." She wiped the wetness from his face with her fingers.

"Do you really love me?"

She nodded. He was easy to love right then. "Come on, it's going to rain and I should be getting back. I'm having Miriam and Ben and the gang to tea."

"You will think about it, won't you?" Chris ran his fingers through his hair and tried to compose himself. "We could be really happy."

"Come on, Chris. Let's go," Ellen said wearily. A week ago she'd been happy and contented. Now she was up in a heap. The dream she'd dreamed for many years was hers for the taking. But now she wasn't sure that she wanted it.

—❦—

"What do you mean they're resigning?" Malachy MacDonald barked down the phone at Ron Evans.

"I'm sorry, Mister MacDonald, to have to be the bearer of bad news. I hope I haven't spoiled your holiday," Ron Evans wittered down the line, like the unctuous, toadying little Uriah Heep that he was, especially when it came to dealing with the chairman.

"Sack 'em. Sack the fucking ungrateful bitches, I say, and don't give 'em a fucking farthing," Malachy swore.

"I can't," Ron bleated. "They've handed in official letters of resignation and – "

"You're hopeless, fucking hopeless, Evans. That bitch Johnston was right. You *are* a Mickey Mouse accountant who could do with a jet-propelled rocket up your arse. You couldn't manage a teddy bear's fucking *picnic*!" Malachy slammed down the phone in fury.

He'd taken a few days off after Christmas and left that gobshite Evans in charge. And on his first day . . . his *first* day . . . two staff members had resigned to take up positions elsewhere.

It was the *where* they were taking up the positions that was getting right up his nose. That walking bitch. That foul-mouthed, unwomanly, sly, two-faced, amoral, unethical *tramp*, Alexandra Johnston, was going to be Arthur Reynolds's personal PR woman and she was stealing two of Malachy's staff, right from under his nose. It was unheard of.

She wasn't down and out. She'd landed on her goddamn feet. It was bad enough having her sending blackmailing, contemptuous, ill-mannered letters – no one had ever told him to *bugger off* before – but to know she had swiped the plum from under his nose! It was enough to trigger an attack of gout!

Crimson with temper, Malachy poured himself a generous whiskey. Tonight he was going to get rat-arsed. And if his hag of a wife didn't like it, tough!

"I want you out of here by the end of the week, Chris."

"What!" Chris stared at Alexandra in disbelief.

"But how are you going to manage to pay the rent?"

"Never you mind. That's my problem, not yours."

"Have you met someone else? Is that it? Have you been seeing someone behind my back?" Chris ranted.

"Oh, cut the crap, Chris. As it happens I've got a marvellous job. I'm Arthur Reynolds's new personal PR. I'll have my own team . . . hand-picked by *moi*. And I've got a salary that would make your eyes water," Alexandra couldn't resist boasting. "So, it was nice while it lasted but *c'est la vie*, baby."

"You sneaky bitch. I'll go when I'm ready to leave and not before." Chris was rabid.

"The end of the week, Chris," Alexandra warned. "And have those kids out of here tomorrow." She swanned out the front door. She was going out celebrating with Karen Finlay and Sarah O'Malley. Her hand-picked team, from her old firm.

Ron Evans had spent an hour in the loo, Karen had gleefully informed Alexandra, when she and then Sarah had resigned after Alexandra had phoned them to offer them the new positions.

Alexandra was delighted with the news. Ron Evans would need to spend *all* his time on the loo by the time she was finished with him.

Tonight, though, the first members of *The Stuart and Stuart's Survivors' Club* were having its inaugural meeting in the Burlington. And not even Chris and his whingeing brats could spoil it for her. He'd be out of her hair soon enough. She wouldn't miss him in the slightest. He was *far* too selfish for her taste. All he ever thought about was himself.

Alexandra sat into her car. She was going to trade it in for a new one this very week, she decided happily.

She couldn't wait to tell all the movers and shakers at the bar in the Burlington her splendid news. It would be the talk of every dinner party of the season. And *how* Alexandra loved to be the talk of the town.

This was serious. He was in deep shit! Chris's heart raced as he poured himself a stiff brandy. Alexandra was kicking him out. So much for loyalty, he thought viciously. She'd used him to pay the rent. That was all he meant to her, the scummy cow. Now that she could afford it herself, he was out on his ear. She was the one who'd seduced him from his wife in the first place. *She'd* invited *him* to dinner. She'd caused all of this and now she was *dumping* him. A man wouldn't behave so crassly. She was a ball-breaker of the highest order.

What the fuck was he going to do? Chris paced the lounge. He wasn't at all sure about Ellen. When he'd started crying in the Botanic Gardens, they'd been genuine tears. And tears of pure panic. He'd felt so sorry for himself. So unsure. Especially when Ellen had said there was another man in her life. That had really got to him. She couldn't possibly love that bearded plank more than she loved him. That was unthinkable. The very idea brought tears to his eyes again. God! She had to take him back, she just had to.

"Daddy, I've a pain in my tummy." Adam stood bleary-eyed at the door. Chris rubbed his damp eyes.

"Adam, go to bed," he said wearily.

"I want Mummy," Adam bawled and then puked all over Alexandra's shag-pile rug.

"Shit! Shit! *Shit!*" Chris swore. This was all he bloody needed. He'd a good mind to leave the mess there and let Alexandra clean it up. It would be good enough for her. Adam was howling for his mother. Christina had just joined in. Chris felt like sitting down and bawling himself.

"Hello, Ellen, Katherine Wallace here. I just wanted to make sure that you were all right. And that yesterday's meeting with Christopher didn't upset you or Stephanie too much. I tried to call you earlier but there was no answer. You've been on my mind, dear."

"I was out, Mrs Wallace," Ellen said guiltily. Glad beyond measure that the other woman couldn't see her red face.

"Well, I am sorry about yesterday. It was most unfortunate. Since Chris has started living with that dreadful woman, he's taken to calling in unexpectedly. I think they have rows and he wants to get out from under her feet," Katherine confided.

Ellen felt the blood drain from her face. "Sorry, Mrs Wallace, I'm a little confused. I thought Chris lived in a flat."

"Oh, it's not a *flat*, my dear, Madam Johnston would have a fit if you called her luxury apartment a *flat*."

Ellen could practically hear Mrs Wallace's nostrils flaring contemptuously.

"Is she the woman Chris is living with now?" Ellen strove to keep her voice from shaking.

"Yes, but it won't last. Too close to the bone," Katherine sniffed.

"How do you mean?"

"Well. Suzy's best friend and all that. Very distasteful. I know I shouldn't say this about my own son, but my dear, although you may not think so, you had a lucky escape."

"I think I realise that." Ellen shook her head in disbelief. Her knuckles were white as she gripped the phone.

"Well, just once again, Ellen, I do apologise. And I'll make very sure it doesn't happen again when you visit."

"Thank you, Mrs Wallace. I would appreciate that," Ellen said quietly. "We had a lovely time yesterday and thank you for your kindness."

"It was my pleasure entirely. Goodnight, Ellen."

Ellen put the phone down. She was shaking like a leaf. The liar! The out-and-out conniving, manipulating, calculating liar! And she'd been feeling sorry for him. For one mad moment she'd actually considered his proposal! He'd never change. *Never.* He was the biggest user she'd ever known.

She didn't feel betrayed. She didn't feel hurt. She felt angry. Damn angry. Angrier than she'd ever been in her life. Tomorrow she was going to have it out with Chris once and for all. This day had been coming a long, long time. It would be a day of reckoning like no other!

Chapter Twenty-Eight

"**S**o when were you going to tell me, Chris? When were you going to tell me that you'd left Suzy because you were having an affair with her best friend? That you're *living* with her!" Ellen was so angry she was trembling.

"For God's sake, keep your voice down. I don't want my secretary to hear." Chris stood up from behind his desk, stunned.

Ellen had just barged in like a madwoman.

"I don't give a tuppenny damn about your secretary. Why did you tell me all those lies about leaving Suzy because you loved me and you couldn't live with her any more? Why did you want to come back to me if you're having an affair with this woman?"

"It means nothing. Honestly, Ellen. I'm telling you," Chris pleaded earnestly. He sat down and rubbed his eyes wearily. He'd had no sleep last night and he was shagged. "I'm telling you, once and for all, Ellen, Alexandra means nothing to me. It was just a fling."

"Don't say *that*. Don't demean that woman like that," Ellen raged. "How can you say that about someone you're sleeping with? Is that all it is to you? Lust? Did you say things like that about me to Suzy? How can you treat human beings the way you do? Are you really that callous? Are you really that calculating? How can you tell lies to people the way you do? How can you look people in the eye and lie to their face? Don't you ever feel guilty about what you do to people, or is it just water off a duck's back to you? Are you really so unfeeling, Chris, that you just use people as it suits you, no matter what hurt and pain you cause them? Do you ever think of how many people's lives you've damaged because you're such a selfish fucking bastard?"

Chris sat through her tirade with his head bowed, shoulders hunched in a typical *Poor-Misunderstood-Me* pose.

Ellen looked at him in disgust.

"You know, I've always given you the benefit of the doubt. I've made excuses for you left, right and centre. I've said that somewhere in the depths of that thoroughly self-centred being there has to be some spark of decency. I even kidded myself that you loved me and Stephanie. But this time, Chris, I have to finally admit it, I've been badly misguided all these years. I've made a huge error of judgement because I'm the biggest fool going. You're rotten through and through and I despise you. You're an out-and-out liar and I hope and pray with all my heart that Stephanie hasn't any of you in her because if she has, I fear for my child."

Ellen leaned over the desk and pointed her finger in his face. "Now this is the last time I'm ever going to see or speak to you again, Chris Wallace. Get out of my life and stay out of it and forget about having anything to do with Stephanie. She's better off without a father if you're all that's there for her. I wouldn't let her be *contaminated* by the likes of you."

Chris jumped to his feet, furious. "When did you become a saint then, Ellen? What the fuck are you so holier than thou about? You've a short memory, haven't you? You had sex with me when we weren't married. And we all know that's a big bad sin. Then you had an affair with me when you knew I *was*

married. Where were your goddamn morals then? There are
different ways of telling lies, you know. There's such a thing as
lies of omission. And you were pretty good at lying to yourself
too. Your behaviour was as damaging to Suzy as mine was! And
don't forget I didn't *make* you have sex with me. It was your
own choice. Do you think you're setting a good example to *my*
daughter by screwing around with that bogman of yours?
Don't you dare lecture me about my faults. You've plenty of
your own. And let's hope Stephanie hasn't inherited any of
those."

"How dare you, Chris," Ellen said through gritted teeth. "How
dare you! Doug and I are not *screwing* around. You're the lowest of
the low – "

"Yeah, I know, I'm a liar and a cheat and I've no morals . . .
spare me. I've heard it all before. I am what I am, Ellen. You
told me you loved me once. Well, you didn't. You loved what
you wanted me to be. So did Suzy. Funnily enough,
Alexandra for all her faults was the only one who took me
for what I am. But you know, no one's ever really loved me.
Not you. Not Suzy. Not my mother. So get off your high
horse."

"That's right, Chris, do what you do best. Justify it to yourself.
Blame everyone else. And feel really sorry for yourself. No one
does it better. You're a master at it. I feel sorry for you. You can't
even be honest with yourself."

Ellen turned and walked out of his office, angrier than she'd
ever been in her life.

⌘

Chris was shaking. He'd blown it big-time. How the hell had
Ellen found out about Alexandra? It was too late for him
now. This really was the end. What was he going to do? He
was practically homeless. Suzy'd have to let him move back
home. There was nowhere else. He picked up the phone and

dialled her number on the off-chance that she'd be there. She was.

"It's me, Suzy. I'll be coming home tonight with the kids. We can't stay at Alexandra's any longer. She's fucked me out," he snarled. It was best to go on the offensive straight away.

"What do you mean she's fucked you out?" Suzy demanded.

"She's got a big new job as Arthur Reynolds's PR woman and she doesn't need me to pay the rent any more. She wants the kids out of the apartment. So whether you like it or not, we're coming home."

"Correction," Suzy snapped icily. "*They're* coming home. You can get lost. Go and get yourself a flat. You're not crawling back here again." Suzy slammed the phone down. Chris stared at the phone in horror. Get a flat! Him! What the hell would he be able to afford? A bedsit in Rathmines was the best he'd be able to manage by the time he'd paid for Suzy to live in their mansion.

He really was up the creek, he thought in panic. She'd shop him to the taxman if he made trouble. Alexandra had turfed him out on his ear. Ellen loathed him. What had he done to deserve this torment?

Chris Wallace buried his head in his hands, a bowed and broken man.

Suzy was shivering. She was so angry she thought she was going to burst a blood vessel. Chris had the nerve . . . the *nerve* to expect her to let him back home because Alexandra had given him the boot. Just what did he think she was . . . a doormat?

That wasn't the way it was supposed to have ended. *He* was supposed to finish it with *Alexandra*.

Maybe – and it was an exceedingly small maybe – if he had given Alexandra the shove she might have considered letting him back. That would have been one in the eye for her erstwhile friend. But not this way. *Never* this way. He could sink or swim now as far as Suzy was concerned.

And what was all that about Alexandra getting a job as Arthur Reynolds's PR? How had she wangled that? It was absolutely infuriating. Beyond belief, even. She was supposed to be on her knees. Never to rise again. It wasn't fair. Suzy had wanted that bitch to live unhappily ever after. Now it looked as though she was on the rise again. And going to rise even higher. That job was prestigious. Arthur Reynolds had the highest profile in town. And Alexandra Johnston would be swanning around at his side. It was too much to take in. She'd won!

Unhappier than she'd ever been in her life, Suzy burst into tears.

Ellen pulled up outside the flat. Stephanie was over in Denise's playing with Lisa and Michelle. She'd make herself a cup of tea and calm down before she went to collect her.

She let herself in and closed the door behind her. It was good to be home in her own place. She was drained. All her anger spent. Everything she'd ever wanted to say to Chris Wallace had been said today. She'd never make a fool of herself over him again. It was finally over.

She didn't hate him. He was too contemptible for hatred. She pitied him. He had no one. He'd lie his way from relationship to relationship. And he'd end up a sad, lonely old man, blaming everyone else for his misfortunes. Unable even to look at himself in the mirror and see himself for what he was.

Ellen took off her coat and walked slowly upstairs. She felt as though she'd been on a long, long journey. He'd got really dirty when his back was to the wall. Accusing her of adultery and screwing around with Doug. She *had* taken him back knowing that he was married. That had been a big mistake. Maybe her actions *had* damaged his wife. That was a guilt she had to accept and live with. Ellen too had been culpable. Closing her eyes to what she didn't want to see. She didn't feel good about it. She had to accept her part of the blame.

Ellen sat down tiredly at her kitchen table. Now, because of her stupidity, she could have lost the best chance for happiness she'd ever have. Would Doug take her back? What should she do? Phone him? Go to his house? She didn't know. Would he take her out to celebrate New Year's Eve, as he'd promised?

How could she expect him to take her back after the way she'd treated him? He might think she was using him.

"Oh Munroe, you fool, you fool," she muttered. Heartsick.

It was New Year's Eve. Doug knotted his new tie and smoothed some aftershave over his neatly trimmed beard. It was Stephanie's aftershave. It smelt good.

He'd waited to hear from Ellen since Sunday but not a peep. She couldn't have taken that swine back! But what other reason was there for her silence? Ellen didn't hold grudges. If it was just a row they'd be talking by now. There must be more to it.

He was going to call on her anyway. He was going to take one last chance on their relationship. Tonight he was going to ask her to marry him and get an answer from her once and for all. At least he'd know where he stood.

He picked up the jacket of his suit and shrugged himself into it. It was do or die. And he had no idea what way the dice was going to roll.

Ellen sprayed *Laughter* onto her wrists and then traced some *Coral Dawn* lipstick over her lips. Her heart was pittering uncontrollably. Her mouth dry with anticipation. She wore her best dress, a crushed velvet, slim-fitting black dress with a sweetheart neckline. Doug's cross and chain lay nestled in the creamy curve of her breasts. She knew without vanity that she looked her very best.

Ellen hadn't told Miriam or her parents about the row with Doug. Stephanie had gone to sleep at Sheila's as planned. She was alone. Waiting. Palms damp. Would Doug call for her or was it over between them?

Doug drove slowly up Main Street. His heart raced uncomfortably. The knot in his tie seemed very tight. He loosened it slightly. This was the worst thing he'd ever endured, he thought grimly.

As he drove up to Ellen's he noticed a big shining black Volvo parked right outside her front door. Doug's heart sank to his boots.

"Oh Christ Almighty," he muttered. That bastard was there. Ellen was celebrating New Year's Eve with Chris Wallace.

He couldn't swallow. He tried to clear his throat as he drove past. He looked up. The lights were on upstairs, the curtains drawn. He kept driving, taking the long way home.

It was the worst night of his life.

Ellen cried herself to sleep. He hadn't come. She'd hoped against hope that he would. Deep down she'd expected Doug to be there. But he hadn't turned up.

Her pride wouldn't let her phone him. If he'd wanted to be

there, he would have been there. She didn't blame him in the slightest. Other men would have run long before he had. She hadn't given him an easy time. But at least she'd always been truthful with him. Now, when she realised that she truly loved him, it was much too late.

Chapter Twenty-Nine

1st January 1970.

Ellen had been lying awake since before six. It was the start of a new decade. And what a start for her. She'd made a hames of her life. She'd been given the chance of happiness and she'd lost it because of her stupidity over a man who'd never valued the love she had for him. A man who cared for no one but himself. Doug had come into her life and offered her a real love. He cherished her, valued her, made her laugh, gave her a shoulder to cry on when she needed it, and she'd been too stupid to accept it.

"It's your own bloody fault," Ellen cursed herself. She tossed and turned restlessly. She couldn't stay in bed. She'd had enough. She had to do something about it.

With a determined set to her jaw, she got out of bed and showered. She glanced at her watch. 7 a.m. She had to do it. She couldn't stand it another minute. She dressed in a warm jumper and jeans, ran down the stairs and hurried out to the car. There was a big black car parked behind hers. She wondered momentarily whose it was but she wasn't really interested. She had other considerations on her mind.

It was still dark. Main Street was deserted. Just the odd light on here and there. Her car windows were covered with thick ice. Ellen cursed under her breath and raced back into the house to get hot water. Finally she got into the car and switched on the ignition. The engine spluttered and coughed.

"Oh no!" she muttered. "Not now."

She tried again. A mournful wheeze. The battery must be low. It had been a bitterly cold night. She tried once more, nursing the accelerator gently. The car jerked and caught. She was off. There was ice on the road so she drove slowly although she was steaming with impatience. The last thing she wanted was to end up in a ditch.

It seemed the longest drive of her life but eventually she drove through the gates of Doug's bungalow. The curtains were all pulled. There wasn't a sign of life. His car was there so he was at home.

Before she could stop to think, afraid that she'd lose her nerve, she got out of the car and rapped sharply on the door. There was no answer. She knocked again, louder. After five more minutes of rapping and calling his name, Doug opened the door, bleary-eyed and dishevelled. Bare-chested, dressed only in his jeans, he had a great body.

"What the – Ellen, in the name of God what are you doing here at this hour of the morning?" His expression changed to one of concern. "Stephanie? Is there something wrong with Stephanie?"

"There's nothing wrong with Stephanie," Ellen said calmly. Now that she'd seen him a measure of calm had returned.

"Well, what's wrong then?" he demanded aggressively.

"Why did you stand me up last night?"

"What?" Doug was taken aback.

"I said: why did you stand me up? You asked me to go out with you on New Year's Eve and then you didn't show up." She felt her composure evaporate. He wasn't in a very good mood. He didn't look at all pleased to see her.

"Excuse me, Ellen. I did show up," he said icily. "Only when I saw that bastard's car outside your front door, I thought I'd be the last person you'd want to see."

"What bastard? What car?" Ellen was mystified.

"Oh, come on, Ellen. Lover-boy Wallace's car," Doug said sarcastically.

"Chris wasn't at my place last night," Ellen protested.

"Well, who owns the car then?" he growled.

"Is it a big black one?"

"Yeah."

"I don't know who owns it. It's still there this morning. It could be someone who's broken down. I had an awful job starting my own car this morning." Ellen shivered in the chilly frosty air. "Look, Doug, are you going to invite me in or not? It's bloomin' freezing out here."

"Sorry! Sorry! Come in." He closed the door behind them and stared at Ellen.

"Why are you here, Ellen?" he asked quizzically. "Does this mean that we're still pals?"

Ellen took a deep breath. "Doug, will you marry me?"

"What!"

"Will you marry me?" she repeated firmly.

He burst out laughing. "Munroe, you're an awful woman!"

"Is that a yes or a no?" Ellen demanded.

He pulled her to him and kissed her soundly. "That's a very definite yes," he murmured huskily when they drew apart.

"Oh good," Ellen grinned. "My mother will worship the ground you walk on for making an honest woman of me."

"Don't mind your mother. As long as you worship the ground I walk on."

"I do love you, Doug. That's why I asked you to marry me. So there'd be no doubts in your mind about it."

"You did me out of my proposal. I had it all planned to ask you last night," Doug chided.

"Did you?" Ellen's face lit up. "Well, maybe it's better today. The start of the new year and a new decade. What a way to start!"

"And is everything settled in your mind about that other yoke?" His tone was dry.

"Doug, I swear. You'll never have a second's worry there. It's definitely over. I know that now. And I'm glad. You just went off at half cock."

"You were pretty fiery yourself," he reminded her.

Ellen laughed. "We'll make a great pair." She reached up and caressed his cheek. "Listen, Buster. I want a proper proposal. You're not getting out of it that easy."

Doug knelt on one knee. "Ellen Munroe, spinster of the parish of Glenree, will you consent to be my wife?"

"Doug!" she protested, laughing. "Do it properly."

He stood up and grabbed her by the waist. "For God's sake, woman, will you marry me?"

"Yes! Yes! Yes!" Ellen's face was wreathed in smiles as he lifted her in the air.

"Let me down," she squealed. "I said yes."

"Say it once more," he ordered.

"Oh yes please, Doug. Yes *please.*"